# EUROPE AFTER ROME

St Andrews sarcophagus (front panel). © Crown copyright. Reproduced courtesy of Historic Scotland.

# Europe after Rome
## *A New Cultural History*
### *500–1000*

Julia M. H. Smith

**OXFORD**
UNIVERSITY PRESS

# OXFORD
UNIVERSITY PRESS

Great Clarendon Street, Oxford OX2 6DP

Oxford University Press is a department of the University of Oxford.
It furthers the University's objective of excellence in research, scholarship,
and education by publishing worldwide in

Oxford New York

Auckland Cape Town Dar es Salaam Hong Kong Karachi Kuala Lumpur
Madrid Melbourne Mexico City Nairobi New Delhi Taipei Toronto
Shanghai

With offices in

Argentina Austria Brazil Chile Czech Republic France Greece
Guatemala Hungary Italy Japan South Korea Poland Portugal
Singapore Switzerland Thailand Turkey Ukraine Vietnam

Published in the United States
by Oxford University Press Inc., New York

British Library Cataloguing in Publication Data
Data available

Library of Congress Cataloging in Publication Data
Data available

ISBN 0-19-924427-8

1 3 5 7 9 10 8 6 4 2

Typeset by SNP Best-set Typesetter Ltd., Hong Kong
Printed in Great Britain
on acid-free paper by
Biddles Ltd.
King's Lynn, Norfolk.

FOR HAMISH

# *Acknowledgements*

WRITING a book is a careful balance of individual endeavour and collective help. While taking full responsibility for the opinions and errors this
one contains, I nevertheless have great pleasure in thanking all those who
have enabled me to undertake and complete it. In the first place, I am
grateful to Simon Mason at Oxford University Press for inviting me to
write it, and, more recently, to Ruth Parr and all her team for their editorial encouragement and expertise. I could not have written without generous amounts of research leave, and for that I thank, in the first instance,
the University of St Andrews, where I am grateful to my colleagues in the
Department of Mediaeval History for accommodating my periods of
withdrawal from teaching, and to the School of History Research Com-
mittee, for a subvention towards the cost of maps and diagrams. External
funding has been essential to its completion, and I have been the privileged recipient of a Fellowship-in-Residence at the Netherlands Institute
of Advanced Study (1999–2000), a fellowship at the Shelby Cullom Davis
Center for Historical Studies, Princeton University (2001), and Arts and
Humanities Research Board Research Leave (2003–4). I thank all those
who elected me to these positions.

In the course of writing this book, I have drawn heavily on the assistance and friendship of many people. At St Andrews, special thanks are
due to Duncan Stewart in Reprographics for preparing nine of the maps,
and to Margaret Grundy and her staff in the Inter-Library Loans department of the University Library for cheerful efficiency in tracking down
the material I needed. I am indebted to Alicia Correa for compiling the
index with expert professionalism. Over the years, dozens of colleagues
have responded generously to email, telephone, and conversational requests for bibliography and advice without necessarily realizing why I was
consulting them: I truly appreciate this help. Julia Crick, John Hudson,
Mayke de Jong, Tom Noble, and Alex Woolf all commented on one or
more chapters in early draft, and I have benefited greatly from their
suggestions. Four people read most or all of it and gave sustenance far
beyond astute criticism and advice. Peter Brown and Chris Wickham
scrutinized the entire manuscript towards the final stages of composition,
and, in saving me from many errors and jejeune remarks, showed me

how to push the argument much further. Over the years, Jinty Nelson responded to most of it, and provided unstinting encouragement in good times and bad. Finally, Hamish Scott is not only the best of friends and, unofficially, the best of editorial critics, but has enabled the good times that have finally brought this book to completion. Its dedication is a small public token of a large private debt.

# *Contents*

# RESOURCES

# IDEOLOGIES

# List of Figures

# Abbreviations

| | |
|---|---|
| *AASS* | *Acta Sanctorum quotquot toto orbe coluntur*, ed. J. Bollandus et al. (Antwerp, Brussels, Paris, 1643–1940) |
| CCCM | Corpus Christianorum, Continuatio Medievalis |
| CCSL | Corpus Christianorum, Series Latina |
| CSEL | Corpus Scriptorum Ecclesiasticorum Latinorum |
| *EHD* | *English Historical Documents*, i: c.500–1042, ed. Dorothy Whitelock, 2nd edn. (London, 1979) |
| *EME* | *Early Medieval Europe* |
| MGH | Monumenta Germaniae Historica |
|   AA |     Auctores Antiquissimi |
|   Epp. |     Epistolae |
|   Epp. Sel. |     Epistolae Selectae |
|   Poetae |     Poetae latini medii aevi |
|   SRG |     Scriptores rerum Germanicarum in usum scholarum separatim editi |
|   SRL |     Scriptores rerum Langobardicarum et Italicarum |
|   SRM |     Scriptores rerum Merovingicarum |
|   SS |     Scriptores |
| *PL* | *Patrologiae Cursus Completus, Series Latina*, ed. J.-P. Migne, 221 vols. (Paris, 1844–65) |
| SC | Sources Chrétiennes |
| Settimane | Settimane di studio del Centro italiano di studi sull'alto medioevo |

# Note on Conventions

*Persons*

Where dates are given in parentheses after the names of rulers, counts, bishops, and popes, they refer to period of office. Dates of birth and death are indicated thus: b., d..

Personal names are given in common English forms, whenever possible.

*Places*

To aid location I have relied on Europe's major rivers and mountain ranges as prominent landmarks; they are marked on Figure 0.1. In addition, I have sometimes used modern nations (Scotland, France, Germany, etc.) as geographical descriptors: the reader is cautioned that these have absolutely no political validity for the period under discussion. Principal places mentioned in each chapter are marked on its first map.

Place names are given in standard English forms, where these exist, and otherwise in the dominant local language.

*Sources*

Notes are confined to identifying the editions of works from which I quote: all translations are my own unless otherwise indicated. Many early medieval texts, especially histories and saints' lives, are readily available in excellent translations, with or without the original language on the facing page, and I acknowledge whenever I have reproduced these. For those texts where the original is not available in the same volume as the translation I have cited, there follows in parentheses a reference to the best available edition. In those cases where I disagree with widely available English translations, I have provided my own translation but have usually noted the availability of an alternative English version.

# Introduction

As concepts originating in the Italian Renaissance, 'Antiquity' and 'the Middle Ages' are deeply embedded in historical consciousness, and few would doubt that these catchwords stand for distinct phases of Europe's past. Scholars during the Renaissance, however, popularized the terms as antithetical poles of European culture, the former positive, the latter negative. When History emerged as a separate university discipline in the middle decades of the nineteenth century, the study of the past for its own sake became institutionalized. This occurred in a way that isolated Antiquity and the Middle Ages from each other in different museums and art galleries, libraries and academic departments. Certainly, serious scholars no longer treat the so-called medieval period as the bleak antithesis of the ancient world, even if the notion of a 'Dark Age' lingers in journalistic vogue. Nevertheless, debates about the relative contribution of 'Antiquity' and the 'Middle Ages' to the complex and problematic phenomenon of 'European Civilization' have persisted in juxtaposing the one against the other. In all this, the centuries in between have remained the poor relations, dismissively labelled as impoverished, barbarian, superstitious, or archaic. If the broad sweep of European history is conceived in linear or evolutionist terms, they are viewed as a period of national origins for narratives whose unfolding requires simple virtues, distinct identities, and suitable foundations for later progress. Alternatively, within a cyclical view of history, they become an interlude of lesser significance between two peaks of political and cultural achievement, the Roman Empire and the cosmopolitan Christian Europe of the twelfth and thirteenth centuries. Both frameworks impose value judgements rooted in the political needs and cultural preferences of post-Enlightenment Europe. This book rejects these hard-worn paradigms. It proposes that the dynamic transformation of Europe's cultures between Antiquity and the Middle Ages is of fundamental significance in its own right.

When did this transformation occur? Periodization can be the bane of historians. Scholarly arguments, each with their own premises, locate the end of the ancient world anywhere between the fifth century and the late tenth or early eleventh century. Where the caesura is placed depends on whether priority is given to political, institutional, social, economic, or

cultural criteria as the basis of periodization: the neat half millennium of
my subtitle is deliberately artificial. It serves as an approximate guide to
the contents of this book, for this contested period forms its subject. At
its opening, around the year 500, Roman imperial rule had already ceased
to be operative in the West, but most other aspects of Roman culture and
practice persisted, little affected by changing political structures: in 500,
Europe was post-imperial, but not thereby post-Roman. By around 1000,
quite different imperial polities dominated the political landscape, and the
Roman cultural legacy had both been transformed and exercised a transforming effect over a vast area of Europe. Those changes are equally evident in the city of Rome itself, the former western imperial provinces, and
the lands far beyond them. In order to establish their main contours, I
pursue themes both before and after the rounded dates of AD 500 and AD
1000. This allows me to demonstrate that, within the overall matrix of
social and cultural development across these centuries, change occurred
at different times and speeds in different places.

Multiple terminologies accompany disputed periodization. The 'late
Antiquity' of the ancient historian, the 'early Middle Ages' of the medievalist, the 'early historic period' or 'late Iron Age' of the archaeologist
of non-Roman Europe reflect different disciplinary presumptions and
analytical perspectives but can all refer to the same century. For simple
convenience, I have generally preferred to use the phrase 'early Middle
Ages' to cover the entirety of the matter discussed in this book, but that
too is arbitrary.

The geographical scope is similarly less self-evident than my title might
suggest. In mythological origin, Europa was a Phoenician princess. But
the god Zeus, in the form of a bull, raped her and carried her off over the
sea: her name came to refer to one of the three continents known in Antiquity. By the ninth century, the name 'Europe' was shedding its use as a
geographical descriptor and acquiring instead strong overtones as a des-
ignator of the zone where Latin Christian traditions found allegiance. Indeed, for much of the Middle Ages, 'Europe' yielded to 'Christendom',
the land of Rome-centred Christianity, as the preferred term of cultural
identification. A legacy of confusion between geographical and cultural
signification has persisted ever since. For most of the nineteenth and twentieth centuries, 'Europe' could be divided along political, religious, and
social fault lines into 'western' and 'eastern' sections, with 'Mitteleuropa'
assigned an ambivalent role and a contested location somewhere in between. Now, in the early twenty-first century, the meaning of 'Europe' is
under renewed scrutiny, its geographical, cultural, religious, and political
connotations more debated than ever before. Even at the most simplistic

level of definition—the member states of the European Union—Europe
has changed while this book has been in preparation.

My frame of reference certainly approximates to the expanded European Union that came into being on 1 May 2004, but with two significant
qualifications. The first is the exclusion of Greece (together with its non-
EU Balkan neighbours). Retaining a focus on the area that by the end of
the first millennium was acquiring an identity as Latin Christendom has
meant relegating the Byzantine world to an offstage role. The second is
imposed by the evidence available. Some parts of 'Europe' were inhabited
by preliterate peoples for part or most of these centuries, while others are
poorly represented in surviving documentation. Scandinavia, the Slav
regions, and the Danubian plain all fall into the former category; much
of Scotland and Wales into the latter. Thus the contours of this book are
inevitably those of the extant written word. I have avoided the temptation
to fill the gaps by using texts from later centuries that purport to offer a
window onto these earlier times, but instead have sometimes turned to
material evidence to complement the textual record. Even so, the very uneven coverage of archaeological research and publication imposes its own
constraints.

The story of the transition from Antiquity to the Middle Ages has conventionally been told in two parts. The first instalment tells of imperial
decline, barbarian invasion, economic stagnation, and the decay of urban
culture; its sequel hails the rise of national monarchies and an inter-
nationally organized Christian church accompanied by the gradual recovery of economic prosperity and civic life. Of the various forms of this
grand narrative, the one most familiar today privileges France, Germany,
and England and allocates occasional episodes to Italy. It defines its subject in terms of significance to the post-medieval history of nation building and high culture, thereby virtually ignoring everywhere that did not
conform to the nineteenth-century paradigm of the nation state. While
this overt teleology has certainly weakened since the 1960s, distinctive
national historiographical traditions nevertheless still inform twenty-
first-century approaches to the early Middle Ages. Additionally, much
scholarly literature continues to take as its field of analysis either the
modern polity or the early medieval ethnic or political grouping deemed
to precede it, whatever specific topic is under investigation. The only place
the reader of this book will find any trace of these approaches is at the
back, in the Further Reading.

I have substituted three revisionist approaches, chosen for their
combined analytical vigour. In the first place, I rebalance the usual

historiographical emphasis on a 'core' region by attention to a much broader geographical field of vision stretching from Scandinavia to Spain and from Hungary to Ireland. As Figure o.1 suggests, this is a region of great natural differentiation between north and south, upland and low-land, coast and interior; this variation forms the backdrop to the chapters that follow. Secondly, I repeatedly move between polities, medieval or modern, cross-cutting national historiographical preoccupations and ignoring modern political boundaries. Finally, I reject any notion that Europe in the early Middle Ages can be characterized as a homogeneous culture-province. My premiss is diversity of experience, not analogy of historical outcome.

In place of teleological determinism, I substitute a comparative ethnog-raphy of the early Middle Ages. This method draws heavily, albeit in-directly, on the work of social and cultural anthropologists; its purpose is to enable questions of general applicability to receive locally specific answers. These cumulatively establish a cross-cultural analysis of early medieval societies and facilitate comparisons and contrasts between them. The organizing problem that I address in this fashion can be summarized thus: how did the men and women who lived between 500 and 1000 order their own worlds in social, cultural, and political terms? In answering it, I emphasize the variety of early medieval experience by highlighting both the omnipresence of localisms and micro-regions and the diversities inherent in gender and status distinctions.

Those around whom power congealed—strongmen, lords, kings, emperors—form the goal of my analysis, not my point of departure. Thus they tend to occur towards the end of each chapter, and especially the end of the book. I have chosen to get at them by addressing issues that pertain to the organization of almost all social groupings: language and communication; kinship and gender; the accumulation and symbolism of wealth; religious practice and ideology; personal and group identity; political legitimation and status. Rather than merely explaining what happened, these concerns analyse how and why things happened, how communities were organized, how people gave meaning to their lives and validated their own ways of doing things.

The book begins by establishing the 'ground rules' for subsequent chap-ters: not only the general limits of what we know about the early Middle Ages and how we can know it, but also the constraints of terrain, climate, and agricultural technology. The first two chapters thus introduce the many and varied environments within which men and women spoke, wrote, and thought, lived and died; together they establish diversity of ex-perience and responsiveness to change as recurrent themes. The next pair

KEY

| | |
|---|---|
| Sea (or lake) | Land between 200 and 1,000 metres |
| Land below 200 metres | Land over 1,000 metres |

0 300 600
km

0.1. Europe: physical features.

of chapters argue that social relationships—between kin-based groups, on the one hand, and between men and women, on the other—organize all communities at every level from household to empire, whatever the locally specific forms of social organization might be. The fifth and sixth chapters turn from the power relationships inherent in distinctions of kin and gender to those organized around immovable and movable wealth— that is, around land and treasure. Once again, situational variety indicates a wide range of responses to the generic problem of maintaining status and hierarchy, of turning resources into enduring political and spiritual advantage. The final pair of chapters focuses on experiences of religious and political change and draws attention to ways in which they were made to seem 'natural' by heavy ideological investment. Both emphasize the importance of Christianity as a transmitter of cultural values derived from an earlier, Roman, age, and the many imaginative uses to which Roman cultural resources were put.

All chapters have the same geographical and chronological parameters, Europe from 500 to 1000. They function like transparent overlays: each one offers a diagrammatic sketch of one aspect of a complex whole, but, as they are placed one upon the other, the lower diagrams remain visible. Each is coherent; together the intersecting perspectives build up a full and nuanced picture. The reader who prefers to take these chapters in a different order to the one in which I have arranged them will find ample cross-referencing between chapters but no repetition of definitions, regnal dates, and so forth.

This is a new cultural history of Europe in several ways. Admittedly a loosely conceived genre of historical writing, the expression 'new cultural history' commonly refers to a diverse cluster of historiographical approaches, many of which have influenced my work. In the first place, it signals an engagement with 'culture' in its widest sense, as the expression of meanings, perceptions, and values by means of which people construct their understanding of reality, organize their experiences, and determine their actions. By implication, this approach prefers to endow the men and women of the past with agency, instead of understanding historical change as a series of forces, trends, or movements that reduce individuals to passive pawns in the grip of impersonal processes. Secondly, new cultural history is founded upon sensitivity towards language. It emphasizes the uncertain relationship between texts and the historical 'reality' they purport to represent—or that some historians aspire to find. While that sensitivity sometimes verges on denial of any relationship, I adopt a more moderate position but nevertheless draw readers' attention to some of the textual problems encountered by historians working on this epoch. There follows the proposition that culture is in the service of power, whether it occludes, displaces, or legitimizes its brute realities. Thus cultural history, so the argument goes, contributes to unmasking the realities of power, and revealing strategies of domination for what they are. Finally, it stems from each of these points, individually or in sum, that new cultural history evinces scepticism of grand narratives. In their place, it substitutes a belief in the value of micro-history and a healthy respect for the pluralism of historical experience.

For these reasons, this is a book not about European culture but about Europe's cultures. My approach allows repeated emphasis to be placed on three interpretative threads, all equally central. I have already indicated my insistence upon recognizing early medieval particularities from many different perspectives. The second is the attention I bring to the role of the Roman heritage in early medieval constructions of power. Whether in Rome's former provinces or in regions that were never within the imperial boundaries, I argue that the reception, reinterpretation, or abandonment of that inheritance made a formative contribution to all the cultures of early medieval Europe. The trace of the former political frontier, marked on Figure 0.2, influenced how that occurred: in cultural formation as well as historiographical periodization, the Middle Ages presuppose Antiquity. They cannot be sundered. The third is the dynamism of early medieval societies. The demonstration that the Europe of 1000 was very different from that of 500 is not an argument for any evolutionary grand narrative, but a recognition that, wherever and however one looks, change and fluidity are evident. Decline, stagnation, and rise have no place here; instead a kaleidoscope of multiple transformations, continuities, innovations, permutations.

One artefact sums up this book more eloquently than an extended introduction could do. At some point in the late eighth or early ninth century, a master sculptor fashioned a large box-shaped structure (177 cm wide, 90 cm deep, and 70 cm high) for the royal Pictish church of *Cennrígmonaid*, in eastern Scotland. Its carved panels of local sandstone slot together to form an object of disputed but indubitably Christian function—perhaps a tomb, an altar, or a shrine. Its richly carved front depicts the Old Testament scene of David wrestling with the lion, represented here in his Christian interpretation as king and saviour (see Frontispiece). He is flanked by an ancient eastern symbol of royalty, a lion-hunter on horseback, and an unmounted huntsman with his dogs, in pursuit of Scottish deer. Artistically, it offers a sophisticated amalgam of distinct stylistic traditions: Eastern Mediterranean, Roman, Irish, Anglo-Saxon, and Pictish.

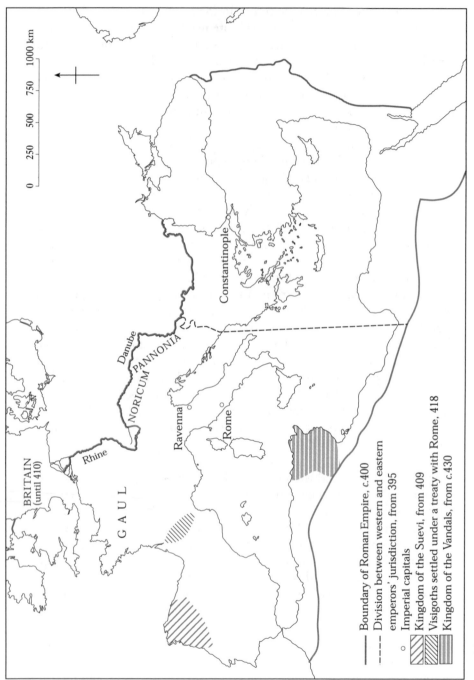

BRITAIN
(until 410)

Rhine

G A U L

NORICUM
PANNONIA
Danube

Ravenna

Rome

Constantinople

0    250    500    750    1000 km

——— Boundary of Roman Empire, c.400
- - - Division between western and eastern
      emperors' jurisdiction, from 395
○     Imperial capitals
▨     Kingdom of the Suevi, from 409
▨     Visigoths settled under a treaty with Rome, 418
▨     Kingdom of the Vandals, from c.430

0.2. The Roman Empire in the early fifth century.

By the time of its manufacture, Roman rule in Britain had receded to a distant and shadowy memory in the minds of an educated few, and even when, in the middle of the second century, it had briefly reached into southern Scotland, the site of future *Cennrígmonaid* (modern St Andrews: see Figure 1.1) lay beyond the imperial frontier. Nevertheless, an urban religion originating on the eastern fringe of the Roman Mediterranean, Christianity, had become integral to the northern political, social, and imaginative world of the Picts. The so-called St Andrews sarcophagus thus represents my three themes of local identities, cultural dynamism, and the reception of the Roman heritage.

It stands as an icon for the issues addressed here in a second way. The Picts were typical of the many peoples of the Atlantic and North Sea regions of Europe north of the Roman frontier whose polities all had fundamentally different and rather simpler internal socio-political organizations than those of the Roman Empire. From a Roman perspective, the contrast was one of civilization and barbarism, of a divide between 'us' and 'them' based upon ancient Mediterranean beliefs that urban communities and the civic culture that they sustained were inherently superior to technologically and politically less complex, rural, warrior societies. From a twenty-first-century perspective, the artificiality of this categorization is painfully evident. 'Civilized' and 'barbarian' are subjective referents based upon perceptions and traditions designed to legitimize one group at the expense of others by affirming a hierarchy of cultural difference and moral worth. The sculptor of *Cennrígmonaid* associated a classically robed David with a traditionally armed Pictish warrior in a way that quite negates any antithesis between 'civilized' and 'barbarian'. European historiography too needs to transcend this ancient polarity: this book offers a contribution to that endeavour.

# FUNDAMENTALS

# I

# Speaking and Writing

What we say passes, what we write remains.[1]

We hear God's books explained and read to us, the Gospel proclaimed, and His glories made known to men.[2]

CENTRAL to the historian's craft are the written relics of the past. Crudely scratched inscriptions, dry bureaucratic prose, inspired poetry, tax lists, abstract theological speculations, or beautifully illuminated manuscripts: these and many other forms of the written word are the materials on which historians base their constructions of past societies. In thinking about Europe's history in the centuries between 500 and 1000, we face at the outset the dilemma that much written material has not survived. Medieval writers sometimes mention or quote texts and documents to which they had access but which have since perished. In copying documents, scribes might struggle to read the handwriting, or might deliberately alter and update the text in front of them, only to throw the old version away when the new one was finished. The ravages of neglect, damp, fire, and warfare over many centuries have compounded deliberate disposal and accidental loss. For all these reasons, we can be sure that the surviving written record for the early Middle Ages is only a fraction of what must once have existed, even though we cannot measure quite how small it may be. The chapters in this book all take their cue from such written material as does remain.

The vagaries of survival are not the only constraint upon our enquiry. Had nothing been lost, we should still not be able to answer all the questions that we might wish to. For part or all of the period under discussion, people in some parts of Europe made no use of any form of writing. Even in those communities that were familiar with the techniques of writing and reading, these skills were practised by only a small proportion of the population: we can study the early Middle Ages through the words of only a few of the men—and even fewer of the women—who lived in those centuries.

Recognition of these limitations should encourage us to begin our enquiry into early medieval culture by exploring the place of writing within it. Let us remember at the outset that writing always happens in a specific language. It encodes speech in a widely shared repertoire of visual signs that represent the sounds that combine to form words. Thus it is never neatly separable from other verbal activities such as talking, reading, and thinking, and is only one of many different means of communication and expression available to any society. Historians of the modern world are often able to exploit a wide range of communicative media, but a more restricted range is available to scholars of the Middle Ages. Visual images were certainly important, as were numbers, gestures, and symbolic actions, but this chapter focuses on words, spoken as well as written—for we cannot consider the one without the other. Early medieval authors commonly composed by speaking out loud to a scribe who took down their dictation, and they generally did so in the expectation that their words would be communicated by being read out loud to an audience or voiced in a murmur by the individual, solitary reader. Knowledge central to a community's identity and functioning might be passed on orally for generations, whether or not its members were familiar with the techniques of writing and reading. Material from that oral storehouse of traditions and information from time to time found its way into written form, and written texts often acquired their social significance when voiced aloud to an audience of hearers. Thus meanings, thoughts, and ideas conveyed by words flowed back and forth between complementary spoken and written media. Although speaking and writing cannot be divorced from one another, historians must remember at all times that only the written words survive for us to analyse and appreciate: in the much-quoted dictum of Pope Gregory I 'the Great' (590–604): 'What we say passes, what we write remains.'[3] The quandary that faces the student of any pre-modern culture is the inaccessibility of the non-written word, despite its central importance in the lives of men and women.

This chapter thus approaches the question of writing from the perspective of spoken language. What languages did people speak in the early Middle Ages? And how readily could they understand one another? Why and how did the linguistic map of Europe change during these centuries? Of defining importance in their own right, these questions provide our starting point. They also introduce a major theme running throughout this book—the diversity of early medieval experience, so different from the universalizing tendencies of the ancient world.

The second section of the chapter analyses the interrelationship between Latin, the language of Roman imperialism and culture, and the local languages of early medieval Europe by asking what was committed to writing and in which language. A world of widely varying customs and local practices, of communities each with their own ways of going about life, acquires firm focus. Against the background of the political collapse of the western Roman Empire, the uses found for Latin in new contexts open up a world of shifting, dynamic cultural processes that contributed to novel forms of power and authority. The section concludes that, in their adoption, adaptation, or rejection of the language of the Roman Empire, early medieval Europeans were making choices about their own identity and about ways of organizing and expressing power in their own world. Here we meet the second overall theme of this book: that interaction with Roman traditions was of fundamental importance to all localities, including those far beyond the former Roman frontiers. The contribution of this legacy to the cultural formations of early medieval Europe cannot be ignored; this discussion demonstrates the point with respect to language and the uses of writing.

The third theme that runs through this chapter, as through all subsequent ones, is power. Building on the analysis of the relative prestige of different languages in the second section, the final part argues that literacy must be understood as a technology of power. There are two dimensions to this. The first concerns individuals and their access to the relevant technical skills that enabled the exercise of authority. The second has an institutional dimension, for ascetic Christian communities gradually emerged as the upholders of a normative, elite literary culture in a way that lacked precedent in the ancient world but nevertheless perpetuated its cultural prejudices. The overall purpose of this chapter is to make clear that the surviving written sources for early medieval history are never naive in conception or transparent in intent: their choice of language, form, and content betrays implicit cultural value judgements and power relationships. This argument is crucial for what follows: once we are aware of the extent to which the surviving written sources are themselves ways of constructing meaning and organizing power, we can proceed to exploit them to different purposes in subsequent chapters.

## The Tower of Babel

Around 850, the wife of Count Hungerius of Langres gave birth to a daughter who was both deaf and mute. Treating her 'like a monster, a brutish animal, more wretched than the slave of one of their domestic

1.1. Principal places mentioned in Chapter 1.

serving girls', her parents rejected her. Somehow the girl survived and, as a grown adult, found her way to the shrine of St Martin at Chablis. Here the saint addressed her: 'Genovefa, my daughter, be not afraid.' As blood poured from her ears and mouth, she was healed. She had never heard speech before, and was Genovefa her name? Shortly thereafter, her brothers' serving-girl happened to visit the shrine and recognized the woman. The servant hailed her as 'my lady Genovefa' and acknowledged the miracle. Cured of her disabilities, Genovefa was restored to human-ity.[4] For the monk who described this miracle, as for other writers in the early Middle Ages, the power of speech differentiated humans from ani-mals. Language was a divine gift to humankind.

But in one part of the origin myth that Christians took over from the Jews, all the peoples of the earth had originally spoken the same language. This tale tells how, having constructed the marvellous Tower of Babel, its builders succumbed to pride in their achievement. To punish them, God 'established for earth-dwellers dissimilar tongues so that they had no success with [each others'] languages . . . nor did any people understand what another said.'[5] To this Anglo-Saxon translator of the biblical myth, it seemed evident that each people spoke its own language. Others were less certain, such as Isidore, bishop of Seville (599–636). He was sure that languages preceded peoples, but could not make up his mind quite how they correlated. 'In the beginning, there were as many languages as peoples, but later more peoples than languages, for many peoples arose out of one language.'[6] This constituted a tacit acknowledgement of the fluid, shifting interrelationship of language to people.

Isidore's intuition was certainly correct. We must dismiss the nineteenth-century misconception that there had ever existed a matching relationship of one people or polity to one language. Equally erroneous is the notion that there was linguistic uniformity within any medieval group that regarded itself as constituting a single people or nation. The rela-tionship of languages to peoples in the early Middle Ages was far too complex to be reduced to simple formulae such as these. As we shall see, languages did not start and stop at political frontiers: they overlapped in various ways that took no account of political allegiances. Moreover, they were always characterized by marked internal dialectal variations and were continually evolving. Naturally, language change continued long after the end of our period, so we must bear in mind that the changes reviewed here form one segment of a much longer story—but it is an era of form-ative significance in European linguistic history, and one that has been central to arguments about the identities of the peoples of Europe since the eighteenth century.

With these points in mind, we can survey the languages of the region on which this book concentrates. Figure 1.2 shows four main language zones at the start of our period. The British archipelago was the main zone of Celtic speech, whose main forms were diverging in important ways in the later Roman period. By the eighth century, two mutually incom-prehensible versions were spoken, Gaelic (or Q-Celtic) and Brittonic (or P-Celtic). Although modern philology has established their close affinity, no one in the Middle Ages was aware of this; to all intents and

**1.2.** Main language zones, *c*.500.

purposes, they were two quite different languages. In *c.*500, Gaelic was spoken in Ireland, as well as by settlers across the Irish Sea. Its use along the western coasts of Cornwall and Wales in the fifth and sixth centuries was relatively short-lived, but not so further north, in what is now western Scotland. We shall return here shortly.

Brittonic, the indigenous language of Britain at the time of the Roman conquest, had remained in use alongside Latin during the centuries of Roman rule, but in the early Middle Ages developed distinctive regional forms, including Welsh, Cornish, Cumbric, and Pictish. Neither regional linguistic variation nor differing political fortunes destroyed a sense of shared identity among the British, and a tenth-century Welsh poet could prophesy that the time would come again when the Cymry, the speakers of Brittonic, would once again

> ... possess all from Manaw [near Edinburgh] to Brittany,
> from Dyfed to Thanet ...
> from the Wall to the Forth. ...[7]

In the fifth and sixth centuries, British speakers were also to be found scattered along much of the Atlantic coast of continental Europe, with particular concentrations at the north-western tip of Spain and the westernmost peninsula of what is now France. Only in this latter region—Brittany—was their linguistic impact enduring: in the eleventh or twelfth century, a Welsh writer commented that the Welsh and the Bretons 'were of one language and one people, although geographically separate'.[8] This was the limit of medieval awareness of linguistic affinity in this region of Europe, for the designation 'Celtic' is a construct of eighteenth-century philological erudition infused with romantic-era political and cultural aspiration: it has no basis in medieval understanding.

As a comparison of Figures 1.2 and 1.3 reveals, the extent of Brittonic within Britain shrank greatly in the course of the early Middle Ages. It faced two challenges. Gaelic speakers applied the name Dalriada both to the north-eastern tip of Ireland and to their settlements in western Scotland. From its relatively modest origins in Dalriada around the year 500, Gaelic gradually diffused throughout almost the entire area north of the estuaries of the Solway and Forth. Its maximum extent, around 1100, corresponded to most of the medieval Scottish kingdom, known to its inhabitants as Alba. Within this area, Gaelic had competed with, and then gradually displaced, local Cumbric and Pictish versions of Brittonic. It remains far from clear exactly how this happened, and, while we know that the Irish monk Columba (b. *c.*521, d. 597) could preach Christianity to the Picts in northern and eastern Scotland only 'through an interpreter', it

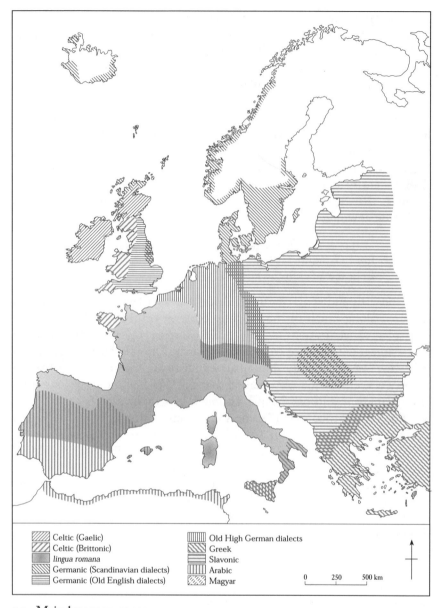

Celtic (Gaelic)
Celtic (Brittonic)
*lingua romana*
Germanic (Scandinavian dialects)
Germanic (Old English dialects)
Old High German dialects
Greek
Slavonic
Arabic
Magyar

0      250      500 km

1.3. Main language zones, *c.*1000.

does seem that, in parts of central Scotland at least, a bilingual elite speaking both Gaelic and Pictish persisted until c.900.[9] Thereafter, the dominant language of the kingdom of Alba was Gaelic.

Germanic is the second language-group to consider, although this too is a post-medieval philological categorization. A version of this posed the second challenge to Brittonic, causing the latter's disappearance from southern and eastern Britain. Germanic-speaking elites, collectively—but anachronistically—designated 'Anglo-Saxons', had certainly established a presence on the eastern seaboard of the island during the fifth century. Thereafter, they gradually established political hegemony over all Britain south of the Firth of Forth and east of the Severn by c.750. How their political successes prompted a linguistic transformation so complete as to eradicate Brittonic throughout this area remains deeply contested, however.

The cluster of dialects spoken by the Anglo-Saxons are collectively known as Old English. They are best assessed within the broad Germanic language zone around the North Sea. It comprised the north-western quadrant of the European continent including southern Scandinavia, as marked on Figure 1.2. In the early centuries of the Christian era, Germanic was the speech of those peoples living along and north of the Roman imperial frontier that followed the Rhine and Danube, and its use had extended as far as the flood plain of the river Elbe in the north-east and the Ukrainian steppes in the south-east. The turbulence of the fourth, fifth, and sixth centuries carried its speakers far and wide throughout the western provinces of the empire, whether as isolated individuals, military detachments, entire armies, or even peoples. Among these were groups who styled themselves Goths, Franks, Saxons, Lombards, Frisians, Bavarians, to name only the most important. We shall meet them frequently in this book, as also the kingdoms they established within Roman imperial territories. One indication of the linguistic unity of the early medieval Germanic-speaking world is a remark of Paul the Deacon (b. c.720/30, d. c.799). He came from Italy to the court of the Frankish king Charlemagne (768–814), where his stay will have familiarized him with the sounds of the Germanic dialects north of the Alps. He recalled how the deeds of the Lombard king Alboin (c.560–72) were remembered 'not only among the Bavarians and the Saxons, but also among other men of the same tongue in their songs'.[10]

Except in eastern Britain, and in a broad swathe of territory in northern Gaul, Germanic speakers gradually became assimilated into the local communities, giving up their traditional language in the course of several generations. Social and political upheaval fostered rapid linguistic change within the Germanic zone, as it did within the Celtic zone: here too one sign of this was growing regional differentiation within the Germanic language continuum, with marked results by the end of the millennium. As divergent strands of Germanic emerged, it must have required increasing effort on the part of speakers of one version to comprehend those using another, particularly when the speakers each came from remoter parts of the dialect spectrum. We certainly should not assume that speakers would have held the same opinion about the degree of linguistic identity they shared, however. In the wake of Scandinavian settlement in England in the ninth–tenth century, some English writers differentiated the Scandinavian language from the English, yet, as late as the twelfth century, a descendant of the Scandinavian settlers in Iceland commented that the Icelanders and English 'are of one tongue'. He emphasized this, despite also acknowledging that 'one of the two tongues has changed greatly, or both somewhat'.[11] Speakers' perceptions of language identity or difference were as subjective in the Middle Ages as they remain today. Figure 1.3 acknowledges the growing differentiation between Scandinavian, Old English, and other Germanic dialect forms collectively known as Old High German.

The growing divergences affecting both the Celtic and Germanic languages had been given impetus by major changes in pronunciation, vocabulary, and word-forms, which were particularly rapid in the fourth, fifth, and sixth centuries. No single explanation of these linguistic changes suffices: complex social and political transformations must all be taken into consideration. Of all the contributory factors, population movement probably played only a minor part. More cogent explanations include conquest and Christianization, for these were both potent agents of linguistic change—and sometimes of language death. Additional stimuli came from the development of written forms of these languages and from the influence of Latin, the language of power, prestige, and Christianity, which influenced Celtic and Germanic languages alike.

With Latin, we reach the third important language zone of the early Middle Ages. In the post-imperial era, it continued to be spoken in those provinces less seriously affected by social or political disruption, and where Christian communities persisted undisturbed. In western Britain, Latin was certainly still spoken in the sixth century but died out thereafter. At about the same time, it ceased to be the dominant language in the Balkans, becoming concentrated in the western half of the Mediterranean and most of its Iberian, Gallic, and Italian hinterlands, as Figure 1.2 makes clear.

The fourth and final language marked on Figure 1.2 is Greek, which had been spoken and written throughout the eastern Mediterranean in

Antiquity. The central Balkans and the southernmost tip of Italy had long since stabilized as its western limits, and although knowledge of Greek had formerly been common among the educated elite of the western Roman provinces, this accomplishment had become rare by *c.*500. The declining use of Greek had an additional cause, however, in the appearance of Slavonic. Despite losing much ground to it during the early Middle Ages, Greek nevertheless remained the main language of the southern part of the Balkan peninsula, and in the course of the sixth century replaced Latin as the administrative language of Constantinople, capital of the Byzantine (eastern Roman) Empire. In Italy, where the southernmost provinces remained under Byzantine rule, Greek remained a language of elite literary culture alongside Latin for as long as the administrative bond with Constantinople persisted.

Slavs are first mentioned by Byzantine writers in the middle years of the sixth century, who located their kingdoms north of the lower reaches of the Danube. It is debatable whether the Slavs ever shared any sense of common identity, however. While it is clear that Slav conquests of the northern and central Balkans fostered the spread of their culture and language at the expense of Greek as far south as Thessaloniki at the head of the Aegean Sea, the causes of the cultural transformation remain contested, as elsewhere. By the eighth century, versions of Slavonic appear to have been spoken throughout much of central Europe east of the Elbe, including areas that had formerly been Germanic—some of which would become so again in later centuries. By *c.*1000, increasing amounts of evidence make the extent of Slavonic more certain, and this is shown on Figure 1.3.

There are two further languages marked on Figure 1.3, both spread by well-documented conquests: Arabic and Magyar. Muslim armies crossed the Straits of Gibraltar in 711 and conquered the southern and central provinces of the Iberian peninsula in the early eighth century; they introduced the Arabic language into Spain. Although Latin continued in use there, it lost its status and prestige as the local population gradually adopted Islam. By the early eleventh century, it remained the language of worship for such Christian communities as remained, but by then Arabic was firmly established as the language of government and elite literary culture. Finally, the Magyars (known to their opponents as Hungarians), in origin nomads from the Asiatic steppes, crossed the Carpathian mountains in the late ninth and tenth centuries on wide-ranging raids before establishing permanent settlements in the Danubian plain, where they introduced their own distinctive language.

Although Latin came under competition from other languages in many parts of the former western Roman Empire, it deserves detailed attention.

In and after late Antiquity, *lingua romana*, 'the Roman tongue', meant Latin, both spoken and written. When it was spoken in Antiquity, pronunciation varied considerably from one region to another and also between elite and non-elite speakers. As a written literary language, the Latin of Antiquity was much less susceptible to change, and retained an inbuilt tendency towards conservatism, standardization, and elitism. The term *lingua romana* referred to all these forms. By the twelfth century, however, *lingua romana* referred only to the spoken forms, 'the Romance tongue'—whether in its French, Walloon, Catalan, Spanish, or Italian versions—to distinguish it from the written Latin language. We can avoid the controversies about how, when, and why spoken Latin stopped and Romance began by referring to the form spoken in the early Middle Ages as simply the *lingua romana*.

It too evolved significantly in the course of the early Middle Ages. Regional divergences in the spoken *lingua romana* gradually become even stronger than in Antiquity, and pronunciation changed too, but not so much as to cause incomprehension between speakers from different regions. That started to happen only around 1200. This meant that, when Abd al-Rahman III, the Arabic-speaking caliph of Cordoba (912–61), exchanged envoys with the German king Otto I (936–73), in 953, they had no difficulty communicating. The caliphal representatives were members of the local Cordovan Christian community, men fluent in both Arabic and the local *lingua romana*. If they had been attentive as they travelled northwards, they might have noticed gradual local shifts of accent and vocabulary, until they finally arrived at Toul, a town still within the north-eastern reaches of the *lingua romana*, but also inside Otto's kingdom. Otto had chosen as his envoy John (b. *c*.900, d. 974), a monk of Gorze, who had been born in the area where the *lingua romana* intermingled with Germanic speech. In all probability bilingual in both these local languages, John travelled south with one of the Cordovan deputation: together they whiled away the long journey by 'talking about everything'.[12] Despite some regional differences, a single language was thus spoken all the way from the Guadalquivir to the Mosel, just as it had been in Roman times. By this date, the descendants of the Germanic speakers who created the fifth- and sixth-century kingdoms had long since abandoned their ancestral language. As a Spaniard who became bishop of an Italian city wrote in the early ninth century: 'Latin, though one language, has within its fold many peoples, like the famous and noble ones of our time: the Franks, the Gauls, the Italians (or Romans), the Lombards; and the Spanish, the Africans, the Asturians and the Basques.'[13] There is an element of linguistic imperialism at work here, for the Basques spoke—and still speak—an ancient language unrelated to Latin, but nevertheless, Claudius of Turin aptly expressed the truism that the *lingua romana* remained a single language spoken by many different peoples.

Latin followed a different trajectory as a written language, however. To track this, we must return from the Mediterranean basin to Ireland, where the spread of Christianity during the fifth century introduced the language of Christian worship used throughout the western Roman world. Irish scholars approached Latin as a language to be acquired by learning to read books in school, not from speaking to parents in the home. They soon developed methods for teaching it as a foreign language, which the new Christian communities in the Germanic parts of Britain also eagerly adopted. For Irish and Anglo-Saxon converts, then, Latin was a written, learned language, not a living, spoken one. They clung to traditional rules for spelling and grammar, in sharp contrast to the fluid usages of native speakers of the *lingua romana*. Only those monks and nuns who travelled to the Continent ever encountered the spoken forms of the language. When they did, they were startled at how different it was from the Latin they had learned to read, write, and pronounce in their schoolrooms. Boniface (b. *c.*675, d. 754) was a missionary from southern England who spent most of his life preaching among the Germanic peoples of the Continent, whose local versions of Germanic he evidently understood without difficulty. But when he visited Rome in 722, he was uncomfortable with the *lingua romana* spoken in the papal court and preferred to communicate important matters in writing. Boniface's written Latin posed no problem for his papal interlocutor, but his experience emphasizes the growing gulf between Latin as a mother tongue and Latin as a language learned in the classroom.

Half a century after Boniface, the Anglo-Saxon scholar Alcuin (b. *c.*740, d. 804) was invited to Charlemagne's court, where he became an influential teacher and counsellor. Among the achievements attributed to him are a reform of the spelling and grammar of the written form of Latin he encountered on the Continent. By bringing it back into line with late antique norms he had learned at school in York, Alcuin initiated reforms that stabilized the written language in a highly conservative way. Though these had no effect on the spoken language, they further exacerbated the growing gulf between the spoken and written language. It seems that preachers who used the learned, 'Alcuinian', Latin were liable to find that they were incomprehensible to audiences north of the Seine, who spoke the orally transmitted *lingua romana*.

This divergence between the spoken and written language, between the 'rustic' or 'vulgar' speech and the Latin of the clerically educated elite, developed only rather later in Mediterranean regions. Not until the very end of the millennium did such a distinction become evident in Rome. When Pope Gregory V died in 999, an inscription was placed above his tomb in St Peter's, commemorating the brief reign of this pope of German origin. Ignoring the turbulent politics of his pontificate, it praised the way he had 'instructed the populace with a threefold eloquence, using German, the vulgar tongue and the Latin language.'[14] Here in Rome, the original home of the *lingua romana*, 'Latin' was no longer the spoken language of the city's inhabitants by the end of our period.

Gregory was the papal name selected by Bruno, cousin and court chaplain to the German emperor Otto III (983–1002). As a career cleric in Germany, he would have acquired his knowledge of Latin entirely in the schoolroom. His elevation to the papal throne took him from the Germanic world into that of the *lingua romana*, which he evidently learned readily enough. Germanic, Celtic, and *lingua romana* were not mutually intelligible; except in the zones where two languages overlapped in frequent use, any bilingualism was an acquired effort, not the product of upbringing. But in the contact zones, the situation must have been rather different. Any place where two spoken languages were in simultaneous use was likely to have been socially complex. Commonly, one will have been the language of the ruling elite and thus enjoyed greater prestige, the other being relegated to the language of the peasantry. This limits the likelihood of widespread, full bilingualism. Active competence in one but general passive knowledge of the other is one possibility; equally probable is partial ability in the second language, for example in restricted spheres of life such as mercantile activity or estate management. Differentiations of social status will have further complicated the picture. Also, scattered communities where the minority language was locally dominant might occur, effectively speech islands.

Although complex linguistic nuances must have characterized areas where any two speech communities overlapped, they are most easily demonstrable where the *lingua romana* shaded off into Germanic. Intensive fifth-century Germanic settlement in areas south and west of the Rhine made Germanic the dominant language far further south than the present-day linguistic frontier between French and German and, for a while, a minority language over much of the northern half of the former Roman province of Gaul. Between the ninth and the thirteenth centuries, however, the border of dominant speech receded to approximately its current position, and any familiarity with Germanic further south faded away. Notwithstanding the dominance of Germanic around Gaul's northern and eastern peripheries, the *lingua romana* continued to be spoken in some cities, such as Tongres, Maastricht, and Trier, as well as in remote valleys in the Ardennes and Jura mountains. How the complex linguistic situation affected the peasantry is impossible to say, but there is good evidence that some members of the aristocracy from this area were bilingual until at least the ninth century. This doubtless facilitated their participation in the far-flung networks of imperial power established by Charlemagne, and, indeed, helped make those networks function. For as long as this empire held together, speakers of *lingua romana* might find themselves sent off to learn Germanic, or married to a husband with a different mother tongue. But the dissolution of the Carolingian Empire that began in the late ninth century lessened the political advantages of familiarity with both languages, except where the bilingual zone persisted along the southern bank of the Rhine. It is symptomatic of the change that, when the German emperor Otto II (973–83) met the leading West Frankish magnate, Duke Hugh (nicknamed Hugh Capet; French king 987–96) in 981, neither spoke the other's language. To communicate, Otto spoke in Latin, and one of the bishops in Hugh's retinue translated for the duke. Evidently Hugh's only language was the spoken *lingua romana* of northern France, and he had neither learned Latin nor understood Germanic.

In sum, we must appreciate the linguistic diversity of early medieval Europe. In this context, some people found it easier than others to strain their ears to make sense of dialectal variations of their own language, or to learn completely different ones. We may contrast the efforts of two Italian missionaries who travelled in 1001 to 'the land of the pagans of horrific-sounding speech'—the Poles. 'With excessive sweat' only one of them tackled the linguistic challenge, learning to understand Slavonic but only to speak it well enough to get by.[15] Although the German-speaking Otto I learned some words of both the *lingua romana* and Slavonic, he nevertheless lacked the confidence to speak them, at least in public. In Chapter 6 we shall meet slave-traders from Verdun who regularly journeyed to Cordoba and German merchants who crossed the Alps to trade in Pavia: certainly these men did not let language difficulties stand in the way of profit. Whatever its diversities and richnesses, language remained the index of humanity. Preaching to the people who dwelt around the southern shores of the Baltic, the ninth-century missionary Rimbert encountered strange dog-headed creatures with two legs. On seeking advice, he was reassured that a key diagnostic was the sound they made: 'humans speak but dogs bark.'[16] Humans shared the facility of language and thus of reason: this united them far more than any language difference divided them.

## Languages of Authority

For centuries, Latin had been the language in which the citizens of Rome made love, scribbled graffiti, commemorated their conquest of an empire in monumental inscriptions, wrote laws, issued tax lists, formulated and preserved rich literary traditions. And, as Christianity spread westwards in the second and third centuries, among communities incapable of understanding the Greek in which the Christian holy texts were written, religious leaders naturally chose to debate, preach, worship, and write in the local language. In preparing Latin translations of the Judaeo-Christian scriptures—the Hebrew Old Testament and the Greek New Testament that comprised the Bible—and in using the same language for worship, fourth- and fifth-century churchmen in the western provinces of the Roman Empire were making their religion as widely accessible as possible. In *c.*500 Latin implied a whole system of learning, a social code, and a technology of power as well as a religion.

As imperial rule crumbled and political systems changed from ancient to early medieval ones, how was the privileged status of Latin as a medium of culture, control, and communication affected? In what language did new converts to Christianity, far beyond the former imperial frontiers, worship? In what ways did the social significance of Latin change, and what political or religious importance did other languages acquire? These are important issues in their own right; together, they help us understand why the surviving written sources for early medieval history take the form they do. This section begins by evaluating the fate of the late Roman bureaucratic apparatus in post-imperial times. It then explores the cultural prestige attached to different systems of writing, and concludes with an extended discussion of the relationship between language and authority. This pays particular attention to the choice of language for written use in contexts where ideology and identity were as important as communication of verbal meaning. By tracking regional variations in the use of Latin vis-à-vis the local languages of Europe, it emphasizes that sacred and secular authority both took many different written forms. The argument  turns on the paradox that the use of Latin spread in geographical terms as the number of people able to understand it, let alone read and write it, diminished. By the end of the first millennium, Latin had become the mark of an elite, inseparably associated with the authority of kings and clergy alike throughout much—but not all—of the early medieval West.

At the outset, it is helpful to distinguish between the western Roman Empire as a political and territorial entity; its administrative and legal apparatus; and Latin as the language in which communication was maintained and authority imposed. Each had a differing fate in the post-imperial centuries: this uncoupling of polity, documentary procedure, and language helps explain some of the characteristic features of early medieval culture. The fate of the polity need not detain us here, for that will be the focus of Chapter 8. For the moment, it is enough to note that the deposition in 476 of the last western emperor, Romulus Augustulus, was of little political significance, and that the disintegration of the western empire into a cluster of kingdoms ruled by local warlords had already begun much earlier in the fifth century.

Understanding the shifting relationship between language and the exercise of power during the early Middle Ages requires attention to the fate of the highly complex Roman bureaucracy of the fourth and early fifth centuries, for this did not cease to function with the termination of imperial rule in the West. Its salient characteristics in western and eastern provinces alike included the linkage of governmental administration to an elite literary culture underpinned by a system of elementary and advanced Latin schooling. Scribal, stenographic, and notarial skills made the humble careers that sustained everything from military provisioning and the law courts to the book trade and estate management. Equally significantly, hard-won mastery of the canon of Latin classics was the access route to high office and the prestige it conferred. The conventional content of this education thus provided a homogeneous cultural code that obliterated heterogeneous geographical and social origins. Simultaneously, its high cost did much to reinforce the social exclusiveness of the ruling elite by making it beyond the reach of the less well-off.

While governing always relied upon direct personal contact and patronage, late Roman emperors also made extensive use of written administrative, fiscal, and legal procedures. Overall, inefficiency and internal contradiction vied with favouritism and corruption as the chief characteristics of the bureaucratic machinery that mediated between the emperors (one since 324 in Constantinople, the other, western, one since 408 in either Ravenna or Rome) and their subjects in the localities. In outlying western provinces, notably Britain and northern Gaul, much of this had probably collapsed rather earlier in the fifth century; further south, in Spain, central and southern Gaul, and Italy, Romulus Augustulus' removal did nothing to interrupt bureaucratic habits. All the kingdoms that emerged on the Continent during the fifth century relied directly on these inherited techniques of ruling. By appropriating traditional mechanisms of government for their own use, fifth- and sixth-century warrior kings asserted legitimacy, collected revenue, made law, and proclaimed their power.

If we take a long-term perspective, however, it is clear that inherited Roman bureaucracy did not endure. To assert that it decayed would be to adopt an inappropriate narrative of 'decline and fall'. Rather, its constituent elements—documentary forms, legal norms, tax accounting, judicial and archival procedures, and so on—disaggregated and thinned out. In places—but only in some places—fragments of the once-coherent bureaucratic regime then perished. Other fragments took on a new life. Men of property freed slaves, negotiated marriage contracts, endowed churches, and arranged their testamentary bequests in formal documents whose wording and appearance owed much to Roman precedent, but they did so in political circumstances that no Roman official would have recognized.

Establishing any precise chronology for these changes is extremely difficult, however, because of the patchy survival of evidence and the problems of dating what we do have. A few broad generalizations are nevertheless possible, if at the risk of oversimplification. Regarding the period between c.500 and c.750, the disaggregation tended to be slower in more southern areas than elsewhere, and was slowest of all in the papal bureaucracy in the city of Rome. Simultaneously, however, the nature of political elites was changing. Martial prowess gradually replaced a lengthy literary education as the quality that kings sought in their secular advisers—and that they rewarded with land and office. The bureaucratic expertise and the literary culture that had characterized the late Roman political elite became increasingly the preserve of Christian clergy, for the mastery of the written word remained as crucial for Christian worship as hitherto. Churchmen were thus becoming the new literate elite, experts in using the written word as a medium for negotiating power.

If we now extend our summary overview to the second half of our period, from c.750 to c.1000, then additional generalizations are possible. After the mid-eighth century, we encounter legal and administrative pro-cedures of Roman origin being adopted, adapted, and transplanted across a wide area, parts of which had never formed part of the Roman Empire. Eighth-century Bavarian dukes promulgated law in self-consciously Roman style; tenth-century German kings made formal grants of land and legal privilege to churches founded amongst the Slavs by means of docu-ments that stand in a recognizable relationship to late Roman exemplars, as do the coins minted by the early eleventh-century Přemyslid rulers of Bohemia. An idiom of power, clearly indebted to Roman precedent, helped bring new kingdoms into being, and clergy played the role of mid-wife, as Chapter 7 will make clear. In brief, Roman bureaucracy and legal procedure were gradually disarticulated from the fifth century onwards, but, instead of disappearing, they persisted in piecemeal fashion as a reper-toire of ways of exercising authority from which Europe's early medieval power brokers could pick and choose.

Against this background, we may turn to the cultural significance of language, and, in particular, to written language. Throughout the ancient world, Latin implied cultural superiority. Like Greek, the *lingua romana* was regarded as the language of learning, law, and rationality—those hallmarks that, Romans opined, raised their own world to a higher level than those around them. To a Roman, the peoples who lived beyond the imperial frontiers were unkempt and ferocious, 'barbarians' whose way of life contrasted unfavourably with that of the inhabitants of the empire. The term 'barbarian' was laden with heavy cultural and linguistic prejudice: 'as much distinguishes a barbarian from a Roman as a four-legged creature from a two-legged one, or a dumb girl from a man with the power of speech', wrote the late-fourth-century poet Prudentius.[17] Above all, the gulf was educational, as we learn from Salvian. A Christian priest from the frontier city of Trier, he was among those displaced in the aftermath of the breach of the Rhine frontier in 406 by Germanic speakers and others, who then made their homes within Roman territory (see Figure 0.2). Writing in the middle years of the fifth century, he characterized the immigrants as 'lacking in Roman learning, indeed in any civilized human education' and 'ignorant of all literature and knowledge'.[18] Education—in the West the mastery of the Latin language in written and spoken form, and in the East, of Greek—entailed the whole cultural formation that underpinned Roman political hegemony. From an imperial perspective, Greek and Latin marked out a superior society that had no respect for the ignorant and uneducated.

Based on education, the distinction between Roman and 'barbarian' was cultural not racial, and thus never formed an impermeable barrier. Except as part of the mental furniture of the Roman elite, we should not take the prejudice too seriously. It is more fruitful to be alert to the ways in which political frontiers functioned as zones of intensive interaction and cultural osmosis, enabling those who originated beyond them to encounter Greek and Latin and either assimilate themselves into the late Roman world or, alternatively, appropriate techniques and uses of writing for their own purposes. Leaders of particular peoples might enter into diplomatic ties and treaties with the emperor that bound their subjects as a group. Assisted by secretaries and interpreters, some warlords, including the Hunnic leader Attila (d. 454), entered into written correspondence with imperial authorities, utilizing Roman norms of written, diplomatic communication to negotiate the standing of their entire following. Individuals often also found personal advancement through trading with the empire or through undertaking military service on its behalf. Priscus, a Greek envoy to Attila, noted that, in addition to the 'barbarous tongues'

spoken by the various peoples under Attila's rule, 'those that have commercial dealings with the western Romans [speak] Latin'.[19] Certainly, a
fair number of military men and merchants would also have acquired
at least rudimentary practical writing skills in the course of their careers.
Although it is impossible to evaluate how this might have contributed to
individuals' professional success, the adoption of Latin words to do with
warfare, writing, and trading into Celtic and Germanic languages is a clear
sign of this acculturation.

In other contexts, those living outside the imperial borders appropriated aspects of the culture of writing to their own use rather differently—
most notably the notion of symbolic representation of the sounds of which
speech is constituted. Runes and ogam are both relevant here. The runic
alphabet was a series of letter forms adapted during the first or second
century AD from the Greek and Latin scripts to represent the sounds of
Germanic speech. It was designed to be cut into wood, metal, or stone.
The earliest surviving runes, on objects scattered sporadically throughout
the Germanic-language zone, were employed for a range of practical and
invocatory purposes, whether inscribing a woman's name on a precious
brooch, announcing the name of a treasured sword blade or spearhead,
invoking good luck, or even naming the gods. Although often hard to
decipher, early runic inscriptions are an example of an important theme,
writing as a form of cultural osmosis around the periphery of the Roman
world.

Later runic inscriptions epitomize new forms of that interaction.
Anglo-Saxon monks standardized the runic alphabet and utilized it for
Christian memorial inscriptions in the monasteries and churches of
late-seventh- and eighth-century Northumbria as a complement to Latin
inscriptions in the Roman alphabet. In tenth- and eleventh-century
Scandinavia, on the other hand, a new and vigorous tradition of com-
memorative inscribed rune stones seems to have been a local reaction to
the pressures of foreign missionaries. In Norway runes coexisted with
Christian, Latin literacy into the late Middle Ages, being turned to new
administrative purposes, although always remaining primarily a script for
carving not penning. Although they gradually lost out to the more prestigious Latin alphabet and authoritative texts introduced by Christian
priests, runes were never condemned for their pre-Christian origins. Quite
the opposite: the ways in which runes were co-opted to Christian uses,
especially in Northumbria, reveal a spectrum of literate practices and a
readiness to adapt to which we shall return shortly.

The history of ogam is not dissimilar, but takes us instead beyond the
far western frontier of the Roman Empire. Around the Irish Sea, fourth-
century speakers of Gaelic were in close contact with the Latin culture of

late Roman Britain; probably on its eastern, British, shore individuals with a precise knowledge of the sound systems and spelling conventions of the Latin language developed an entirely new sequence of marks to represent the Gaelic language. Specifically designed for stone monuments to commemorate deceased persons of elite status in direct imitation of Roman epitaphs, ogam is testimony to the impulse to appropriate—on local terms—the evident association between writing and power. In the kingdom of Dyfed in south-west Wales, as elsewhere in western Britain, it was used until the seventh century for the Irish part of bilingual Old Irish–Latin epitaphs, in public assertions of the direct equivalence and high status of these two minority languages, and in Scotland, both Gaelic and Pictish ogam inscriptions occur. Across the Irish Sea, the many fifth- and sixth-century ogam stones of south-western Ireland are an idiom for emulating Roman memorial practices while shunning its language and script. They demonstrate the resonances of Roman hegemony beyond the empire long after its western half had ceased to exist as a political entity.

Like runes, ogam was adapted to Christian contexts, lingering longest in Scotland, into the tenth century. Its abandonment in eighth-century Ireland and replacement by Latin as the language for the display of secular status became possible only once Latin itself was no longer associated with powerful neighbours just across the Irish Sea. By then, Latin had acquired a completely different significance as a mark of Christianity. On any evaluation, the diffusion of this Roman religion beyond the boundaries of empire had a defining cultural significance in European history; crucial here is the stimulus to reading and writing presented by this book-based creed, for Christianity prompted the development of ways of writing local languages that had hitherto remained wholly or largely pre-literate. It also introduced more ways of exploiting writing to enhance power and authority than either runes or ogam had ever expressed.

Over the course of the early medieval centuries, there emerged a richly textured and widely varying repertoire of languages of authority, of which Latin was only one. We can best survey this region by region, paying particular attention to the languages of Christian worship, of law, and of the expression of claims to landed property. To commence, we should remain in Ireland, where the impact of Christian book learning was startling, for two reasons. First, although the details of the conversion of the Irish during the fifth century in large part elude us, it is clear that the Irish had mastered 'Latin as a foreign language' by *c.*600. During the following century, they not only began composing their own texts in Latin but also adapted the Latin alphabet to writing in their own language. With the ability not merely to carve short inscriptions on stone but now to write lengthy Old Irish texts in fluent documentary hands, Irish *filid*—scholars, poets, and legal experts—appropriated the Roman alphabet to their own uses, creating a large corpus of Old Irish texts side by side with Christian Latin ones. This took many forms, including Old Irish poems, genealogies, mythical tales, but also a very large number of legal treatises, setting out the complexities of Irish social organization and detailing the norms that regulated everything from bee-keeping to the treatment of hostages or the qualifications for poets of different ranks. These law books were the work not of legislators making new law, but rather of judges and scholars systematizing past procedures and existing social practices into generalized normative statements whose impact on everyday living is unknown. How far the Irish ever supplemented these law tracts with practical administrative forms of writing cannot be said. It is impossible to determine whether the almost total absence of tribute lists, land documentation, and the like is the result of massive documentary losses or of a persistent preference for oral modes of remembering and regulating community affairs. We are left with only the vivid insights into how the elite of highly trained scholar-poets and jurists thought their communities ought to operate, but very little evidence about how they actually did. We shall encounter some of these ideal societies later.[20]

Secondly, the Irish preferred to keep their Bible and their worship in a foreign language. Hitherto, the seepage of Christianity beyond the frontiers of the Roman Empire had been accompanied by translation of the Bible into the local language, often also accompanied by development of a new script so as to keep each language in its own script. In the mid-fourth century, the priest Ulfilas (b. *c.*311, d. 383) had done exactly this for Christian Goths living north of the lower Danube and in the steppes north of the Black Sea.[21] But in Ireland, nothing comparable occurred. The Irish chose to keep their sacred books in Latin. They seized with enthusiasm upon the dictum of Isidore of Seville, that, among the variety of tongues after the Tower of Babel, there were three 'sacred languages', those of the sign posted over the dying Christ on the cross (John 19: 19–20) and of the Bible: Hebrew, Greek, and Latin.[22] For the Irish, the sacred books remained in the sacred language. To be sure, poetry, hymns, saints' lives, homilies, and a range of other religious texts composed in Old Irish mediated Christian stories and values to unlearned audiences, as tales of secular heroes composed by Christian authors also did indirectly. Moreover, Old Irish words were sometimes jotted above or beside difficult Latin words to aid comprehension (glosses), but the central texts of worship— the liturgy of the Mass, the Creed, the Lord's Prayer, and the Gospels— remained unintelligible to all except those who undertook the long rigours of learning Latin in the schoolroom.

By the later sixth century, Irish Christians were themselves active as preachers and missionaries outside Ireland, taking their sacred books in their sacred language to western Scotland, the Continent, and the Anglo-Saxons of eastern and central Britain. Among the Anglo-Saxons, their paths criss-crossed those of seventh-century missionaries sent out either from Rome, men whose native language was the *lingua romana*, or from Frankish Gaul, whose dialect of Germanic was fairly readily intelligible to the Anglo-Saxons but who also knew Latin. In the cultural melting pot of early Anglo-Saxon Christianity, the languages of authority underwent another reconfiguration.

Unlike western Britain, where Christianity, spoken Latin, and Roman techniques for documenting property rights continued uninterrupted throughout the sixth century, most or all of the Roman cultural apparatus of religion and bureaucracy had collapsed in eastern Britain during the fifth and sixth centuries. Aided as much by Irish as by continental missionaries, the Anglo-Saxons too developed a written version of their own Germanic dialects, supplementing the letters of the Latin alphabet with a few runic characters. England's early convert kings turned this towards law. Unlike those of the Irish jurists, however, their law books contained not only specifications of existing social conventions but also royal law, a promulgation of power that had Roman overtones but used the local language to spell out the king's command. In addition, from the late seventh century at the very latest, Anglo-Saxon kings began assenting to formal Latin documents that reorganized and recorded for posterity claims to landed property. Issued in the king's name but drafted by churchmen, these documents—known as charters—adapted the forms of Roman provincial bureaucratic documentation with which continental missionaries were familiar. That seventh-century Anglo-Saxon kings could neither have read nor understood these Latin documents mattered little: from a royal perspective this was symbolic writing and an assertion of a new form of power; from an ecclesiastical one a means of securing a landed endowment, establishing enduring institutional structures and enhancing the clergy's political influence.

Like the Irish, the first Anglo-Saxon Christians adopted the new religion as a Latin religion. But they approached the cultural and linguistic chasm differently. By the early eighth century, Christian texts began to acquire a new, Old English penumbra, sometimes in the form of an Old English interlinear gloss or 'crib' added in small letters between the lines of a magnificent Latin gospel book, at others in the form of explanations of the meaning of the Creed and the Lord's Prayer by educated priests to the people 'in their own language'.[23] Bede (b. *c.*673, d. 735), the most influential of early Anglo-Saxon scholars and teachers, even provided written Old English translations of these two central texts for priests and monks who knew no Latin 'in order that the faithful may learn how to be faithful'.[24]

Here we meet the central issue. Was Christianity a religion confined to a symbolic, prestigious language, incomprehensible to all except the few who, like Bede, had been intensively schooled in it since early childhood? Or was an effort to be made to make its sacred texts directly intelligible? Even in the tenth and eleventh century, by which time Old English had developed a sophisticated written form capable of being turned to a wide variety of legal, administrative, pastoral, historical, and poetic purposes, the words of the Mass itself always remained in Latin. As for the Bible, strategies included the reworking of biblical narratives into Old English, either in traditional poetic form or as homilies. By the late Anglo-Saxon period, Old English versions existed of the most frequently read parts of both the Old and the New Testaments, although these cannot have been widely available. Nor was translation uncontentious. Ælfric (b. c.950, d. c.1010) did translate the first part of Genesis for his noble patron Æthel-weard, but warned him that this was an 'exceedingly dangerous' thing to do, for the polygamous habits of the Old Testament patriarchs ran counter to Christian teaching and needed to be made 'safe' by an experienced ex-egete.[25] Ælfric was one of a generation of scholars who shaped a distinct-ive Old English culture in late Anglo-Saxon England. The Anglo-Saxons never went as far as the Irish, who claimed that their own language was the best of all because their mythical ancestor Fénius Farsaid had invented it by combining the best features of all other languages. But they were far more willing to put their native tongue, the language of royal power and law, to the service of Christianity as a tool for teaching and preaching than seems ever to have occurred in Ireland.[26]

In brief, the imported Latin culture of early Anglo-Saxon England steadily mutated into a bilingual one in which Latin and Old English complemented each other as languages of power and authority. Tenth- and early eleventh-century kings and their counsellors legislated in Old English but heard Mass in Latin. They issued charters composed in Latin, with the property concerned specified in Old English. They sent out administrative letters (writs) in Old English and may perhaps have recited the Lord's Prayer in Old English as well as in Latin. One king, Alfred (871–99), took delight in books of Old English poetry—but that verse was as likely to be about biblical heroes as traditional Germanic ones. Another, Edgar (957–75), gave lavishly decorated Latin gospel books to favoured churches, whose clergy he also commissioned to translate key Latin texts into Old English. The powerful late Anglo-Saxon polity drew strength from finely calibrated linguistic strategies.

In the eighth century, Anglo-Saxon missionaries such as Boniface took to preaching and founding churches in the Germanic-speaking regions of continental Europe, north and east of the Rhine. Naturally, they took with them their appreciation of the advantages of using the local language to assist in training priests and explaining Christian doctrine, and, under Anglo-Saxon influence, the various dialects of Old High German began to be written in the Latin alphabet. As in England, vocabulary lists and glosses, to both religious and legal texts, preceded the composition of works entirely composed in the local language. When produced, these were mostly for classroom and pastoral use, helping to make sense of, but not replacing, the Latin of religious services. Thus alongside the Creed, the Lord's Prayer, and baptismal formulae, we find some sermons, prayers, and blessings. Slightly later, German poetic paraphrases of parts of the Bible, especially the Gospels, extended the repertoire of Christian German literature, although, as in England and Ireland, the Mass itself always remained in Latin.

Yet the churches and monasteries founded on the Continent by Boni-face and his compatriots lay in the lands of rulers who legislated in Latin, unlike the Anglo-Saxon kings. It had been self-evident that fifth-, sixth-, and seventh-century kings of the Goths, Burgundians, Franks, and Lombards should legislate and govern in Latin, not only because they often relied on the assistance of late Roman legal experts but also because they were deliberately insisting upon their role as successors of the Roman emperors. Moreover, their Germanic followers were all, more or less rapidly, abandoning their traditional language in favour of the *lingua romana*. To issue laws and charters in Latin was to do so in the language of most, if not all, of their subjects, and, if kings themselves did not fully understand, interpreters were always to hand. So the Carolingian dynasty of kings who seized the Frankish throne in 751, though themselves speakers of the Frankish dialect of Germanic, asserted their legitimacy by continuing to legislate in Latin. As their kingdom expanded through political manœuvring and outright conquest in the late eighth century, it became a huge, multi-ethnic and multilingual conglomerate, ultimately extending far beyond the area of Anglo-Saxon missionary activity. The subjects of the Carolingian kings and emperors spoke a wide variety of languages, from the Brittonic of Brittany through the full dialectal spectrum of the *lingua romana*, the Germanic of the Rhineland, Saxony, and Bavaria through to the Slavonic speakers of the eastern borderlands of the empire. Royal officials and preachers alike certainly used local dialects and languages to communicate with their audiences in the localities; on arrival at the royal court, they entered a multilingual environment. But Latin defined everyone's wider cultural identity, and, most especially, their religious identity. Latin law and Latin worship gave the Carolingian Empire a coherence that it otherwise lacked: the sacred language was also the language of imperial power.

From the middle years of the ninth century onwards, Carolingian preachers were active among the Slav principalities that lay along the empire's eastern flank. These lands were also sought out by Byzantine missionaries, most notably the brothers Constantine and Methodius, both bilingual in Greek and Slavonic and excellent linguists. It was they who first gave the Slavonic language written form, when the Byzantine emperor sent them to preach to the Slavs of Moravia in 863. Before departing, Constantine invented an entirely new alphabet, and began to produce Slavonic translations of the Greek Bible, the liturgy, and other service books all written in this, the Glagolitic alphabet. After his death in 869, his brother Methodius continued his missionary and literary endeavours, now working in Pannonia, until his own death in 885. Thereafter, German missionaries gradually succeeded in displacing the fledgling Slavonic liturgy in favour of the Latin liturgy and alphabet; the cultural project of Constantine and Methodius endured only among the Bulgars in the south-east Balkans and, from the eleventh century, far to the north-east among the Rus of Kiev. Amongst Bulgars and the Rus, another alphabet, this time directly adapted from Greek—Cyrillic—vied with the Glagolitic for writing in Slavonic, eventually winning more widespread acceptance. For the Slavs, the adoption of Christianity brought with it books for worship in their own language and distinctive scripts that were adaptable to a wide range of purposes, including laws, chronicles, spiritual and exegetical works, and inscriptions.

The achievements of Constantine and Methodius proved contentious in a way that casts a sharp light on the relationship between languages and power in the early Middle Ages. For the Byzantines, the use of a local language and writing system for Christian worship was normal; as Ulfilas's activities indicated, eastern Christianity was characterized by linguistic pluralism. Carolingian clergy, however, insisted that there were only three sacred languages. Moreover, they regarded Moravia and Pannonia as within their exclusive sphere of influence. En route to Rome from Zalavár, seat of Prince Kocel, Constantine and Methodius stopped in Venice in 867, where the bishop and clergy of the city met them with hostility, attacking Constantine 'like ravens against a falcon' for his translating enterprise.[27] When Methodius returned to Pannonia after his brother's death, he too came in for criticism, being disparaged by the clergy of Salzburg on the grounds that, 'behaving like a philosopher, he displaced the Latin language and Roman doctrine as well as the venerated Latin alphabet with a newly invented Slavic alphabet, and in that region he rubbished for everyone the Masses and Gospels and church services of those who conducted them in Latin'.[28]

What was at issue? Neither the clergy of Venice nor of Salzburg found it acceptable to use anything other than one of the sacred languages for worship. Resentment of the Greek brothers' intrusion into their own territory doubtless fuelled their antagonism, but their response betrayed deeper cultural anxieties about language and power. Like all Christians who spoke the *lingua romana*, the Venetians conducted religious worship in the language of their everyday speech, albeit in a register that may well have sounded old-fashioned. Similarly, everywhere in the zone of the *lingua romana* except that part of the Iberian peninsula governed by the Arabic-using bureaucracy of the caliphs of Cordoba, secular rulers and their officials issued laws, arbitrated disputes, administered property in Latin, simply the written form of local speech. In this respect, nothing really changed here during the early Middle Ages. The clergy of Salzburg, by contrast, were Germans. Their Latin had been learned from schoolmasters in monastic and cathedral schools. They read the Bible and conducted religious services in Latin but also used it to administer their estates, remember their dead, receive and respond to royal orders, record the outcomes of lawsuits, and fulfil a host of other purposes. Knowledge of Latin set them apart from their congregation, tenants, and servants, many of whom spoke the Bavarian dialect of Germanic while a number spoke Slavonic. Disparate in linguistic background, the clergy of Venice and Salzburg were united in feeling that Constantine and Methodius had impugned the sacredness of the Latin Bible and liturgy.

The two brothers must have been puzzled by the hostility they encountered. But their assumption that the sacred Christian texts could be translated into any local language highlights the peculiarity of western Christianity. From the conversion of the Irish onwards, western Christianity was essentially Latin Christianity, whatever the local language. First in Ireland, then in England, there was one language for religion and another for law. But in the Carolingian lands, the indispensability of Latin as the language of both sacred and secular authority was affirmed. Assisted by their clergy, tenth- and eleventh-century German kings and emperors enthusiastically followed suit and, through sponsoring missionary activity amongst the Poles, Hungarians, and Scandinavians, made sure that Latin was exported as the language and symbol of both German kingship and German Christianity. Everywhere north of the linguistic divide between Germanic and the *lingua romana*, the language of authority had to be learned from schoolmasters brandishing the cane. The rod thus instilled a technology of power, for Latin not only communicated information, ideas, commands: it conveyed status, prestige, identity, and allegiance. As for the British Isles, it took the onslaught of the Norman Conquest in 1066 to trigger the displacement of the local languages by Latin for the purposes of governing.

Despite its inherited cultural prestige and the mass of surviving manuscripts written in it, book-learned Latin was not the only language of power in the early Middle Ages. In using schoolroom Latin as the language of religion, law, and property, the clergy of Salzburg were out of step with large parts of the Europe of their own day. That this only much later became the normal experience must not be allowed to obliterate the fluid, multiform relationships between language and authority in early medieval Europe.

## Local Literacies, Elite Literacy

In 721, Gregory, later bishop of Utrecht, visited his aunt Addula, the abbess of Pfalzel near Trier. As was common for noble youths, he spent his formative years in the retinue of the Frankish king—an education in courtliness, arms, and rudimentary literacy. Dinner at Pfalzel was accompanied by religious readings in accordance with monastic custom, and on this occasion Addula handed the Bible to her 14- or 15-year-old nephew. The dinner guests included the missionary Boniface, who, as Gregory's disciple Liudger later told the tale, addressed Addula's nephew. 'You read well, my son—if you understand what you're reading.' Gregory asserted that he did, so the holy man questioned him more closely. The youth began to read the passage again from the beginning, just as he had done before. 'I'm not asking you to speak out the passage like that, my boy. Explain your reading to me in your own language and in the everyday speech of your family.' Gregory confessed that he could not do this, and so Boniface began to expound the text, preaching to the whole family.[29] This encounter set young Gregory on the path to his own missionary career. It sets us in pursuit of the complexities of 'literacy' in the early Middle Ages.

The term is a capacious one, referring to individuals and social practices. It embraces many skills that were taught and learned separately in the early Middle Ages: the graphic art of wielding a pen, whether with unpractised effort or calligraphic fluency; the transformation of speech into text with or without the intermediary of a scribe between author and parchment; the cognitive skill of the reader, not always extending to comprehension of the text. The term also invites us to enquire into the contexts in which texts were read, written, and consulted, to consider the importance attached to these activities, and the mentalities associated with them. Gregory's encounter with Boniface exemplifies several of these strands. It reminds us that, wherever the *lingua romana* was not spoken locally, learning to read was accomplished in a foreign language. Furthermore, in its locales of palace and monastery, his early career draws our attention to the relationship between literacy and elite status, secular and ecclesastical. Finally, the tale cautions us to avoid creating a false antithesis between 'literacy' and 'orality'. For Gregory, reading was an oral performance in front of an audience of hearers, the usual way of experiencing a written text in the early Middle Ages. And the flow of words from speech to text always worked in both directions: in composing his life of Gregory, Liudger relied as much on stories narrated by the saint's family as on literary models of missionary sanctity. Literacy thus requires attention to both social situation and individuals.

It is immediately clear that not all communities regarded writing in the same way. A predisposition to utilize writing for a host of purposes from the most mundane to the most formal was certainly characteristic of many regions once within the Roman Empire. The spread of written language did little to encourage that predisposition elsewhere: some places remained more text-minded than others. Moreover, the relationship between literacy and power was liable to be reconfigured, as power relationships within and between polities themselves shifted over time. Aspirations towards intensive government commonly fostered the use of administrative writing more than geographically extensive assertions of power. Thus the two most powerful polities of the early Middle Ages—the Frankish empire of Charlemagne and his son Louis the Pious (814–40), and the late Anglo-Saxon kingdom of Edgar and his successors—were also those that relied most on written modes of government. In both these cases, subsequent political change brought with it different attitudes towards and uses of the written word. Comparable diversity is evident when we turn to the religious contexts of literacy. Though the sacrality of the Latin Bible was universal, its local cultural milieux varied both in the ways that churches received and adapted the literary heritage of late antique Christianity and in the ways in which they used administrative literacy in pursuit of their institutional goals. In short, early medieval Europe manifested a kaleidoscope of cultures of literacy, combining and recombining in localized patterns that shifted over place and time but that steadfastly resist ordering into a linear series from 'less' to 'more' literate.

It helps to distinguish between the reading and/or writing skills possessed by an individual and the access to those skills enjoyed by those who lacked them themselves. Personal literacy is direct, the consequence of education; participatory literacy is indirect, mediated through a scribe or reader. The extent of the former is hard to assess even within a religious context: not only is the patchy evidence susceptible to widely differing interpretations, but also there can be no generally applicable criterion of assessment. On balance, it is safe to conclude that significantly more monks, nuns, and clergy than laity could write their name or vocalize the letters on a page and that even in Italy, certainly the most 'literate' place in the early Middle Ages, only a small minority of the population possessed either skill. Since personal literacy was uncommon, we shall focus for the moment on participatory literacy. This was far more widespread, as a sermon preached by Caesarius, bishop of Arles (502–42), suggests. He told his congregation about merchants who, although unable to read and write themselves, hired the services of those who could. With their employees to keep their accounts, they made a huge profit. By the same token, Caesarius argued, illiteracy was no impediment to the spiritual profit of reading the Bible. 'You who don't know your letters, whoever you are, why don't you seek out for a fair price someone to read holy scripture to you so that you can gain the rewards of heaven through them? Certainly, brothers, he who goes about this diligently believes that he can benefit from it in eternity; but he who neither wants to read the Bible nor to hear it being read to him certainly does not believe that any good can come of it.'[30] Here was a culture where personal literacy was never universal but participatory literacy was extensive.

At other times, individuals might be caught up in a world of written texts without it necessarily being to their own advantage. As a young child, Fructuosus of Braga (d. 665) accompanied his father, a Goth of elite birth and rank, on a trip to the family sheep pastures in the mountains of north-western Spain. The boy wandered off while his father 'wrote down [details of] the flocks and discussed the accounts with the shepherds'.[31] Even if the shepherds could not themselves maintain written stock lists, they nevertheless had contact with, and contributed to, the managerial documentation necessary to the smooth running of a large landed estate.

Examples such as these could be multiplied throughout the early medieval centuries, from many different secular and religious contexts. But we should remain in the central-northern regions of the Iberian peninsula for further evidence of text-mindedness in the seventh and eighth centuries. Here, the discovery in archaeological contexts of over 150 slate slabs used as writing tablets reveals a distinctively local literacy. Although their badly chipped, poorly decipherable, condition prohibits conclusions about their scribes or readers, the slates nevertheless allow unmatched insight into the social contexts in which some people employed writing to conduct their affairs. They also exemplify the kind of particularities that gave early medieval practices of literacy such marked regional diversity.

Several of these slates are exactly the sort a landowner such as Fructuosus's father would have needed to run his estates—lists of livestock, slaves, and dues owed by tenants. Others relate to different aspects of property management, but had similarly short-term usefulness: a letter from an estate steward to his master, an inventory of stolen domestic objects and clothing complete with the monetary value of each item. Some slates have a religious rather than an administrative purpose: curses against named individuals, texts of prayers and psalms, invocations to archangels and saints; others again are classroom writing exercises—all lost or discarded when no longer needed but nevertheless revealing of local religious mentalities or individual efforts to acquire personal literacy. One group would have been of more lasting importance: formal documents of sales and exchanges of land between individuals, details of the guarantees that secured a deal, and precisions of the oaths sworn to complete them. Documents in this last category conform to late Roman legal provisions for validating property transactions and use standard local conventions for phrasing such documents. Indeed, legal procedural norms offer one of the most characteristic markers of regional particularity in the social uses of writing.

Elsewhere, the best surviving evidence for regional documentary practices mostly concerns landed property. And, since these records have survived only in ecclesiastical archives, they reveal most about local literacies in the spheres of influence of major churches. The insights such archives can offer into local social organization and landed economies are deferred until Chapter 5; here let us focus on the textual habits of one locality: eastern Brittany in the ninth century. This was a document-minded world of a few large landowners and many peasant proprietors who bought and sold land amongst themselves, bequeathed property to their heirs, raised loans, argued and settled disagreements, or stood surety for each other's behaviour. They took care to make their transactions in front of witnesses and announce them to their neighbours with public formality. They also ensured that local scribes recorded the deals in Latin formulae sanctioned

by time-honoured local usage and included the names of those who had
witnessed the transaction and affirmed its validity. When the monastery
of Redon was founded in their midst in 832, the ensuing donations to the
monks were equally precisely specified in writing. In turn, the monks exploited local documentary practices for their own interests, in so doing
conserving hundreds of charters for their—and our—benefit.

A member of the region's elite of petty landowners, Riwalt functioned
as local bigwig in villages close to Redon during the 830s and 840s. He
and other members of his family epitomize the participatory literacy of
this social group. Riwalt regularly witnessed the gifts, sales, and pledges
of his neighbours. In 840, he had the donor, witnesses, and scribe assemble in his own house for the formalities and recording of Catworet's gift
to Redon; when his own son Deurhoiarn killed Catworet a few years later,
he made public recompense in a carefully documented pay-off. He took
pains to have his own donation to the monks witnessed, including having Deurhoiarn attest and thus assent to his father's generosity. Whether
Riwalt could read or hold a pen well enough to make his own mark of attestation is unimportant. The formal gesture of touching the parchment
sheet with the hand commonly counted as the equivalent to a graphic
mark of attestation or a signature, so Riwalt had no need to be able to
write his name to keep his affairs in good order. Nor does it matter that
he probably spoke Brittonic and so perhaps did not understand the Latin
of his charter of donation, for he most certainly knew its gist. Riwalt
shrewdly regarded written records of customary format as central to his
activities, and knew how to turn the local documentary conventions to his
own advantage.

In the 850–60s, Deurhoiarn, his wife Roiantken, and their son
Iarnwocon all continued Riwalt's relationship with Redon, making sure
valid records of their gifts were drafted in conformity with local conventions. The surviving documents include a charter recording a donation
that Roiantken made with the agreement of her husband and son: it draws
attention to women's participation in the documentary literacy of a rural
community such as this. To the extent that married women had land under
their own control or were central to wider family strategies for the disposition of property, they were in a position to issue and attest charters in
conjunction with their husband or son, as Roiantken did. Only in widowhood or if vowed to a celibate life did they sometimes issue charters in
their own name. The wider issues of management of the familial patrimony will be discussed in detail later, but, to anticipate briefly, women's
opportunities to control land were universally limited.[32] As a result, their
opportunities for active participatory literacy were commensurately few, a
restriction reinforced by a widespread reluctance to call women to witness

other people's transactions. With a few notable exceptions of rulers' wives, charter witness lists suggest that the meetings at which land transactions were completed, conflicts resolved, and community affairs regulated were essentially men's gatherings.

Here, then, was a culture that regarded both the verbal testimony of male eyewitnesses and the written record of charters as overlapping ways of proving ownership or settling a dispute. Across Europe, local communities might put more emphasis on the one rather than the other. Even in Ireland, where documentary forms of Roman origin (such as those in the Redon area) seem to have made little impact, 'godly old writing' was recognized along with valid witnesses, sureties, and ogam-inscribed boundary stones as a form of proof.[33] And in southern France, where Roman legal procedures with their heavy emphasis on written documentation persisted throughout the early Middle Ages, the sworn oral testimony of witnesses remained a vital complement to lost, falsified, destroyed, or disputed charters: judges ruled only after they had 'seen and heard' the evidence.[34] Whether in the reading-aloud of a disputed charter or the writing-down of witnesses' oaths, document-mindedness always presupposed an oral, spoken milieu. It never presumed the personal literacy of all participants.

Provided that a few individuals had the necessary skills to draw up records in the approved manner, widespread reliance on documentary practices was as possible for modest freeholders as for lay or ecclesiastical proprietors of vast landed estates. Such document-mindedness characterized the small social elite, either lay persons of sufficient wealth and standing to own land and command the services of others, or the bishops, abbots, and abbesses who represented the institutional interests of cathedrals and monasteries. This general truth offsets the wide variation in local literacies. There is far more at issue here than simply a well-resourced lifestyle, however, for writing was integral to the functioning of political power in the localities and royal courts of Christian Europe alike. Whether as a medium for communicating, expressing an ideology, transmitting specialist legal knowledge, maintaining king-lists, proclaiming royal pedigrees, or keeping fiscal records, literacy was widely implicated in the articulation and maintenance of authority in the Christian regions of early medieval Europe. This is particularly true of those polities that actively sought to promote a degree of centralized control, but everywhere literacy had the potential to enhance legitimacy, build consensus, and convey intense symbolic meaning.[35] Those who were accustomed to dealing with documents and understood the social conventions surrounding their use could contribute what rulers sought. Like the landowner with a personal notary or village scribe at his elbow, the churchman skilled at drafting letters, charters, or estate memoranda contributed to the exercise of authority at local and central levels. Especially where Latin was one of the languages—or the only language—of power, but regional communities spoke Celtic or Germanic, only the elite had the necessary savoir-faire or technical assistance to participate in ruling and to mediate between courts and localities. Whether personal or participatory, document-mindedness was thus both a precondition for and a consequence of membership of the power-broking elite.

Early medieval literacy had a religious as well as a documentary aspect. By the fifth century, the conventions of Christian worship had crystallized into written form, reproduced in service books that encoded considerable regional variations in liturgical practice. Wherever adherence to Christianity was formalized into local congregations led by officially appointed, male priests, worship required the presence of such books and of a man capable of reading aloud from them. As a late-tenth-century Anglo-Saxon preacher put it, during worship 'we hear God's books explained and read to us, the Gospel proclaimed, and His glories made known to men'.[36] Christian liturgy was a verbal and visual drama, at the centre of which were God's books.

To complete the full annual cycle of services, a priest required several different books for fulfilling a community's sacramental needs, with additional books for any pastoral work he might undertake. How many minor rural churches, as distinct from cathedrals, monasteries, and other regional centres ever possessed the full set of texts in this period is open to question, but the uncertainty does not detract from the encounter with the written word that church attendance implied for everyone, of all social ranks. The form of that encounter doubtless depended, in part, on whether the language of worship was comprehensible in that locality, how effectively trained the officiating priest was, and whether he was separated from the congregation by a screen. Far more than the communication of verbal content was at stake, however. The centrality of books to the words and gestures of Christian ritual grounded religious authority and truth in writing. It thereby devalued unwritten opinion and oral tradition, and gave men but not women the opportunity to put their literate skills to work in public.

Emphasis on the Christian tradition of the written word found its fullest expression not in scattered local churches but in monastic communities. The roots of the early medieval monastic tradition lay in the distant past, in the early Christian impulse to reject land, wealth, sexuality, and family in favour of a life devoted to living out biblical precepts, sometimes accompanied by spectacular forms of self-denial and a reputation for miraculous achievements. This movement found expression wherever Christianity gained adherents, whatever the local social and political conditions. By the fifth century, those who withdrew into ascetic communities often found themselves balancing the self-discipline and social distancing that their commitment demanded with the popularity and flow of landed gifts that their reputation encouraged. Intense engagement with the culture of the Bible required that at least some members of the group could read and comprehend Latin—but this might also entail exposure to the vast non-Christian Latin literary tradition, as well as to the fourth- and fifth-century authoritative works of biblical interpretation. By the seventh century, and in some places rather earlier, monastic communities found themselves the main guardians of the educational traditions and literary heritage of Antiquity.

Ascetic existence turned on the Word of God—written in sumptuously decorated Bibles bound with gold and jewels, sung and spoken during worship, recited aloud and heard by all, read silently or in a low murmur for meditative reflection on its inner meaning. Monastic organization and ideology were sometimes codified in writing, but the monastic rule always functioned as a spoken text. 'Listen, my son, to the teachings of your master, and incline the ear of your heart,'[37] began what became the most popular and, by the ninth century, the most authoritative of such written rules, composed by Benedict of Nursia (b. c.480, d. 560). In monastic culture, words shifted endlessly back and forth between spoken and written form, but the fixed point of reference was always holy scripture, the oral teaching of Christ transmitted in words on the parchment page.

'The foundation, form and perfection of discretion is knowledge of the holy scriptures.'[38] Thus wrote Hrabanus Maurus (b. c.780, d. 856) in 819, the influential schoolmaster of the monastery that Boniface had founded at Fulda in the forests of central Germany. His parents and older brother were typical of the charter-using regional aristocracy of the central Rhineland, but, in contrast with their participatory literacy, Hrabanus became one of the most literate men of his age, a prolific author of works of biblical exegesis and monastic instruction as well as of complex Latin verse. Later, as abbot of Fulda (822–42), he presided over the largest monastic community north of the Alps (some 600 men). In this position, he developed its library into a major collection of both Christian and classical texts and oversaw the management of the monks' vast landed endowment of over 8,000 farmsteads, before ending his career as archbishop of Mainz, the counsellor of kings (847–56). Whether for poetic, pedagogical, spiritual, administrative, or political ends, Hrabanus always expressed himself in polished Latin. All this was possible because his parents had placed him in the monastery as a child of 7, young enough for extended years of schooling to foster his abilities and instil full mastery of the 'sacred language'.

Under Hrabanus's aegis, Fulda developed a distinctive literary culture. Although the common wellsprings of monastic learning encouraged monasteries to collect similar foundational texts of Latin grammar and biblical interpretation, even monastic literacy assumed characteristically local or regional forms. This only partly resulted from the sheer difficulties of obtaining books from far away; equally important was the continual reformulation, revision, and alteration of texts to suit local needs and preferences. Fulda, however, evinced additional particularities, for its abbots also fostered the formation of a written literature in Old High German, primarily but not entirely for pastoral uses. Their diligent searches also built up a unique collection of rare classical works, several of which have survived only thanks to the activities of the monastery's ninth-century copyists. Fully consonant with the common ideals of monastic life, Fulda nevertheless enjoyed a literary culture with its own, local quality.

Fulda was not alone in this. However widespread the Rule of Benedict had become by the ninth and tenth centuries, monasteries maintained locally traditional styles of liturgy. They also built their own intellectual life within the context of regional cultural norms, using whatever resources, opportunities, and contacts they could. In the Christian kingdoms of northern Spain monasteries such as the Catalonian houses of Ripoll and San Millan de la Cogolla benefited from their relative proximity to the brilliant intellectual culture of the tenth-century caliphal court at Cordoba, acquiring scientific and mathematical treatises unavailable elsewhere in the Latin West, including some translated from Arabic. Meanwhile, in tenth- and eleventh-century England, the monks and clergy of Exeter, Winchester, Ramsey, and elsewhere copied and collected books in Old English as enthusiastically as Latin works, pursuing eclectic tastes in Old English heroic poetry as well as biblical exegesis. When Gerbert, a young monk of Aurillac, travelled across the Pyrenees to Ripoll in 967 and Abbo, monastic schoolmaster of Fleury in central France, went to teach in England at Ramsey in 985–7, each encountered a familiar monastic lifestyle and liturgy offset by novel resources for study. Even the elite literacy of a monastic library displayed local particularities.

All this came at a price. Books required expert scribes and an abundant supply of high-quality animal skins for the parchment. Consider two of the most famous works from eighth-century Northumbria: Bede's

*Ecclesiastical History*, available today as a paperback of 290 pages, required the skins of about thirty animals for a single copy, while the magnificent, exceptionally large Lindisfarne Gospels was made from the skins of over 150 calves. Hildemar of Corbie (d. *c*.850) intimated that his monastery could sell a book made from thirty skins for 60 *denarii* (silver pennies), a sum approximately equivalent to the value of four fleecy sheep or fifteen piglets: Corbie's own library possessed over 300 titles, most of them recently copied. Stocking a library of this size was extremely expensive—and helps explain Hrabanus's care in organizing bound registers to preserve copies of the thousands of individual charters that witnessed Fulda's rights to land and income. Nor does this take into account the illustrated liturgical books that Fulda also produced in the ninth and tenth centuries, a single one of which might consume over sixty skins in addition to costly, imported pigments and gold leaf for the paint.

Despite the huge size of the Fulda community, its famous school, and the vast resources that sustained the monks and their library, few others of its ninth- and tenth-century monks authored works in Latin or Old High German, and none of them was nearly as prolific as Hrabanus. In any monastery, male or female, full participation in the monastic life demanded the ability to read. Community affairs would be aided if a few of the monks or nuns could copy books and draft charters. But compositional literacy remained a rarity throughout the early Middle Ages, an intellectual achievement that required exceptional resources as well as exceptional talent. Little wonder, then, that abilities of this sort were confined to an elite, or that Hrabanus and others like him graced rulers' courts. A privileged status and a privileged voice: theirs are the voices that have best survived the centuries.

> No work of men's hands but the weary years
>   Besiege and take it, comes its evil day:
> The written word alone flouts destiny,
>   Revives the past and gives the lie to Death.[39]

Hrabanus's words themselves flout destiny. But for the energy of a seventeenth-century printer, these verses would have been lost to us, long since destroyed along with the majority of the manuscripts in Fulda's medieval library. In these lines, Hrabanus expressed a perspective inherited from the Christian writers of late Antiquity and affirmed much that was central to the Christian, Latin culture of the Carolingian Empire: indebtedness to the past, respect for a culture of Latin book learning, profound conviction that no other medium, no other language, conveyed authority and truth. But we should not allow him to trap us into perpetuating that prejudice or replicating its presumption that Latin literacy necessarily represents a superior level of cultural attainment. Rather, we should view it as an agent of political transformation. As this chapter has argued, writing, and with it literacy, was deeply implicated in the exercise of power by strengthening, shaping, and justifying social hierarchies, ecclesiastical control, royal rule. Not for nothing did a freed slave receive a document confirming his or her manumission, for writing constructed power relationships of all sorts and ensured that they were remembered.

Nor should we allow Hrabanus to drown out other voices from other places. While Christianity certainly provided a powerful impulse to the written word, older, epigraphic runic and ogam habits persisted in Atlantic and northern Europe for some centuries after the arrival of Christian forms of literacy. We have also seen that, in practice, early medieval communities were extremely diverse in what they chose to commit to writing, in which script and in which language. Only a common attachment to the Latin Bible and liturgy helped create a degree of shared identity and enabled those who knew Latin to communicate wherever they travelled in Christian Europe.

Certainly, if we are looking for generalizations, we may conclude that it was in the early Middle Ages that Latin first emerged as an international mandarin language throughout most of Europe and, equally, that during these centuries education, book learning, and literacy became the overwhelming preserve of Christian churches. But this chapter has emphasized additional conclusions. It has drawn attention to the interplay between Latin and other languages. It has shown the facility with which lay landowners manipulated traditions of written documentation, whether in their own language or in Latin. In outlining some of the ways in which rulers relied on writing in legislating, governing, and evoking their authority, it has introduced themes to which the final two chapters of the book will return.

Finally, it has emphasized that a kaleidoscopic variety of local cultures of speaking and writing characterized early medieval Europe. Although our understanding of them is constrained by the erratic loss of books and documents sustained over the past millennium, it is beyond doubt that their characteristics were contingent upon individual preferences and needs as much as on local resources and precedents. Exceptionally, rulers intervened to encourage schools and book learning, in the hope of fostering correct Christian behaviour and tighter royal administration. But the written remains from the early Middle Ages introduce us to the localities as much as to the royal courts, and it is with these that we shall stay, as we turn in the next chapter to investigate matters as equally fundamental to human existence as speaking—birth and death.

# 2

# Living and Dying

A storm-bowed maple,
I sorrow for my son,
My boy, who has bent
His body to earth:
Unhappy, he
Whose kin is hewn down
And must bear away the bones
From the bed.[1]

There came also a certain woman almost dead of starvation with a
small child among the others seeking help. Before she could cross the
threshold she collapsed from weakness and died. The child tried to
pull the breast of his dead mother out from her clothes and suckle,
which caused many of those who saw this to groan and weep.[2]

A FATHER mourning the drowning of his son, an infant suckling its
famished mother's still-warm corpse: men and women in early medieval
Europe lived intimately with deprivation and death. In the face of inter-
mittent climatic disasters, periodic epidemics, and harsh everyday living
conditions, the population of Europe laboured to produce a living from
the land and to raise children to carry on their efforts. Most lived at or
near subsistence level; others reflected on the meaning of human existence
and its moral qualities amid the fearfulness of unexpected death and the
likelihood of dearth. As in all cultures, the fundamental rhythms of living
and dying framed human experience, not only shaping the age profile of
any community, its members' life expectancy, and their search for security,
but also affecting politics, informing understanding of the natural world,
and situating humans in the cosmos.

This chapter enquires into the interaction of humans and their natural
environment. It also reflects upon their understanding of it. It introduces

questions that are not all amenable to textual enquiry but that can be addressed by the archaeological recovery and scientific analysis of material remains. Preliminary cautions are in order, however. The archaeological research necessary to answer environmental and demographic questions by tracking changes in climate, land use, and population levels is painstaking and expensive. It has been conducted only at a limited number of sites: to extrapolate beyond them is to risk overgeneralizing. Whereas the discovery of hitherto unknown textual evidence for the early Middle Ages is rare, new archaeological excavations and surveys are frequently undertaken and novel techniques of scientific analysis developed: conclusions based on data currently available remain liable to subsequent review.

With these provisos in mind, this chapter integrates archaeological evidence with the extant textual record in order to place the perceptions and social responses of early medieval men and women within the context of the landscapes in which they lived and the lifespans that they enjoyed. It thus approaches living and dying as both biological and cultural phenomena. The first section addresses the environment: climate, landscape, and settlement distribution. Against this background, the second turns to demographic questions, to estimate population levels and to suggest explanations for the fluctuating rates of fertility and mortality that seem to have been characteristic of the early Middle Ages. The final part asks how men and women coped with deprivation, disease, and death, and seeks answers in a range of cosmologies and curative strategies. In all these respects, a pattern of intense localism emerges.


## Habitats

Early medieval men and women lived, worked, and died in environments affected not only by natural resources and climate but also by a long prehistory of settlement and exploitation. Over the millennia, human activities had created many landscapes out of Europe's complex physical geography. Always a dynamic process, that interaction continued throughout the early Middle Ages, shaping human habitats out of the natural world and lending a characteristically heterogeneous aspect to life in the early Middle Ages.

Let us take a brief glance at the richness and diversity of that natural world. Some aspects of its variegation are as obvious today as in the Middle Ages—for instance, the contrasts between the agricultural potential of the lowlands of the south-eastern corner of Britain and the upland economy of the mountainous zones to the north and west, or between the

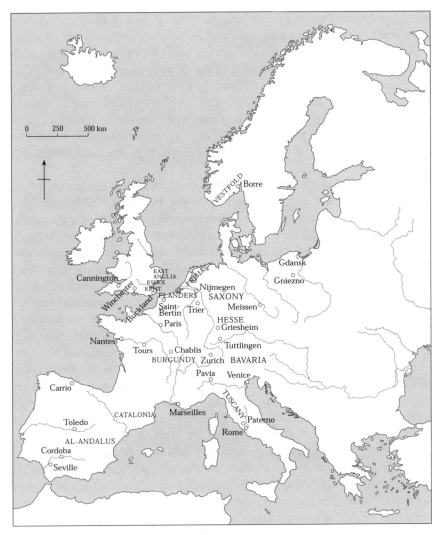

**2.1.** Principal places mentioned in Chapter 2.

olives and vines of the Mediterranean littoral and the cereal cultivation of
northern France. Differences such as these reflect a combination of geo-
logical structure and soil type interacting with the characteristic climatic
patterns of the regions in question. Intensely local differences—between
the soil in one field and the next or the amount of sunshine on one side
of a valley rather than the other—are no longer so obvious in an age of

urban sprawl and intensive mechanized farming. But in the early Middle Ages the distinctive nature of one small locality as compared with another was often as significant as the differences between entire regions, for each community was intimately attuned to the potentials and limitations of its own immediate environment. Farming, diet, textiles, clothing, pottery, building materials: all responded to locally available resources in this world of micro-regions. Interconnections came from the social, economic, and political bonds that later chapters will explore, as also from the rivers and coasts, roads and trackways that afforded contact between one settlement and the next.

Other aspects of the diversity of the early medieval landscape reflect the evolving impact of humankind upon the natural environment. One token of this was the push to bring new land under arable cultivation. Along the river Po, the northern Italian plain was still largely covered with oak forest at the end of Antiquity, and disafforestation made a major impact here only from the ninth century onwards. Likewise, the lands east of the Rhine and the Danube remained heavily wooded, and, although newly arrived settlers began making clearings in these wooded regions from the eighth century onwards, extensive felling did not reach east of the Elbe before the twelfth century. By the tenth century, drainage and the canalization of rivers were transforming landscapes dominated by rapidly shifting coastlines and low-lying salt marshes, such as the polderlands of Frisia, the East Anglian fens, and the Po delta. Although an anonymous ninth-century writer claimed that the Frisians 'almost live like fish in the water, by which they are surrounded on all sides',[3] archaeological evidence confirms that the coastal region of early medieval Frisia supported densely populated communities. Their inhabitants lived on artificially raised mounds (*terpen*), where they combined intensive agriculture with extensive exploitation of the surrounding salt marshes and waterways. From these settlements, they began to make inroads into the peat bogs that lay just above the tidal flood plain, digging drainage channels to carve small arable fields out of the bog from the ninth century onwards and founding new settlements on recently dried sites. The transformation of the Frisian landscape was well under way long before large-scale drainage efforts began in the late eleventh century. In regions such as this, a particular effort of imagination is required to envisage the changing aspect of the early medieval landscape.

In other circumstances, changes resulted from the spread of new crops and technologies. The Iberian peninsula is particularly notable in this respect, for the Arabs and Berbers who settled here in the wake of the Muslim conquest of 711 introduced new plants and techniques of irrigation. After the Umayyad dynasty had been ousted from power in Damascus in 750, leading members of the family fled to Cordoba and in 756 established the independent polity of al-Andalus in Spain. Encouraged by Umayyad amirs such as Abd al-Rahman I (756–88), who is said to have sent for pomegranate seeds and date palms familiar from his Syrian homeland, parts of southern Spain took on a new aspect, as a result not only of the introduction of new plants for cultivation but also of the establishment of the systems of intensive irrigation widely practised elsewhere in the Islamic world. Under Muslim rule, belts of irrigated fields around the cities of al-Andalus enabled the cultivation of such water-dependent crops as sugar cane, rice, and cotton, all of which were widely farmed in southern Spain by the late eleventh century. With the introduction during the tenth century of the orange, much appreciated for its ornamental qualities in formal gardens, Cordoba, Seville, and other cities in early medieval al-Andalus recalled to visitors' minds the landscapes of Syria.

Changing landscapes also need to be assessed in the context of climate and weather. Early medieval writers certainly had an intuitive notion of meteorological normality, and extreme aberrations in the weather drew comment. In 748, Ireland was afflicted by 'snow of unusual depth so that nearly all the cattle of the whole of Ireland perished, and the world afterwards was parched by unusual drought'. And in northern France in 874, a 'long, hard winter' produced 'such a tremendous amount of snow that no one could remember seeing anything like it'.[4] Commentators also noted the connection between climate and disease or harvest failure. Exceptional rains in 820 led, we are told, to widespread disease among humans and livestock, caused grain and vegetables to rot in the fields, and left that year's grape harvest small and bitter. Worst of all, perhaps—and certainly unusual for the precision with which it is recorded—was the 'great flood far beyond the usual coastal tides' that inundated Frisia on 26 December 838, breaching all the dunes, spilling sand everywhere, and washing away homes, cattle, and 2,437 people.[5]

However perceptive, early medieval observers could not have been aware that sudden crises such as these betokened a cycle of long-term climatic shifts that very gradually changed the world in which they lived. Only the combination of documentary witness and modern scientific techniques allows an outline of the climatic history of Europe in the first millennium AD to be reconstructed. Midway through the millennium (very approximately the years c.400–600), a significant drop in average temperatures of about 1.5°C throughout the northern hemisphere produced increased rainfall and flooding. Additional manifestations included rising sea levels along low-lying coasts of the North Sea, expansion of the peat bogs of south-western Ireland, the advance of Alpine glaciers, and the extension into the Mediterranean of the Atlantic climate pattern of wetter winters than had characterized the first part of the millennium. By c.700 a more continental climatic pattern, of hot, dry summers and severely cold winters, was leaving its mark. (The frequent heavy snows and frozen rivers of north-west European winters in the ninth century are among the indications of this.) Only in the last century of the millennium did temperatures again rise above their long-term average, building gradually to another climatic optimum in the twelfth century, nearly 2°C higher in northern Europe than in c.500.

Climatic change might affect the ability of marginal land to sustain cultivation and certainly contributed to some of the shifts in settlement sites noticeable in the early Middle Ages. The abandonment and rebuilding elsewhere of early medieval Frisian *terpen* corresponded with phases of marine transgression and regression. Likewise, as peat bogs expanded in upland areas of south-western Ireland and north-western Britain in the early Middle Ages, communities ceased to cultivate hillside fields, leaving them to revert to scrub and woodland. In Ireland, archaeological evidence for increased cereal production and pastoral farming activity on the fertile central and eastern lowlands suggests a redistribution of population in favour of these areas. A particularly well-studied example is the chalk hills of southern England. Here, a progressive lowering of the water table in the seventh to eighth centuries seems to have contributed to the abandonment of hilltop settlements to the south-east of Winchester. Combined with steady erosion of the soil on the hill slopes, this may have helped prompt communities to relocate to the heavier and more fertile soils of the coastal lowlands. By contrast, the climatic amelioration of the last third of the first millennium may help explain a notable increase in cereal cultivation in Scotland, and also its introduction to north Atlantic islands, notably the Shetlands and Outer Hebrides.

Changes in land use and rural settlement frequently also resulted from altered political and economic relationships between and within communities. Archaeological evidence suggests that in parts of southern Scandinavia, for example, intensification of agricultural production in the seventh century accompanied widespread political changes. A well-studied example concerns Borre in Vestfold, where larger fields and new crops signalled enhanced cultivation in association with the emergence of a new centre of elite occupation evidenced by massive, richly furnished burial mounds. Powerful chieftains were evidently forging larger kingdoms by imposing themselves upon the lesser farmers in the region, extracting produce or tribute by means we can only surmise, but leav-ing a changed landscape as evidence of their new-found power. Similar but less dramatic restructuring contributed to the well-known 'wandering-settlement' phenomenon that affected many rural habitation sites in much of north-western Europe. Until *c.*700 Anglo-Saxon settle-ments were liable either to shift gradually within their territorial bound-aries or to relocate entirely; in Denmark settlements continued to wander around in this way until the eleventh or twelfth century. In all these cases, the emergence of less egalitarian, more exploitative social relationships, coupled with changing ecological conditions, manifested itself in spatial reorganization and agrarian change.

Towards the end of our period, the Italian peninsula provides a particu-larly well-studied variation on this theme. Textual and archaeological evidence agree that almost all rural Italy from Tuscany southwards un-derwent a redistribution of habitations in the tenth and eleventh centuries. In a process commonly known as *incastellamento*, dispersed rural house-holds gathered together into a single fortified village. These were usually built on a previously unoccupied site located on higher ground than the former dwellings. Relocation to defended sites was only partly a response to the growing insecurity of the tenth-century Italian countryside, which was suffering persistent attacks by Saracens (Arab pirates from North Africa) and highly mobile Magyar raiding parties. Weakened princely au-thority also contributed, for it freed landowners to build and garrison their own fortifications, from which they could intimidate their neighbours. At least as important as threats of violence, however, transformations in the nature and organization of the agrarian economy stimulated *incastella-mento*. Burdensome new rents and labour services enhanced landowners' domination of their rural workforce at a time of rising population, mak-ing it advantageous to rehouse tenants directly under the lordly gaze.

A different aspect of population movement is migration, whether voluntary or forced. Temporary or permanent population displacement probably accompanied much of the inter-ethnic violence of the early Middle Ages. We hear, for example, of the Daleminzi Slavs from around Meissen on the upper Elbe, who suffered repeated Magyar attacks in 906. This region was 'reduced to such miserable penury that the Daleminzi abandoned their own land and took service with other peoples in order to have something to eat'.[6] Largely unrecorded because lacking in political consequence, sufferings such as these must have been far more frequent than the evidence makes explicit. We occasionally also learn of deliberate ethnic cleansing, and it too must have had a temporary impact on settle-ment and land use. The fate of the Saxons living east of the Elbe is the best-known case: in 804 Charlemagne consolidated his conquest of Saxony by the mass deportation of many thousands of men, women, and children, whom he relocated in interior parts of his empire.

Displacements such as these are a sad but straightforward manifest-ation of settlement mobility. Much more controversial is the extent to which long-distance migration in northern Europe accompanied the col-lapse of the Roman frontier in the fifth century. The idea that entire peoples trekked south in search of new homes was first promulgated in the origin tales that the Franks, Goths, Lombards, and Anglo-Saxons told about themselves after they had successfully established their own king-doms within former imperial provinces. As we have seen, however, there are additional powerful explanations of the social and cultural changes of the fifth and sixth centuries.[7] While settlement archaeology does suggest that between the fifth and seventh centuries there was some reduction in the population around the base of the Jutland peninsula and along the North Sea coast of modern Germany, and, in places, an associated ex-pansion of forests, migration may not have been its sole, or even main, cause.

We are on safer ground if we turn our attention to what happened within frontier provinces of the empire, for organized evacuation formed a recognized instrument of imperial policy, and supplemented the flight of refugees away from zones of conflict to safer parts of the empire. The gradual collapse of the Danubian frontier was accompanied by deliberate evacuations of towns, starting along the southern bank of the river's upper course in the last two decades of the fifth century and then, a century or so later, along its lower, Balkan, reaches. In the 480s, townsfolk, clergy, and saints' relics from Noricum were resettled in Italy, and then, in the 580–90s, evacuees and refugees from Slavic attacks in the Balkans found safer homes in Greece, the Aegean islands, southern Italy, and Sicily. North-eastern Italy was not exempt from this disruption. Repeated in-vasions and raids across the eastern Alps from the Balkans and Danube basin created an atmosphere of insecurity, which lasted into the later seventh century. Vulnerable to attack, the cities and settlements on the dry lands above the head of the Adriatic Sea steadily declined in importance. Their inhabitants found safer refuges on the islands surrounding the Adriatic lagoons, where new communities developed, first temporary refuges and then permanent settlements. From c.800 onwards, the independent and increasingly powerful trading settlement of Venice grew rapidly on the island of Rialto: its rise marks the new predominance of island settlements over the depopulated *terra firma* in this region.

In situating the men, women, and children of the early Middle Ages in their habitats, two points emerge. First, we must envisage rural and urban settlements as dynamic and ever-changing, not static and timeless. Habitation sites were rarely stable or permanent: they occupied a landscape littered with the debris of former generations and ages, whether buildings, field walls, cemeteries, or monuments. As men and women shifted their dwellings and modified their farming practices, they left their mark on the continuously evolving European landscape. Climate, exploitation of natural resources, availability of cultivable land, choice of crops, habitation sites, forms of settlement, and modes of exploitation all gradually changed, each contributing to the European environment familiar today. Some of this evolution can be detected in the year-by-year events recorded by written documentation, but much of it occurred slowly, over decades and centuries, and is not readily identifiable except by intensive regional archaeology. That we now know as much as we do about the evolution of Europe's landscapes is the fruit of close collaboration between historians and environmental scientists, and a broadening in historical perspective beyond the events of political or ecclesiastical history towards a complementary focus on longer-term structural change in human societies.

Secondly, wherever we look, we encounter the regionalism, even localism, that is the dominant characteristic of the early Middle Ages. Landscape, natural resources, climate, farming systems, settlement distribution, and population density not only changed over time; they also differed from one part of Europe to another, from one locality to the next. The variation and diversity of habitats is of fundamental significance: although subsequent chapters will explore the human endeavour expended in overcoming the limitations of micro-regional living by forging networks of social association, economic contact, and political allegiance, the next section of this chapter will demonstrate ways in which human experience remained constrained by local conditions throughout the early Middle Ages. By thinking in local rather than generalized terms, we can make sense of the dynamics of living and dying in the early Middle Ages.

## Birth and Death

After three years of marriage, Vilithuta, wife of Dagaulf, died in about 590. Aged 17, she passed away in childbirth, 'pregnant with her own doom'. 'Born in the jaws of death', her child died with her; her sorrowing husband 'in one death . . . grieved for burying two'. We know of Vilithuta's brief life and Dagaulf's grief only from the verses of consolation that her death occasioned, but this poem nevertheless reminds us that, however inextricably linked, birth and death are both the cultural experience of individuals and the biological fundamental of collective human existence over time.[8] The case of Vilithuta and Dagaulf invites us to consider a wide range of demographic questions about birth and death in the centuries between 500 and 1000. This section explores the nature of population change in the early Middle Ages. It then moves on to enquire into life expectancies and sex ratios in order to sketch the demographic profiles of the communities who form the subject of this book: Vilithuta's life story turns out to be not uncommon. Against the backdrop of regional and micro-regional landscapes outlined above, it also argues that birth and death are best comprehended in local contexts.

Inasmuch as they are both cultural and biological phenomena, birth and death are, in principle, amenable to study through both cultural and biological evidence—that is, through textual representation and human remains. In practice, however, neither separately nor even in conjunction do the two categories of evidence easily yield answers to the questions historians might wish to pose. We immediately find that things that seem important to us rarely mattered in the same way in the early Middle Ages. Take the question of age. One late Roman habit maintained by the literate urban elites of Italy, Gaul, Spain, and the Balkans until c.700 was the practice of erecting epitaphs to commemorate the dead. Many of these tombstones state the age of the deceased. The ages given are occasionally downright impossible, sometimes explicitly approximate—'Demetius lived more or less thirty-seven years'[9]—and often rounded off to a suspiciously neat number that was socially appropriate rather than factually accurate. It seems that few people knew exactly how old they were, and that age was more a matter of social role than a precise period of time. Analysis of skeletal remains offers an alternative approach, but, even so, can offer only approximations of the age at death of individuals whose remains have been excavated.

Nor was anyone concerned to count people, for the question about how many people lived in a place never arose in the early Middle Ages, and, even if it had, no one would have had the means to answer it exactly. Thus there is a fundamental absence of evidence for calculating Europe's early medieval population—not that this has prevented efforts at guessing. For what they are worth, estimates of the population from Scandinavia to the Balkans c.1000 fall either side of the 40 million mark. The nearest thing to a population census is a handful of estate surveys and descriptions of the workers on great ecclesiastical estates in the ninth-century Carolingian Empire. As will be seen, if used with care these can provide approximations of the density, sex ratios, and age profile of the specific settlements concerned. Even so, this evidence is exiguous and unreliable, for the compilers' aim was not a population census but a record of fiscal exactions and labour services in which individuals were generally recorded only in so far as they were burdened with taxes or labour services. This is the nub of the problem with the available evidence: statistical records of a population and its obligations are the product of cultures featuring both sophisticated document-mindedness and intensive government. As the previous chapter has indicated, extant documentation from such environments survives only from parts of the ninth-century Carolingian Empire and late-tenth-century England, and none at all remains from the highly bureaucratic regime of the amirs of al-Andalus. In Scandinavia, where any written documentation is absent before the eleventh century, there is nothing to fall back on except extrapolations from indirect evidence offered by burial archaeology, to the extent that such cemetery evidence has survived and been analysed. The same situation pertains in Ireland, for, if Irish uses of writing did extend to forms of record keeping, no traces of them have survived. As for the Slavs, who generally disposed of their dead by cremation rather than inhumation until at least the late tenth century, archaeological assessment of demographic questions necessarily excludes any skeletal analysis. It is best to accept that we cannot say what the population of early medieval Europe was.

Although we cannot measure numbers of people, we can deduce something about relative changes in population levels in the course of the early Middle Ages. Tracking these starts in the cities of the sixth-century Mediterranean, certainly crowded but many of them less so than they had been a couple of centuries earlier. Each town was not only the focal point for its rural hinterland but also a hub in inter-regional trade networks.[10] Thus the epidemic of bubonic plague that broke out at Pelusium on the Nile delta in 541 was able to spread rapidly from one seaport to another. Recurring frequently during the remainder of the sixth century, and thereafter at lengthening intervals, its demographic impact was especially severe in the eastern Mediterranean, where ongoing long-distance grain shipments facilitated its persistence. The disease reached the western Mediterranean basin in 542, repeatedly ravaging the cities of the Italian, French, and Spanish littoral as well as North Africa during the next two centuries, until a final outbreak in southern Italy in 767. But long-distance shipping declined somewhat earlier in the western Mediterranean than in the east, and this may have reduced the severity of the epidemic's impact here. On occasion, plague reached inland along major trade routes such as the Rhone, the Ebro, and the Po, but its virulence faded as it spread; only once did it reach north of the Loire valley.

Bubonic plague had unmistakable symptoms and killed fast. 'It was a sudden death. A wound like a serpent's bite swelled in the groin or armpit and those affected were so consumed by its poison that they died on the second or third day. The strength of the poison robbed sufferers of their senses.'[11] At its most noxious, the epidemic might have dramatic consequences: shortages of coffins, mass burials, flight, civic collapse. In the summer of 654, plague hit several Italian cities. Nearly 150 years later, the devastation seemed apocalyptic to Paul the Deacon. 'So great was the multitude of those dying that even parents with their children and brothers with their sisters were placed on biers two by two and conducted to their tombs in the city of Rome. And in like manner too this pestilence also depopulated Ticinum [i.e. Pavia] so that all citizens fled to the mountain ranges and to other places and grass and bushes grew in the market place and throughout the streets of the city.'[12] Whatever the actual death toll may have been, an outbreak such as this left traumatic memories and enduring perceptions of social dislocation.

In demographic terms, the impact of the plague undoubtedly varied from region to region and city to city. Locally severe on several occasions in Rome and Marseilles, a passing anguish in Trier and Toledo, non-existent in Nantes or Paris, these epidemics caused regional but not global decline in population. Indeed, bubonic plague rarely reached much beyond the busy trading ports of the Mediterranean and their immediate hinterlands, where the preconditions for its spread existed. Nevertheless, spasms of virulent disease certainly visited the more rural and sparsely populated areas of Atlantic Europe and the British Isles. Mentions of 'yellow pestilence', 'mortality of children', 'great mortality', and 'pox' occur in Irish and Anglo-Saxon sources for the sixth and seventh centuries, but these phrases cannot be reliably translated into modern medical terminology. Whatever their precise nature, these epidemics had serious consequences. Several kings succumbed to disease, their deaths inevitably plunging fragile kingdoms into turmoil. On occasion, it seems that whole localities were devastated too, as in 664, when one of these outbreaks ravaged first southern England, then northern regions, and finally spread to Ireland. According to Bede, in Northumbria, this 'most grievous pestilence . . . brought with it destruction so severe that in some large villages and estates once crowded with inhabitants, only a small and scattered remnant, and sometimes none at all, remained'.[13]

In assessing whether epidemics had a significant effect upon European population levels, we have no means of moving beyond literary impressions of disaster such as Bede's to any measure of how many people actually died or fled to uncontaminated places. Nor is it possible to determine whether the population level was reduced for more than a couple of generations. We should avoid any temptation to overgeneralize, and, rather than postulating any overall fall in population, it makes best sense to interpret the decline and dislocation induced by epidemics as short term and locally specific, varying from place to place.

The same holds true for the food shortages that are such a marked feature of the historical record from *c*.800 onwards. Famine recurred on average one year in four throughout the ninth century, dropped to only one year in ten in the tenth, but rose again in the eleventh century. Many of these were of regional impact: the Rhineland in 850, Saxony in 853, Bavaria in 882, 'here and there' in 889, for example.[14] In contrast, Ireland, a country especially dedicated to animal husbandry, endured recurrent bouts of murrain among cattle in the course of the early Middle Ages, with a profound impact on food supply and human resistance to disease. In 700, 'cattle mortality' broke out early in the year, with extreme consequences: 'famine and pestilence prevailed in Ireland for three years, so that man ate man.'[15] Only on one occasion is it clear that all Europe was affected simultaneously, however. In the famine of 1005, so great that 'no man ever remembered one so cruel',[16] cannibalism was again reported: this famine ravaged everywhere from the British Isles to Bavaria. The terrible hunger of 1005 was nevertheless exceptional. In general, dearth and disaster struck here one year, there another year. No long-distance trade in foodstuffs evened out the oscillations of scarcity and plenty; equally, no general cycle of misery afflicted all early medieval Europe.

The same emphasis on regionality also applies to the circumstances that might be conducive to population growth. A critical prerequisite for sustaining demographic advance is a regular and adequate food supply. Either extension of the area of cultivation or intensification of agricultural techniques might increase the availability of foodstuffs—to the extent permitted by climate and soil fertility, supply of labour and agricultural technology. Did agricultural change enable more intensive cultivation, and thereby population growth in the early Middle Ages? The most appropriate answer is again one that stresses regional distinctions. Consider a small part of France: watermills studded the area west of Paris from at least the late eighth century onwards, yet they remained rare until the eleventh century just 50 kilometres to the south, where different geology and patterns of landholding delayed their introduction. Whether the issue is the use of a heavy plough or the introduction of new crops, both of which are attested in many different places, the same picture emerges: change was localized, and dependent on many factors besides technical expertise. At the very least, as Chapter 5 will argue, the arrival of a new, energetic landlord could make a considerable difference. The one thing that seems not to have altered anywhere is extremely low grain yields, even on the most fertile soils. Although the quality of harvests was doubtless extremely erratic, to reap no more than two to three times the amount of grain as had been sown appears to have been common: and out of this harvest came next year's seed corn. If the population of rural areas grew in the early Middle Ages, more intensive food production was not the main cause.

By contrast, many different parts of Europe provide evidence to suggest that land clearance was common, certainly from the eighth century onwards, and in places perhaps from the seventh. Archaeological traces of new settlement sites, palaeobotanical analysis of pollen deposits, and documentary references to the extension of cultivation into areas of woodland all point in the same direction. Whether the evidence comes from Ireland, southern England, Scotland, central France, Catalonia, northern and central Italy, the Ardennes, Hesse, eastern Bavaria, or the western Polish heartland, it is consistent in suggesting the extension of cultivation and, in particular, of cereal-growing. Whether small-scale clearance on individual initiative, or larger projects pushed forward by the energy of lords, churches, and even kings, the felling of scrub or woodland constituted the main form of agricultural change in the early Middle Ages.

The extension of arable land should probably be associated with growth in the rural population of Europe inasmuch as it both presumes a supply of labour adequate to the task and results in an increased supply of foodstuffs. Certainly, those few ninth-century estate surveys that provide a snapshot of their workforce at a particular moment reinforce the view that there was considerable pressure on landed resources by this date. On the lands in southern Flanders belonging to the abbey of Saint Bertin in the middle years of the ninth century, the population probably reached an average density of twenty inhabitants per square kilometre. On the estates belonging to Saint-Germain-des-Prés in the Seine basin around Paris, the average was even higher, up to forty persons per square kilometre on certain estates.

To the suggestion that the cereal-growing lowlands of northern Europe were already supporting dense settlement in the ninth century can be added clues from the mountainous fringe of the Mediterranean. Indeed, in the upland valleys of Catalonia, the rural population may well have been as high as nineteenth-century levels. The only documentation that allows an estimate of demographic growth to be hazarded comes from the Provençal lands of Saint-Victor at Marseilles in 813–14. The evidence of this estate survey indicates that the population increased rather faster on some properties in the region than on others. Extrapolations suggest an overall growth rate on Saint-Victor's estates equivalent to a doubling of the population in the course of a century. If these calculations are at all reliable, they imply that, in at least some parts of ninth-century Europe, the population was capable of brief spurts of growth almost at the rate sustained in England towards the eve of the Industrial Revolution. In all, there are firm signs of considerable, if short-term, demographic growth in parts of Europe at various times from the ninth century onwards.

The summary picture for the eighth and ninth centuries is one of patchy, regional changes in agricultural methods and technology, widespread land clearance, and the capacity for substantial population growth. Yet these developments had only modest cumulative impact, for not until c.950–1050 is there clear evidence of widespread, prolonged population growth. Medieval Europe's sustained demographic upturn commenced, approximately, with the millennium. In the preceding two or three centuries, land clearance and population growth were tempered by outbreaks of disease, frequent famines, and the effects of climatic deterioration.

The most likely explanation for the lack of steady population growth in the early Middle Ages is that spasms of subsistence crisis, marked by food shortages and natural calamities, interrupted periods of growth and expansion. Since famine rarely struck universally, and since heavy rains, drought and other climatic disasters were similarly regional or local in impact, the oscillation between population growth and stagnation (or even short-term decline) is likely also to have been regional and inconsistent. All this suggests that, in the early Middle Ages, the resources were not widely available to sustain steady population growth over long periods of time. A population on the brink of subsistence crisis was not well equipped to withstand years when the crops failed or cattle murrain was rife. While there certainly were dense pockets of population, that density was neither uniform nor stable. In short, throughout the early Middle Ages, the rate of change in the population level fluctuated unpredictably from place to place. If the impact of dearth and disaster was erratic and uneven, so too was population growth.

For a population to grow, a sustained surplus of births over deaths is required. In the assessment of fertility and mortality, cemetery evidence is invaluable, for painstaking analysis can induce the bodies of the early medieval dead to yield up much valuable information on the sex ratios, life expectancies, patterns of disease, and forms of mortality prevalent within particular communities. With the caveat that skeletal analysis is not an exact science, and that a cemetery does not necessarily hold all (or even a representative sample) of a community's dead, burial evidence nevertheless throws into sharp relief the circumstances in which men and women lived, endeavoured to reproduce themselves, and died. Two cemeteries, widely separated in space and time, illustrate its potential.

The first is a site in south-eastern England, in use from the late fifth century until the middle of the eighth. At Buckland, at least 20 per cent of all the community died before they reached the age of 18, and only about 6 per cent lived to an age of 60 or more. Of the adult population, women outnumbered men by 3:2, but had a significantly shorter life expectancy, for the average age at death of adult women was 31, as compared with 38 for men. Approximate though these figures are, they indicate a population faced with very heavy child mortality, a high rate of female mortality in the child-bearing years, a surplus of women, which may imply that men frequently died away from home—at war or out hunting—and a community whose elderly members were far fewer and much younger than in recent centuries. Furthermore, since the people who lived in the vicinity of Buckland buried their infants under about age 5 somewhere separate from this communal cemetery, the real child mortality rate must have been very much higher. The sixth-century cemetery at Cannington in south-western Britain suggests a likelier figure: there 64 per cent of the entire population died before they reached 18 and, indeed, 15 per cent did not survive their first year.

The second example is the Münsterhof cemetery in the centre of Zurich. This served as the burying ground for the proto-urban settlement that formed around the Frauenmünster nunnery founded in 853, and it remained in use until the end of the twelfth century. Figure 2.2 indicates its overall population profile. Unlike Buckland, young children and some infants were buried here, but it seems that, before the eleventh century, stillborn babies and those dying in the first weeks of life continued to be laid to rest elsewhere. Of those who were buried in the Münsterhof, almost 50 per cent failed to reach age 18 and at least 30 per cent died in the first five years of life, two-thirds of whom died within their first year. In terms of perinatal, infant, and child mortality, the population of ninth- and tenth-century Zurich was depleted at a rate broadly comparable with that at Buckland or Cannington. By contrast, the adult population of Zurich was quite different. The ratio of women to men was much more nearly even, with six women for every five men, a ratio in line with many other cemeteries of the high Middle Ages. Also, the average age at death of the adult population suggests that the security of existence was measurably greater in Zurich than it had been in Buckland, for most adults died between 50 and 60 and a few lived on above 60. There was,

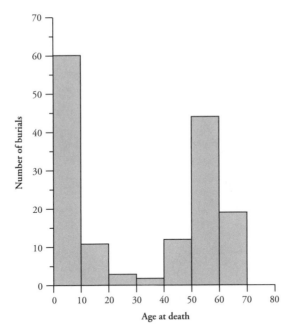

**2.2.** Age profile of the burials in the Münsterhof cemetery, Zurich. This graph emphasizes the very high rate of infant and child mortality and, for those who survived into adulthood, the likelihood of dying in their 50s. Based on J. Schneider, D. Gutscher, H. Etter, and J. Hanser, *Der Münsterhof in Zürich: Bericht über die vom städtischen Büro für Archäologie durchgeführten Stadtkern-forschungen 1977/78* (Olten, 1982).

nevertheless, a clear difference between men and women, which Figure 2.3 reveals, for the average life expectancy of a 20-year-old male was 57, as compared with 49 for women of the same age. This was an environment in which childbirth remained an appreciable danger, for over one-third of adult women died during their fertile years.

Approximate though these figures are, they nevertheless suggest a few general observations. In the first place, regional and temporal variation is again noteworthy: the striking fluctuations in general population levels reflected locally varying fertility and mortality rates. Further, if on average one-half of the population died during infancy or childhood, this means that women underwent pregnancy and childbirth twice for every child that reached adulthood. For population levels to remain steady each couple had to produce four offspring, of whom two would survive; for the population to grow, even more. There is also the inescapable observation

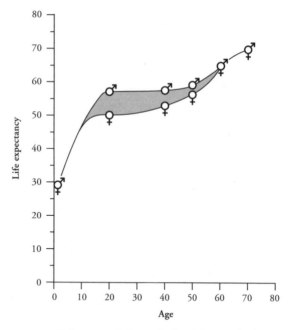

**2.3.** Life expectancy of the population of the Münsterhof cemetery, Zurich. Average life expectancy at birth was about twenty-eight years, but those who survived their first year of infancy might expect to live on to 36. By age 20 a clear gender differential is evident, which diminishes only in old age. Based on J. Schneider, D. Gutscher, H. Etter, and J. Hanser, *Der Münsterhof in Zürich: Bericht über die vom städtischen Büro für Archäologie durchgeführten Stadtkernforschungen 1977/78* (Olten, 1982).

that birth and death were intimately associated. The risk of death was always greatest within the very first year of human life—probably even the first weeks—and, for adult women, around the time of childbirth. In this respect, early medieval Europe was little different from those twenty-first-century communities that lack any access to modern hygiene and medicine. The population profile thus contrasts starkly with that of contemporary western Europe, as Figure 2.4 emphasizes.

Cemetery evidence from Buckland, Zurich, and elsewhere reveals something of the quality of life in the early Middle Ages. Among the symptoms betrayed by skeletal remains are: dental problems such as badly worn teeth and abscesses; broken limbs that had healed crooked or shortened; long-running inflammation and infections in joints whose sufferers had lived deformed from pain; uncomfortable and debilitating skeletal

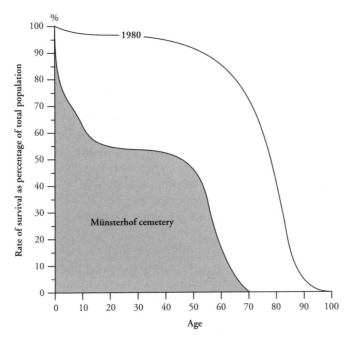

**2.4.** Population profile of early medieval and modern Zurich. This graph con-trasts the demographic profile of the early medieval Münsterhof cemetery with the much lower rate of infant mortality and much longer life span of late-twentieth-century western Europe. Based on J. Schneider, D. Gutscher, H. Etter, and J. Hanser, *Der Münsterhof in Zürich: Bericht über die vom städtischen Büro für Archäologie durchgeführten Stadtkernforschungen 1977/78* (Olten, 1982).

conditions such as arthritis, osteoporosis, or spondylosis afflicting men and women in the middle and later years of life. Cemeteries sometimes also hint at communities in which diseases such as tuberculosis were endemic as well as at personal life stories otherwise unknown to us: an adult woman at Tuttlingen whose bow legs were the result of malnutrition in childhood; a man at Griesheim whose left leg had been amputated below the knee, but who had lived on into his 50s with a wooden leg fitted with a rust-proof bronze cap; a congenitally malformed child at Zurich who had been born with a severely twisted spine; a man in Kent who had been stabbed in the left eye and then sustained three decapitating blows on the back of his skull. Skeletal remains evoke a world pervaded by illness, pain, and de-formity, exacerbated from time to time by the violence of personal hatred and warfare.

Cemetery evidence on its own does not, however, fully explain early medieval patterns of fertility and mortality, for both are also shaped by social conventions of a type not amenable to archaeological enquiry. For example, archaeology cannot elucidate whether fertility rates were affected by deliberate limitations of family size. From the earliest Christian times, churchmen had inveighed in vain against both contraception and abortion, and there is no doubt that common herbs with effective contraceptive and abortifacient properties were well known throughout early medieval Europe. Occasional instances of infanticide cannot entirely be dismissed, although arguments that systematic female child killing was practised in some ninth-century peasant communities and in Viking-age Scandinavia remain quite unconvincing.

There are two interrelated issues here. First, unlike the numerous cemeteries that suggest a sex ratio in favour of women, the ninth-century estate surveys consistently report more men than women. To explain this by invoking female infanticide is to ignore the good reasons why women tend to be under-recorded in surveys of agricultural estate workers. Secondly, deliberate measures to limit family size are more plausibly associated with the constraints of poverty than those of gender. To the extent that it is possible to estimate the number of surviving children born to each couple, only amongst the royal dynasties or the most rich and powerful continental aristocracies of the ninth and tenth centuries are families of more than three or four children at all common. A frequently repeated pronouncement against abortion offers vital evidence of the way in which the conscious limitation of family size might correlate with poverty: after imposing differential penalties for termination of a pregnancy within the first six weeks or after a foetus has quickened, the ruling continues: 'but it makes a great difference whether an impoverished woman does it on account of the difficulty of feeding the child or a prostitute for the sake of concealing her crime.'[17] Other texts too impose a much lighter penalty on the impoverished woman who slays a child. The recognition that poverty might drive a woman to abortion or even infanticide gradually became an established aspect of ecclesiastical law, but cemetery evidence can never reveal the extent to which this was practised.

If poverty constrained fertility at one end of the social spectrum, then lifestyle may have influenced mortality at the other. Analysis of animal bone remains from high-status sites suggests that early medieval elites enjoyed a diet rich in the meat of domesticated animals raised for early slaughter when the flesh was of optimum quality, supplemented with wildfowl and game such as boar and deer. Food remains from peasant sites, on the other hand, point to the consumption of the flesh of much older animals, livestock whose primary function may have been to provide wool, milk, or traction rather than meat. Better diet and access to such medical expertise as was available may have helped elite women survive the traumas of childbirth a little more readily than other women, but their menfolk were perhaps more susceptible to early death than the men of other social groups. The German aristocracy of the tenth century offers a well-studied and extreme example of this. Hunting, war, feuding, and judicial duels thinned out the ranks of the men of the Ottonian aristocracy, who were often long outlived by their female relatives, whether sisters dedicated to a life of Christian celibacy or widowed wives and mothers. In this context, mortality might have serious political repercussions. When the ruling dynasty itself was involved, a bitter succession dispute or the accession of a minor, usually under the tutelage of his mother, was the likely consequence.

In any society, demographic changes reflect a complex interaction between external factors such as climatic disaster and famine, on the one hand, and, on the other, such internal social conventions as constraints on family size, attitudes towards contraception and abortion, medical knowledge, and the prevalence of dangerous lifestyles among certain social groups. Fragmentary and impressionistic though the early medieval evidence is, it shows clearly enough the main patterns of fertility and mortality. The physical discomfort of chronic illness probably affected most people; endemic disorders were exacerbated from time to time by epidemics of infectious diseases, of which the plague was only one. Amid these difficulties, infants, women in labour, and aristocratic men all faced an enhanced risk of death, yet Europe's population nevertheless managed to increase in the course of the early Middle Ages. Although individual communities experienced fluctuating patterns of fertility and mortality, the overall upward curve is clear.

Moreover, as the millennium approached, erratic demographic change was giving way to a steadier rate of increase as the constraints on growth eased. Certainly, the climate was generally improving by the year 1000. Documentary evidence suggests that land clearance projects were taking place on an enhanced scale. Local and regional trade networks were intensifying, transporting foodstuffs to towns whose growth, especially in northern Italy and the Low Countries, must have relied upon surplus rural population.[18] By the opening years of the eleventh century the population and economy of Europe were entering an era of sustained growth that would last into the thirteenth century. The developments of the high Middle Ages did not suddenly develop out of nothing; but they did consolidate changes that had hitherto been faltering or spasmodic.

## Responses to Calamity

For any early medieval community, everyday life involved facing death and disaster. Enduring this ever-present threat, men and women not only raised children and eked out a living; they also strove to make sense of the world in which they lived and to do whatever they could to ameliorate their lot. Their responses were informed by ideas and assumptions about the causes of good or bad fortune, about the place of humans within the cosmos, about what happened after death. But it remains virtually impossible to recover most of these mentalities, partly because of the difficulties in extrapolating from material culture to attitudes, beliefs, and rituals, partly because attempts to suppress older explanations for the fates of humankind accompanied the spread of Christianity. As will be seen, we can nevertheless pick up some traces of those other views, despite the dominance in the textual record of a Christian cosmology. What emerges from this survey are the variety and versatility of early medieval responses to the calamities that constrained existence.

Many different ways of dealing with ill health, disability, and disease are particularly well evidenced. It would be possible to categorize the range of curative techniques and resources thus: professional doctors, trained in book-learned medicine inherited from the ancient world; practitioners of local wisdom concerning herbal remedies; Christian faith healers, living and dead; clerical specialists expert in manipulating ecclesiastical rituals for curative purposes; traditional practices such as amulets, talismans, invocations, and charms. Yet, in practice, these were not clear-cut distinctions, for some holy men possessed medical knowledge, while clergy sometimes carefully copied out herbal recipes that were to be applied with a mixture of Christian prayers and charmlike incantations. What the evidence generally fails to offer is a sense of healing as practice rather than as textual strategy, not least because of the paucity of direct evidence for the application of most of these methods. It would seem, though, that the more specialist resources were thinly and unevenly distributed, and thus that the curative options available in any one locality were in all likelihood restricted. For all except the wealthy few, cost would anyway have prohibited virtually all forms of external help, for professional doctors charged fees for their services or for rare drugs; the nearest shrine might be far away and hard of access, its custodians likely to expect a significant gift. Most people were thrown back on whatever expertise was locally available—and free.

Far more is known about one form of healing than all the others, however: that offered by the shrines of Christian saints. Some were the tombs of men and women who had been martyred in the second and third centuries. Others were the graves of holy men or—less frequently—women, persons who had acquired a reputation in their lifetime for mitigating human affliction through their own religiosity and whose achievements had commonly included healing the sick through prayer and ritual, sometimes also identifying and expelling the demons whom Christians deemed to inhabit the bodies of the suffering. Whether martyred or not, all saints were understood to have the ability to intercede successfully with the God of Christian tradition to win beneficial intervention in human affairs: their importance reflected a clearly articulated cosmology that identified certain humans during and after their lifetimes as special conduits of supernatural assistance.

As Christianity spread, so clergy established new shrines, either by moving body parts of established saints to new locales, or by encouraging the veneration as saints of recently deceased religious leaders. In some places, these shrines perpetuated pre-Christian healing powers once vested in potent springs and trees or attributed to sites sacred to the local gods; in others, a quite new religious landscape emerged, competing with, and ultimately replacing, earlier ritual sites. Thanks to the clerical custom of keeping written records of the cures, exorcisms (expulsions of demons), and other intercessions attributed to the saints, the healing available at Christian shrines is far better documented than any other of the curative possibilities of the early Middle Ages.

We have already met one such saint, Martin, also one of the many cures achieved through his intercession. After a spectacular and controversial career as bishop of Tours (371–97), healer, and wonderworker, he had become the best-documented and most widely revered saint of the early Middle Ages, venerated from Scotland and Ireland to Spain and Germany. Although his tomb in the magnificently decorated fifth-century church just outside the city of Tours always remained the focal point of his cult, Martin's bodily remains had been removed to a church in Chablis for safekeeping between about 872 and 885, a time of threat from the Vikings, seaborne Scandinavian raiders.[19] It was there that Genovefa had been cured of her congenital deafness and lack of speech when she spent the night in silent prayer outside the doors of the church, along with other pilgrims congregated there. The clerical author who noted the details of her visit drew on commonplace religious motifs when he represented her cure in terms of a confrontation between a fire-spitting devil and the resplendent, white-haired saint, a conflict easily won by the latter. In so doing, the author relied upon the widespread

Christian understanding of the world as one in which the cosmic struggle of good and evil manifested itself in the symptoms displayed by the human body, a struggle in which Christian salvation was synonymous with physical healing. The fundamental tenet of Christian belief, that this redemption came through belief in Christ, easily accommodated saints as the channels through which divine beneficence or retribution flowed. 'I am Martin, through whom Lord Jesus Christ deigns to restore you to health' declared the saint as his healing touch cured Genovefa.[20]

Christian teaching relied on a cosmology that explained far more than the physical afflictions of individuals: it supplied reasons for death and disaster too. For one thing, the Bible provided a frame of reference and comparison. In 873, the 'ancient plague of the Egyptians' afflicted much of Europe—an infestation of locusts. When the swarm flew, it filled the air with the thrumming of wings: 'one could scarcely see the sky, as if looking through a sieve.' Clergy processed with crucifixes and the relics of saints through stricken areas, 'beseeching God to defend them from this plague'.[21] Above all, however, the Bible presented an exemplum of suffering and destruction as symptoms of a wrathful God angered by personal immorality or social disarray. No one contributed more to interpreting the afflictions of this world through the lens of Christian doctrine than Gregory I. Wracked by pain and illness for much of his life, he drew inspiration and comfort from the Old Testament story of Job, a man who exemplified persistence in faith undeterred by disease and suffering. What held good for Gregory in his private life held good also for the world around him. Elected pope in 590 as plague raged through Rome, claiming among its victims his predecessor Pelagius, Gregory explained the reason and remedy for this epidemic to his congregation:

Behold! The sword of heavenly anger strikes down the entire Christian community, as one after another they are laid low by sudden slaughter. No infirmity warns of the approach of death, but, as you see, death overtakes the onset of sickness. The smitten person is struck down without time for conversion to tears and penitence. Think, therefore, how the person who has had no time to repent of their actions will come into the presence of the stern Judge [at the Last Judgement]. Our townsfolk are not taken away piecemeal but they all collapse together: houses are left empty, parents attend the funerals of their children, their heirs precede them to the grave. So let each of us take refuge in repentance and lamentation of our sins whilst there is still time to weep before death strikes. Let us recall to the mind's eye how we have gone astray and what wrongdoings we have done and let us punish ourselves with tears. 'Let us come into God's presence in confession' and, as the prophet urges, 'Let us lift up our hearts with our hands to the Lord'.[22]

Whether the tribulation was induced by epidemic, famine, Viking attack, or any other calamity, the appropriate responses were fasting, prayer, and penance. From Rome to Ireland, wherever the Christian religion found adherents, Christians instinctively reacted by propitiating their God through penitential processions and prayers of intercession, as did the local clergy in the areas overrun by locusts in 873. Such measures could be universal as well as local. Faced with severe and widespread famine in the winter of 792–3, Charlemagne commanded all bishops, priests, monks, nuns, and clergy throughout the Frankish lands to say Masses and sing psalms, ordered everyone to fast, and required all lay and ecclesiastical landowners to give alms to support their tenants until the next harvest time. Similarly, with his kingdom under threat of imminent collapse from Viking invasions in 1009, the Anglo-Saxon king Æthelred II (978–1016) ordered identical action by 'all the nation' in order that 'we may obtain God's mercy and his compassion and that we may be able through his help to withstand our enemies'.[23] Prayer, penance, and almsgiving were the practical manifestations of a mentality that attributed human suffering to spiritual deficiency and found the remedy for physiological, environmental, and political dislocation in the rebalancing of relationships between humans and the divine.

Of the various crises facing early medieval communities, one in particular raised a host of moral and practical problems: famine. One issue was that of lawful foodstuffs. Christian teaching urged a concept of a community whose social boundaries had various markers. Among these were food laws, behavioural prescriptions whose transgression would pollute both the individual and the group. The flesh of several categories of animals was commonly proscribed as unclean: those who shared their living space with humans, such as cats, dogs, and rats; those contaminated by wrongful contact with blood or semen; those that had eaten carrion or human corpses; those found already dead. But, when food was scarce, few starving people can have thought in these terms. In the summer of 869, for example, famine hit central France especially severely. 'A huge number of people died a bitter death, to the extent that men are said to have eaten human corpses. And some are also said to have eaten the flesh of dogs.'[24] A rather different moral issue was the fair price for grain. In the spring of 585, as grain stores ran out long before the next harvest, merchants 'grievously despoiled people' by selling such wine and grain as remained at vastly inflated prices. Struggling households eked out what little flour they had by drying and grinding grape pips, hazel catkins, the roots of ferns, or the young shoots of corn in the field. We also know how those who could not afford any grain at all fared: 'many others, who had no flour

at all, gathered and ate various grasses, but they swelled up and died. . . .
The impoverished gave themselves into slavery in order to receive
a scrap of food.'[25] It was to alleviate situations like this that, in 792–3,
Charlemagne regulated grain prices in a move to prevent landlords from
pursuing profiteering rather than their almsgiving obligations. As
expressed in this legislation, prices and profits were more a matter for
religious concern than economic planning, but at least almsgiving had the
effect of redistributing food to those most in need.

However, Christianity monopolized neither explanations of disaster
nor available remedies. In places where it was of recent introduction,
the validity of the new religion might itself be at issue. The political elites
of southern England had accepted the new faith only a generation or so
before the epidemic of 664: in reaction to the spread of disease, the
East Saxons 'deserted the sacraments of the Christian faith and aposta-
sized. . . . They began to restore the derelict temples and to worship images, as if they could protect themselves by such means from the plague.'[26]
Centuries later, the German missionary bishop Bruno of Querfurt
(1002–9) preached to the Magyars, Poles, and Pechenegs of eastern
Europe. He also wrote an account of the missionary Adalbert of Prague,
using his own experiences to present insights into the difficulties Adalbert had faced immediately before his martyrdom near Gdansk in 997. In
describing the Prussians' hostility that culminated in Adalbert's death at
their hands, Bruno represented their opposition to Christianity as an
equation of the evangelizers' presence with the sterility of the land: '"On
account of these men," the Prussians said, "our land will not yield a
harvest, our trees will not bear fruit, new animals are not born and old
ones die".'[27] A sensitive missionary such as Bruno understood that, in the
struggle for prosperity, religion and disaster were as integrally associated
for non-Christians as for Christians.

Many men and women in early medieval Europe, however, neither enjoyed the learned outlook on the world of a man such as Gregory the
Great nor lived in non-Christian communities. Rather, their Christianity
was richly varied in its understanding of and responses to the world, for
the spread of the Christian religion was a slow process of extended cultural encounters that left its everyday content open to centuries-long negotiation. As Chapter 7 will argue, leading churchmen certainly had their
own firm views about appropriate Christian practice for addressing the
pressing concerns of a rural population struggling with subsistence—the
fertility of animals and fields, the health of children, good weather. They
met limited success in imposing them, however: local communities and
their rural priests persisted with a much wider range of solutions for deal-

ing with the difficulties of a harsh existence. This emerges clearly when we consider the problem of weather, and especially the summer hailstorms that could devastate a harvest. Two complementary beliefs are widely attested throughout the early Middle Ages: that the devil was responsible for unwanted rain and hail; and that 'storm-makers' existed, men and, occasionally, women who could be invoked to deflect bad weather—or to rain hail down on a hated neighbour's lands. Techniques for achieving the desired weather addressed saints, storm-makers, and others deemed able to intervene through prayers and incantations; charms both spoken and written, adjurations and invocations; the payment of protection money, and much else.

Many of these are principally known from their repeated condemnation by clergy, but an exceptional text from north-western Spain does allow us to see what one individual actually did to ward off hail. In the late eighth or early ninth century, the 'servant of God' Auriolus wrote, or had written out for him, a talisman to keep hail off his and his neighbours' fields. He folded then fastened its two slate leaves together, text inside; after nine incantations to ensure its efficacy, he buried it in his field near Carrio, where it remained until unearthed by farmers in 1926. Auriolus adjured 'all you patriarchs Michael, Gabriel, Cecitiel, Oriel, Raphael, Ananiel, Marmoniel, who hold the clouds in your hands' that they 'go across the mountains and return neither when the cock crows nor the hen clucks, neither when the ploughman [ploughs] nor the sower sows'. He also adjured Satan not to harm the trees, harvest, vines, or fruit bushes and added prayers to God attributed to St Christopher before ending 'in the name of the Father, the Son and the Holy Spirit, amen, amen, ever amen, alleluia'.[28] Auriolus's slate not only indicates the persistence of enduring regional textual habits;[29] it also suggests a broad-spectrum approach to eliminating hail, simultaneously invoking archangels, saints, and Satan while mixing prayers, incantations, and adjurations in a powerful cocktail of diverse traditional practices and local wisdom.

Auriolus's concerns were practical, but, to many in the early Middle Ages, bad weather, pestilence, and other caprices of nature also had a portentous place in human experience. The appearance of a comet, for example, 'betokens famine or pestilence or war or the destruction of the earth or fearful storms'.[30] Experts—in astronomy, in the sinfulness of the kingdom—then pronounced upon its significance, while annalists and commentators with a political point to make offered their own opinion about the meaning of a comet, as they also did for locusts, disease, and other such omens. Indeed, writers at ninth-century Carolingian courts so frequently reported natural disasters as the immediate precedent of a revolt, Viking attack, or the death of a king that some of these 'disasters' are as likely to have been rhetorical signals as actual sufferings. Disorder in the natural world had become a sign of decay in human society, a mirror image of perturbation and chaos. For some of the learned men who reflected upon the right ordering of human affairs, it was also a possible sign that the cosmic struggle of good and evil might be nearing conclusion in the manner of the prophetic vision of the biblical Apocalypse.

In the decades either side of AD 1000, reflection upon the end time (eschatology) and scrutiny of signs potentially suggestive of its approach both intensified. Archbishop Wulfstan of York (1002–23) was no stranger to these. Writing in the aftermath of the harsh famines of 1005 and in the midst of extreme political turmoil facing England in 1014, he circulated a sermon that summed up early medieval thinking about the relationship of natural calamity, the social order, and the end of the world.

> Beloved men, realise what is true: this world is in haste and the end approaches; and therefore in the world things go from bad to worse, and so it must of necessity deteriorate greatly on account of the people's sins before the coming of Antichrist, and indeed it will then be dreadful and terrible far and wide throughout the world.
>
>      . . .
>
> For it is clear and manifest in us all that we have previously transgressed more than we have amended, and therefore much is assailing this people. Things have not gone well now for a long time at home or abroad, but there has been devastation and famine, burning and bloodshed in every district again and again; and stealing and killing, sedition and pestilence, murrain and disease, malice and hate and spoliation by robbers have harmed us very grievously, and monstrous taxes have afflicted us greatly, and bad seasons have very often caused us failure of crops. For now for many years, as it may seem, there have been in this country many injustices and wavering loyalties among men everywhere.

Wulfstan concluded his address with the time-tested remedy: 'turn to the right and in some measure leave wrong-doing, and atone very zealously for what we have done amiss.'[31] However near the end of the world might seem, there was always time for repentance.

In the face of scholarly disagreement about when exactly it fell, the millennium came and went without the world coming to an end. That did not invalidate the point that calamity had meaning, whether as portent or punishment, for the association of human behaviour with the behaviour of the elements was far too fundamental to be so easily severed. Whether we address the theologically informed thinking of the learned elite, seek to comprehend the mentality of those for whom conversion to Christianity threatened to bring disaster, or survey the means by which hard-pressed peasants sought to control the hostile forces of nature, we find everywhere deeply rooted assumptions that human affairs were but one aspect of a much vaster cosmic order, an order that could be disturbed by wrong action or rebalanced by the appropriate mental effort and actions. In this light, the practical and intellectual responses to calamity surveyed here all make sense to us, even though many of them were dismissed or even ridiculed by high-minded bishops and legislators.

On 24 January 1002, Emperor Otto III died of a sudden fever at Paterno, just north of Rome, aged 21, unmarried and without an heir. Contemporaries ascribed his death to the 'Italian sickness', in all probability malaria.[32] Both his own early demise and that of his father Otto II eighteen years earlier at the age of 28 are sharp reminders that even the most powerful rulers of the early Middle Ages were as likely to succumb to disease and sudden death as anyone else. Otto II had at least secured the succession by having his infant son elected co-ruler six months earlier, but Otto III had made no provision for the succession: his untimely death threw into turmoil his empire, a sprawling conglomerate of lands from the Baltic to central Italy. Indeed, the political impact of death and disaster on this and countless other occasions during the early Middle Ages cannot be underestimated, for famine and disease could as easily halt a vital military expedition as sudden death could trigger a succession crisis. Perhaps because of his awareness of this fragility, perhaps the result of an outlook instilled by those who had tutored him as a boy, Otto III interpreted his rule as a renewal of the right political, religious, and social order needed to defer the beginning of the end time. To that purpose, his actions were decisive. He made Rome, the eternal city, the capital of his transalpine empire, the first ruler since the fourth century to pay anything more than a passing visit there.[33] In 1000, he travelled to Gniezno, where he inaugurated the cult of a new miracle-working saint, Adalbert of Prague. And as a reminder of what would happen when the world came to an end according to biblical prophecy, he surrounded himself with apocalyptic imagery. At his imperial coronation in Rome in 996, he had even clothed himself in a mantle 'on which the entire Apocalypse was embroidered in gold'.[34]

Otto's reign encapsulates many of the themes of this chapter. His sudden, fevered death was a characteristically Italian one in an age where disease, like famine, almost always hit locally rather than universally and where forms of morbidity varied from one region and habitat to another. From his birth near Nijmegen to his death at Paterno, he had travelled

vast distances both north and south of the Alps, and had a personal experience of the mosaic of landscapes and localities that constituted
Europe everywhere from the modern Nertherlands to Poland and Italy.
His preoccupation with eschatology was an effort to give his reign meaning in terms of Christian cosmology and to situate himself within the
grand narrative of human history, past, present, and future. His distribution of the relics of Adalbert of Prague expressed the universal Christian
view that healing and other forms of divine beneficence flowed from the
bones of sainted patrons. Yet, for all his acute sense of his own mission to
guide his empire towards Christian expansion and Roman renewal, Otto
cannot have been aware that he ruled a population now steadily growing
in number, as elsewhere in Europe, or that the climate of Europe was
improving. Nor, in his brief life, is he likely to have taken note of the
changing appearance of the landscape, as forests were cleared, new settlements founded, and old ones relocated. And, although Rome was central
to his politics and his world view, Otto cannot have realized the extent to
which this city had been transformed in the course of the centuries that
separated him from the last of the western Roman emperors. When we
visit Rome in Chapter 8, we shall find its population a fraction of what it
once had been, its cityscape ruralized and its topography transformed.
More than any other city, Rome epitomizes the highly localized changes
that made the world in which early medieval Europeans lived and died so
complex and, at the same time, so dynamic.

# AFFINITIES

# 3

## Friends and Relations

In happy times a man's near relative will be fond of him; neverthe-less each of them will have to turn from the other, since the Lord means, by his sentence, to commit the wretched body to the earth.[1]

It befits as many things as nature has bound together to be in har-mony—nature who joins to herself the friendship of kinsmen.[2]

THEY are indeed happy times in any community when a man's relatives are fond of him, but, as an anonymous Anglo-Saxon poet recognized, death severs and restructures familial relationships. Similarly, the affection of kinsfolk, and in particular their friendship for each other, may be fit-ting, but reality rarely matches the myth of what is 'natural', for, though the ties between parents and children, brothers and sisters, uncles and nephews are some of the most cogent bonds in any human society, they can also be amongst the most fraught. To explore the significance of kinship in the early Middle Ages is thus to investigate one of the most important ways in which men and women structured human relationships, made choices about their social world, expressed emotions and ideals. Reflection upon these ties also elucidates personal identities, forms of affinity, and deeply ingrained habits of thinking.

Three themes run throughout this chapter: the locally varied social forms and cultural expressions of kinship; their ubiquity as a matrix within which to assert—or contest—power and authority; and the balancing of affinities of blood with those of friendship. Different aspects are explored in each section. In using patterns of name giving, modes of religious com-memoration, and genealogical records to demonstrate that familial tradi-tions helped construct individuals' sense of social identity, the first section emphasizes the tendency for paternal traditions to take precedence over maternal ones. The second turns to the situations in which men and women might, in principle, expect support from their relatives, but argues that, in practice, ties of friendship were at least as important as those of family in the giving and getting of help. The final part explores the separate norms of honourable behaviour for men and women, arguing that the latter were far more grounded in familial relationships than the former. All three sections dismiss generalized assumptions about the functioning of kinship as a form of social process, stressing instead the importance of individual choices and contexts as well as wider power relationships.

We must be aware at the outset, however, that 'kinship' has two different, but not unrelated, connotations: first, the affiliation of an individual to a group defined in terms of consanguinity—that is, of shared blood—and, secondly, the alliances between groups of consanguineal kin effected by marriage or other strategies of association. In the early Middle Ages, both were important. In addition, we must note these affinities can be both objectively and subjectively defined—on the one hand, those people to whom an individual is deemed related in accordance with a clearly stated set of social rules, but, on the other, the persons whom an individual chooses to acknowledge as kin at any particular moment. As will become evident, early medieval men and women used both, often for different purposes. Much of the challenge of studying early medieval societies stems from the fact that the latter group was generally more important than the former.

Clearly, then, 'kinship' is a matter of socially constructed interrelationships, not simply of biologically determined ones. This is true at several levels beyond the answer to the question 'who are your kin?'. Adoption, common under Roman law but absent from other early medieval cultures except Ireland, is a particularly clear case in point where biological paternity and legally recognized fatherhood do not coincide. Fosterage, particularly important in early medieval Wales, Ireland, and Scandinavia, created another form of 'artificial' kinship, where the emotional bond between a boy and the adults who raised him did not coincide with his tie to the parents from whom he in due course inherited property, legal rights, and obligations. Christianity came to place great emphasis on the spiritual kinship created at baptism between godparents and godchild and between a child's natural and spiritual parents. It deemed the former bond as strong as that between a child and its natal parents; the latter—between 'co-parents'—it regarded as equivalent to that between full siblings. 'Nature', then, made a relatively modest contribution to early medieval 'kinship', which was in reality a far more complex and flexible notion than it may seem at first sight.

Full appreciation of all these nuances is hindered by the nature of the surviving sources. Jurists' and law-makers' preoccupation with property, violence, and the protection of the defenceless led them to take far more interest in the interactions between relatives than those between friends. Although there survives ample guidance on kinly affairs issued by kings or codified in lawyers' compilations, it is not distributed evenly either geographically or chronologically. Nevertheless, for some places and periods, such as sixth-century Gaul, seventh-century Ireland, or tenth-century Wessex, it allows us to construct a schematic model of how kinship relations (as also other forms of social relationship) were ideally supposed to work. Even so, to get beyond norms and expectations to social practices and conventions takes very different forms of textual record. Documentary forms of evidence are often anecdotal but provide only a narrow snapshot of a much wider picture. Other sources are either dramatized, poetic evocations of plausible but not historical situations, or clerical diatribes suffused with the authorial prejudices and narrow perspectives of a celibate elite trained to despise all aspects of family and sexuality. The historical reality of interactions among friends and relations is exceptionally hard to pinpoint, the more so because, when we can grasp that reality, it is usually only for upper social levels—local bigwigs, nobles, royalty—and virtually never for peasants.

We may take Lombard Italy of the seventh to eighth centuries as an example of some of these challenges. Ample royal legislation touching on familial interactions survives, most notably the Edict issued in 643 by King Rothari (636–52). In legislating on issues where the king had an active concern in the affairs of a free Lombard, such as the inheritance of property, the proper procedures for betrothal and marriage, or accusations of plotting the death of one's relatives, Rothari's laws are all framed in terms of relationship to the individual in question: father, mother, stepmother, brother, sister, uncle, cousin, nephew are all mentioned. The laws also refer frequently to other 'near relatives' without specifying exactly who these might be. As envisaged by legislators, therefore, Lombard kinship not only took the individual person as its point of reference but also acknowledged the needs of a particular situation. On occasion, however, much more distant relationships might matter, most particularly when the inheritance of property was at issue. Anyone claiming property, Rothari decreed, had to be able to proclaim the names of all ancestors for seven generations, and had to provide kin who would swear to the precise nature of their relationship in front of the judges of the royal law court. In the vital matter of ensuring that land was inherited only by those with a provable claim by blood, Lombard law, therefore, took as its definition of 'kin' a descent

group of seven generations. How many Lombards could name their ancestry for seven generations, trace those related to them by descent from
a common great-great-great-great-great-grandfather, and—crucially—
make their own story agree with that of their relatives? In claiming title
to land, then, legal theory fixed the limits of entitlement at seven generations, even though recorded court cases suggest that claims to kinship
may have worked very differently in practice.

Rothari's Edict shows clearly how multiple notions of kinship could
function simultaneously in one community, according to situation and
purpose. Lombard Italy was not unique: analogous conclusions can be
drawn for all early medieval cultures. But we may remain with Lombard
laws for the moment, for they exemplify a further general point. Rothari
assumed that free Lombards resided in households including domestic
slaves and semi-free men and women as well as their free members.
Although the king certainly envisaged that these households might be
focused on a husband, wife, and their children, his laws also take other
familial patterns for granted. A household might, for example, consist of
a brother, his widowed sister, and some unmarried sisters, in addition to
slaves and other dependants. It might be a group of brothers remaining
together in their father's house after his death, or it might be father and
grandsons, sons of a deceased son, perhaps also a still unmarried son. Another permutation mentioned by Rothari is father, children by a former
wife, and their stepmother. This last may have been a particularly common pattern: given what we know of early medieval mortality rates, many
children are likely to have grown up in households lacking one or both
natal parents.

Simply stated, Rothari's Edict makes clear that the main medieval
social unit was not the nuclear family. Rather, it was the household.
Modern thinking identifies the co-residential descent group as a discrete
social element consisting of parents and children, occasionally with the
addition of close relatives of a third generation (grandparents) or collat-
erals (a brother, his wife, and children, for example). But this way of
thinking has been habitual only since the eighteenth century. The
medieval word *familia* translates most effectively as household and there
is no term equivalent to the modern 'nuclear family'. Although in practice a *familia* commonly had a conjugal unit at its core, both the word
and the social grouping embraced servants, dependants, and sometimes
other close kin. Its precise membership will have been fluid, as older
members died, a widowed sister returned to her natal kin, foster sons
joined then left, or new slaves were purchased and dependants reallocated

to duties elsewhere. In practice, then, a *familia* comprised all those who were under the authority of the male head of the household at any one time and who resided, if not in his house itself, then elsewhere on his property.

That we must think in terms of households not nuclear families is clear wherever we inspect the residential patterns of the men, women, and children of the early Middle Ages. Even royal courts were but households writ large. Consider the exceptionally large empire of Charlemagne. At its domestic and political centre was his queen or concubine of the moment, his daughters but not his sons (for after infancy they were sent off to govern subkingdoms far from the parental palace), several grandsons in the emperor's latter years, and a staff of officials, domestics, stewards, clerics, scribes, huntsmen, cooks, and whoever else was needed for the maintenance of such a large household and the central governing of a huge empire. At the other end of the scale, the peasants of the early Middle Ages lived in households too, usually with their wife and perhaps offspring, and sometimes also with slaves or other semi-free dependants. If they were tenants on a large estate, their household may even have included spare or aged serfs allocated to it by the lord or his bailiff. Modern assumptions about the meaning of the word 'family' do not, therefore, map easily onto the Middle Ages; the following pages use the word 'family' exclusively as a diffuse and ill-defined shorthand term for all those with whom an individual acknowledges association by shared blood, ancestry, upbringing, or marriage.

Although 'family' in the sense of 'mum, dad, and the kids' was not a recognized social unit, this group nevertheless formed the core of most households in both affective and juridical terms at all social levels. Within this narrow group, children were raised in an environment shaped by maternal love and paternal authority, for the rights enjoyed by the male head of household over his dependants intersected with the complex emotional realities of family life. Early medieval sources reveal a world of strong affections between parents, children, and siblings—a world of joy at a safe and healthy birth, grief at the untimely death of a child, mutual conjugal love, maternal anxiety for the well-being of an adult son launched on his own career, fraternal help and friendship. By the same token, they also indicate the equally powerful disappointments, rivalries, and jealousies that could lead parents to reject a disabled infant, husband to abandon wife, brother to feud with brother, or son to kill father. Then, as now, parents, children, brothers, sisters, uncles, and aunts were relations, but not necessarily friends.

# Identity

> . . . 'or of what ancestry are you?
> Name but one, the others I will know,
> Youth, in the kingdoms all the kindreds are known to me.'[3]

With these words the hero Hildebrand challenged his younger opponent according to a ninth-century poetic epic. He expressed a common sentiment, for in the early Middle Ages social identity remained firmly associated with kin throughout life for all except those who, like Bede or Hrabanus Maurus, had been given over to a monastic life as small children. Since the shaping of the social person commenced when the parents chose a name for their newborn child, enquiry into the significance of kinship should start with naming. The customs and preferences that influenced early medieval name giving varied over time and from region to region, but the broad outlines are reasonably clear. There certainly were no hard-and-fast rules to follow; rather, parental decisions often reflected deeply ingrained cultural habits. Except in the naming of some royal babies, where the name was of the utmost political importance, we cannot usually recover the precise reasons why parents chose a particular name. Nevertheless, it is clear that the naming of an infant gave the newborn an identity that situated him or her within a circle of relatives and might even single the child out for a future as a cleric or as the heir to ancestral lands. Another strategy, less common but certainly deployed, especially in Ireland and Scotland, named a child after a particular saint or religious patron.

The close association between kinship and name giving deserves particular attention. In the early imperial period (first–second centuries AD), formal Roman naming procedures used three names to identify each citizen as a member of a subset of a particular patrilineal clan—that is, a descent group in which fathers but not mothers transmitted membership and identity to their offspring. In response to social and political changes, more fluid usages had superseded these rigid conventions by the fourth century, enabling names to signal not only social rank but also, at least among the elite, maternal as well as paternal ancestry. In the late Roman West, aristocrats of the fourth, fifth, and sixth centuries typically bore two, three, or even more names, selected to transmit pride in illustrious ancestry and a strong sense of identity with close kin. The sixth-century historian Gregory, bishop of Tours (573–94), typifies these practices. His full name was Georgius Florentius Gregorius, and he was the descendant of rich, influential Gallic aristocrats on both paternal and maternal sides. His first

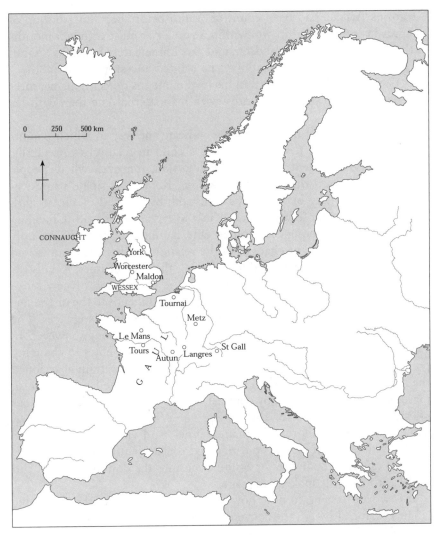

**3.1.** Principal places mentioned in Chapter 3.

name, Georgius, was the name of his paternal grandfather (d. 502/6), almost certainly a member of one of the wealthiest and most prestigious aristocratic lineages in fifth-century Gaul. The second name was his father's, but the third, the name by which he chose to be known, was the name of his mother's paternal grandfather. That Gregory of Tours went by the name of this maternal relative can have been no coincidence.

Gregorius Attalus had been count of Autun before becoming bishop of Langres in 506; he died in 539, within a year or at most eighteen months of the birth of his great-grandson, and was immediately hailed as a saint. By harking back three generations to a sainted ancestor on his mother's side, Gregory of Tours stressed in his own name his descent, his nearness to a saint, and his stronger identity with his maternal line than with his father's kin.

Gregory of Tours's multiple names indicate the way in which parents might choose names that would locate a child in relation to its family. But they also represent a weakening tradition, for, even where people continued to regard themselves as *Romani*, Romans, a single name was becoming customary by Gregory's time and, by the end of the seventh century, had become universal even in the Byzantine world. Changing onomastic habits among old Roman elite families are nevertheless only one of several important changes in the relationship between names and identities at the start of our period. During the fifth century, the dissolution of Roman governing structures and the coagulation of new kingdoms around Germanic-speaking elites gave prominence to the distinctive patterns of name formation shared by all the Germanic languages. The two pools of names did not remain separate for very long, however. In sixth-century Gaul, names reveal the adaptation of old elites to changing political circumstances, for some individuals of Roman origin abandoned their traditional naming habits in favour of those of their new Frankish masters; in Spain and Italy, by contrast, Goths and Lombards sometimes selected Roman names for their offspring. When parents with Roman names gave their children Germanic names, and vice versa, they made local decisions about cultural prestige and social identity that had everything to do with the desire for assimilation into the dominant group and nothing to do with spoken language.

It is worth pausing to note how names were formed in the Germanic languages, for, although the convention that a name associated a newborn with his or her ancestors and kinsfok was as strong among Germanic-speaking communities and their descendants as amongst the Romans, different linguistic and social principles were nevertheless at work. Germanic names (non-royal and royal) commonly consisted of two elements, a root and a suffix, which were transmitted and recombined in various ways, and through which ancestry, ethnicity, and social identity might all be signalled. Some of these elements were common to all Germanic languages, but others, characteristic of one language, became valued indicators of ethnic identity.

An example from the end of our period illustrates both the way in which

Germanic names were formed and the complex connotations that one name might have. In about 1008, a well-to-do Anglo-Saxon couple, the priest Æthelstan and his wife Wulfgifu, had a son, possibly their first. The child became a bishop and a saint, and his biographer records: 'He was given the name Wulfstan, made up of the first part of his mother's and the second of his father's. The child had fair hopes, and fair too the omen which gave him a name taken from both parents, considering that he was destined to pour into himself the sanctity of both, and perhaps to surpass it beyond all comparison.'[4] The omen of future sanctity emphasizes how parental name elements had been used to form the new name, but it seems also that the child was named after his maternal uncle, the famous archbishop of York. The name presumably marked the young Wulfstan out for an ecclesiastical career. When it came to naming the future bishop's two brothers, Æthelstan and Wulfgifu again signalled the boys' paternity, naming them Ælfstan and Byrcstan, but selected other elements to combine with the paternal suffix -stan. These decisions about the names of their children may be summed up as freely chosen variations around a common familial theme.

The young Wulfstan did indeed become a bishop (of Worcester, 1062–95). His name exemplifies the way in which elements were recombined to form a new name that nevertheless associated the child with his parents; it also emphasizes that name elements were handed down bilaterally—in other words, they might be as easily derived from the mother or maternal relatives as from the father or paternal relatives. Despite this, wherever a large enough sample of names has been preserved in ways that permit statistical analysis, it is clear that parents usually chose to associate a child with its paternal rather than the maternal kin. Certainly, among the aristocracy of the Carolingian Empire, almost all children were named after a close relative (parent, uncle or aunt, grandparent), yet fewer than one in five can be shown to have carried the name of a maternal relative. Not entirely shunning the use of other names, Frankish name-giving habits nevertheless preferred the names of close kin, and, within the circle of close kin, preferred to indicate paternal affiliations more frequently than maternal ones. Only when the maternal line was of more prestigious ancestry did parents tend to select names that associated a child with its mother's kin.

By the time Wulfstan, the future bishop of Worcester, was born, the custom of coining a name by varying the two elements had become archaic. In the sixth century, ruling dynasties in continental Europe had started to name their offspring by repeating the entire name of a deceased relative rather than varying the name elements. This custom spread gradually from kings to aristocracy, and, by the end of the tenth century, crossed the English Channel and began to influence Anglo-Saxon naming conventions too. By *c.*1000 it was universal for continental elites to use a restricted pool of names to identify members, and for the emphasis on patrilineal transmission of names to be even greater. When Hugh 'Capet' was crowned king in France in 987 after the demise of the old Carolingian ruling dynasty, he bore a name that clearly identified him as a member of one of the leading aristocratic families that had been prominent in France since at least the middle years of the ninth century. His male forebears all bore the names Hugh, Robert, or Odo; their sisters were commonly called either Emma or Adela. By the millennium, then, names remained a sign of identity, for parents continued to choose ones that associated their offspring with their close relatives and immediate ancestors. But, more than ever, names associated a child with its father's relatives rather than its mother's.

If naming a child at birth placed a newborn within a narrow familial circle, stretching to include cousins, grandparents, and occasionally great-grandparents, then death gave a new twist to the patterns of kinship and social identity. Within the Christian communities of the eighth century and later, concern for the welfare of the soul in the afterlife led many to enter on monastic registers the names of their relatives, living and dead, for whom they requested prayers of intercession. Such prayer bound the living and the dead together in a liturgical community that invoked the presence of the dead by naming them in the company of the living. Massive lists of names registered at several ninth- and tenth-century monasteries in France, Germany, and England survive, and they provide us with a complementary perspective on the ways in which individuals associated themselves with their kin. The German king Henry the Fowler (919–36) is typical: in 932 he requested prayers from the monastery of St Gall for himself, his wife, their three sons and two daughters, together with the husband of one of the daughters, his wife's parents, and her three sisters. Henry's concern for the spiritual welfare of his kin embraced three generations and extended beyond his own wife and offspring to include those associated with him by various marriages. In the context of religious commemoration, 'family' extended beyond an individual's natal family and the conjugal unit of which he or she formed one element, to include a wide, but still selective group of relatives. With the fate of the soul in the afterlife rather than the transmission of land or worldly office at issue, this form of kinship readily recognized women—mothers, wives, daughters— on the same terms as men.

In obtaining religious commemoration and in naming a child, differing ideas about the bonds of kinship thus came into play. Their most significant shared characteristics were, first, the recognition that kinship embraced two to three or, at the very most, four generations; and, secondly, an acceptance that women might sometimes make a significant contribution to the definition of familial identity. Neither of these points obtains in the third main way in which individuals used the associations of kinship to construct their social identity: genealogies. Genealogies are statements of descent modelled on biblical precedents. They usually take the form of 'X was the son of Y, son of Z', and, unlike most of the evidence discussed so far in this chapter, they cast a shaft of light on the cultures of the British Isles, particularly Wales and Ireland. Several royal genealogies survive from the Continent, but none traces the ancestry of non-royal personages before the end of the tenth century; in Ireland, by contrast, the many thousands of genealogies that survive from the eighth to tenth centuries pertain to Christian holy men and aristocrats as well as to kings. These genealogies present a form of kinship that is vertical (they may extend from a handful of generations to thirty or more), almost without exception totally male, and ruthlessly oblivious of siblings or collateral relatives.

Although many such genealogies have sections where the claimed relationships can be proven to be historically accurate, they are more important for the cultural and political assertions that they make. In all early medieval societies, claims to secular power, wealth, and status rested in large part upon descent: a genealogy legitimized those claims. The ties of kinship presented were those of immediate political significance and were thus liable to be remade and rearranged as political dictates demanded. Such manipulation could involve excision or augmentation of both the length of the pedigree and its collateral branches. The Carolingian dynasty (751–987) not only hitched itself onto the Merovingian dynasty (c.480–751), which it eventually replaced, but also appropriated the Roman past into its ancestry by a genealogy that claimed that its sainted (and historically attested) founder, Arnulf of Metz (d. c.643), was the grandson of the (mythical) Merovingian princess Blithild and her (equally mythical) husband Ansbert, hailed as a Roman senator. Two aspects of this are noteworthy. First, a fictional bride formed the key link in an otherwise male statement of descent. The deliberate omission of the historically attested women through whom the dynasty had, in reality, built up its position confirmed women's exclusion from formal authority, while the inclusion of a mythic ancestress nevertheless acknowledged women's essential contribution to dynastic reproduction and the transmission of family memories. Secondly, beyond the span of accurate human memory, seventh- and eighth-century historical fact shaded off into inventive ideological optimism, aided by access to textually transmitted knowledge of the distant Roman past. The political imperative to manipulate a genealogical statement by whatever means best suited the occasion is clear. As a way of using the past to assert contemporary political claims, this Carolingian genealogy was nevertheless relatively restrained. In Ireland, the need to stress the ancient length of a pedigree resulted in the common ancestor of the Érainn and the Dál Fiatach being named as 'Old son of Very Old son of Strong son of Very Strong'.[5] With this, we reach the apogee of biological fiction in the service of political legitimacy.

Genealogies make the point that kinship can be as much about socially constructed relationships, expressed in the fictions of biological descent and mythical ancestry, as it can be about genetic parentage. Further, they express more clearly than anything else the patrilineal inclinations of all early medieval cultures: pared down to bald statements of the descent of one powerful person after another, they emphasize that all that counted was the succession from 'father' to 'son'. But those masculine norms operated in a world that at no time had a single, stable understanding of kinship. Name-giving customs and the rituals of commemoration remind us that, in these situations, those who were acknowledged as kin were a close circle of relatives on both the male and the female side. Kinship, in effect, meant different things in different circumstances.


## Friends by Blood

It is time to turn to the wider implications of kinship, for an extensive range of sources—legal, documentary, narrative, poetic, hagiographical— all confirm that interactions with relatives commonly had great social and political significance. They also insist that kinship cannot be disentangled from friendship. The practical expressions of these affinities were, however, immensely varied, and the reasons for this help explain the many roles that relatives—and friends—might play in each others' lives.

One manifestation of the cultural heterogeneity of early medieval Europe was the coexistence of diverse social norms. Much of our detailed knowledge of these derives from records of law, whose contents are as varied as their textual forms and sources of authority. Broadly speaking, three legal cultures can be identified, with widely differing expectations of social relationships, including those among relatives. In Mediterranean Europe, the legislative codifications of the late Roman Empire remained in force wherever continuity of population and administration enabled people to continue to think of themselves as *Romani*. To the north, Germanic-speaking settlers introduced their own social customs, which began to take normative, written form from the sixth century onwards. No hard-and-fast division separated these two legal cultures, for in one way or another all the law codes issued by post-imperial kings betray the influence of Roman law, and this is especially true of those originating from the more southerly areas of enduring Roman presence, notably the Burgundian, Lombard, and Iberian Gothic kingdoms. Much less amenable to Roman influence in either format or content was the third legal culture, that of the Celtic-speaking regions fringing Atlantic Europe, where direct Roman influence was limited or non-existent. Each of these three traditions proposes a different view of the social implications of kinship.

With the proviso that law only ever offers an oblique and highly schematic view of social reality, each of these legal cultures can be said to approximate roughly to a distinctive form of social organization. As codified in the fifth century AD, Roman law was intensely concerned to regulate marriage and to confirm the authority of the male head of the household over his wife and children; but it explicitly rejected any notion that an adult male's juridical identity was bound up with his relatives. Secular Irish legal treatises, by contrast, make clear that the kin group was the most fundamental form of social organization; they stipulate norms and procedures in such detail that elaborate reconstructions of the ideal interactions between relatives are possible.[6] Both late Roman and Irish juridical expectations of the roles relatives should play in each others' lives emerge clearly. Between these two extremes, however, lies much debate over the significance of kinship within Germanic-speaking communities.

Nineteenth-century historians constructed grand schemes of early Germanic society (first–seventh century) and organized it into large clans that functioned as political entities, peacekeeping and judicial organizations, units of military recruitment, and settlement groups. They endowed these kin groups (usually referred to by the German term *Sippe*) with constitutional importance and accorded them a prominent place in an evolutionist progression of European society from the clan to the nuclear family, and from the tribe to the state—in other words, from 'primitive' to 'civilized'. This paradigm of cultural advance has long since collapsed, but the underlying view of the social organization of early Germanic

peoples has been slower to disintegrate: it too must be definitively discarded. In its place, we must substitute individuals, each of whom had a
web of consanguineal relatives shared with no one except his or her full
siblings, and a somewhat different range of interactions with the in-laws
to whom he or she was related by marriage.

In practice, kin never endured as a group. Rather they every where existed as a category of persons, a web of latent affinities to be activated and
mobilized as each separate situation required. Two aspects are deferred for
discussion in the next chapter—namely, the conventions surrounding marriage and the strategies of inheritance. Here we shall draw on poetic, documentary, and legal evidence to emphasize the ambiguity and uncertainty
inherent in kinship in a range of other situations.

Surviving in a single manuscript from around the year 1000 but probably of much earlier origin, the Old English epic poem *Beowulf* is set in
a mythic Scandinavian past. Its ideals and values nevertheless resonated
with its Anglo-Saxon audience, and also have close parallels in vernacular poetry from other parts of the early medieval west—Ireland, Wales,
and Germany, for example. *Beowulf* derives much of its dramatic vigour
from the tension between theoretical obligation and practical unreliabil-
ity between kinsfolk. Although 'the bonds of kinship | nothing may re-
move for a man who thinks rightly', the poet also knew well enough that
the time would come 'when the blood-feud should bring out again |
sword-hatred in sworn kindred'.[7] For insight into how the tension between obligation and animosity between relatives might play out, we can
turn to the Frankish *Pactus Legis Salicae*. Probably put together in the reign
of Clovis (c.481–511), this is a compilation of customary procedure and royal
pronouncement for Franks who now lived between the Rhine delta and
the Loire but whose culture was not yet overly influenced by Roman
norms and legal procedures. The *Pactus* makes it clear that kinsmen were
expected to offer support to each other in a variety of ways. If a man
needed to establish his status, or perhaps his insolvency, on oath, he had
to find people to co-swear with him: these 'oath-helpers' were drawn from
among his male relatives. Furthermore, if someone was killed, the slayer
had to find a monetary compensation for the lost life or risk a blood-feud
(to be discussed in the last section of this chapter), and the payment was
to be divided between the dead person's children and relatives on both the
paternal and maternal sides. If the slayer, on the other hand, could not
raise the entire sum himself, then his relatives had to help out: first, his
father and brothers, then, if the obligations still could not be met, his
maternal and paternal kin.

Which kinsfolk were involved here? Certainly children and parents—

the close-knit conjugal group, central to identity, inheritance, and indeed survival. Beyond that, the laws did not specify, referring simply to 'relatives' both paternal and maternal. Any individual, then, was in a particularly close relationship with parents and offspring, but also had to negotiate to acquire whatever support was needed from a wider, bilateral circle of relatives. The composition of that circle was unlikely to be constant, as death removed parents and uncles, and as marriages introduced in-laws at different points in an individual's life. Furthermore, the *Pactus Legis Salicae* envisaged that an individual might formally sever the ties of kinship, and outlined how to achieve this:

He who wishes to remove himself from his kindred should go to court and in the presence of the thuningus or hundredman [a local judicial official] break four sticks of alderwood over his head and throw them in four bundles into the four corners of the court and say there that he removes himself from their oath-helping, from their inheritance, and from any relationship with them.[8]

Freed from obligation to provide cash (or its equivalent in land and livestock), oaths, or any other support for kinsfolk, whoever went through this procedure would find that henceforth neither help nor inheritance would be forthcoming; such a person would face the world alone and unaided. On this evidence, Frankish kinship was not a cohesive bond among a specified range of people who functioned as a group in all circumstances. Rather, beyond the immediate parent–child tie, it was an undefined web of potential supporters, to be persuaded to action in time of need. At its bleakest, it was a network of unwelcome obligations and social embarrassments to be negotiated and, in the last resort, rejected.

Other potential supporters in time of need might be a man's neighbours, his lord, and his dependants within his *familia*. Since some of these people might well be related to him, kinship commonly overlapped with and reinforced other highly localized relationships. Those who could be relied upon to rally round in a crisis were thus all 'friends' of the hard-pressed individual, and it is striking how often sources refer to 'friends and relatives' without differentiation. Indeed, in Anglo-Saxon England the distinction at times collapses completely, for among the many Old English words meaning 'kin' one of the most commonly used, especially in law codes, is *freond*, the word from which the modern English 'friend' directly derives. The kinship that mattered was not the technicalities of precise genealogical relationship, but rather the kinship that made a difference in practice. As the late-eleventh-century biographer of Theoderic, bishop of Metz (963–84), affirmed, 'kinship without goodwill is an empty word, and friendship is inseparable from goodwill'.[9]

In Marc Bloch's memorable phrase, 'friends by blood' were the kin who could be relied on.[10]

In contrast to kinship, with its aura of being a 'natural' relationship, friendship is entirely socially constructed. As Chapter 5 will argue, social relationships in the early Middle Ages were predominantly ordered in hierarchical ways; friendship offered horizontal bonds of solidarity that softened the harsher contours of domination and subordination. The *Beowulf* poet knew this too; he makes Hrothgar, king of the Danes, describe his murdered friend Ashhere thus:

> 'He was my closest counsellor, he was keeper of my thoughts,
> he stood at my shoulder when we struck for our lives
> at the crashing together of companies of foot,
> when blows rained on boar-crests. Men of birth and merit
> all should be as Ashhere was!'[11]

So friends, in the early Middle Ages, were those men who provided each other with advice and support when needed, affirmed their loyalty, and backed it with appropriate action, even in battle. They might be neighbours, in-laws, members of a peer group, even kinsmen. Especially amongst the elite, friendship could be of great social advantage, its loss of gravest consequence. Heorot, Hrothgar's royal hall, had known happy times whose end *Beowulf* chronicles; as the poet also prophesied, friendship was no more reliable than kinship:

> Heorot's floor was
> filled with friends: falsity in those days
> had no place in the dealings of the Danish people.[12]

Kinly friendship might be of considerable political importance, and its consequences cannot be dissociated from forms of power and authority. There are two extremes to note here. On the one hand, fifth- to sixth-century Ireland contained hundreds of small lordships and kingdoms, whose rulers had only modest executive influence. Here, where the Old Irish word *fine* also means both 'kin' and 'friend', the loyalties of kinship tended to reinforce the loyalties of lordship, and the two together helped foster social cohesion and order. On the other hand, where royal authority was vigorous and largely effective, as it was in Carolingian Francia and in Anglo-Saxon England by the tenth century, the support that kin offered each other might be to the detriment of the kingly view of law and order. The English king Æthelstan was only one of several rulers vexed by criminals whose relatives protected them from the rigours of royal justice. He confronted the problem of thieves who were being sheltered by kindreds 'so strong and so large' that they were beyond the reach of royal officials. Clearly, local bosses and bigwigs were enforcing their grip on a locality by taking cattle-rustlers and the like into their retinue and *familia*; Æthelstan's solution was to authorize mounted posses of armed men to overawe and smash these local kin-based protection rackets.[13]

By the same token, the withdrawal of friendship between kinsfolk might have serious political repercussions, especially when the rifts occurred within the ruling family itself. The German emperor Henry II had died in 1024, leaving no son or other designated heir. Members of the German elite negotiated among themselves, and some weeks later agreed that there were two most suitable candidates to succeed to the throne, both called Conrad, who were cousins. During tense bargaining between the two, the elder Conrad—who prevailed and was duly crowned as Conrad II (1024–39)—is reported to have told his kinsman: 'it befits as many things as nature has bound together to be in harmony—nature who joins to herself the friendship of kinsmen'.[14] But the accord was fragile, and no one can have been surprised when Conrad the Younger was among those who rebelled less than a year later, and remained long thereafter a threat to his crowned cousin. On inspection, many of the most bitter political rivalries of the early Middle Ages turn out to be similar, for nothing bred competition more than kinship.

But what of individuals whose kinly rights and obligations had been severed, leaving them effectively kinless? These were most likely to be men, who had either exhausted their relatives' goodwill by habitually thieving, brawling, and stirring up feuds, or whose treachery and violence had been turned against their immediate family in acts of patricide, fratricide, or even incest with their own mother. In Anglo-Saxon England and on the Continent, those whose relatives were no longer prepared to support them by co-swearing or contributing to a hefty compensation payment were left to answer with the only thing left to them—their life—by penal servitude or hanging. In Ireland, the man guilty of betrayal, theft, or the slaying of kin was labelled a wolf and treated as such: he was left to wander in exile as a hated outcast, a feared outsider, devoid of status, identity, help—of humanity.

In the final analysis, kinlessness reduced the free man close to the abject social situation of a slave, lacking in rights or relatives. In a Christian society, it was a fate worse than death, for the man who had remained friends with his relatives could expect a decent burial and prayers for the sake of his soul. Social outcasts were flung out on the dung heap when they died; the kinless exile endured the living equivalent. Such utter degradation points up the central importance of kinship not for its genealogical affiliations but for its social importance, as the 'friendship' that helped keep communities together.

Nowhere did kin form a defined group with clear criteria of member-ship and invariable rules of behaviour; everywhere a person's relatives were a social resource to invoke, a source not only of identity but also of support as the situation demanded. Yet kinly relationships presupposed uncertainty, for the support had to be negotiated, coaxed into action. Such an interpretation of kinship takes little for granted, for it counter-balances reciprocity with unpredictability and affinity with rejection. It ac-cepts that, in principle, a person's loyalties and obligations extended to both paternal and maternal relatives, and recognizes that kinship was es-tablished by marriage, godparenthood, or fosterage as well as by descent. And it helps explain how, notwithstanding the cultural and social hetero-geneity of early medieval Europe, the bonds of kinship remained a fun-damental source of social cohesion, whether in isolated villages or among wide-ranging imperial elites. By the same token, however, their rupture threatened the essence of the social fabric. No wonder that hell was a place 'where there is not any recognition of anyone closest to one . . . where a mother does not love her son or daughter, and a son does not respect his father'.[15]

## Honour and Vengeance

As the *Pactus Legis Salicae* had elaborated, one of the ways in which relatives might help each other out was by paying the compensation owed by a slayer and his kin to the relatives of the person he had killed. Except where Roman legal principles remained vigorous, all early medieval communities put a monetary value on redeeming a person's life, termed wergeld in the Germanic languages. Its amount varied with rank, making explicit the much greater worth of a king or noble than of a peasant or slave; women and children generally enjoyed the wergeld of their father. Wergeld did not only apply in cases of homicide, however. Homicide certainly explains why wergeld is the price of a life, but either the wergeld itself or a proportion of it was due in less than fatal circumstances in which injury was suffered. That injury might be either physical or verbal: the Lombard laws of Rothari tabulate the compensation due for a huge range of injuries ranging from cutting off the little toe to gouging out the eyes, while the Frankish *Pactus Legis Salicae* stipulates a scale of penalties for verbal insults. These included accusing a woman of being a prostitute, and impugning a man's martial courage and loyalty by accusing him of being 'covered in shit', calling him a 'fox' or a 'hare'—accusations, in other words, of having soiled himself with fear, behaved treacherously, or fled the scene of battle.[16] We need, then, to assess how the value ascribed to a person's life encompassed social as well as physical selfhood, and to explore how different expectations of male and female conduct informed the behaviour of family and friends. As we shall see, these insults suggest a world of touchy pride that turned on women's sexual propriety and men's aggressive valour.

Since wounding words and injurious blows assailed social standing, wergeld was far more than a payment for physical damage. It expressed in monetary terms the slight done to familial pride, reputation, and integrity: the obligation to pay a wergeld imposed upon the offender and his relatives an equivalent degradation. In effect, wergeld recompensed a person's family for the damage done to their collective social esteem. Its dual nature both as reparation for loss and as a means of restoring respect is sharpened by comparison with the Irish procedure of making two discrete payments. The one compensated the dead, injured, or insulted person's paternal relatives for the loss or damage; the other, termed 'the value of a face' or the 'face-cleansing' payment, counterbalanced the affront done to both paternal and maternal relatives. That 'cleansing' a besmirched face removed the stain of loss, injury, and insult suggests a culture that intimately associated reputation with the human body: recovery of a person's social standing was 'saving face'. That both wergeld and the Irish value of a face were graduated according to rank indicates that those of high social standing risked a far greater loss of face than those lower down the social hierarchy. The following discussion focuses on these well-documented, high-value elites.

The mid-eighth-century Bavarian law code takes us a little further. It names five elite families ranked immediately below the ducal lineage who were entitled to 'double compensation' because they were granted 'double honor'.[17] 'Honour' is not susceptible to brief definition—except that, unlike compensation payments, it follows no tariff schedule. Anthropologists use the word as a short-hand term for a complex bundle of personal social attributes that together facilitate political influence and the accumulation of material wealth. Its essence combines the self-esteem of an individual with the respect accorded by others. Both self-regarding and other-regarding, it tends to dissipate unless constantly reasserted and reaffirmed through both general conduct and particular actions. By extension, therefore, it is never stable and cannot be hoarded. Further, the

association with compensation payments hints that early medieval honour was as much familial as personal: it inhered in persons-in-groups and
placed the individual firmly at the centre of a web of social relationships
with relatives, friends, lords, and kings. And, since some forms of conduct
were more liable to affirm or restore respect than others, the elite men and
women of the early Middle Ages were acutely aware of the consequences
of the wide range of words or actions that might tarnish or destroy it
entirely. A rich vocabulary of shame, infamy, humiliation, and disgrace indicates ways in which dishonourable actions could lead to an infamous
reputation in the eyes of others. At the negative end of the spectrum of
social values, shame attached to actions detrimental to the pride and
reputation of both individual and family. And, when the family in question was a royal one, the erosion of honour might be politically disastrous.

Early medieval writers rarely used a single word to sum up this abstraction. They preferred to think in terms of the action—to honour, show
respect to someone. Honourable conduct emphasized generosity and the
display of wealth, loyalty, sexuality, martial prowess, revenge. Running
through these seemingly disparate aspects of behaviour are two interlocking themes, one concerning the correct disposition of the human body,
whether in sexual or military affairs or through resplendent attire, the
other concerning obligations towards others, whether of generosity, loyalty, or revenge. Leaving aside social display and generosity to Chapters 5
and 6 respectively, we can use other forms of honourable behaviour to pursue further our theme of interactions between friends and relations in the
early Middle Ages.

Sexual conduct offers the most immediate indication of the way in
which the activities of individuals affected the collective standing of their
kinsfolk. At issue here were notions of sexual propriety, and the allocation
of blame for the breach of deeply rooted conventions and taboos. The
*Pactus Legis Salicae*, for example, regarded illegitimate children as 'marked
with disgrace'.[18] In general, however, celibate Christian churchmen form
our greatest source of information on early medieval sexuality. While it is
certainly hard to disentangle lay social behaviour from the complaints of
clerics quick to condemn whatever did not accord with their own ethical
views, it is nevertheless clear that early medieval codes of strict sexual
conduct commonly pertained to women much more than to men. 'In
Old Saxony [i.e. in still-pagan northern Germany]', the Anglo-Saxon
missionary Boniface reported in 746/7,

if a maiden stains with adultery her paternal home, or if a married woman breaks
the bond of matrimony and commits adultery, they sometimes force her to end

her life by her own hand, hanging herself by a noose; and when she has been burnt and cremated, they hang her violator over her pyre. Sometimes a crowd of women is gathered, and the matrons scourge her and lead her all over the district, striking her with rods and cutting off her garments to the girdle; and cutting and pricking all her body with wounds with their knives, they send her from village to village bloody and lacerated. And new scourgers are always joining them, prompted by their zeal for chastity, until they leave her dead, or barely alive; that others may be afraid of adultery and lasciviousness.[19]

Admittedly, Boniface had a point to make to his Christian audience, whose morals he considered far too loose, but his words nevertheless hint at a mentality that equated adultery with pollution of the integrity of a family.

Not only pre-Christian families responded to unsanctioned female sexual activity by putting the guilty woman to death or imposing an extreme form of censure. Le Mans had long been a Christian city when in 584 a woman of good birth dressed as a man to elope with her lover, a priest. When her relatives found out, they rushed 'to avenge the humiliation of their family' by burning the woman alive and imprisoning the priest.[20] Her behaviour had affected the reputation of all her kin, who took the only step open to them to redeem it. For the most part, early medieval societies left the punishment of errant women in the hands of their male kin, whether father and brothers or husband. Summary, familial retribution for a woman's flagrant breaches of her relatives' integrity counterbalanced the procedures for expelling a man from the kin group and condemning him to the life of an outcast.

'If a woman during her husband's lifetime commits adultery with another man, and it becomes known, let her afterwards become herself a public disgrace and her lawful husband is to have all that she owns, and she is to lose her nose and ears.'[21] Shame, loss of face (literal and metaphorical), family dishonour, and even death followed from female sexual activity outside recognized unions. They provided the largely unwritten sanctions that regulated women's conduct, and they mark out the intimate connection between the reputation of a family, on the one hand, and the control of women's sexuality, on the other. Women and sexual intercourse were so essential to the reproduction of any kin group that the honour of kinsmen was inextricably identified with the sexual purity and self-control of their sisters, wives, and daughters. Moreover, just as adultery brought dishonour through the way in which a woman used her body, so too retribution was visited upon her body, by stoning, disfiguration, or death.

A woman's sexual misdemeanours challenged the paternity of a man's

heirs and thus threatened her entire family's social standing. But a woman
could also make a positive contribution by controlling her own sexuality.
'A chaste and prudent wife, diligently attending to useful matters with a
humble demeanor and cheerful speech,' one ninth-century writer opined,
'peacefully manages her children and family; and, on behalf of her husband's welfare, if necessary, she sets her life against death and defends his
wealth with an honorable reputation'.[22] If a woman's honourable reputation contributed to the esteem in which her kin was regarded, it was
also incumbent upon her male relatives to protect her from risk and to defend her good name. This point emerges from a lawsuit that came to the
attention of Liutprand, king of the Lombards (712–44), in 733. A woman
had been bathing alone in the river, having laid her clothes aside on the
bank. 'A certain perverse man' took them, and she was forced to walk
home naked, 'blushing with shame'. But the shame was not her fault, and
Liutprand decreed that the thief had to pay his full wergeld in compensation for such a 'shameful' act on the grounds that, if the woman's father,
husband, or other male relatives had been on hand, they would have
jumped on the man and killed him. Having escaped unseen and
unscathed, the thief therefore was required to provide the monetary equivalent of his life.[23] Implicit in the king's ruling was an acknowledgement
that the woman's kinsmen had both the obligation and the right to defend her modesty and thereby her honourable reputation, if need be with
violence.

  A woman's conduct epitomized the way in which honour stood at the
heart of relations between family members. Any sexual impropriety she
committed brought disgrace to herself and her relatives; her chaste conduct upheld the social esteem of her husband, father, and brothers. In
return for maintaining her—and their—honour, she could expect them to
defend her from shameful treatment and false accusations. The maintenance of honour and the avoidance of shame suggested the conduct that
would help maintain cordial relations among close relatives.

  In defending their wives, sisters, and daughters from verbal or physical
assault, early medieval men were quick to resort to violence. Indeed, masculine honour was as intimately associated with displays of aggression,
courage, and martial skill as feminine honour was bound up with sexual
propriety. By contrast, however, masculine honour was less exclusively attached to familial honour, at least among the elite. It was also a quality
inhering in the right relationship between a warrior and the lord under
whom he served, complementing rather than displacing the honour that
associated a man with his family. As such, it was an avenue to social
advancement and political influence.

In 843, an Aquitainian mother named Dhuoda wrote to her much-loved 15-year-old son, resident at the court of the West Frankish king, Charles the Bald (840–77), and learning the ways of courtly society. In pouring out moral and religious advice to William, Dhuoda touched upon the theme of honour, and its relation to family and lord. She opened her chapters of advice on how to be successful in the tense atmosphere of mid-ninth-century politics with the injunction that William 'should fear, love and be faithful to [his] lord and father, Bernard, in all things', and then, by linking honour towards his father with obedience to the Christian God, Dhuoda developed the point that honour and respect in the secular world might be achieved by this dual loyalty. She expected her son to be loyal to his lord, King Charles, but stressed that other loyalties would also bring William honour: 'I urge you to strive to act among your associates, peers, and faithful friends so that your life may hold to a good course, marked with no shame of disloyalty to your lords but with eagerness for good action, in a laudable fashion, worthy and proper.'[24] William's task was to earn respect by his loyalty and his actions towards not only his father but also the king and his courtiers. Separated now from his family, William had to uphold his own and his family's honour in the competitive environment of the royal court. Dhuoda's summary of her advice put the giving and garnering of honour at the centre of the precepts that, she believed, should govern upright behaviour in a world of turbulent politics. 'Therefore, my son William, cherish and show respect to whatever one or many persons you wish to respect you. Love, revere, stand by, and honour all, so that you may be found worthy to receive from everyone an appropriate return with the honour that pertains to it in the changeable situations of the world.'[25]

Dhuoda did not elaborate upon the acquisition of respect through martial prowess. To explore the connection between masculine honour and military skill, we can do no better than to turn to the epic poetry of the early Middle Ages. The problem of determining an honourable course of conduct in situations where loyalty to kin conflicted with loyalty to lord, and the demonstration of the hero's fearless courage in the face of his adversaries are twin themes that repeatedly preoccupied early medieval poets and their audiences across the entire spectrum of early medieval languages. In *Waltharius*, a Latin epic probably written in the late ninth or tenth century, the anxieties of honour versus shame and kinship versus lordship intertwine to offer a compelling glimpse of the imperatives of early medieval masculinity. The stuff of legend, not history, the events of the poem concern the deeds of a hero named Walter, who, like Dhuoda's son William, was an Aquitainian. Walter grows from youth to manhood as a hostage at a foreign court, that of Attila the Hun. Attila has also taken as hostages the Burgundian heiress and Walter's betrothed, Hildgund, and the Frankish nobleman Hagen, who has been surrendered in lieu of the still-infant Frankish prince Gunther. The three share Attila's hospitality and grow up to positions of eminence and importance in his court, Hildgund as companion to the Hunnish queen, Walter and Hagen as victorious commanders of Attila's army. But when Gunther becomes king of the Franks, Hagen flees back to serve him. Rather later, Walter and Hildgund also make their escape, taking as much of the Huns' treasure as they can manage. To reach Aquitaine, they must cross Gunther's kingdom, but the Frankish king learns of their presence in his lands and, with a squadron of twelve proven and courageous warriors, he marches out to seize the treasure Walter and Hildgund carry. Hagen is compelled to accompany Gunther. Walter makes his stand in a narrow gorge, and, when Gunther sends out his twelve warriors one by one, Walter slays each in turn. As Gunther's fury grows, there remains only Hagen, who has hitherto refused to fight against his friend. Anguished by the decision, he finally agrees to help Gunther tackle Walter, and, in the final combat of two against one, all three warriors are maimed but none dies.

As Walter works his way through the twelve single-handed combats, several themes preoccupy the poet. One, of course, is Walter's heroism, valour, and apparently limitless strength, for he is a man of 'accustomed bravery' who was 'utterly unmoved | by any fear'.[26] Another is the instinct to seek revenge as the warriors fall one after another, and most especially the impulse to avenge a relative's death. A third is the role of verbal boasts of prowess and courage, in combination with taunts and insults hurled at the opponent; a fourth, the imperatives of honour and manliness. All strands come together after the twelve warriors have been killed and when only Hagen and King Gunther remain alive to face Walter.

Before the combat had started, Gunther had tried to rouse Hagen to fight by insulting him, his family, and, by implication, his reputation as a man.

> 'As I observe, you are the image of your father;
> Hagathie also bore a timid heart inside
> A frigid chest, avoiding war with many words.'[27]

But Hagen had not risen to the taunts and instead remained at a distance, watching the fighting but not participating, even when his nephew fell to Walter's sword. But when only the two of them remain, Gunther intensified the taunting:

'Are you not shamed to disavow your manhood, with
So many friends and kinsmen killed?'[28]

The implications are clear. If Hagen will not fight, the price of failure
to avenge his nephew and his companions in arms will be the shame of
cowardice. Only women do not fight, so, in his shame, Hagen will be
reduced to womanliness. And yet,

> Still Hagen wavered and considered in his breast
> The faith so often pledged to Walter, and he pondered
> The outcome of the matter as it had transpired.
> But now the luckless king begged more insistently.
> Moved by the fervor of his pleading, he avoided
> His sovereign's gaze and thought about his reputation
> For valor, that it might be sullied if he should
> In any manner spare himself in this affair.[29]

Here, at the moral crux of the poem, all the conflicting values are laid bare.
Hagen's decision, reluctantly taken, is that manly honour demands that he
maintain his reputation as a valiant warrior prepared to risk his life in the
pursuit of glory. Only by agreeing to fight Walter can he avoid shame,
avenge his nephew, retain his king's goodwill, and remain a man. In the
last analysis, the unambiguous need to prevent the collapse of his reputation makes clear the course of action that Hagen must take.

In 991, a band of Anglo-Saxons were defeated by the Vikings in a well-
attested battle at Maldon on the Essex coast. Their leader slain, some of
the Anglo-Saxons had fled the battlefield. A contemporary Old English
poet recast the defeat in terms of traditional epic values, emphasizing not
the Anglo-Saxon reverse but the heroism of those who chose to stay and
fight on to the end:

> Proudly the thanes pressed forward,
> uncowed the warriors crowded eager
> for one of two things: each man wanted
> either to requite that death or to quit life.[30]

Stripped of their political ambiguities, the events at Maldon offered an
opportunity to restate a familiar theme—the inseparability of honour,
courage, vengeance, and loyalty to the point of death—and thereby to
remind a fast-changing world of age-old values. In real life, as distinct
from poetic representation, such conduct brought acclaim—and enhanced
dangers. In 801, Alcuin interceded with Charlemagne on behalf of
the Northumbrian nobleman Torhtmund, one of 'our friends'. In 796

Æthelred I, king of Northumbria, had been assassinated; Alcuin spoke up for Torhtmund as 'the faithful servant of King Ethelred, a man proved in loyalty, strenuous in arms, who has boldy avenged the blood of his lord'.[31] Torhtmund's act of vengeance can have left him no option but to flee abroad beyond reach of further reprisal. Alcuin was evidently confident that Charlemagne would not only take the imperilled man into his protection, but would regard his avenging valour as a mark of commendation.

An Irish prophecy of doom foretold social collapse into a world of 'women without modesty, men without valour'.[32] In pursuit of social order, early medieval men chose their course of action with reference to an ethic that was different from but complementary to the constraints of sexual modesty imposed upon women. Masculine honour was not only the avoidance of shame, for it also implied an aggressive pursuit of martial prowess and the constant reassertion of manliness in both speech and action. Those who failed, fleeing from the battlefield, behaved 'like women'.[33] Nor was it exclusively kin-centred, like feminine honour, for it demanded the approbation of a wider public, that of a man's friends as well as his relatives, his lord as well as his peers. Yet it too was concerned above all with reputation in the eyes of others, and was as closely bound up with speech, gesture, action, and body as was a woman's honour. Furthermore, masculinity often found expression in boastful vaunting and in the exchange of insult. Sometimes, especially in the intoxicated atmosphere of a feast, verbal aggression turned out to be the foreplay that preceded the exchange of physical blows and even killings. When honour demanded that shaming insult, injury, or homicide had to be requited, the threat of feud might loom on the horizon.

Except to the extent that the Roman juridical principle that an individual was solely and uniquely responsible for his own actions may have remained enforceable in some parts of the Mediterranean, early medieval Europe was a feuding culture, for feud is the manifestation of a notion of honour that associates virility with vengeance. It also encapsulates both the moral obligations amongst relatives and their fragility; for that reason it deserves consideration here. It should be said immediately that feud is neither a state of anarchy, whether temporary or persistent, nor one of constant bloodshed. Rather, it is an attitude of potential, latent, or actual hostility between groups, in which the very threat of vengeance killings may itself help to discourage violence and promote more orderly means of resolving conflict. Only when the spilling of blood seemed more honourable than the acceptance of honourably offered wergeld—or when sage advice could not temper young hotheads—did early medieval feud become bloody retributive justice. Much of the time, however, it seems that wergeld was paid in order to deflect the risk of vendetta. That land was sometimes sold off explicitly to raise the large sums needed to pay a wergeld suggests that a slayer's kin frequently saw the advantages of providing monetary compensation in the hope of placating the slain person's aggrieved relatives. Within small communities, where most neighbours were probably also relatives, the threat of violence may well have seemed far too terrible to contemplate.

Feud, then, is a form of managing conflict. It follows conventions that are more often embedded in social practice than articulated in explicit principles of action. A state of mind as much as a code of action, feud results in bloodshed only when other methods of repairing the insults done to injured honour have failed. Rarely do the written sources allow us to trace the beginning, course, and resolution of a vendetta or enable adequate assessment of the wider social context, but they do reveal clearly that feuding was about the reciprocal exchange of enmities, and that, once a blood-feud had developed, a desire for retribution contributed to its persistence and to the lack of any easy resolution. In seeking Charlemagne's protection, Torhtmund knew this well. For this reason, vendettas might be of brief duration, or might flare up spasmodically over years, sometimes over generations. Whereas decisions to sell off family land and settle financially are not the stuff of chronicles or heroic epics and achieve only fleeting mention in deeds of sale, conflicts that escalated into violence catch our attention—as they did that of early medieval chroniclers—because of their exceptional narrative allure.

Two incidents, approximately contemporary but from quite distinct cultural milieux, encapsulate the complexities of honour, compensation, and revenge. Both occurred around the year 590, one in western Ireland, the other in northern Gaul. Librán, a man from Connaught, tells his own story first:

While I still lived in my own district I killed a fellow. After this I was held in chains as a guilty man. But a relative of mine, in fact one of my immediate kindred, who was extremely rich, came to my rescue in the nick of time. He paid what was needed to get me off though I was bound in chains, and he saved me, though guilty, from death. After he had bought my release, I promised him with a binding oath that I should serve him all the days of my life.[34]

Librán had committed homicide and must have surrendered himself in admission of his guilt. That he was not at large minimized the risk of the dead man's kin setting out to undertake a vengeance killing, but equally Librán was evidently unable to raise the compensation and face-cleansing payments due in accordance with Irish law. His life was therefore at the mercy of the dead man's kin, who could slay him or sell him into slavery. That Librán had been rescued by a wealthy kinsman suggests the interest that kin had in each other's continued existence. Nevertheless, the price of that rescue was to be bondage to his own relative. In fact, he broke his oath and fled into exile a few days later, and it took the intervention of the holy man Columba to find a resolution that satisfied the honour of all of Librán's kin and also purged Librán's conscience of his guilt at the slaying and the broken oath.

In this instance, one slaying did not precipitate a chain reaction of counter-killings. Rather, all the pressures towards a peaceful settlement combined to restore honour without further dislocating the social order. But, in the other incident, the initial offence involved no bloodshed at all, yet it escalated into a protracted and vicious feud. Gregory of Tours's account is worth quoting in full:

A dispute arose among the well-born Franks of Tournai because the son of one was insistently rebuking the son of another, who had married his sister, angrily chiding him for having abandoned his wife for a prostitute. Since the accused man did not change his behaviour, the brother's anger [at the slight to his sister] became so intense that the lad fell upon his brother-in-law and killed him along with his own men. Then he himself and those who had come with him were cut down and no one from either group remained alive except only one man, who lacked a slayer. As a result, the relatives of both men feuded among themselves. They were repeatedly urged by Queen Fredegund to end their hostility and make peace, lest the continuation of their strife create even greater disturbance.[35]

Here, the heady cocktail of familial honour, sharp words, and hot blood triggered a sequence of vengeance killings that was finally ended only when Fredegund had the three ringleaders beheaded while drunk.

Its dramatic quality exposes some of the complexities of feuding to our attention. In the first place, although the immediate cause was the shaming of a woman by her husband, this vendetta, as all others, was conducted by men. Women's participation was at best indirect, either (as here) as the precipitating cause or in an instrumental role in rousing their menfolk to take action, as is especially well documented in Iceland and Ireland. Feuding was men's business, and was conducted by groups, not individuals. Those groups had to be assembled on an ad hoc basis if there was revenge killing to be done. As this Tournai example again shows, the ill feelings that manifested themselves in feud involved men in the same social network, neighbours who knew each other well. In Tournai, where brother feuded with brother-in-law, the dispute forced men to take sides within their own familial circle. Indeed, as many feuds occurred between men related to each other as between two distinct kin groups. Further, the circle of kinsmen who were liable to be sucked into a feud was not defined by social practice or explicit rules, whether in late-sixth-century Tournai or anywhere else. It depended on how successful the chief contestants were in persuading others to join them, and on how far the honour of those not directly involved might be impugned. And each time someone was killed, the circle of those affected would be recomposed. The shift from ill-feeling to violence in Tournai was the work of a hotheaded, unmarried young man, able to mobilize a group of supporters, not explicitly his kin. In the first bout of fighting, he and his brother-in-law with all their followers but one were killed. At that point, the circle of feuding men widened, as (other? older?) kinsmen of the antagonists became involved and the level of violence escalated. Entirely typical of other feuds whose details caught the attention of early medieval chroniclers, this one seems to have involved not only kinsmen, but also other associates of the two brothers-in-law. Ties of friendship, cameraderie, neighbourliness, or loyalty to a lord could as easily sweep men up into a feud as the obligations of kinship. But, just as feud could also range kinsmen against one another, so feud could also force apart sworn friends, much as Walter and Hagen were finally forced apart by Gunther. The outbreak of a feud, then, called into being a group in which the imperatives of kinship could either meld or conflict with other forms of association and obligation.

Finally, this conflict over a perceived slight to a woman's honour makes the point that feuding coexists with other forms of social regulation, in this case royal command. It would be mistaken to regard feuding as necessarily antithetical to royal authority, and, indeed, some of the best evidence for feuding procedures comes from the legislation of particularly powerful kings, such as the ordinance on feuding issued by the West Saxon king Edmund (939–46). All early medieval kings accepted the principle of feuding: their concerns were to prevent vendettas escalating to the point where they caused serious political disturbance and to reap the fiscal benefit for themselves by fining men for breaches of appropriate procedure. Rather than prohibiting feuding, they tried to co-opt the impulse towards vengeance and turn it to royal advantage. To that end, royal legislation made it advantageous and honourable to settle by accepting compensation. Rothari, for example, increased the level of compensation for a wide range of injuries 'in order that the faida, that is the blood feud, may be averted after receipt of the . . . composition, and in order that more shall not be demanded and a grudge shall not be held. So let the case be concluded and friendship remain between the parties.'[36] A strong king of firm will could mobilize the full vigour of royal anger to force hostile parties to make peace with each other to the general enhancement of their honour and royal power alike. Where royal authority was tenuous (as in tenth-century southern France), or where kings were themselves implicated in the feuding (as in tenth-century Germany), vendettas functioned as an integral aspect of politics, as a way of asserting dominance and grasping power in a highly competitive and unstable environment. If, for some, the pursuit of resources, followers, status—of honour—encouraged feuding, for others there remained the hope that feuding might undermine the power of regional strongmen and remake the local realities of dominance and subordination.

The last word goes to the Frankish king Guntram (561–92), mourning the assassination of his brother, King Chilperic, in 584: 'I ought not to be regarded as a man if I am unable to avenge his death this year.'[37] Early medieval kings were driven by the need to defend their manliness, family, and reputation as much as other men, and vengeance could be as much the mainspring of royal policy as it was of the quest for individual or familial honour. In the early Middle Ages, men participated in a culture that encouraged them to prove themselves in exchanges of boasts, insults, blows, and killings. Through defence of his honour, the individual asserted his place in the community of adult warriors: in so doing his reputation redounded to the credit of his entire family. Alternatively, his actions might drag his family into turbulent relations with other kinsmen, neighbours, even the ruler. With so much at stake, masculine honour was volatile, virile, and vengeful. It had to be: the essence of 'friendship by blood' was the willingness to lay down one's life in defence of family, or perhaps of lord. Without kinsfolk, a man had no one to help defend his honour; without honour, he lacked manliness; without manliness, he had no social existence.

At its simplest level, kinship is about parents and children, husbands and wives, and about the associated endearments, tensions, hatreds, and obligations that result from such fundamental human pairings. Yet it is also much more than that. As this chapter has repeatedly demonstrated, discussions of kinship as a form of affinity are in effect discussions of politics at every level from the local to the imperial. The convergence enables us to avoid simply pigeon-holing early medieval kinship as 'social history', allowing us to recognize that it forms one of the fundamental ways in which power was distributed and disputed, social control maintained or challenged, legitimacy asserted and achieved. Early medieval politics turned on the imperatives of kinship as much as on ideologies of authority, the benefits of office holding or sheer military force: to ignore that is fundamentally to misunderstand the nature of all early medieval societies. Prestigious ancestry offered a cogent rhetoric of legitimacy. Relationships between relatives provided identity, support, and legal standing. Among the elite, the urge to stop honour seeping away—and to enhance it—informed dealings with friends and relations, lords and neighbours. All these, at root, were issues of politics and power, whether or not kings were directly involved.

Yet at no stage has a simple definition of early medieval kinship been supplied, with good reason. In matters of name giving, 'friendship by blood', honour or feuding there were no hard and fast rules. Rather, kinship was a habitual amalgam of the conventions of a particular cultural group, the pressures of the moment and of individual strategies and choices. It was a resource to exploit, an identity to affirm, a custom to confirm, a norm to challenge. Its particular significance depended on the specific context.

Its social practices were neither uniform nor unchanging. In the Mediterranean areas where Roman law persisted, individuals had no formal right to seek support and help from their kinsfolk. Their only recognized recourse was to a judicial system that left the individual to face the force of the state alone and unassisted—but that did not stop people pursuing personal and familial interests by whatever means, peaceable or violent, they preferred. Elsewhere, customary law envisaged that kinship would fulfil some of the functions that the Roman state had once arrogated to itself, particularly in matters of regulating the behaviour of members of the group and in offering the means to resolve grievances and disputes. North of the Alps and in Anglo-Saxon England, the bonds of kinship sometimes competed with and sometimes complemented royal power and formal legal processes: here, aristocratic kinship and royal power coexisted in an unstable equilibrium that could as easily promote a ruler of exceptional power such as Charlemagne as it could throw formidable obstacles in the way of efforts to consolidate the authority of Æthelstan or Otto I. In the Celtic-speaking regions, where there was little or no direct Roman heritage, no contribution of Germanic settlement, and no stable, powerful, wide-ranging monarchies, the self-regulatory pressures of close ties of kinship—reinforced in all probability by close residency—provided much of the cohesion needed for ordered existence. It has sometimes been argued that royal authority grew in the course of the early Middle Ages by attacking and weakening the bonds of kinship. Such a sharp opposition is untenable, for ties of kinship were fundamental to all the different cultures of the early Middle Ages at all social levels: they were never the antithesis to strong royal government. Rather, the most successful rulers were generally those who could manage tensions amongst their own close family, co-opt the support of a wide circle of relatives, and turn all the strategies of kinship to their own advantage. An effective king was one who knew how to turn his own relatives into friends.

# 4

## Men and Women

'Man' is the word for any strongminded and discerning person, but 'woman' refers to a mind that is weak and lacking discernment.[1]

Two people are mates. A man and a woman will bring a child into the world through birth.[2]

MINDS that are 'weak and lacking discernment' rarely figure in accounts of great deeds and political achievements. Conventionally told, the history of the early Middle Ages was one of men's politics, economics, and religion, where women were largely absent from the politics and economics and marginal to the religion. This presentation not only rested on the presumptions and prejudices of earlier generations of scholars, but also reflected the tenor of many early medieval chronicles, annals, and histories. But much has changed. Historians now realize that women are more likely to be mentioned in other types of medieval text, such as saints' lives, charters recording land transactions and law codes, than in narrative sources. Also, when the enquiry broadens to acknowledge the local and familial contexts in which people lived, then women take their place beside men as central subjects of historical and archaeological research. Undertaking this is not just a matter of drawing attention to the wives, mothers, and daughters of the kings, princes, bishops, and warriors who feature prominently in chronicles. This approach demands that we explore the disparities between men's and women's social roles and expose their underlying assumptions, values, and prejudices. In other words, it demands that we pay attention to gender as an integral aspect of both social organization and cultural expression during the early Middle Ages. As we do this, we find ourselves studying forms of domination and subordination in every aspect of daily existence in peasant huts as much as imperial palaces. That is the task of this chapter.

It has two premisses. The first has already been established: that literacy justified, promoted, and defended sacred and secular authority.[3] It follows that early medieval scribes and authors were never disinterested, neutral, or innocent reporters of the world around them. In serving the vested interests of those with most at stake, they were selective in their reporting, imbued with attitudes common to their place and time, and adroit at shifting attention away from those who were partly or entirely excluded from rights, resources, prestige, power. These rhetorical strategies easily reduced women to partial or complete invisibility alongside children, slaves, and peasants; this chapter draws attention to some of the gender games that early medieval writers played.

Its second premiss was implicit in the previous chapter but must now be made explicit: that, although most early medieval texts marginalize women, they are nevertheless crucial to the reproduction of any community. Their role is not only the biological reproduction of pregnancy and childbirth, but also the social reproduction of cultural assumptions, modes of behaviour, and mores from one generation to the next. Family names and advice from mother to son are aspects of this that we have already encountered.[4] Equally fundamentally, women contribute their labour to the task of sustaining a community, producing clothing, food, and much else. For the time being, it suffices to note that women's economic contribution complements their cultural and social role.

This chapter thus extends the exploration of the patterning of men's and women's behaviour begun in the previous chapter by taking gender disparities as its focus. It argues that, although early medieval gender relationships varied widely from place to place and changed greatly in the course of the centuries under discussion, there were nevertheless fundamental commonalities in mental attitudes and social practices throughout the early Middle Ages. Wherever we look, these turned on the inferiority of women to men. We shall begin with explicit statements and manifestations of the differing social worth of men and women, before moving on to two important subjects where the disparities between men and women were particularly marked, sexual partnerships and the negotiation of marriage, on the one hand, and access to landed property, on the other. In all three areas, the Roman legacy turns out to be vital.

## Differences of Gender

Of all the forms that social distinction may take, gender is but one. Class or rank, age, ethnicity, and religion can also be prominent categories for

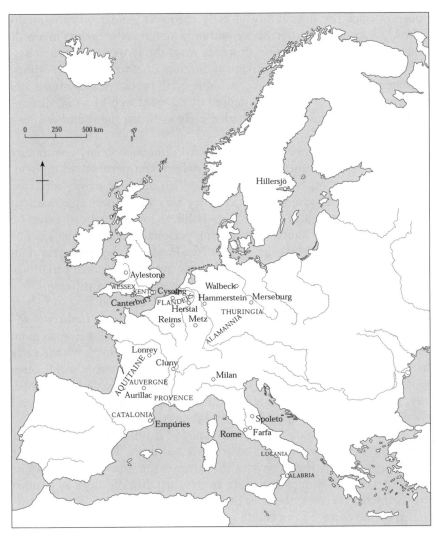

4.1. Principal places mentioned in Chapter 4.

regulating membership of a group, determining access to resources and formulating identities. Alternatively put, these are all ways of privileging some while restricting and demeaning others. In the early Middle Ages, gender was arguably the most protean and the most pervasive of them, the least amenable to alteration in the course of a lifetime. The fluidities of social, religious, and ethnic identities will become more readily apparent once the inflexibility of early medieval gender order is established.[5] Since gender differences commonly manifest themselves in a wide range of ways, this discussion proceeds from the most to the least obvious by starting with visible markers of difference before turning to explicit statements of social norms and concluding with persistent stereotypes and prejudices. We shall see that a dense but nuanced web of social distinction and cultural meaning surrounded early medieval men's and women's lives.

Perhaps the most visible aspect of social difference in any community is dress. Types of garment, forms of jewellery and personal adornment, ways of cutting, concealing, or displaying hair all carry strong messages about rank, wealth, age, and gender. They may also convey signals about ethnic identity, religious vocation, or political loyalty. All can easily be changed, whether to announce changing personal situation or as a deliberate disguise. Archaeological and art historical evidence indicates that, while early medieval costume showed many local and regional variations, and, especially for the wealthy elite, also evolved over time, different dress codes for men and women nevertheless remained universal. By *c.*500, short tunic and trousers had long since lost their opprobrium as 'barbarian' apparel and replaced the classical toga as the dress of choice for Roman men; they remained the universal basis of men's clothing throughout the early medieval West, except for clergy and, from *c.*800 onwards, royal ceremonial. Women, by contrast, always wore a calf- or ankle-length robe, and, for the few who could afford them, silks, fine woollen cloths, and changing fashions in display jewellery brought added variety.

Gendered distinctions of apparel cannot be isolated from the other meanings encoded in personal adornment and dress. This becomes clear if we pause to note the life cycles that shaped the experiences of almost all early medieval women and men. In the early Middle Ages as in most pre-industrial societies, the lives of women at all social levels were dominated by the passage from childhood to marriage at or soon after puberty and a move away from the parental home to reside with their husband, however near or far that might be. Then, if death in childbirth did not intervene, came another transition, from motherhood to old age. If widowed as young brides and mothers, they commonly entered a second or even third marriage, moving to wherever their new husband lived. Widowhood in later years commonly meant a different sort of move: an elderly peasant woman was liable to find herself shifted by her lord to a minor outlying dwelling on his estate, whereas elite widows often entered religious communities, which afforded protection and companionship. Only those girls whose parents committed them to the religious life in early childhood are likely to have resided in the same place for almost all their lives.

Men's lives followed a somewhat different rhythm, whatever their social status. Early years were shaped by the acquisition of the physical skills appropriate to their rank, whether the use of weapons or agricultural expertise, but, unlike their sisters, marriage did not intervene as soon as they reached physical maturity. By now sexually active, they commonly enjoyed a phase of full but unmarried adulthood. At the upper end of the social spectrum, they served as warriors in their lord's retinue and lived in his household, receiving training in courtliness and martial skills, as Gregory of Utrecht did at the royal court.[6] At its other end, young unmarried workers were vital members of a lord's agricultural workforce, often put to work on the main parts of an estate, but sometimes sent off to distant places to clear new land for cultivation. Marriage occurred at an older age than for their sisters, adding the roles of head of household and father. If his wife died young, a man was likely to remarry another woman significantly younger than himself: for him, old age brought physical senescence but far less commonly a lonely widower's existence. Even in old age, men still filled a valuable social role, for 'an old man knows most things, a man made wise by distant years, who has experienced a great deal before'.[7] They were the 'elders' whose knowledge and advice were frequently sought in the regulation of community affairs.

With these gendered life cyles in mind, we may return to dress and personal accoutrements. For the many preliterate communities of the early Middle Ages, funerary archaeology provides the crucially important evidence for these life cycles as well as for changing modes of apparel. When the men, women, and children of the fifth and sixth centuries died, they were sometimes buried in graves equipped with a rich variety of objects, commonly of great beauty, splendour, and wealth. Furnished burials are particularly characteristic of the social dislocation and fluidity that accompanied the arrival of peoples such as the Franks, Lombards, Goths, and Anglo-Saxons inside the Roman Empire. Later examples occur in places that, although distant from the former Roman lands, were nevertheless witnessing profound political and social reorganization, such as the western Slav lands in the ninth century and Denmark in the tenth century. They are not, it must be stressed, a product of a pagan, pre-Christian society whose beliefs presumed that the deceased would need the accoutrements of everyday life in the afterlife, for Christians carefully placed some of the most famous of these burials in churches. Rather, they are a symptom of unstable communities where economic, cultural, and military pressures were fostering stressful social change and competition for status and legitimacy. In such circumstances, the living frequently chose to affirm both their own and their dead relatives' social worth through this form of funerary provision. Especially where entire cemeteries of furnished graves have been excavated, they reveal ways in which the standing of individuals within their community fluctuated according not only to rank, but also to age and sex—in other words, according to the point in the gender-specific life cycle at which an individual died.

Sixth-century cemeteries from the region around Metz in north-eastern Gaul are a well-studied case in point. They reveal a world where families responded to the loss of a woman of adolescent or childbearing age with lavish burials containing specifically feminine objects—notably, necklaces, bracelets, earrings, and brooches, sometimes also spindlewhorls and bunches of household keys. Deposition of these objects both reflected the dead woman's social status and value to her family, and unequivocally identified her social value as one derived from her female, childbearing capacities. Both children and women over about 40 years of age, by contrast, were buried with either no grave goods at all, or only a few non-gender-specific items. Men, on the other hand, did not receive a furnished burial until aged about 20, by which time they would have reached the peak of their physical strength and be already fully established in adult male society. Their grave goods were, typically, sets of weapons such as throwing axes, swords, or spears; older men (above 40 or so) usually had far fewer objects buried with them, but nevertheless still ones of characteristically masculine nature. In effect, these graves suggest that women of marriageable or childbearing age, and male warrior heads of households, were in some senses more valuable to their families and communities than the very young and the very old. They also confirm the importance of dress and personal accoutrements in distinguishing men and women from each other and in signalling social role.

As we have seen, early medieval law codes are another valuable indicator of social norms and ideologies. They make explicit some of the disparities at which the material record hints, endowing them with durable, authoritative vigour. Many of these legal provisions pertain to rank, but, of those that deal with distinctions of age and sex, two are especially relevant here, wergeld and legal capacity. First, wergeld. In addition to putting an explicit value on a person's life according to social rank, it could also vary according to age and gender.[8] This is particularly clear in the *Pactus Legis Salicae*: roughly contemporary with these north-eastern Frankish burials, it offers a strikingly similar picture, using the heavy gold coin of late Roman imperial coinage (*solidus*; plural: *solidi*) as a unit of value. The standard wergeld for a free Frankish man or woman was 200 *solidi*, but a threefold increment to 600 *solidi* marked a woman who was pregnant or of childbearing age. After her fertile years had ended, a woman's wergeld dropped again to 200 *solidi*. A man's wergeld, by contrast, increased to 600 *solidi* when he was below 12 years of age or if, as an adult, he was in royal service. In juridical terms, the value of a life varied substantially across an individual's life cycle; in gender terms, the social worth of a sister was sometimes greater, sometimes less, than her twin brother's.

The second important distinction in this context is legal capacity. Early medieval law codes take the free, adult male as normative, and specify variations on the norm that apply to other groups, including women, children, semi-free, and unfree persons. In this context, several distinguish the legal capacity of adults from children and of men from women. Roman law had granted far fuller rights to bring a case or testify in a lawsuit to adult men than to minors or women, and of the post-Roman laws that impose similar restrictions, Rothari's Edict is firmest about restrictions on women's freedom of action, especially in property transactions. Rothari required a male protector or legal representative, normally father, brother, or son, to regulate a woman's interactions with the wider community, especially in any property transactions. In default of any male relative, the king would take on this responsibility—and doubtless benefit from the opportunity to intervene in family affairs. 'No free woman who lives according to the law of the Lombards within the jurisdiction of our realm', he declared, 'is permitted to live under her own legal control, . . . but she ought always to remain under the control of some man or the king. Nor may a woman have the right to give away or alienate any of her movable or immovable property without the consent of him who possesses her *mundium* [i.e. the right of legal authority over her].'[9] Although Rothari subjected the women of early Lombard Italy to greater legal disabilities than are found anywhere else, surviving early eighth-century charters indicate that his legislation did not reduce Lombard women to complete passivity. In practice, they retained greater freedom of manœuvre and somewhat more control over their own landholdings than the letter of the law would suggest possible. Like other early medieval legislators, Rothari had seen women's position as an opportunity to extend his own sphere of action under the guise of protecting them: women's affairs provided a useful excuse for royal intervention. Taken on its own, Rothari's Edict might suggest that rigid gender distinctions infused all aspects of Lombard women's lives. In the context of the more

nuanced picture provided by charter evidence, it provides another
reminder of the importance of law as a statement of ideology not a
description of social reality.

A similar slippage between prescription and practice emerges when we
turn to peasant labour. Ecclesiastical efforts to impose Sundays as a day
of rest began in the late sixth century; as the stipulations gradually became more specific, they incorporated explicit statements about the distinct but complementary roles for men and women. They culminated in
Charlemagne's frequently copied declaration:

Manual labour is not to be carried out on the Lord's day—that is, men are not
to engage in rural work by cultivating the vines, ploughing the fields, reaping,
hay-cutting, hedging, assarting, tree-felling, stone-working, house building or
gardening. . . . Women are not to engage in cloth-working or to cut out clothes
or to sew or embroider; they are not to be allowed to card wool, to break flax, to
launder in public or to shear sheep, that the *honor* [respect] and repose of the
Lord's day may in all ways be preserved.[10]

Although the association of women with all aspects of cloth production,
whether from wool or from linen, is confirmed throughout all parts of early
medieval Europe, in practice the division of agricultural tasks varied
according to local tradition—and changing technology. In some places the
preparation of bread fell to men, in others to women, and, wherever
village watermills were constructed for grinding grain, the allocation
of domestic labour will have been affected by the abandonment of individual querns. Likewise, harvesting seems to have been men's work on some
estates, but, on others, women went out into the fields too, and were sometimes explicitly charged with making sheaves and stooking them. In practice, then, rural labour was gendered, but neither inflexibly nor uniformly.

Not even powerful early medieval kings such as Rothari and
Charlemagne could bring social reality fully into line with prescriptive
norms. In practice, women characteristically lived their lives in the inter-
stices of ideology and convention. As we shall see, that gap was often considerable, a cause of vulnerability for some but of opportunity for others.

To what extent did the spread of Christianity affect this? It is easy to
point to institutional consequences—a valorization of celibate life that in-
verted the secular norms of masculine and feminine conduct; monastic
alternatives to some or all stages of the male and female life cycles; an
officialization of men's exclusive access to sacred power in the priesthood.
The shifting nature of marriage, to be discussed shortly, fits here too.
Equally importantly, however, Christian engagement with the Roman
literary legacy reinvigorated deeply rooted stereotypes, while the fostering

of literacy provided a new means for articulating prejudice among formerly preliterate communities. Gregory I's comment that '"man" is the word for any strongminded and discerning person, but "woman" refers to a mind that is weak and lacking discernment' typifies this.[11] The massive work in which he made this remark was much copied by medieval scribes. Approximately 500 manuscripts of it survive, giving the aphorism a permanence and universality that belie its origins. In effect, the comment recycles commonplaces of Roman tradition.

Isidore of Seville is our best guide to these. With a straightforward play on Latin words that is lost in translation, he summarized conventional ancient wisdom on the qualities of men and women thus:

Man [*vir*] is named because there is greater force [*vis*] in him than in women, whence also strength [*virtus*—the word means both physical strength and moral uprightness] takes its name, or because he rules over women by force. Woman [*mulier*], however, is named from softness [*mollities*], as if 'softer' [*mollier*] with a letter changed and one taken away were 'woman' [*mulier*]. They differ from one another in bodily strength and weakness, for the man's strength is greatest and the woman's is less, so that she may be subject to the man.[12]

Isidore instructed his early medieval readers to regard the human body as the key to moral disposition, much as it was in classical ethics. Since women were softer or weaker than men, their moral strength was less than men's—and so they were subject to men.

This position works by justifying moral differences between men and women as the consequence of natural, physiological difference. And since, from a Christian perspective, the entire natural world was a divine creation, ancient thinking was easily transposed into a Christian framework. Social differentiation and the gender order originated with God and 'nature' alike. Weaving his thoughts around a string of biblical quotations, Ambrose, bishop of Milan (374–97), had declared:

Thus it is written: 'A woman shall not be clothed with man's apparel, neither shall a man use woman's apparel: for he that doeth these things is abominable before God.' If you think about it hard, whatever nature herself abhors is incongruous. Why would a man not want to be seen to be what he was born? Why assume an alien appearance? Why pretend to be a woman, or you, woman, a man? Nature clothes each sex in its own garments. Men and women have different habits, complexion, movements, gait, strength and voice. Thus it is amongst other species of animals: the lion and the lioness have different appearance, different strength, different voice. . . . Male peacocks are beautiful, but the females are not adorned with the same varied plumage. . . . Surely they never change their appearance? Why should we want to change ours?

...

But I think one would say it's not so much in clothing as in manners, or habits and behaviour, that one action is fitting for a man and another for a woman. Hence the apostle Paul says, as an interpreter of [divine] law, 'Let women keep silence in the churches: for it is not permitted them to speak, but to be subject, as also the law saith. But if they would learn anything, let them ask their husbands at home.' And also, 'Let the woman learn in silence with all subjection. But I suffer not a woman to teach, nor to use authority over the man: but to be in silence.' How disgusting it is for a man to perform woman's work![13]

Ambrose had neatly conflated divine command and the animal world to argue for inflexible gender distinctions of dress and behaviour. His and Isidore's words echoed through the early Middle Ages, copied or quoted by many who read them. From the Christian writers of late Antiquity, early medieval scholars inherited a ready-made view of normative gender relations whose subversion would threaten divine order, and they saw little need to develop it further.

But real life was not as straightforward as early medieval moralists might wish. One spring, the holy man Gerald of Aurillac (b. c.855, d. 909) encountered a woman ploughing. On being asked why she was doing this 'man's work', she explained that her husband had been ill for a long time and that, if she did not do the sowing, no one else would. Gerald's response was to give her enough money to hire a labourer to finish the work. His biographer Odo, abbot of Cluny (927–42), knew his Ambrose, however, and made a moral of the tale. 'Nature flees from everything artificial, as Ambrose says, and its author, God, abhors what is unnatural.'[14] A peasant woman's crisis had given a pious Christian the opportunity to give alms; a monastic moralist presented his readers with a tale of the restoration of the divinely ordained gender order.

Appeals to 'nature' constitute one of the common rhetorical gender games of clerical authors in the early Middle Ages—and for centuries thereafter. Another, as we shall see, was to withhold the name of a woman from the reader or audience of a text, for anonymity obliterates identity. Those who resorted to textual tricks such as these doubtless did so out of force of habit. But the habit itself is revealing—of ingrained assumptions about women's marginality, weakness, or inferiority. As a powerful cultural reflex, the notion of women's natural weakness served many purposes— political, legal, religious, literary. It could encourage exploitation as easily as protection; it could be turned to praise or slander at will. It made fame and good reputation hard to acquire and easy to lose. Above all, it reinforced other social disparities, of age, rank, or resources, leaving women who did succeed in making their way in the world through whatever means available always vulnerable, caught within a web of meaning not of their own weaving.

## Pairings of Conception

Sexual partnerships are essential to the reproduction of human society, not only as the means of procreation but also because the intimate group of parents and children is the forum in which cultural assumptions and values are most often transmitted from one generation to the next. Yet to speak without qualification of 'marriage' in the early Middle Ages is too simple. The word does not adequately describe the full range of accepted sexual partnerships that men and women made for themselves. By the end of the millennium, something recognizably similar to our modern notion of marriage as an enduring relationship between one man and one woman had developed in parts of Europe, but not without controversy. Examination of these issues will make clear the social organization of gender relations and take us to the heart of early medieval ideas about sexual mores. Building on the discussion of kinship in the previous chapter, it opens to scrutiny additional varieties of men's and women's experience.

Underlying early medieval cultural diversities, however, lay a persistent and universal imbalance. The less access to legal rights or economic resources a woman had, the more she was at the sexual disposal of men of higher status: everywhere elite men had sexual access to women of low social standing on their own terms. These informal liaisons were nothing to do with the partnerships through which property and cultural values were channelled or with the bonds of affection and familial identity that formalized partnerships enabled; they thus are rarely visible in the sources. Lacking in any political significance or ideological value, they seldom came to the attention of the lawyers and legislators whose models of social relationships expressed dominant values in terms of marriage and sexual conduct, as in much else.

Of the three legal cultures outlined in the previous chapter, the inherited Roman tradition provides our starting point, because it proved fundamental. It recognized two mutually exclusive forms of sexual partnership, concubinage and marriage. The former involved no property transactions and was simply an acknowledged, long-term, sexual partnership between a man of high status and a woman of vastly inferior rank; a concubine's offspring lacked any inheritance rights. Concubinage was an alternative rather than an adjunct to marriage, a sexual outlet for young, unmarried men or widowers who preferred not to remarry. As defined by Roman law, marriage expected husband and wife to be of equal rank, and it required a betrothal contract, the formal consent of both parties, and endowment of the new couple by the bride's parents. It thus defined a man's heirs as only those of his offspring whom his wife had born. Fourth- and fifth-century imperial legislation put an unprecedented emphasis on it as a permanent partnership, only dissoluble if one of the partners committed the sacrilege of grave robbing or resorted to witchcraft, or if the wife had intercourse with someone other than her husband. Idealized as a consensual partnership based on mutual affection and respect, these legal provisions remained in practice throughout the Mediterranean areas of the early medieval West. As we shall see, they also informed the views of a succession of bishops, and thereby came to influence ecclesiastical teaching throughout the Middle Ages.

Into this late Roman world, Germanic-speaking settlers introduced rather different values and conventions, in marriage as in kinship. Notably, both written law and social convention recognized several types of marriage, in contrast to the single definition of Roman law. Of these, only one involved property transfers and thereby rights of inheritance. The groom's family commonly paid a marriage price to the bride's father, which the groom supplemented with a 'morning gift' on the day after the consummation of the union. In addition, it became normal, by the ninth century at the latest, for the groom to specify a marital endowment out of his own property at the time of the engagement. Especially if she lacked brothers, the bride might also contribute property inherited from her own parents. Negotiated between the aspiring groom and the girl's father and kinsfolk and celebrated in a public ceremony with the participation of friends and relatives, this was a transaction between two groups of kin that not only endowed a new household but might also seal a political alliance to mutual advantage or even end a feud. As such, it could generally only be ended by the man, with serious economic implications for both partners. Well described as 'conjugal domination',[15] this first form of union had two further features. First, it also required the transfer of the father's *mundium* over his daughter to her husband, so that he acquired the rights to represent her legal interests and to exercise authority over her. Secondly, the bride went to reside on her husband's estate, however near to or far from her natal home that might be. By the very nature of its property transactions, this was a form of partnership characteristic of the wealthy elite.

Equally accepted, long term, and publicly celebrated was a form of marriage in which the woman's move to the man's home was unaccompanied by any transfer of *mundium*, even though she might have property of her own. Men had no need to choose between these two forms of union: the rich and powerful could easily afford to support more than one woman, and indeed multiple partnerships became an expression of status and a way of accumulating socially prestigious resources. One such man was the wealthy and influential Rhineland landowner Pippin of Herstal (b. *c.*650, d. 714), who is known to have fathered sons by three women. His two simultaneous wives Plectrude and Alpaida both came from powerful families of the Ardennes region, although possibly only the extremely wealthy Plectrude had been transferred to Pippin's *mundium*. In due course, their sons contested their father's inheritance. Much less is known about Pippin's third partner, but the lack of any record of her name and the exclusion of her son from any share in Pippin's inheritance both strongly suggest that this was a much more informal partnership.

This brief survey does not exhaust the ways in which men competed for status by attracting women, for early medieval law codes recognized a range of supplementary relationships. Women could be taken without their parents' consent either in enforced abduction or in a seduction in which they themselves were willing accomplices. Although the parents had to be compensated for the loss of their daughter, such unions were nevertheless recognized, and might also be made more formal by a subsequent property settlement. Finally, at the bottom of the social hierarchy, it was left to lords to authorize whatever marriages among their slaves and serfs best suited the exigencies of efficient estate management.

In sum, the descendants of Germanic speakers generally preferred to maintain their traditional spectrum of sexual unions long after they had assimilated into many other aspects of post-Roman provincial life. These unions were differentiated by their degree of permanence; by the ways in which the transfer of a woman from her natal kin to her husband was achieved; by the nature of the attendant property transactions, if any; and by the arrangements for legal authority over and protection of the woman. While it remains uncertain whether a girl had much opportunity to voice her opinion of a proposed union, high-status men certainly could foster their interests by strategic marriages and find ample scope for sexual satisfaction and the begetting of heirs. When, towards the end of the eleventh century, Adam of Bremen (d. *c.*1083) commented that among the Swedes 'a man according to his means has two or three or more wives at one time, rich men and princes an unlimited number. And they also consider the sons born of such unions legitimate', he was only reporting, with perhaps modest exaggeration, a centuries-old pattern of powerful men exploiting these opportunities to 'hoard' women and thereby confirm their superiority not only over the women but also over less successful men.[16]

In the third place, we should return to Ireland, where lawyers' treatises blended elements of Christian, late Roman marriage law with indigenous practices to delineate a range of types of sexual union. Seventh- and eighth-century Irish scholars categorized nine 'pairings of conception' and ranked them from the most to the least honourable.[17] In the most honourable form of union, the woman's kin gave her to the groom, and the new household was supported by substantial property endowments. Foremost among these was the union to which both sets of kin contributed property and livestock, establishing the bride as a 'wife of joint authority'.[18] Less conducive to enhanced status, the property could come solely from either the husband's or the wife's kin. The constitutive element of these three unions was a contract regulating the property provisions and the division of responsibility for administering it. Despite their complexity, such contracts could be terminated. In contrast with other early medieval cultures, Irish laws permitted a wide range of grounds for separation. In theory at least, a man could part from his wife if she betrayed him, damaged his honour, persisted in adultery, killed their children, or neglected household tasks. She could leave him if he were impotent, sterile, or homosexual, too fat to have intercourse, gossiped about her sexual performance, took a mistress, circulated a satire about her, or if, in exercising his right to rebuke her, he struck a blow that caused a blemish. Unfortunately, we lack the sort of evidence that would reveal whether Irish social reality corresponded at all closely with these idealized schemes.

Next in the Irish ranking of sexual unions came those that the woman's kin accepted but in whose negotiation they had not been actively involved. The 'pairing of conception' in which a man visited a woman in her parents' home with their consent was less formal and less honourable; even less honourable were unions in which the woman went away with a man with neither the participation nor the consent of her kin, or was secretly visited by him. At the very bottom of the scale came the 'pairing of conception' to which the woman herself had not consented (rape) or the union of two insane people. All these provisions potentially had important consequences for the distribution of property, for only if a women's kinsfolk had not recognized the union did the sons of that alliance lose their right to inherit from their father, yet these sons could nevertheless inherit if their father chose to acknowledge them as his.

This spectrum of relationships allowed for multiple simultaneous relationships even more readily than in the successor kingdoms, for Irish law distinguished between the *cétmuinter*, the 'chief wife', and lesser-status wives.[19] The 'chief wife' had entered into a marriage contract in which her kin had fully participated, and which bound her more closely to her marital family than to her natal kin. Thus she was under the rule of her husband, and responsibility for two-thirds of her legal liabilities now lay with her sons and only one-third with her natal kin; her sons and her kin stood to inherit her property in equivalent proportions. Other wives, however, remained largely or fully within their natal kin in matters of legal liability, and enjoyed only half the status and entitlements of the chief wife. It was quite acceptable for a high-status man to have a chief wife, then acquire a second wife (on whom the *cétmuinter* was entitled to inflict non-fatal injuries during the first three days of this additional union), and also be visiting one or more women in their parental home. In the face of Christian clerical disapproval, Irish lawyers turned to the Old Testament for justification of traditional habits. 'There is dispute in Irish law as to which is more proper, whether many sexual unions or a single one: for the chosen people of God lived in plurality of unions, so that it is not easier to condemn it than to praise it.'[20] For those who could afford it, multiple sexual partnerships were normal.

Those who condemned a plurality of unions, in Ireland and elsewhere, were the clergy. The Christian doctrine of marriage was based firmly on the practice of the later Roman Empire, as encapsulated in a ruling of Pope Leo the Great (440–61) that a legitimate marriage was one between a free man and a free woman of equal rank, and that it involved the kin of the girl giving her in a formal betrothal into a marriage that was endowed with property and publicly celebrated. Leo's view, that 'not every woman joined to a man is a "wife" because not every son is heir to his father', asserted a distinction between the woman who was partner to the only form of sexual union recognized in Roman property law, marriage, and a woman in any other form of sexual liaison, such as a concubine or mistress.[21] To this legal definition of Roman origin, fourth- and fifth-century moralists had added a strong dose of a rigorous sexual ethic based largely on the New Testament. Paul of Tarsus (d. *c*.65) had declared that 'On account of fornication let every man have his own wife and every woman have her own husband' and 'Know ye not that the unrighteous shall not inherit the kingdom of God? Be not deceived: neither fornicators, nor idolaters, nor adulterers, nor effeminate nor abusers of themselves with men, nor thieves, nor covetous, nor drunkards, nor revilers, nor extortioners, shall inherit the kingdom of God,' and pronouncements such as these became the basis for a Christian morality of male and female sexual restraint that recognized heterosexual marriage as the sole legitimate relationship in which intercourse was permissible.[22] Promulgated by the clergy, this combination of Roman legal premises and uncompromising Christian morality cut across local conventions everywhere.

But to what extent did ecclesiastical opinions alter social practice? In Ireland, the Latin word for a woman having illegal intercourse, *adultrix*, supplied one of the Old Irish words for the secondary wife, *adaltrach*. Lexical borrowing by no means signalled the end of multiple sexual part- nerships, however. The success of attempts to restrict the learned caste of poets, clerics, and judges to only one wife cannot be ascertained, and the view that 'lords, poets, commoners are impaired by illicit cohabitation' seems to have made little impact.[23] Genealogies certainly suggest that multiple partnerships remained common at least amongst kings, and, when the full force of high-minded continental clerical reform reached Ireland in the twelfth century, reformers were vigorous in their condem- nation of the marital practices they found there.[24]

Outside Ireland, local habits and ecclesiastical expectations also diverged, as the experience of a seventh-century man named Barontus indicates. A nobleman from Lonrey in central France, he decided to end his days as a monk. Having entered his local monastery, he participated in its daily round of prayers and psalms. Then, in 678/9, he is reported to have had a near-death experience. On his return to full consciousness he recounted how devils had taken his soul on a tour of heaven and hell. At one of the gates of heaven, the apostle Peter asked the demons what charges they had against Barontus. 'They replied: "He had three wives, which was not permitted. He has also committed other adulteries and many other sins which we persuaded him to." '[25] Until he retired to the monastery, Barontus's behaviour was just like that of his contemporary, Pippin of Herstal. The difference is that we know about Barontus's mul- tiple marriages from the perspective of a critical monastic author from whose high moral vantage point the normal behaviour of rich men seemed like the work of the devil.

Visionary literature was not the only means of censure, or elderly men its only targets, however. On the occasions when ecclesiastical disapproval turned against kings, the stakes were high, for dynastic succession could be at risk. 'Know that these boys will never bear the royal sceptre, for they were begotten in sin' prophesied the Irish ascetic Columbanus in 610, ful- minating against the marital habits of the Merovingian Theuderic II (596–613).[26] Many Merovingian kings of Gaul, Theuderic included, had multiple sexual partners, most or all of whose sons they recognized as heirs. Those, like Columbanus, who dared to criticize, struck out at the practices that helped perpetuate the dynasty.

The stakes were raised even further during the eighth and ninth cen- turies, when councils of bishops in Italy and the Frankish lands launched a concerted effort to redefine marriage and to establish it as a religious, sacred undertaking. Starting at a synod in Rome in 721, ecclesiastical coun- cils gradually added three further elements to Leo the Great's ideas: an emphasis on the permanence and indissolubility of marriage, a refusal to countenance more than one sexual relationship at a time, and a very much broader definition of incestuous, forbidden marriages. In this context, bishops were emphatic that both the spiritual kinship established through baptism and the relationships created through marriage were impediments to marriage. Godparents, god-siblings, co-parents, and all in-laws thus fell into the vast pool of prohibited marriage partners. In addition, some bishops tried to impose an additional disqualification—consanguinity extending all the way to a common ancestor within seven generations, way beyond the widely acceptable four-generation limit.

It remains contentious why some Carolingian clergy sought to extend the circle of incestuous relationships to such extremes, especially since there is no evidence that marriage to close relatives was common, let alone normal, prior to the middle of the eighth century. Whatever the underlying motives, the result was that, during the century and a half from 721, marriage, and sexual relationships of all sorts, became politicized in a new way. There are two main reasons for this. First, by the later eighth century, good kingship meant fostering Christian conduct.[27] Thus Charlemagne and his successors supported ecclesiastical efforts to enforce a revised marital morality, while finding their own sexual conduct and marital alliances open to new scrutiny. Indeed, as Lothar II (855–69) discovered to his great cost, bishops could turn these prohibitions against a king, leaving him heirless. Secondly, beyond the immediate context of the politics of kings' bedrooms, bishops' only real chance of changing marital practices came if they worked in alliance with rulers: they thus handed wily kings an effective weapon for asserting control over their powerful subjects.

A case that came to the attention of a council of Frankish bishops in 860 allows us a rare glimpse of the social complexities, emotions, and conflicting political interests involved in betrothal and marriage. It concerned Stephen, count of the Auvergne, and its setting was Aquitaine, where his royal lord Charles the Bald was having difficulty building a stable, loyal regime. The story was one of 'very great scandal to the church and detriment to the kingdom'. In Stephen's own words: 'In the weakness of youth, as was the custom, I had my way with a young woman.' Then, in about 857, acting 'with the consent of my family and friends', he negotiated with another leading Aquitanian count, Regimund, to be allowed to marry the latter's daughter. They reached agreement about the marital endowment Stephen would provide, and the couple were formally betrothed. But, before Regimund could publicly hand over his daughter or Stephen could effect the property transfers, Stephen had discovered that his fiancée was related to his previous sexual partner. He had then consulted his priest, who informed him that the proposed marriage would be incestuous, and therefore forbidden. Stephen's ensuing efforts to back out of the betrothal aroused the wrath of both the king and Regimund. Fearing exile and ruin, Stephen felt 'compelled by necessity' to take Regimund's daughter as his wife in a public ceremony, and to hand over the endowment intended for her. But he nevertheless declined to consummate the marriage, and his obduracy made the confrontation with Regimund increasingly violent. Angered and humiliated at his daughter's treatment, Regimund finally lodged a complaint with the bishops in 860.[28]

Faced with such complex issues of honour, property, contractual obligation, sex, and sedition, the council decided that the case should be heard simultaneously by a secular assembly presided over by the king and by an ecclesiastical assembly led by the archbishops of the provinces where both Stephen and Regimund had their lands, the former to deal with the issues of property and politics, the latter with the nature of the marriage. The council also had a report on the case prepared by Hincmar, archbishop of Reims (845–82), one of the most vigorous lawyer-bishops of the entire Middle Ages but in this, as much else, also Charles the Bald's agent. The archbishops' ruling has not survived, so we do not know the final outcome, but, if they did follow Hincmar's advice, their solution would have been a face-saving one for Stephen and Regimund, with scant regard for the well-being of the unwanted bride, whom the briefing never bothered to name. Hincmar's concern was not sex outside marriage, but sex within it. He advised the provincial ecclesiastics to interrogate the girl: if the marriage had indeed been consummated, it was incestuous and therefore invalid; but, since consummation was necessary to complete a marriage, it was not a proper marriage if the pair had not had intercourse. Either way, Stephen was released and the royal assembly must deal with the broken betrothal contract, the insult to Regimund, and the threats of political unrest.

Why had Stephen acted thus? He claimed that fear of losing face and encountering the king's wrath played their part, but there seems to have been more to it than this. He may have been an innocent victim of the recent rigorous prohibitions against marriage to anyone related to a previous sexual partner, or he may have been cleverly manipulating the law to wriggle out of a marriage alliance no longer politically convenient for him. Whatever the case, Charles the Bald's grip on Aquitaine was in question. However we choose to adjudge Stephen's behaviour, a conflict such as this would have been hardly conceivable a century earlier. Whether the tale of a hapless victim or an adroit schemer, the case is important for several reasons. In the first instance, it is a reminder of the importance of elite marriage as political negotiation. Secondly, in a society that more commonly consigned a girl of marriageable age to a role as pawn than as an active strategist, a woman's opinion and well-being mattered little. Indeed, to Hincmar, they meant as little as her name. Thirdly, it testifies to the reformulation of definitions of kinship in the service of a changing ethic of sexuality and marriage.

Finally, it is no coincidence that Stephen of the Auvergne was a man of high status, a member of the king's retinue. His prominence exposed his marital shenanigans to the critical gaze of courtier-bishops and a king quick to spot any potential way of exerting leverage over his followers. Far to the south, beyond the Pyrenees, his Catalonian contemporary Dela, Count of Empúries (862–94), had married his first cousin Quixilona, daughter of his father's brother. Cousin-marriage was the norm for the counts of late ninth- and early tenth-century Catalonia, for it reinforced the familial grip on power. Had they known, bishops at the Carolingian court might have been perturbed—but Catalonia had never enjoyed close contact with Carolingian centres of power and, by the late ninth century, was rapidly losing all contact with the northern lands. When, in the middle years of the tenth century, Catalonian counts did begin to look further afield for their brides, it was for reasons of political advantage rather than the result of any moral pressure. Similarly, in Wessex, King Edward the Elder (899–924) assured his claim to the throne by marrying Ælfflaed, daughter of his first cousin and rival Æthelhelm. Not for another fifty years or so did the Carolingian notion that close kinship was an insuperable impediment to marriage even begin to alter English practice. And it did so only because late-tenth-century Anglo-Saxon kings found a strategic political advantage in supporting moralizing bishops who had familiarized themselves with stringent continental ideals. In effect, the Carolingian redefinition of marriage—indissoluble, exclusive of any other simultaneous sexual partnership, prohibited to couples related to each other within at least four generations—began to affect people's behaviour only when the full resources of king and church were united in trying to enforce it.

Elsewhere, either beyond Carolingian purview, or where the will and the means to effect change were lacking, definitions of marriage long remained much more flexible. Scandinavia is a case in point, as Adam of Bremen reliably informs us.[29] The Dane Cnut conquered England and seized the throne in 1016, then shortly thereafter acceded to the Danish crown: in having two concurrent wives, Ælfgifu and Emma, he maintained the older, Scandinavian ways, while nevertheless bowing to ecclesiastical

pressure and legislating to fine those Anglo-Saxons who married close relatives or did not confine their sexual activity to marriage. Even further
away, quite beyond the sphere of Carolingian influence, Ireland remained
untouched by continental norms until the very end of the eleventh century. Indeed, an Irish woman who was her father's sole heir was likely to
be married off to her closest male relative precisely to prevent her property leaving the kindred, and, despite lip-service to the patristic ban on
marriage within four generations, Irish churchmen evidently acknowledged the need for cousin-marriage for heiresses.

To change marriage customs required both political persistence and
consistent norms on the part of aggressive kings and bishops acting in
tandem. But for long after the high tide of Carolingian moralizing, neither the alliance nor the will to action were much in evidence. Instead, at
least among the political elite, marriage long remained an uneasy balance
of political exigency and divergent norms, only sometimes tempered with
personal morality. A poignant early medieval love story from the close of
our period emphasizes these contradictions. Count Otto of Hammerstein
and his wife Irmengard were distantly related—Irmengard's great-
grandparents were Otto's great-great-grandparents. Their long-standing
marriage was interrupted when the vengeful German emperor Henry II
(1002–24) set out to destroy Otto, fearing he was becoming an over-mighty
subject. Henry attempted this by encouraging a renewed mood of moral
rigour among German bishops, some of whom were seeking to put new
force into the ninth-century proposals for a seven-generation definition
of incest. In 1018, Henry II presided over an ecclesiastical council that
excommunicated the couple and ordered them to separate. 'Blazing with
blind love', Otto nevertheless remained with Irmengard, and in 1020 he
assaulted his leading ecclesiastical opponent, the archbishop of Mainz.[30]
Henry II retaliated, besieging Otto in his castle at Hammerstein, razing
it, and then seizing all Otto's extensive lands. Still the couple clung together until, in 1023, another ecclesiastical assembly again ruled against
them. Fearful of the emperor, Otto finally submitted, but Irmengard remained defiant. In breach of the German bishops' refusal to let her
appeal to the pope, she journeyed to Rome in 1023 and successfully pleaded
her case. In affirming the validity of her marriage and denouncing the
German bishops who had annulled it, Benedict VIII (1012–24) provoked
a storm of protest for his interference. The following year, both king and
pope died, and with them, the controversy: Otto and Irmengard remained
married and enjoyed the favour of the new king, Conrad II, whose own
marriage elicited strong clerical criticism.

The travails of Otto and Irmengard reveal much about marriage at the turn of the millennium. In the first place, their own acceptance of it as permanent and monogamous indicates the long, slow reorientation of social assumptions that took place in large parts of early medieval Europe under Christian influence. They embodied the ideal that ecclesiastical teaching advocated, of marriage as an exclusive partnership of equals. Secondly, despite agreement on the principle that marriage should be between partners who were not related in any way, uncertainty persisted about where to set the limits of kinship. Thirdly, kings, bishops, and popes contested the right to arbitrate marriages. Originating in the era of vigorous Carolingian moral idealism, a distinctive notion of marriage had been formulated whose presuppositions had massive implications for local conventions about the nature and number of tolerated sexual partnerships, and for the social units in which women raised their children. Sometimes reinforced by royal promulgation, it spread wherever handbooks of Carolingian ecclesiastical legislation were copied, primarily on the Continent and, by the later tenth century, into England as well. But, as we have seen, formulation of that notion was one thing, its implementation quite another, and attempts to turn aspiration into reality remained fitful, controversial, and inconsistent long beyond 1050.

## Women, Family, and Inheritance

If marriage long remained more a matter of politics than of Christian morality, it did so because it involved far more than regulation of sexual activity. At the very least, the arrival of a wife and daughter-in-law into a man's home increased the pool of labour available for women's work—the spinning, weaving, sewing, embroidering to which women of all social levels devoted their energies, and the food preparation and other tasks that slave and peasant women undertook. Among the elite, marriage also involved calculations about conserving, distributing, and augmenting family property so as to arrange its disposition across generations. With land came the wherewithal to survive and, for all property-owners above the meagre subsistence farmer, the possibility of a surplus. The next chapter will emphasize how rights over landed property opened the way to status, political power, and influence; here the focus is on inheritance of the patrimony as a means of negotiating gender disparities. This analysis argues that, while the distribution of resources among heirs reinforced men's and women's differential access to wealth, influence, and power, women's access to property was nevertheless crucial to early medieval familial interactions.

Open to the influence of political pressures, ecclesiastical opinion,

evolving local legal procedures, and changing ideas of family, early medieval inheritance customs varied widely from place to place. Yet, despite
widespread regional and temporal variation, some general points are clear.
The first is that sexual partnerships transmit property (movables and land)
from parents to children, and that the right to inherit is generally closely
related to the nature of the parents' partnership. The formal and publicly
acknowledged unions in early Ireland gave sons a greater right to their
father's property than those of less formal partnerships; elsewhere the
developing notions of Christian marriage strengthened the inheritance
rights of a man's child by his wife against claims by the children of less
formal unions. Secondly, the normal patterns for inheriting land diverged
from those for movable property such as cattle, slaves, or jewellery, and
procedures for inheriting political office might be different again. Thirdly,
parental property was in principle partible—in other words, was shared
between some or all children, albeit usually in unequal amounts. By the
eleventh century, however, some families were beginning to develop strategies for channelling most or all of their patrimony to a single son, as notions of family and identity continued to evolve. Fourthly, the transmission
of property from one generation to the next was rarely the concern of
parents and children alone. Kings were watchful, keen for an excuse to
intervene, and, except where Roman property law persisted, the wider kin
group was also involved. This discussion therefore locates men and women
among their relatives and also keeps an eye on the broader political contexts within which they lived. Finally and fundamentally, men's right to
inherit land was one of the commonalities of all early medieval cultures;
women's access to the family patrimony, on the other hand, varied greatly
from region to region, and from generation to generation. By tracing
women's differential access to land vis-à-vis their brothers, a gendered pattern of immense political significance emerges.

Identifying strategies of inheritance inevitably depends upon the
surviving documentation. In this context, it is germane to reiterate several points made earlier. On the one hand, the norms articulated in law
codes about the transmission of property are not an adequate guide to
how people behaved in practice: to get at that, we must juxtapose them
with the records of transfers of specific, named estates such as charters
of donation, wills, and bequests. Further, not only did the degree of
document-mindedness vary markedly from region to region, but the rate
of documentary survival has been much better in some places than others. A final point to recall is the gradual adoption across northern Europe
of testamentary practices of Roman origin, practices that affected methods of transmitting and recording title to property.[31] Overall, records

detailing land transfers generally survive in some numbers only from the late seventh century onwards in Italy and the Frankish lands, the late ninth century in northern Spain, the mid-tenth century in England, and even later elsewhere.

It is nevertheless possible to sketch some of the most obvious regional distinctions in inheritance custom. The two extremes are, as so often, Ireland, on the one hand, and the southern, enduringly Roman areas of continental Europe, on the other. In Ireland, the paternal land was divided equally between all recognized sons, but daughters were entitled to an equal share of movable property, most notably slaves and cattle. If a man died leaving a daughter but no sons, she might have a life interest in his estate, but on her death the property reverted to her male kinsmen on her father's side. These practices operated within a culture that emphasized that land was the property of a four-generation kin group, known as the *derbfine*, and in which alienation of land away from the *derbfine* was discouraged and difficult to achieve. Female inheritance would pose a threat to the kin group and its land, for recognized sons belonged to their father's *derbfine*, not their mother's: were a woman to inherit land and pass it to her sons, it would pass from one *derbfine* to another. This is why an heiress would find herself pressured to marry her father's nearest male relative.[32] By contrast, Roman property law of the fifth and sixth centuries operated on two quite different principles, which remained intact throughout the early Middle Ages, and long beyond. First, land was owned in full and outright ownership only by individuals: there was no notion of any collective interests or rights over land. Secondly, the law of the late Roman Empire was based upon the assumption that daughters had the right to inherit on equal terms alongside their brothers in the event of intestacy. Overall, it posed no legal obstacles to the full control and free disposal of property by women independent of any guardian. In areas such as Calabria and Lucania in southern Italy or Aquitaine and Provence in southern France, where Roman practices persisted throughout the early Middle Ages, women's access to property gave them in principle a degree of economic independence quite unthinkable in early Ireland.

But what of those regions between Ireland and southern Italy, in other words in the kingdoms where Germanic-speaking settlers and their descendants persisted in their own customs? Here, it is important to acknowledge a wide range of local differences, but with two significant common factors. First, rights to private, individual ownership of property were balanced alongside the interests of the kin, who might wish to claim it or to be consulted if its owner desired to sell or donate land to anyone

other than his offspring. Secondly, these traditions clearly preferred transmitting land to male heirs, and generally acknowledged inheritance rights
of daughters or sisters only when sons were lacking. More hostile to
women owning land than any other law code, the mid-eighth-century
compilation of Thuringian law specified that, in the absence of a son, the
property would go to the father's nearest male relative. The Thuringian
law is also useful for making more explicit than any other law code the
differential routes to be used in passing on movable goods as distinct from
land, for it stipulated that, although the latter went to the father's nearest
male relative, livestock and slaves went to his daughters, who would also
be the ones to inherit their mother's clothing, jewellery, and personal
ornaments.

And yet: prescribing written rules for inheritance and drawing up documents confirming individual land transactions were both devices adopted
from Roman tradition. The result of this is that, from the earliest moment
when the written record first allows us to glimpse inheritance strategies
in the post-imperial kingdoms, they are already touched by Roman norms.
This trend intensified only in the seventh, eighth, and ninth centuries.
The Lombard kingdom in northern Italy is a particularly clear instance
where the inheritance rights of Lombard women altered significantly
under the heavy pressure of the customs of their Roman neighbours, and,
by the end of the eighth century, Lombard daughters had a far greater
chance of inheriting a part of their father's property than did their predecessors who had lived under Rothari's rule. In effect, wherever the
documentation survives to reveal the specificities of property transactions,
women in the successor kingdoms could and did inherit land as well as
movables.

That is not to say, however, that women's access to property was ever
as great or as secure as men's. Rather, it remained limited, insecure, and
liable to be contested. Although statistical deductions are notoriously unreliable for the early Middle Ages, several rough calculations may help
focus this discussion. Late Roman women, it has been optimistically suggested, may have owned 30–45 per cent of all the landed property in the
empire. Admittedly, this is little more than guesswork, but it may be contrasted with figures for later centuries derived from differing types of
material. First, analysis of continental charters from the eighth century
onwards suggests sharp regional differences in women's access to land. In
areas where the influence of Roman legal traditions remained strong,
women may have controlled significant amounts of land—approximately
17 per cent in tenth-century northern Spain and 13 per cent in adjacent

regions of southern France. North of the Loire, in Germany and in Lombard Italy, women had less than 10 per cent, and probably less than 5 per cent of all land. For England, the evidence is rather different: Domesday Book, the national survey of landholding compiled for William the Conqueror (1066–87). In addition to reporting on landholding in 1086, Domesday records the pattern of landownership in Anglo-Saxon England on 'the day when King Edward was alive and dead', that is in 1066, and it offers a snapshot of property rights immediately before the Norman Conquest. Anglo-Saxon custom strongly preferred land to pass from man to man, and, in general, women's access was conditional and restricted. Domesday records only about 5 per cent of all the land in England as being owned by women in 1066: and there are good reasons for believing that somewhat more land was in female hands by 1066 than it had been in c.1000. These figures suggest—however tentatively—that, subject to the influence of legal cultures and local traditions, female property rights varied tremendously and that, even on the best possible estimate in the regions most favourable to women's property rights, the vast majority of all land remained under men's control.

Access to landed wealth was not only conditioned by the constraints of local social practice or legal restrictions. Specific familial circumstances were of equal significance, and might affect women just as much as men. First and foremost, the uncertainties of birth or the vagaries of sudden death might throw into confusion even the most carefully planned property distribution. Abba, the reeve—king's official—in Kent, had a childless marriage. Between 833 and 839 he drew up a will in which he made arrangements for several possible futures. 'It is my desire', he stated at the outset, 'that if God will give me a child, he shall have the land after me, and enjoy it with my wife; and similarly, and that after him my descendants shall continue to hold it as long as it is God's will that there be any of them able and qualified to hold land.' But Abba also envisaged a childless old age: 'If, however, it is my lot not to have a child, then I desire that my wife shall have it [my land] as long as she is willing to keep it without marrying again.'[33] Another possible future was that his widow Heregyth remarried. In that case, the land was to return to his own kinsmen, leaving her with only whatever property she had herself brought into the marriage. Finally, he made provisions in case Heregyth wished to enter a convent, provisions designed to ensure that she had adequate wealth to be accepted into the community but that the land remained with his own kin. Abba also gave some thought as to which of his kinsmen might expect to benefit if he did indeed die childless. His brothers were to pass the property to their heirs, if they had any; failing them, one Freothomund (cousin? uncle?) would inherit if he were still alive; if he had already died, then one of Abba's sisters' sons could claim the land. If his family died out completely, the land was to go to the local cathedral church, Christ Church in Canterbury. Abba had stared into an uncertain future, not knowing whether his wife would ever conceive, or which of his relatives might predecease him.

How did things turn out? We do know that, in her widowhood, Heregyth surrendered Abba's lands to his kin in a way that diverted some of the produce from them to Christ Church, Canterbury, to enable both their deaths to be properly commemorated there with regular intercessory prayer for the sake of their souls. She herself may have retired to a convent, or perhaps secluded herself back in the home of her natal family. Such a fate for a widow was far from unusual. Abba had left her a life interest in his lands, but had directed that ownership of those should be restricted to his male blood relatives. Abba's decisions exemplify a practice particularly common in, but not confined to, Anglo-Saxon England, a practice that channelled property from man to man through women. Heregyth and Abba's sisters could transmit the title but not hold it in their own right.

Occasionally, family circumstances might work out very much to a widow's advantage. The characteristic demographic profile of early medieval communities must have meant that it was not uncommon for adult children to die before their parents.[34] Whenever offspring who lacked children of their own predeceased their parents, their heirs were normally either siblings or parents. Reverse inheritance from children to parents is well attested, and may not have been all that unusual. An eleventh-century runic inscription from Hillersjö in Sweden reflects conventions widespread in northern Europe in the preceding two centuries. It runs as follows:

Read! Germund took Gerlög, a maiden, as wife. Then they had a son before he (Germund) was drowned and then the son died. Thereafter she had Gudrik as her husband. . . . Then they had children but only one girl survived, her name was Inga. Ragnfast of Snottsta had her as his wife. Thereafter he died and then the son. And the mother (Inga) inherited from her son. Then she had Erik as her husband. Then she died. Then Gerlög inherited from Inga her daughter. Torbjörn the skald carved the runes.[35]

Gerlög had outlived her first husband (Germund), her son by him, her second husband (Gudrik), her only surviving child by her second husband (her daughter Inga), her son-in-law (Ragnfast), and her unnamed grandson. Directly or indirectly, she was the heir to all of them. In the course of her long life, she accumulated by reverse inheritance from her own children the lands of her first husband, her second husband, and her son-in-law. Marriage normally transmits property from the older generation to the younger, and no one would plan for the grandmother to be the sole heir of all the wealth of the younger generations of her family. But, with all the uncertainties of mortality in the early Middle Ages, it could and, on this occasion, certainly did happen.

More commonly, widows found that their access to the property left to them by their husband either with a life interest or in outright ownership was contested by their dead husband's relatives. Abba had certainly foreseen that his brothers would prowl around his widow Heregyth, and had tried to co-opt their support for her. But, on occasions, the opposition might come not from the husband's kin, but from a woman's own son, eager to take immediate control of his paternal inheritance without having to wait for his mother to die. A famous dispute occurred at Aylestone in Herefordshire in the reign of Cnut (1016–35), when a man called Edwin brought a lawsuit against his unnamed mother. In consigning her to anonymity, the charter scribe nevertheless recorded that she successfully defended her right to bequeathe 'my land and my gold, and my clothing and my raiment, and everything I possess' to her kinswoman Leofflæd.[36] Such conflicts between a man's widow and his heir were hardly unusual, but, in all probability, widows won them infrequently. In this instance it may well have been the fact that Leofflæd was the wife of an important local landowner and power broker that enabled mother to fend off son.

Partible inheritance did not require a parent to divide land equally among heirs, whether sons and daughters, or just sons. The chances of squabbling were therefore high. Siblings might find themselves jockeying for more favoured treatment from one or both parents; cousins might also be eyeing lands formerly the possession of their common grandfather; the brother of a dead man might dispute with the adult sons of the deceased for control of his lands. Such tensions could spill over into hostility, even feuding, notoriously in Ottonian Germany. Although chronicles may narrate these familial animosities, charters normally only hint discreetly at them. An unusual example of frankness, and unusual too in revealing the strategies available to parents, comes from Spoleto, in central–southern Italy. Pando had given his wife Taneldis a life interest in his estate of *Cicilianus*, with directions to pass it on to their son Benedict if he behaved well towards his mother in her widowhood. But, Taneldis declared, Benedict 'insulted me and was hostile to me and inflicted many wrongs on me, as is known to many people', and so in 768 she gave his father's land in its entirety to the monastery of Farfa.[37] She doubtless acted not so much out of spite for her son but to secure her own income in her widowhood, for she nevertheless retained a life interest in the land that she had donated. Typical of many women who achieved relative security in their widowhood by associating themselves in one way or another with a monastery, Taneldis could live out her days assured of an adequate income and the assistance of an influential patron and protector in the person of the abbot of Farfa.

Although negotiating an elite marriage had always involved designating specific resources for a woman's maintenance, it was generally only in widowhood that she acquired direct control of its landed component. Like her marital endowment and her morning gift, any land she had inherited in her own right would have been administered conjointly with her husband's property for the duration of her marriage. Widowhood brought an end to 'conjugal domination' and inaugurated her direct access to landed resources, whether the widow enjoyed outright ownership of them or a life interest. For Taneldis, as for all the other identifiable early medieval women of property, access to land—and with that the potential for independent wealth and influence—came at a major turning point in the female life cycle. Indeed, wherever women did transfer property by written document in their own name, as Taneldis did, they only ever did so as nuns or widows, never as wives or daughters.[38] But widowhood might nevertheless entail social isolation, and it certainly left a woman vulnerable to challenge from the aggressive or the unscupulous. It is little surprise that Taneldis secured powerful and effective protection of her own interests.

The example of Taneldis makes the point that women's access to property in the early Middle Ages was conditioned by a complex cultural matrix, within which each woman had to negotiate as best she could. On the one hand, that matrix was influenced by local legal tradition, royal power, and ecclesiastical pressure. On the other, it was resolutely familial. Whereas men stood a chance of acquiring property from their lord or king as well as by inheritance, women generally had access to land only as a result of inheritance from their parents (and sometimes from their dead children) or under the terms of their marriage settlement. The effective result of this was to leave women as the conduit through which land was channelled from one generation to the next, or from a family to a church, with minimal opportunity for them to own it securely in their own name, unfettered by any other interests in it or claims to it. Women's access to property is therefore inherently an aspect of the wider question of men's strategies of heirship: once again, discussion of women cannot be separated from that of the families, natal and marital, to which they belonged.

However distinctive any particular family was—and no two families were ever the same in composition, ancestry, identity, or affections—all had roughly similar aims as they transmitted land from one generation to another. Two goals predominated. In the first place, families strove to maintain status from one generation to the next. Since status was in large part dependent upon access to wealth, the preservation of status called for the preservation of patrimony. For families who managed to raise more than one child to adulthood, however, the custom of partible inheritance and the familial frictions that it encouraged had to be carefully managed. Complementary to this goal, and of equal importance, once the Christian custom of prayer for the dead had become universal, was provision for commemoration of oneself and one's family in the afterlife. Liturgical commemoration made the dispersal of wealth an imperative, whether as charitable almsgiving or as endowments to monasteries. Strategies of heirship, then, had to be formulated to balance a range of competing priorities.

From at least the ninth century onwards, it is possible to glimpse some of those techniques and women's place in them. One obvious approach was to limit the number of heirs. Whether sexual self-restraint was practised in addition to the use of readily available herbal contraceptive or abortifacient agents cannot be said. What is clear, however, is that parents made decisions that directed their children either into a secular life of marriage, inheritance, and the perpetuation of the family or into a religious life of committed celibacy and asexuality. Born in 975, the historian Thietmar, bishop of Merseburg (1009–18), was the third of five sons of Siegfried, count of Walbeck, and his wife Kunigunde. The first two sons were raised for marriage and the life of an aristocratic warrior, the eldest succeeding to his father's countship in 991, the second achieving a more modest political career. Thietmar and his two younger brothers were all sent into the church and all eventually became bishops. The count of Walbeck thereby made a calculated gamble that, even if one of his secular sons died before producing an heir, the other would succeed and continue the family line. With three sons in the church, he was also attending to his family's spiritual needs.

Daughters too had an integral place in family plans. A century or so earlier, in 864, the ageing Eberhard, marquis of Friuli, and his much younger wife Gisela made a will, distributing their huge wealth in northern Italy, Alamannia, and Flanders amongst their children. The couple catches our attention for many reasons—and especially for the opportunity that their will affords for examining familial strategy in some detail. Of their five sons and four daughters, the eldest son, named after his father, had died in infancy. Of the surviving eight children, marriages were arranged for two sons, Unruoch and Berengar, and one daughter, Heilwig. A further two sons, Adalard and Rudolf, were sent into the religious life, becoming abbots of religious communities in Flanders. One daughter, named after her mother, was also dedicated to God and raised as a nun in northern Italy. The fate of the third and fourth daughters is unknown, but there are grounds for suspecting that they never married. In planning their children's futures, Eberhard and Gisela had shaped the family long before the time came for the children to inherit.

The testamentary disposition of their property evinces an equally firm parental strategy. Under the terms of their will, all eight surviving children stood to inherit precious objects and books from their parents; all except one daughter (of whom more in the next paragraph) received land as well. The lion's share of the patrimony, including all his father's land in Italy and Alamannia, went to Unruoch. As the eldest surviving son, he was intended to succeed to his father's political status and influence: as a token of this, he was allocated his father's sumptuous jewelled and gilded weaponry and gold-embroidered clothing, the symbols of high status and imperial office. The other three sons, two of them already in religious orders, all received much smaller portions of land in Flanders, as did Heilwig, the only married daughter. Her inheritance would have been indirectly intended for the grandchildren—and indeed, she was the only one of the three married offspring fortunate enough to succeed in raising another generation to adulthood.

The three children sent into the religious life also contributed to the family's future, for their share of the landed inheritance helped fulfil the family's need for religious commemoration. The gift of a child to a church established close links between parents and the religious house through the child; property conveyed via that child confirmed the link and made provision for intercessory prayer and Christian remembrance of all members of the family. Such arrangements rarely removed land entirely out of a family's sphere of influence: to the contrary, they established strongly reciprocal interests that often endured over generations. All this was at work in the planning undertaken by Eberhard and Gisela, and, since a daughter's monastic vow was customarily accompanied by a gift of land to the convent in question, provision for the religious daughter, Gisela, will have pre-dated her parents' will, whereas the property assigned in their will to Adalard and Rudolf simply took longer to enter ecclesiastical management. Of the three churches in question, one had strong associations with

Eberhard's family, another with Gisela's; the third they founded together at Cysoing, in Flanders. Eberhard and Gisela will have considered the land that followed Adalard, Rudolf, and young Gisela into their respective religious communities as effective an investment in their families' future as the estates distributed to their other children. Finally, we should note the place in these arrangements of the elder Gisela after her husband's death in 866. Widowed, she used her own inheritance to build up Cysoing as a place where the members of her family might be buried and remembered in prayer, and she appointed as its abbot first Adalard, then Rudolf. Some of her land was to be held by her sons before passing, on their death, to this family monastery, again meeting both the goals of immediate economic sustenance and long-term prayer.

In the generations after the deaths of Eberhard and Gisela, some aristocratic families began to develop another strategy for limiting the fragmentation of their property among an ever-expanding number of descendants. Tentatively and erratically, some experimented with appointing only a single heir and leaving the patrimony intact from one generation to the next. Precocious in this respect were the aristocratic families that rose to princely and even royal power as the Carolingian dynasty faltered after 888. Like their Merovingian predecessors, the Carolingian kings had tended to treat the kingdom as a partible familial inheritance. But the last few Carolingian kings, ruling western Francia from 898 until 987, had too little power or land to risk splitting it up. They, like the Ottonians who succeeded them as rulers of the East Franks, pioneered a tradition of appointing a single heir, leaving younger sons to find a career in the church or in service to their elder brother. A high-risk strategy, this laid the eldest son open to challenges and revolts by his siblings.

Where kings and princes led, aristocrats followed, especially in the heartlands of the former Carolingian Empire. Here, a gradual reconfiguration of the relationship between family and land began during the ninth century, encouraged by demographic and economic growth. By the twelfth century, elite families in north-western Europe commonly passed land undivided from father to one son, usually the eldest surviving one. The practice never became universal, however, for partible inheritance remained widespread in large parts of Europe up to the end of the Middle Ages and even beyond.

One thing never altered: access to land brought opportunities for status and influence. For men, that meant the possibility of participating in the political life of a kingdom, and seeking further reward in the service of a lord or king. For women, access to land as heiresses or widows certainly might bring influence, but it also reinforced vulnerability.

However wealthy, women could never combine their influence with formal office holding in royal government in the early Middle Ages. Institutional positions such as count, duke, sheriff, or reeve were bestowed on, or inherited by, men, as indeed were royal thrones, but women could only be the channel through which these offices passed from one man to another, their guarantor of status and legitimacy. Even when, from the late tenth century, counts' wives were increasingly referred to as 'countess', and when those of them whose widowhood involved governing on behalf of an infant heir began to use this as a formal public title, the shift in titulature did not signal any new ability to be appointed to office in their own right. Instead, it confirmed marriage and motherhood as the sources of their prestige and influence. Just as a queen might exercise huge political influence as the wife of a sickly or incompetent king or as mother of an under-aged monarch but could not inherit the throne or be elected to it in her own name, so, throughout the aristocracy, women's access to power came as wives, mothers, or widows. Landed wealth, then, might bring a woman wealth and influence; it could not bring her institutionalized power and authority.

Too much has been made in recent years of a shift in familial structures in the early eleventh century—from the amorphous, bilateral kin groups of the early Middle Ages to tightly focused patrilineal families in the high Middle Ages within which property passed from eldest son to eldest son to the increasing detriment of daughters and younger sons. To the extent that changes did occur, they happened neither abruptly nor universally, and were only ever one of a range of ways to accumulate land. Younger sons might maintain their status by finding an heiress to marry, receiving gifts from living relatives, benefiting from royal patronage, or finding other ways to acquire property—for example, by emigrating. Unexpected death might as easily upset a father's planned distribution of his lands in the twelfth century as it did in the eighth. From the perspective of women's place in familial strategies, they always remained the channel by which property flowed from one generation to another, and from one familial group to another. As daughters, they had just as good a chance of succeeding in default of brothers in the twelfth century as in the ninth. As wives, their marriage still required a carefully calculated property transaction agreed between their father and their husband. As widows, they remained in control of significant proportions of a family's land, vulnerable to others' interest in it but central to its transmission.

Family, sexual partnership, and, if wealthy, property inheritance: these formed the matrix within which early medieval men and women lived their lives. Despite changing notions of marriage, shifts in inheritance strategies, and wide regional variations in social practice, two themes have remained constant throughout this chapter. The first is the centrality of women to the affairs of their family. A girl dedicated to the religious life in childhood; a mother dead in her prime years and buried in a richly equipped grave; a magnate's daughter betrothed—then discarded—to suit her father's politics; a son's inheritance blocked by his mother; a wife's ride to Rome to save her marriage; a widow vacillating between the demands of her husband's relatives and shelter in a convent: all have emphasized the familial context of women's lives and the affinities that shaped them. The second theme is the disparities, sometimes negotiable, sometimes not, between women's experiences and men's opportunities. Despite the individuality of every family, the temperaments of individuals, the unpredictability of long life or early death, men were almost always at an advantage. Tacit social assumptions and explicit legal principles alike worked in their favour, whether in terms of sexual access to women and inherited access to land, or in terms of authority over their wives and daughters. Above all, when a boy was sent off into the household of an influential relative, his father's lord, or even the king, he left the immediate familial circle and started to find his way in a world where friends mattered as much as relations. For him, marriage and fatherhood supplemented other equally important affinities and political relationships.

As kings, magnates, and bishops, it was men who legislated, revised social norms, passed sentence. It was mostly they, or their subordinates, who copied charters, wrote histories and chronicles, composed moral treatises, delineated ideal social relationships. Legal, intellectual, and religious traditions inherited from the Roman world provided powerful justification for a world tilted in their favour. It is no wonder, then, that their voices are the loudest, or that many generations of historians found it easy to see the early Middle Ages as a man's world, or, at least, from men's perspectives. To some extent, this accurately reflected communities where men were indeed more likely to have far more wealth and power than women. But, as this chapter has stressed, there was often a considerable disjuncture between ideological expectations and social realities: we must not confuse or conflate them. If early medieval men and women occasionally found themselves hard up against stringent legal requirements or inflexible moral expectations, customary expectations and unvoiced assumptions shaped their interactions on a daily basis.

# RESOURCES

# 5

## Labour and Lordship

'What do you say, ploughman? How do you go about your work?'
'Oh my lord, I work extremely hard. I go out at daybreak, driving the oxen to the field, and I yoke them to the plough. There is no winter so harsh that I dare linger at home, for fear of my lord. . . . Yes, the work is hard because I am not free.'[1]

> Let each man cleave to his lord;
> let each man protect his territory.
> The top of each man is his lord;
> the root of each man is his territory.[2]

LAND, those who laboured on it, and those who lorded it over them are themes that take us to the heart of social, economic, and political relationships. The overwhelming majority of Europe's inhabitants between c.500 and c.1000 lived on the land and worked it directly: their lifestyle was constrained by the physical toil needed to maintain the rhythms of the agricultural year. Equally importantly, control of landed property and the extraction of surplus produce were central to relationships between individuals and groups. The previous chapter has shown how social distinctions between men and women in the early Middle Ages often turned on differential rights over land; this one takes up the theme of social stratification and the ways in which landholding underpinned untidy hierarchies of inequalities.

It contends that control over people and control over land cannot be neatly separated. The combination was an essential aspect of political organization in almost all early medieval communities, for lordship embraced them both, separately or together. The owner of cattle, slaves, or land was a lord by virtue of the power he exercised over them. So too was the master of a household, by virtue of his authority over all members of his *familia*, from the most menial to the most distinguished.

Lordship was thus essentially a form of social power, rooted in relationships between persons and control of resources, especially land and livestock. As a term of address for a master, chieftain, king, emperor, or the Christian God, 'lord' acknowledged that power, implied deference, and showed respect for the one who was first and foremost. So a woman too could be a lord, when she controlled estates or ruled in her own name. In brief, early medieval inequalities were not simply those of material wealth and the lifestyle it brought, but of social influence and political power as well.

Our starting point is the straightforward observation that the groups into which people formed themselves in the early Middle Ages reveal differentials of resources, wealth, legal rights, and status, whether those groups were isolated village communities or large kingdoms and empires. These inequalities did not neatly correspond to each other, for legal rights were no guarantee of material wealth, any more than juridical rank reflected subjective perceptions of status. Although men and women lived in a world of domination and subordination, the gradient was never neatly ordered or systematized, except sometimes in the tidy-minded wording of law codes and schematic legal treatises. Rather, it resulted from the reality of power over others: those at the bottom were subordinated to those at the top by custom and tradition; legal constraints and sanctions; a wide range of forms of dependency and clientage; menacing behaviour and actual violence, or simply fear.

'The work is hard because I am not free': the ploughman's lament alerts us to the fact that the history of land, social hierarchy, and power also raises emotive issues of freedom and servitude. For this reason, it has often been contentious. History emerged as an academic discipline in an environment saturated with heated debates about the appropriate political order for modern times—absolutist or aristocratic, liberal or conservative, bourgeois or Marxist. Social theorists, polemicists, and historians alike found in the early Medieval past harbingers of the freedoms they yearned for, causes of the oppressions they fought against, or justifications of the privileges they defended. In this atmosphere, they constructed schematic, generalized overviews of the early medieval centuries, and readily perceived them as either a golden age of peasant freedom or a crucible of exploitation and oppression—that is, a prelude to subsequent 'better' or 'worse' phases of human existence: the shadow of these older passions still lingers over debates about the early medieval peasantry.

The approach adopted here is different. It presumes that diversity of experience is characteristic of the early Middle Ages. Instead of seeking a unified story of the relationship of land, labour, and lords, it looks for varied localisms by following the fluid terminologies and multiple perspectives of the early medieval sources themselves. In referring to a wide range of political structures—large empires, small chiefdoms, compact, intensive polities, developing kingdoms—it argues that regional diversity and change over time were the hallmarks of all early medieval social hierarchies. The chapter starts at the bottom of the ladder by exploring slavery and serfdom and the implications of freedom. The first section argues that, although the distinction between free and unfree was of fundamental legal importance, social realities were far more complex than this neat antithesis suggests. The central section focuses on social inequalities organized around the control of land. In looking at the many different forms of lordship that touched peasants' lives, it argues for responsiveness to changing local situation and political context. The final section moves to the upper social echelons, to ask how high status was perceived, maintained, or contested, and how lordship also expressed political relationships.

## Servitude and Freedom

'There is nothing other than the freeman or the slave': thus ran a Roman legal adage that Charlemagne found useful in adjudicating the status of children with one free and one unfree parent.[3] As in the ancient world, the distinction between freedom and servitude remained the fundamental legal cleavage in all early medieval communities. This was a pairing of opposites, a radical statement of juridical extremes. At its simplest, it distinguished the person inviolable in life and limb from the person whose physical well-being and existence remained at the mercy of others.

In practice, however, servitude and freedom did not constitute polar opposites. Rather, they formed the ends of a spectrum. Just as there were degrees of dependency, so there were degrees of freedom and the advantages it brought, for both servitude and liberty were relative notions. A sliding scale of domination and subordination ran the entire length of the spectrum: at the top, forms of dependency organized the elite's political relations with their ruler, and, at the bottom, structured the exploitation of the rural workforce. While the demeaning obligations imposed on the unfree lacked any honourable aspect, the service that a magnate rendered to a king enhanced status and honour. Both offered *servitium* to their superior. Service and lordship were two sides of the same coin at every point in the social gradient: only their form and social worth differed. In any case, dependency and freedom were not so much singular terms as bundles of restrictions and privileges that could be associated in many different combinations. Prominent among these were: freedom of movement;

5.1. Principal places mentioned in Chapter 5.

control over one's own body and its labour; the right to carry weapons; access to law courts; ownership of property; entitlement to marry or inherit; the recognition of one's own children; and the pursuit of honour. Each of these could be denied or recognized in more than one way, by judicial proceedings, custom, or social regard.

Crucially, however, one disability did not imply all of them. Wherever we look, we find a huge range of intermediate statuses that combine aspects of freedom with degrees of dependency. These defy classification; it is better to recognize the immense variety of local practice in this, as in so many other respects. It was possible to be servile yet of high status, as were the *adalschalks* (the 'noble unfree' of eighth-century Bavaria), and the *ministeriales* of late-tenth- and early eleventh-century Germany. Both groups lacked legal freedom but carried out honourable and skilled services for their lords. It was also possible to be free, yet dependent; we shall shortly meet examples of free men who made annual payments to a major church or monastery in recognition of its lordship.[4] A variant on this were the riding men (*radcnihts*, *geneats*) in western England in the tenth and eleventh century. These were propertied dependants, substantial enough to own horses, like those on the estates of Bath abbey at Tidenham, whose duties included the obligation to 'ride and furnish carrying service and supply transport and drive herds and do many other things'.[5] They were far from the condition of the slave girl whose lord was himself an unfree peasant and who exploited her sexually—and this suggests an even more abject female experience of subordination than men ever suffered.

Charlemagne's memorandum to his officials had used the traditional words for freeman and slave: *liber* and *servus*. The former is relatively straightforward: the *liber* enjoys liberties, in the sense of freedom to exercise certain rights, whatever his economic condition may be. The latter term is notoriously difficult. The ancient meaning of *servus* had been a chattel slave, an object possessed by a master, usually captured in war and imported from afar, who would be replaced by another human import when his working life ended. In the course of the early Middle Ages, it came to mean an unfree serf, recognized as a person though with minimal rights and, commonly, bound hereditarily to the land on which he laboured and on which, in due course, his offspring would work too. For much of this period, however, the word could mean either, or both. The new meaning did not displace the older one, and individual writers were not always consistent in exactly how they used the word. Nor is context always a reliable guide. There are two main reasons for the linguistic imprecision: first, its ancient meaning had specified a juridical condition but early medieval texts commonly used the word to describe a socio-economic situation, not a legal one. Secondly, its shift in meaning was closely associated with changing ways in which lords used dependent labour to work their estates. For both these reasons, it has left a residue of controversy about whether the early medieval economy can be classified as a 'slave economy'.

The debate is unhelpful, for several reasons. Importantly, it risks reducing the social relations and agricultural economy of these centuries to a single, paradigmatic model and discourages appreciation of the immense variety of forms of dependency and unfreedom that coexisted even within a single locality. It also distracts attention away from a group of undoubted importance in many places, the free peasant proprietors, who are often hard to track in the sources except at the moment when they surrendered either their land or some of their freedom to a lord. Further, it tends to obliterate the wide range of other words in common use for dependent workers in Latin and in local languages, words that were used separately or in conjunction with *servus* and that had their own fluid meanings.

But the most important point is this: although the vocabulary of servitude hardly shifted, its social and political dimensions were quite different in the early Middle Ages from those of the ancient world. Some of the vast agricultural estates in Italy and other Mediterranean provinces of the Roman Empire had been worked by large gangs of imported slaves, who were housed in barrack-like conditions and denied any family life, but that method of exploitation and of human degradation had disappeared before the fourth century. Settled on individual plots of land, fourth- and fifth-century slaves came increasingly to resemble tied, dependent peasants in two ways: their recognition as persons, not objects, and their impoverished economic situation, social subjection, and heritable status. Yet there remained a fossilized juridical vocabulary, redolent of former times, that did not correspond with newer socio-economic realities.

By the time that early medieval records begin to show us the characteristic forms of lordship and subordination in any detail, agricultural slavery had become a thing of the past in the post-imperial provinces. In Christian regions of the Continent, the only slaves to be found were in aristocratic households and high-status urban residences, where they worked as either domestics or skilled craftsmen. By contrast, in England, agricultural slavery existed alongside other forms of servitude, as social practice and Old English vocabulary both make clear. Elsewhere in the British Isles and in Scandinavia, slavery formed the main source of unfree labour, its supply replenished by raiding and purchase. It persisted until northern French conquerors took their own traditions of agricultural exploitation and long-established moral strictures against the selling of humans to England after 1066, to Wales at the end of that century, and then finally to Ireland after 1169. The end of the slave trade points to a practical difference between early medieval serfs and slaves: although both could be put to work in the fields, the former generally remained tied to the particular estate on which they were born and were transferred with the land, whereas the latter could also be bought or sold in the marketplace, and made to work far from their place of birth.

Whether slaves or serfs, the unfree population entered lordly domination in various ways. As well as hinting at the harsh realities of subjection, these introduce us to some of the insecurities and uncertainties of life in the early Middle Ages. Many were subjected to a lord from birth, simply because their parents had been: from a lord's point of view, the distinction between freedom and servitude mattered most when, as commonly happened, sexual relationships or marriage across the legal gulf produced offspring whose status had to be decided. From a lord's perspective, the issue was to maintain control of the workforce. Some individuals lost their freedom as the penalty for a crime for which they were unable to scrape together the compensation owed; we have encountered others who gave themselves into servitude when desperate hardship and starvation made enslavement an acceptable price for a little grain and perhaps even some protection.[6] Being on the losing side in a war could result in capture and enslavement, and, indeed, around the periphery of Christian Europe, warfare and slave raiding were inseparable. 'I captured that slave beyond the border where the duke led the army': this declaration was adequate proof of ownership in eighth-century Bavaria.[7]

An individual could move back and forth between freedom and servitude, sometimes more than once in a lifetime. The altered status would touch future generations too, as this poignant text from northern England in the late tenth century bears testimony: 'Geatfleda has given freedom for the love of God and the sake of her soul [to] Ecceard the smith, Ælstan and his wife and all their children born and unborn, and to Arkil, Cole, Ecferth [and] Aldhun's daughter and all the people whose head she took for their food in those evil days.'[8] These starving men and women had stooped down, placing their heads between Geatfleda's hands to symbolize their subjection to her lordship: in return, she fed them. Later, she freed them in another, equally symbolic, ceremony at the altar of Durham cathedral.

Practised throughout Christian Europe and encouraged by the clergy as an act of piety, manumission was probably the most common way in which an individual's legal status was altered. Emancipation was nevertheless an act of lordship that, in religious terms, benefited the lord whose initiative it was. In legal terms, it removed several disabilities endured by the unfree person. On the Continent, Roman documentary forms were widely available, and the newly freed, clutching their charters, might be referred to as a 'charter-people'. In the British Isles, by contrast, records of manumission were commonly entered into Gospel books, and divine sanctions invoked to uphold them. This is what the four sons of Bleddri did in the early ninth century when they granted freedom 'in per-petuity' to Bleiddudd ap Sulien and his offspring. In the margins of an old Gospel book kept in the church of St Teilo at Llandeilo Fawr in Wales, they declared: 'Let he who keeps this grant of liberty to Bleiddudd and his sons be blessed. But let he who does not keep it be cursed by God and St Teilo, in whose Gospel this is written.'[9]

On other occasions, free status came not from lords but from servile peasants' own actions. Reports of uprisings are rare in the extreme, but references to the flight of individuals are much more common. Sometimes a local church provided sanctuary—and, in these instances, flight was probably a prelude to renegotiation with one's lord. On other occasions, a nearby frontier provided an opportunity, and pacts regulating boundaries between kingdoms sometimes made explicit provision for the return of fugitives. In addition, anyone who aided and abetted the fleeing man or woman was liable to harsh penalties. Since freedom of movement was itself one of the marks of the free person, successful removal to a new region might transform an individual's status. Less commonly, an enter-prising lord in a sparsely inhabited region would offer freedom to all those coming to settle there: thus, in 880, Wifred, count of Cerdanya, offered freedom to all slaves or serfs who could escape their masters to settle south of the Pyrenees in the frontier district of Cardona.

To win freedom was worth one's life savings or the perils of flight. To defend it might be worth slaying an unfree relative who might disprove one's status: Charlemagne prescribed the death penalty for anyone who went to such lengths, and for good measure ordered that any free relatives would fall into servitude too. But freedom could be defended by litig-ation, especially since one of its privileges was access to royal law courts. It also conferred the right to carry weapons. Freedom was not all advant-ages, however. It is as likely to have brought greater insecurity as any im-provement in living conditions, for, in times of dearth, the independent, free peasant had little chance of handouts from a lord's granary. So peas-ants who acquired their legal freedom often renegotiated another form of subordination in return for their lord's continued protection. The legal advantages and economic disadvantages of freedom were finely balanced, since the distinction between freedom and servitude was slight by some criteria but substantial by others, rendering the social barrier between the two conditions permeable.

In principle, gaining freedom lessened the risk of being subjected to the violence that accompanied subordination. While laws often stipulate mutilations, floggings, and even capital sentences for serfs or slaves caught stealing, damaging property, or breaching the peace, the equivalent pun-ishments for freemen involved monetary compensation, although, in the event that they were unable to meet it, they were liable to be reduced to servitude. Beyond the remote world of legal prescription, however, lay a more immediate culture of customary violence. Occasionally, law codes themselves refer to it, such as this Bavarian provision: 'If a slavewoman is maimed by any person in a way that causes her to lose the child she is carrying, if it had not yet quickened, let him pay four *solidi* in compens-ation. If, however, it had already quickened, let him pay ten *solidi*.'[10] More commonly, however, the fulminations of Christian moralists alert us to its ubiquity. Only human society creates inequalities between persons, who are all alike at the moment of birth, Jonas, bishop of Orleans (818–43), re-minded Count Matfrid in about 820. 'Lords who are roused by their slaves' mistakes to violent indignation and tremendous fury and who either beat them with savage blows or mutilate them by cutting off their limbs' should not be mistaken into thinking they could get away with it—but should remember that there is only one God in heaven.[11] Such masters were un-likely to have cared much about the niceties of legal distinction between an unfree serf and one whom he had freed but who remained in his dependency. Precisions of legal status can have meant little when living in extreme subjection meant living under the shadow of violence and, for women, of sexual exploitation too.

In an effort to mitigate the more brutal realities of a hierarchical world, late antique churchmen had preached the ethics of responsible power, linking it to hopes of Christian salvation for the elite. One aspect of this was emphasis on the redemptive effect of charitable giving. Bertechildis was the wife of a notable at Bingen on the Rhine, who lived at an un-known point in the sixth or seventh century. She had absorbed this ethos, and when she died aged 20, only one year into her marriage, an inscrip-tion was placed over her grave. It commemorated her pious generosity: 'loved by the people, she gave alms to the widows, orphans and the poor, for the sake of her own sins.'[12] Such direct testimony to lay almsgiving is rare, but it reveals what we know to have been common: a perspective that attributed to the poor a role in assisting the salvation of the wealthy. By accepting alms, the poor helped tilt the economy of salvation in favour of the rich.

Early medieval bishops and moralists continued to take for granted the existence of the *pauperes*, 'the poor', meaning not only widows, orphans, and the impecunious, but all those who were vulnerable to exploitation by the powerful and who lacked the resources of lordship with which to defend their own interests. From the ninth century onwards, they broadened the responsibilities towards the poor that they urged upon the *potentes*, the powerful. The latter could not eliminate social inequalities, but they could protect the poor; buy peasants' wine and grain at fair prices and without rigging the measures; and give alms to the destitute—and, in so doing, save their own souls.

The distinction between servitude and freedom, then, had social and moral dimensions that were at least as important as any juridical difference or economic reality. Firm in legal theory, but highly permeable in social practice, the one implied the possibility of the other. Lordship lay at the heart of the relationship, for servitude presupposes domination, and subjection was not restricted to those who were legally unfree. All early medieval moralists accepted the gulf between the powerful and the poor. They simply urged that each fulfil their allotted role and respect the rights of each rank. In an ideal world, the unfree would labour to support the free, and the lords would protect and defend everyone:

> For no free man can live without the unfree.
> When there's a job that they really want to see done,
> The king and bishops seem to serve their serfs.
> The lord is nourished by the serfs whom he should nourish.

In a Christian moral economy, lordship rested upon a careful use of power, for it brought social responsibilities as well as rights, privileges, and wealth. But Adalbero, the elderly bishop of Laon (977–c.1031), who penned these lines in the early eleventh century, also knew better. He immediately added:

> The groans and tears of the unfree have no end.[13]

The ploughman who dared not linger at home in the midwinter cold would have agreed, and since, in an agricultural economy, lordship depended on the exploitation of land, we now turn to that.

## Peasants and Lords

How then were social relationships organized around the need to produce an agricultural surplus? In practical terms, how did peasant labour uphold lords' position? What were the social and economic realities of lordship? A remark of the fourth-century writer Palladius that 'there cannot be one way of organizing the work when there are so many different types of land'[14] offers a helpful starting point. Palladius explained this heterogeneity in terms of different soils and climates; we should add that practices varied from small to large estates, and that they changed over time too. Late antique and early medieval landholding was characterized by a profusion of regional and local realities that we should keep in mind at all times.

One of those diversities was scale. Small-scale landowning was widespread but very unevenly distributed, mostly visible in the documentation only at the moment when ecclesiastical institutions took control of some or all of smallholders' property. Large-scale landowning was possible only within large polities, and the context of Palladius's observation was the huge size of late Roman elite landownership. Some members of the senatorial aristocracy of the western half of the empire had owned huge scatters of properties throughout the Mediterranean in the early fifth century, but the growing insecurity and the gradual collapse of unified Roman rule in the western empire in the course of that century eroded their landed fortunes: the establishment of the post-imperial kingdoms was accompanied by a shrinkage in the scale of property ownership.

The ending of Roman rule in the West had additional repercussions. In late Antiquity, the landed urban oligarchy of each region (the *curiales*) had been responsible for collecting taxes from proprietors of modest estates and independent smallholders, and passing their payments on to the state. Their intermediary role enabled them to extend their influence through extortion, threats, or false generosity. This is how Caesarius of Arles described what happened in early sixth-century Provence:

If [the rich man's] neighbor is a poor man who has been put in the position of having to sell or who can be pressured and forced into selling, his eye turns in that direction, and he hopes that he can take away either the estate or the tenant farm of his poor neighbor. He therefore inflicts troubles on him. For example, he secretly convinces those in power to have tax collectors entangle him or to appoint him to some ruinous public office. . . . Driven by necessity, [the poor man] goes to the rich man through whose wickedness he is being oppressed and afflicted, and ignorant of the fact that he is suffering because of his actions, says to him: 'I ask you lord to give me a few *solidi*, for I am in need; I am beset by creditors.'

Having tried to raise a loan, the poor man is finally forced to sell up. 'The rich man says that he will help his so-called friend', and buys the poor man out for far less than the true value of his land.[15]

As influential landowners interposed themselves between local men and the state, both peasant freeholders and small proprietors found their independence eroded. Their payments evolved into customary dues, and, on this basis, large landowners could gradually pull them into more tightly defined and subordinated positions of dependency. The transition from small freeholder to dependent peasant was rarely reversible; great estates expanded everywhere between the sixth and eleventh centuries, and small men lost out.

The process was hastened in another way. Insecurity in the fifth and sixth centuries blurred the difference between the parallel civilian and military professional cadres of the fourth century. Standing garrisons gave way to peasant militias, landowners began to offer armed protection to their tenants in times of invasion and insecurity—or to run protection rackets themselves. To ensure their own position, landlords became war-lords. And, following the precedent of the settlement of a Gothic war-band in Aquitaine in 418 (Figure 0.2), several armies originating north of the imperial frontiers were relocated under their own leaders in the coun-tryside of western Roman provinces, perhaps initially only drawing a por-tion of the tax revenue generated by rural estates, but sooner or later developing into a landowning military elite. This further enhanced the control of a lord over his dependants and neighbours. Thus the associ-ation between social elites and military leadership that characterized European society throughout the Middle Ages and beyond was cemented during the rapid changes that accompanied the disintegration of the Roman political order.

Relations between peasants and lords always implied a wider political environment. Military service, royal patronage, and, at times, additional financial levies had a direct effect on the leading men who had found their way into their rulers' entourage. Indirectly, peasants felt the impact, for the pressures of lordship trickled down to them in various ways. Shifting settlement patterns in north-western Europe in the seventh and eighth centuries are suggestive of tighter lordly control, probably coupled with demands for larger renders of produce and higher dues, and also enhanced artisanal production of specialist items. Peasants must have been adversely affected, although the details are elusive. By the late eighth century, lords were commonly demanding direct labour services as well, certainly in the Carolingian heartlands and possibly elsewhere. Although there was always pressure on peasants to produce more than sufficed for their own subsist-ence, so that the lord could profit from the surplus, trends in estate man-agement nevertheless varied, and, by the tenth and eleventh centuries, it seems that many lords preferred rents and payments in kind to direct labour services.

Beyond these generalities, we know frustratingly little about the details of secular landownership in the early Middle Ages, because no lay or royal collection of title deeds, charters, surveys, or estate memoranda has re-mained intact. Documents issued by the laity have generally survived only when they accompanied donations of property to churches. The archives that have endured are those of cathedrals and monasteries: as the following pages demonstrate, our fullest perspective on landownership and exploitation is thus an essentially ecclesiastical one. As we proceed, we can nevertheless keep an eye on relations between secular lords and their peasants.

Wherever the Christian religion was established, major churches had been acquiring land since the fourth century. Early phases are extremely hard to trace in any detail, in part because papyrus, the main late antique material for record keeping, is easily perishable. It is clear, however, that the rate of pious donation increased sharply from the early eighth century, as strategies for the disposition of familial resources shifted and the search for posthumous religious commemoration became more urgent. The spread of document-mindedness that accompanied this upsurge coincided with a switch to the highly durable medium of parchment in many parts of Christian Europe, and, as a result, both lay donation and ecclesiastical landholding become very much more easily visible from the eighth century onwards, especially on the Continent.

By the ninth century, approximately one-third of all cultivated land in the Carolingian Empire belonged to churches, although there was wide regional variation and not all these estates were retained in the long term. In England, on the eve of the Norman Conquest, the figure was similar— about one-quarter of all land. These imprecise, but nevertheless striking, figures have several implications that deserve attention.

First, as their landed wealth grew, churches became central to the economic organization of the landscape and its inhabitants. Regional specialization on ecclesiastical estates—in wine, salt, or wool, for example, and artisanal manufacture of cloth, pottery, and the like—gave a major impetus to regional and inter-regional trade. From the wealth that churches derived from their property, they also acquired ever-growing political clout. No study of lordship can afford to ignore this institutional dimension.

Secondly, whereas secular landed property was liable to be redivided, reallocated, and contested on the death of each owner, ecclesiastical estates commonly enjoyed enduring institutional ownership. To be sure, spasmodic and piecemeal rapacity by kings and local bigwigs caused losses, but, even so, a lord who was notorious for seizing the land of one church was often commemorated as a generous benefactor by a different one. A lesser form of attrition came through the tendency of tenancies to become hereditary; it took continual managerial vigilance and strong-mindedness to limit this form of quiet erosion. But nevertheless, ecclesiastical estates were on the whole islands of relative stability in a sea of tenurial fluidity. Supported by long institutional memory in the form of carefully stored archives of title deeds, church lands had a far greater permanency than early medieval secular estates.

Finally, because churches had developed into propertied institutions under imperial aegis, they functioned in accordance with late Roman property law. Wherever they went in the early Middle Ages, Christian missionaries took with them its presumptions of individual title in full ownership, forms of written documentation, and technical vocabulary. These often cut across traditional property relations, especially where rights over land were closely tied to membership of a kin group and were preserved in social memory by oral tradition. Everywhere from the mountainous hinterland of Rome itself to the rolling hills of Ireland, the Romanizing language of early medieval records frequently obscures tenurial practices considerably adapted to indigenous conventions.

For many reasons, then, relations between lords and dependent workers, whether slave, serf, or free, conform to no single pattern. Some customs were fairly widespread, but there was no norm, no paradigmatic system. Multiplicity, fluidity, and evolution were the hallmarks of early medieval landed estates, and we must recognize this. Since the spectrum of practices does not lend itself to summary presentation or representative examples, there follows a single case study chosen to illustrate this diversity.

The area in question is northern Flanders, and is shown in detail in Figure 5.2. Just within the former Roman border, it straddled the early medieval (and modern) linguistic frontier zone between Germanic speech and *lingua romana*. For the moment, our concern is with a religious community founded between 629 and 639, and dedicated to St Peter. Its site was the hill called *Blandinium*, overlooking the old Roman settlement of Ghent at the confluence of the rivers Scheldt and Leie, and close to the

-------------------------------------------------------------→

5.2. Landowners in ninth-century Flanders. This map indicates the intermingling of the estates of Ghent's two abbey's, St Peter's and St Bavo's, along the rivers Leie and Scheldt. St Peter's, in particular, attracted many small donations here, consisting of tiny fields interspersed with meadows and, on the slightly higher ground, woodland. By contrast, the large estates of southern and western Flanders included extensive areas devoted to grain growing. Sheep pasturage in the coastal salt marshes was eagerly acquired by all monasteries, including more distant ones such as St Amand and Lobbes. In addition to Eberhard and Gisela, many other lay persons doubtless owned land in the region, but this is much harder to document.

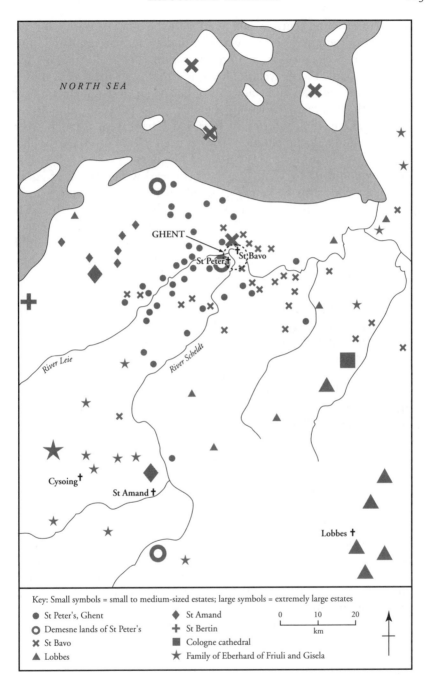

Key: Small symbols = small to medium-sized estates; large symbols = extremely large estates

● St Peter's, Ghent
○ Demesne lands of St Peter's
✖ St Bavo
▲ Lobbes

◆ St Amand
✚ St Bertin
■ Cologne cathedral
★ Family of Eberhard of Friuli and Gisela

0    10    20
km

spot where a trading centre would develop by the ninth century. Like most monasteries, it enjoyed periods when its endowment accumulated, interspersed with periods of stagnation or erosion. These fluctuations were commonly coupled with cycles of 'reform'—that is, of the overhaul of ecclesiastical observances and standards of behaviour of its inhabitants conducted with an eye to widening the difference between religious and secular life. Over the centuries, St Peter's at Ghent went through several of these; from the documentation that has been left we can trace the shifting patterns of lordship in this corner of Flanders.

Initially endowed by King Dagobert (623–39) with a block of land in its immediate vicinity, St Peter's gradually acquired other estates further up the Scheldt and the Leie, and among the forests to the north and the coastal salt marshes beyond. As Figure 5.2 indicates, its lands were modest, and almost all lay within 30 kilometres of the abbey church—unlike many other monasteries, whose possessions were much more widely scattered. Later Merovingian kings seem not to have maintained interest in the new church. By the eighth century, as rival magnate power brokers contested for control over northern Gaul, St Peter's tried but failed to remain neutral. Inevitably, perhaps, it became sucked into the patronage of one of them, but seems to have lost lands in consequence.

Royal control was reasserted in the reign of Charlemagne. For St Peter's, Ghent, as for many other monasteries and cathedrals, Carolingian lordship brought immediate access to the royal court in any lawsuits. Further, within its own lands, the abbot substituted for local imperial administrative and judicial officials: in effect, he became the king's agent here. By the same token, Carolingian control meant vulnerability and obligation, as became evident when Louis the Pious appointed a new abbot in 815, whose task was to 'reform' the community. This was Einhard, loyal courtier, famous biographer of Charlemagne, and layman. He represented royal lordship within the very confines of the community, and was the channel through which the emperor tapped into the monastery's wealth. Administering some of its landed estates for personal or imperial advantage, Einhard nevertheless set aside specified lands for the upkeep of the twenty-four clerics who resided in St Peter's. He carefully registered their share, and associated documentation reveals how this particular ecclesiastical community organized and exploited its lands.

Although Einhard or one of his ninth-century successors as abbot assigned to the brothers a farm nearly 50 kilometres to the south, most of their land lay adjacent to the abbey itself, a modest unit comprising arable, hay meadows, a wood where pigs were kept, and part of a tiny vineyard. Associated with this were outlying sheep pastures in the coastal salt marshes. All this was called the *terra indominicata*, the demesne, meaning that it would be cultivated directly for the profit of its lord, in this case the community of St Peter's. The clerics also had assigned to them a larger block of land, adjacent to their demesne, which had formed part of the original seventh-century endowment. How it had been organized then remains unknown, but it is clear that by the early ninth century the tenurial arrangements had evolved considerably. By then, it was subdivided into units each cultivated by a dependent worker who had specified obligations to fulfil.

Let us look at one particular dependent, Folcric, who held one unit of land, one *mansus*. Each year he owed the abbey specified quantities of bread, beer, pigs, wood, roofing shingles, flax, eggs, and grain. In addition, every third year he paid two *solidi* (= 24 pennies) at harvest time instead of contributing his own labour to the demesne, on one of the intervening years he paid another two *solidi* towards meeting the abbey's military expenses, and in the other year he had no cash payments to make, only a shirt to stitch. Since we know neither the size of Folcric's *mansus*, nor whether he had a wife and children to help him, we cannot estimate the severity of these obligations, nor calculate how much produce would have been left to feed himself and any family. But we can be sure that bailiffs would have ensured that the brothers received a steady supply of bread, beer, and other produce; and that their managerial tactics would include graft, extortion, and flogging.

Folcric's daily routine must have been bounded by the fields he tilled, the woods he visited to chop and cart wood, and the flax he harvested for (presumably) his wife to make into linen cloth and then clothes, but he was nevertheless part of a much larger and more complex economy. His predecessors in the days of Charlemagne had possibly been subjected to labour services on the demesne, but, if so, these had been converted into a cash payment by Folcric's time. In the late eighth and ninth centuries, dependent peasants frequently owed labour services (of varying onerousness) on an estate's demesne, thus integrating the different parts of an estate, but this was far from universal. Landlords might substitute demands for cash in a move to exploit their lands more effectively and to provide a more flexible income. But they could do so only when peasants had access to a market where they might exchange small quantities of surplus produce for silver pennies. Living so close to the growing market centre of Ghent itself, St Peter's dependants evidently had no difficulty with this, especially after the establishment of a royal mint there after 840.

Beyond Folcric's fields, the local market, and the control over his life exercised by the abbey, royal power made itself felt. In paying two *solidi* every three years towards St Peter's military commitments, Folcric contributed to the cost of the Frankish army. Although details of the ways in which troops were levied in the ninth century remain controversial, great ecclesiastical landowners and secular aristocrats alike had to provide contingents. The core of each group was probably the landowner (or, in the case of a church, its lay representative), with his retinue of heavily armed, mounted followers. The impact of military obligation can be glimpsed at St Peter's. The fifty cartloads of hay produced each year by the demesne meadow would have sustained horses through the winter, as would the oats grown on part of the demesne. Some of the timber received from tenants may have been directed to the upkeep of the coastal defence fleet that had been built at Ghent in 810. And did the abbot pool the small sums the abbey's many dependants each paid and use the proceeds to buy in the equipment, pack animals, and warhorses needed to send heavily armed, mounted warriors off to the army? Or had he contracted to pay a regular lump sum into royal coffers in lieu of actually sending troops? From Folcric's point of view, it can have mattered little: he simply had to pay up. In this and other ways, the abbey's lordship mediated between himself and the ruler.

Some twenty-four other dependants each held a *mansus* on identical or similar terms to Folcric. During and after Einhard's abbacy, St Peter's acquired further plots of land for the clerics' own use that were organized on the same basis of demesne with dependent tenancies. The records of these gifts indicate that along with the land came its workforce, and that the peasants passed from the lordship of the donor to the beneficiary. These men and women can only be described as servile. Their children came with them, and inherited their status. By the end of the ninth century, the marks of their extreme subordination to the abbey were even clearer: in addition to their annual obligations, they had to make a payment when they married, and another upon their death. St Peter's domination thus had three chief qualities: it was patriarchal in that it touched all members of the monastic *familia*; patrimonial in that it was exercised over the entire monastic landed endowment; and obligatory in that it could not be avoided. Whether the lord was a church, a secular lord, or a king, these were the three main characteristics of all early medieval lordship.

Other men and women stood in quite different relationships to St Peter's. The demesne lands were farmed by twenty-nine unmarried people—young men and women and a few milkmaids to whom no individual plots of land had been assigned, and who must have been housed in the abbey's outbuildings. Whether we choose to call them serfs or slaves does not affect their position of total dependency. At the other end of the spectrum, some people enjoyed much looser and more honourable relationships with the abbey. Several 'free men' owed only substantial cash payments accompanied by limited dues in kind, usually of beer. They may have held tenancies on a basis whose details elude us. Or they may have been small freehold proprietors on land that had once been under loose subordination to the king but who now paid their customary dues to the abbey instead. Ecclesiastical lordship sat fairly lightly on these men, but St Peter's nevertheless asserted rights over their land and its profits.

Different again were the relationships between the clergy and some recent donors. Nordbert was one such: he had purchased an estate that he gave to St Peter's. But then in 830 he arranged with Einhard to continue to occupy and profit from the land, in return for the nominal annual sum of twopence in recognition of the abbey's lordship. Only on his death would the clergy acquire direct control: until that moment, Nordbert and the clergy had overlapping rights over the estate. Such an arrangement was made to the church's advantage, or benefit, and the land in question commonly designated a 'benefice'. Those advantages would have been social and political rather than economic. Did Nordbert act as Abbot Einhard's armed escort or fight in St Peter's detachment of troops? Did he use his influence in local affairs to protect and foster the abbey's interests? Might Einhard have used his position to help Nordbert? We shall see in the next chapter that he did that for others of his personal followers. These speculations simply reflect what we know of similar benefices elsewhere in the ninth century, but they also remind us that lordship could be about personal loyalty and political service as well as about managing land. It consisted of a spectrum running from economic exploitation through social links to political patronage.

Thus the relations between the community of St Peter's, Ghent, and its dependants fit no single, simple pattern. There were many ways of organizing the land and its workforce. A shrewd abbot such as Einhard was flexible, balancing local custom with a drive for efficiency. The natural resources available provided one set of opportunities and constraints, the accessibility—or remoteness—of markets another. It suited the abbey to impose heavy renders and obligations on some men and women, much lighter ones on others. The effective lord responded to changing circumstances, whether economic, demographic, or political; individually and collectively, lords' decisions helped shape a changing society.

How did the lands of St Peter's fit into the pattern of landowning in northern Flanders as a whole? There were other major landowners in the vicinity, notably the much richer abbey of St Bavo located at Ghent itself, whose lands up and down the Scheldt and Leie intermingled with those of St Peter's. For the most part, however, small-scale proprietors dominated the locality, each man or woman owning a few small fields that they worked with the assistance of a couple of dependants, or at most five or six. Fragmented landholdings were the rule: wealthier owners held their properties scattered in several locations. The overall effect was a patchwork of tiny fields and meadows cut out of the woodland, with water meadows along the rivers. And, as these peasant proprietors made their small donations to St Peter's, so the abbey's acquisition of a field here and a field there contributed another element to the changing landscape.

The valleys of the Leie and Scheldt were ideally suited for growing flax, and were notable for their very heavy concentration of linen production. Elsewhere in Flanders, the natural environment and its modes of exploitation differed, as Figure 5.2 makes clear. To the north, in the coastal salt marshes and peat bogs and on the islands in the Scheldt estuary, St Bavo's owned estates each large enough to support upwards of 1,000 sheep. Perhaps, like the monasteries with sheep-ranching interests further up the coast in Frisia, they made few demands on the peasants here, except for annual renders of finished cloth, for pastoral economies generally encouraged very different forms of lordship.

To the north-east, as well as to the south up the Scheldt around Tournai, lay some of the lands that Eberhard and Gisela would distribute in their will.[16] These were large, intensively farmed agricultural estates, which in all probability had been royal land for centuries until assigned to Gisela as her dowry by her father, Louis the Pious. They followed a mixed agricultural regime, producing several types of grain but also raising cattle, large numbers of pigs, and some sheep, in addition to poultry—and even peacocks.

Also to the south-west, the abbey of St Bertin was another major landowner. In the gently undulating countryside of southern Flanders, St Bertin had huge cereal-growing estates whose tenurial arrangements had been systematized in the first half of the ninth century. This monastery's peasants had a more onerous relationship with their lord than those of St Peter's, Ghent. In addition to specified payments and renders, each holder of a *mansus* was required to work three days a week on the abbey's demesne if he was servile, two days a week if he was free. This was the most efficient way of farming large cornfields. If there had ever been farms belonging to independent peasant proprietors here, they had disappeared by the mid-ninth century, swallowed up by their powerful ecclesiastical neighbour.

We can let this corner of Flanders stand as a microcosm of early medieval rural society as a whole. It demonstrates the interplay of arable and pastoral economies: although they complemented each other throughout Europe as a whole, few regions were as intensively devoted to sheep raising as the Flemish and Frisian coast—or to grain as the cereal-growing estates that stretched southwards from Flanders to the Paris basin. Inter-regional trade redistributed their surpluses; elsewhere other specialist regional products, such as wine or salt, were also transported to markets considerable distances away. Flanders also reminds us of the economic importance of woodland—here for both timber and fodder for pigs. And, above all, it demonstrates the ways in which tenurial regimes adapted to different environments. In this particular region, the forms of control over dependent labour varied according to the differing requirements of animal husbandry and tillage; in Mediterranean Europe, the cultivation of vines and olives was characterized by other, more suitable forms of tenure and, in the next chapter, we shall encounter quite different ones again in the cattle country of Ireland.

Throughout Europe, lords exploited their local natural environment as best they knew, controlling peasants and other dependants by balancing local possibilities with their own changing priorities. But we should also remember that they responded to the wider political environment as well. Einhard's administration of St Peter's, Ghent, was characteristic of the heyday of the Carolingian Empire, when royal patronage was the dynamo that temporarily converted fluid regional networks of lordship into an exceptionally large polity. By the end of the ninth century, however, the Frankish polity was in crisis, the result of competition for power within the royal dynasty rapidly followed by the failure to produce male heirs. In the mid-ninth century there were too many kings' sons, each hopeful for a kingdom, but by the end of the century not enough to maintain existing subkingdoms. As the dynamo faltered, regional elites turned to different power brokers and reconfigured themselves into multiple, smaller polities.

Flanders was one of these, its counts related by marriage and common political interests to the last Carolingians, the tenth-century West Frankish kings. By the end of the ninth century, Ghent emerged as the central stronghold from which the counts ruled a nascent polity, basing their power in a new wooden castle there. Within its confines, they behaved as power brokers in exactly the same ways as the Carolingians had done within their empire, and managed to maintain an effective grip on the ebb and flow of patronage—of land, office, and honour—within their region until the twelfth century.

With that in mind, we can return to the clergy of St Peter's, the

secular landowners and peasantry of the vicinity, to see how the changing
political context affected relations between peasants and lords. Another
phase of 'reform' in the 940s has left a deposit of documentation that suggests not only losses of properties to be recovered, but also a rapidly changing world. St Peter's was now governed by Count Arnulf I (918–65) in his
capacity as patron and lay abbot, and Ghent was a rapidly developing
town. In 941, for example, Count Arnulf's benefactions to St Peter's included revenues from town houses and levies on cargo boats that passed
through the port. Outside the town, the landscape was changing too, as
lordship acquired a new, commercial, dimension. Mills were being built,
and sheep raised in vast numbers throughout Flanders: St Peter's profited
from both. As the tenth and eleventh centuries progressed, Arnulf's successors did much to encourage the clearance of woodland and the drain-
ing of the coastal floodplain.

We can deduce the implications for the Flemish peasantry. They found
themselves participating in a growing cash economy, for lords now preferred money payments to labour services or renders in kind. Mills meant
an end to the domestic grinding of corn and the release of peasant labour,
usually female, for other tasks. But they also meant the obligation to pay
for their use, an example of the spread of lordly 'customs' that created new
forms of subordination. Land clearance implied a growing population,
altered dealings with lords, and a degree of rural mobility. Other peasants
must have been leaving the countryside altogether, for the rapid growth
of Ghent and other Flemish towns can only have been the result of
immigration from the countryside, with all its dislocating effects. Those
that remained in the countryside will have been involved in producing
enough food to feed the townsfolk as well as their families and lords.
Finally, the emergence of an urban artisanal cloth industry introduced new
forms of labour and lordship.

In these various ways, Flemish peasants were touched by wider economic currents and by the changing lordship of St Peter's abbey and the
counts of Flanders. Though these developments were specific to the region around Ghent, peasants everywhere were caught up in and affected
by the spread of lordly 'customs' and the ever-shifting networks of political power among the elite. We cannot ignore the great diversity of these
customs by generalizing any more than this, for all lords, secular or
ecclesiastical, instituted their own preferred techniques of extracting surplus from the land to sustain their lordly position. That different routes
led to similar outcomes would not have surprised contemporaries. After
all, an early eleventh-century Anglo-Saxon writer on estate management

had echoed Palladius when, after summarizing the organization of a particular property, he continued: 'This estate-law exists on certain estates; at
some places, as I have said, it is heavier, at some places also lighter; for all
estate-customs are not alike. . . . He who looks after the administration is
to take care that he always knows what is the ancient arrangement of the
estate, and what the custom of the people.'[17] Local custom in a changing
world: this was the matrix within which peasants answered to lordly
domination.

## In Search of Status

'Tell me, in what do your riches lie?' the tenth-century moralist Rather of
Verona (d. 974) asked a fictional rich man in a literary dialogue. 'In my
possession of estates, male serfs and female slaves, horses, oxen and other
animals, in the obedience of my followers, in my delight in dogs and
hawks, in my abundance of clothes, fine tableware, grain, wine and oil, of
arms, silver, gold, jewels.'[18] Landed property, a servile workforce, a loyal
retinue, costly possessions, and ostentatious display: the rich man's reply
suggests the complexities of achieving high social status. He was asked
about riches, and answered by combining power over people and material
resources in just the way that was typical of lordship, as we have seen. He
alluded to the lifestyle he so enjoyed, one of hunting, feasting, personal
finery, and other forms of conspicuous consumption that set him apart
from others. Naturally, his words presume a hierarchical view of human
relationships, from the slave to the wealthiest, most powerful lord. This
section explores some implications of this self-perception for those at the
top of the early medieval social order.

Great diversity was also to be found at the upper end of the scale. Those
who were designated by a wide variety of terms that simply mean leading
men, bigwigs, the powerful, the best (*primores*, *potentes*, *optimates* in Latin;
there is an equivalent range of terms in Old English and other languages)
enjoyed the greatest possible cluster of liberties, but even so served a
princely, royal, or imperial lord. Lesser notables, well-to-do free men who
enjoyed privileges on a regional level, served them sometimes voluntarily,
sometimes under duress. In some places, tight hierarchies bound each
group tightly to those above and below, but, in others, the contacts, obligations, and forms of service were looser and lighter. Additionally, those
who served a lord renowned for territorial expansion had quite different
opportunities from those whose lord ruled a stable, or even shrinking

polity, for royal or princely patronage depended, in part, upon available resources.

Take four men whom we have encountered earlier, all alive in the 830s: Abba, Eberhard, Riwalt, and Nordbert.[19] Riwalt and Nordbert were both locally substantial men who nevertheless chose to enter into dealings with an important local church, Riwalt with Redon and Nordbert with St Peter's, Ghent. In Brittany, any superior lordship sat very lightly on local landowners such as Riwalt, but, as we have just seen, tightening obligations of lordship were affecting Flanders in Nordbert's day. Abba and Eberhard both served their king directly, the former as reeve of Kent, the latter as marquis of Friuli, but the scale of their landholding, wealth, and political influence bears no comparison. Powerful and wealthy though he was in Kentish terms, Abba was puny in contrast with Eberhard of Friuli. The latter's family ranked among the Carolingian super-elite, and this had enabled his father and himself to benefit from the Franks' territorial expansion under Charlemagne, resulting in landed possessions stretching from Flanders to Italy.

Other than ownership of land, there is little in common between these four elite men and their families, except the fact that they all used land to establish an association with churches—and that, indeed, is why we know about them. The diversity suggests we should look carefully into what additional markers of status there may have been in the early Middle Ages. We shall see that the vastly disparate resources and variable terminology reflected the social fluidity of the upper echelons, and the lack of any firm criteria for membership of the elite. In the absence of any precise prescription for gaining or losing high status, we have to search for it in various ways. So, as we shall see, did early medieval men.

In the first place, it was visible to others. Leovigild, king of the Iberian Goths (568–86), gave an estate near Merida to an abbot called Nanctus, to support his monastic following. Its inhabitants went to visit their new master, and were appalled: 'When they went and had seen him in his wretched clothes and with his hair uncut, they despised him and said to one another, "it would be better for us to die than serve such a master"'— so a few days later they killed him.[20] For Nanctus, lack of personal grooming was a sign of asceticism, but his workers were not prepared to serve a master who looked like an abject slave, however holy he might be. A master had to look the part.

In addition to appearance, deportment and speech also conveyed high rank, as the seventh-century Northumbrian Imma found out. Taken prisoner in battle by the Mercians in 679, he pretended that he was not a king's retainer but only a poor peasant. His captors kept a close eye on him and, after a while, 'realized by his appearance, his bearing, and his speech that he was not of common stock as he had said, but of noble family'.[21] Evidently, attendance at the royal court promoted elegant manners and refined speech as well as the dress code that set the elite apart from peasants.

Courtliness fostered a distinct appearance in other ways too. By the time of Charlemagne at the latest, the royal entourage dressed with an eye to fashionable display, investing in costly silks and furs, together with jewelled, gilded weapons for the men and brooches, armbands, girdles, and necklaces for the women. Louis the Pious had to persuade his bishops and abbots—almost all of them men of high birth—not to dress like secular nobles. He urged them to give up 'the ornaments of secular glory'— namely, 'belts weighed down with golden sword-mountings and jewelled daggers, exquisite clothing and footwear decorated with spurs'.[22] These were exactly the prestigious items that Eberhard of Friuli bequeathed to his children and that, as we shall see in the next chapter, were used to cement bonds of patronage and favour. All signalled elite status, but sword belts had a special significance, for, jewelled or plain, they were badges of office as well. And this form of courtliness was catching: the trend that began at the Carolingian imperial court developed still further at the Ottonian court, and both set a fashion for luxurious high-status apparel that others emulated elsewhere. By the late tenth century at the latest, Anglo-Saxon kings and queens together with the nobles and their wives were following suit, dressing in patterned silks with ample gold embroidery overlaid with jewellery and heavy furs.

Attention to display extended to fine mounts and their harnesses, decked out with 'decorated medallions'.[23] Only the 'most renowned horses', plump, strong, and 'praiseworthy in every aspect', would do for Pope Hadrian I (772–95) to ride in processions.[24] And when (between 1036 and 1038) the 50-year-old Boniface of Canossa journeyed across the Alps to collect Beatrix, his bride of about 18, he shod his horses in silver. He deliberately attached the shoes so loosely that they were shed en route for the local populace to gather up: 'this way the people might find out who he was.'[25] No opportunity was lost to make status obvious.

Fine food was another aspect of elite lifestyle, as we saw earlier.[26] In addition to game and the succulent meats of domesticated animals reared especially for slaughter, a well-stocked table had fish from the sea, such as porpoise and herring, and dishes prepared with imported spices. It had all these in great abundance: to judge by preachers' complaints, bigwigs liked to eat and drink to excess. Despite this, food intake could, in principle, mark out graduations of status, for, when Louis the Pious specified the rations for his representatives going about imperial business, he stipulated precisely 'how much should be given to each according to his rank', whether bishop, abbot, count, or retainer.[27]

Membership of the elite also implied social distance. One expression of that was a personal retinue of armed men, domestic officials, and hangers-on. Another might be a defended residence, such as the tenth-to eleventh-century Anglo-Saxon hall at Goltho, where the main hall, outbuildings, and courtyard were enclosed by an earthwork rampart and ditch. It also demanded deference and the avoidance of threatening gestures. 'Servants are accustomed to hand knives to their masters [holding them] by the tip of the blade.'[28] Careful tactics might reinforce hierarchy: Tagino, archbishop of Magdeburg (1004–12), simply preferred 'nobility of lineage and manner' and declined to admit the low-born into his company.[29] Social climbers set out to erode that distance, however, for to emulate nobility was to court the deference due to it. Thus estate stewards of the monastery of St Gall 'learned to blow their horns in a way that made a different sound from the other peasants' and started carrying polished weapons and going hunting with dogs—at first just hares, but then even wolves, bears, and boars. '"The cellarers can look after the fields and meadows," they said. "We must look to our own advantages and indulge in hunting, as befits real men."'[30]

Elite status, then, implied a lifestyle and mores characterized by personal display and conspicuous expenditure. An eighth-century Irish treatise, surely over-systematizing but nevertheless true to its spirit, sums this up. The man who had twenty-seven clients in his retinue, a house 29-foot long with a 19-foot outhouse, lavish furnishing including eight beds and couches with cushions and rugs, a cauldron in his kitchen large enough to stew an entire ox, twelve gilded bridles and hunting dogs, and whose wife had a pet lap-dog, was a 'noble of the first rank'.[31]

In these terms, the fictional rich man with whom we opened had a good claim to be regarded as elite. He had the necessary wealth, lifestyle, and retinue. But were great riches and appropriate behaviour sufficient? Not necessarily. What defined the elite in early medieval perception was being 'noble'. An early eleventh-century Anglo-Saxon treatise on status acknowledged that, 'if a trader prospered, that he crossed thrice the open sea at his own expense, he was then afterwards entitled to the rights of a thegn [i.e. in Anglo-Saxon terms, a noble: see below]'.[32] Maybe some early medieval merchants did manage to ease themselves into the ranks of the thegns, but we have no evidence to prove it. What we do have, however, are many indications that more was involved in being noble than just luxuriating in wealth, as the rich man did.

'Noble' was yet another flexible term. It often described a person's high rank and position of power and privilege, but it could also refer to distinguished, upright conduct within the religious and social expectations of the day. One or both of these meanings might be intended in any particular context: they shared the implication of being notable and well known. While the rich man had a claim to be noble in the former sense, not all his peers would necessarily have regarded him in this light. There is a fundamental reason for that: despite its key place in medieval and early modern European social hierarchies, 'nobility' was not, in the early Middle Ages, a rank defined by objective, agreed criteria.

Rather, it was a quality. Conduct often mattered, as the word 'noble' itself suggested. But, in addition, ancestry counted, for two reasons. In the first place, there was a strong presumption of inherited status: knowledge of a person's parentage confirmed his or her nobility. A woman, in particular, inherited her father's rank, and was often the custodian of familial genealogical details. Secondly, except perhaps for the occasional merchant who made good, the main way of acquiring the resources necessary to support a noble lifestyle was inheritance. Since only nobles had the opportunity to assemble or inherit resources on anything more than a very modest scale, the possession of wealth did not automatically ennoble. Rather, it confirmed it. Conduct, ancestry, wealth: all contributed towards being hailed as noble.

Consider Gerald, count of Aurillac, whose celebrity as a holy man stemmed, in part, from his refusal to indulge in the ostentatious lifestyle of his noble peers. He was, nevertheless, of true blue blood: 'he was so illustrious by the nobility of his birth, that among the families of Gaul his lineage is outstanding both for its possessions and the excellence of its life. . . . And indeed the great quantity of estates endowed with serfs, lying in various places, which came to Gerald by right of succession, testifies to the extent of [his ancestors'] riches.' 'Excellence of life' in the form of 'modesty and religion' also ran in the family.[33] Gerald took nobility of living to new extremes, however. In general, nobles were expected to behave in the ways that brought honour to themselves, their family, and their lord: courage and martial prowess for lay men, sexual modesty and careful household management for women.[34] By shunning vengeance and the force of arms, and keeping himself quite chaste, the count of Aurillac simply stood traditional paradigms of gendered conduct on their head. Gerald, then, had all the tokens of nobility: ancestry, great landed estates, and that other, elusive, criterion—distinguished conduct, albeit of a rather odd sort. He was so noble, his biographer implied, that he did not need to confirm the fact by flaunting his wealth.

There remains one important additional avenue to nobility or its enhancement to consider: royal service. It is not by accident that many of the words that came to denote high rank originally meant a servant or domestic retainer: this is the root meaning of 'thegn', 'thane' (the main elite rank in Anglo-Saxon England and Scotland respectively), 'knight' (Old English *cniht*), and 'vassal' (Old French *vassallus*). At the very least, since that service was often military, the death in battle of one man might open the way for the rise of another at court; conversely, distinction in battle might bring reward, patronage, and higher social esteem. Service might also be more peaceable, in the secular and ecclesiastical administrative positions of great responsibility that supported the monarchies and empires of the early Middle Ages. And its rewards—prestige, influence, landed estates, even a royal bride—could be great indeed, as Eberhard of Friuli appreciated.

Access to these posts created a group of insiders, those who enjoyed and could exploit their closeness to the king for their personal and familial advantage. Further, while noble ancestry conveyed noble rank (or did so for so long as memory of that ancestry was cultivated and a noble lifestyle maintained), it need not be a prerequisite for access to high office. Liutward, bishop of Vercelli (880–900), exemplifies both these points. Of low birth, he rose through ability to hold the highest ecclesiastical positions in the court of Charles the Fat (876–87) and 'was honoured and feared by all more than the emperor'. He was also successful in promoting his family, and 'he carried off the daughters of the most noble men in Alemannia and Italy without opposition, and gave them to his relatives in marriage'.[35] Marriage to a woman of higher rank was an established means of social advancement, for women could transmit status as well as resources from one generation to another. We should remember, however, that privileges, wealth, and the power that arose from closeness to a ruler by no means always went together. Great noblemen often had obscure brothers, men of equally high birth and comparable wealth but of little political standing or influence.

Nor was royal confidence in a valued courtier necessarily matched by the trust of his peers. In the 570s, Leudast was count in Tours. He had acquired the position by winning the attention of King Charibert (561–7) and then his brother King Chilperic (561–84). The office brought responsibility for fiscal, military, and judicial administration on the king's behalf, and carried a presumption of nobility, but we only hear of Leudast through the eyes of his rival for influence in the town, Bishop Gregory. The latter asserted that Leudast was the son of a slave in a royal vineyard, who was put to work in the royal kitchens. As a scullion, Gregory alleged, Leudast had his ear mutilated for attempting to escape, but nevertheless managed to ingratiate himself at court, catching the eye of Charibert's queen, Marcofeva. Once appointed count, Leudast 'strutted around, bursting even more with prideful glory in his high office. He showed himself to be a rapacious plunderer, a brawling braggart, and a filthy adulterer. By sowing discord and fomenting malice, he amassed no small fortune.'[36] This may be a story of unusually successful upward social mobility; it was certainly Gregory of Tours's desperate attempt to vilify a dangerous political rival by denying him any nobility, despite his undoubted wealth, power, and royal favour. It was also the contest of a parvenu self-made through royal service with an aristocrat of ancient, inherited status often at odds with Leudast's royal patron.[37]

In the absence of any hard-and-fast criteria of nobility at any point in the early Middle Ages, tension between old and new blood probably characterized royal courts more often than not. After all, noble status was jealously guarded, to be defended against newcomers attempting to encroach upon it. 'The emperor made you a free man but not a noble, for that is impossible', was the accusation hurled by a ninth-century polemicist at a man whom he hated, an archbishop who coupled humble origins with loyal service towards his imperial patron, Louis the Pious.[38] The charge of humble origins could also be turned against those who were noble, but not of the right sort, as Hagano discovered in the early tenth century. He came from an important landed family in Lotharingia, a part of the East Frankish kingdom that the West Frankish king Charles the Simple (898–922) seized in 911, and rapidly won the trust of his new royal lord. In his native circles, Hagano would have undoubtedly been treated with all the respect due to someone known to be of distinguished nobility. But, at Charles the Simple's court, he encountered the rivalry of those with vested interests in the West Frankish networks of power, who resented the intrusion into their midst of an outsider—this 'man from the middling sort whom the king had made powerful'. The old elite complained to Charles about his habit of discussing royal affairs in private with Hagano, excluding his other—rightful—counsellors. They threatened to withdraw their own participation unless Charles dropped 'this man of obscure parentage [who] was doing immense damage to the king's dignity by giving him advice as if there were no nobles'.[39] Charles persisted in trusting Hagano—and, in 920, his critics finally rebelled and deposed the king shortly thereafter.

With these cases, we come to the crux of the matter. No distinguished conduct or pedigree, no amount of royal favour, wealth, social climbing, or power, could necessarily make a man noble in the eyes of his rivals. The essence of noble status was social acceptance by one's peers. No legal formula quantified the relative proportions of its constituent elements: in the absence of agreed, explicit status qualifications, nobility remained in the eye of the beholder. For that reason, it could be fragile, even evanescent. It encouraged the proclamation of pedigree through the reuse of ancestral names. It needed constant reaffirmation through conspicuous displays of wealth, influence, and appropriate conduct, and it needed defending against the risk of being upstaged by social climbers. Careful cultivation of friends and relations; a watchful eye for ways of enhancing honour; strategic marriage alliances for oneself and one's offspring; a reputation for generosity towards churches; careful disposition of the family patrimony; navigating the shifting sands of patronage and favour: all were means of advancing or, at least, of striving to contain the erosion of nobility.

That nobility was in large part a matter of social perception is crucial to one of the most important shifts to affect medieval elites: the emergence of knighthood. Although the roots of this gradual process are traceable in the ninth and tenth centuries, it was not complete until the twelfth, or in some places even the thirteenth century. There are three major strands to this, one ideological, one sociological, and one semantic. First, the warrior aristocracy of the Carolingian Empire embraced a specifically Christian ideology of martial values. Among the ninth-century nobility who fought on horseback, heavily armed, against the foes of Christendom, there developed a rhetoric that exalted and justified warfare. They delimited membership of this elite group by rituals of weapon giving, which were sometimes accompanied by religious ceremonies. Secondly, as tenth-century lords began to build castles and garrison them with armed followers, a group of free but non-noble men dedicated to warfare as a way of living became more prominent. These men were styled *milites*, meaning, in accordance with the word's classical usage, simply 'soldiers'. Thirdly, in a complex semantic shift that began in parts of France towards the end of the tenth century but can be traced elsewhere only rather later, the noble elite began to regard itself, and to be regarded by others, as *milites*. At the same time, the garrison *milites* began to claim noble status for themselves. From being a word of non-noble connotation, *miles* thus became a reputable status that nobles were keen to adopt. Only gradually did these three developments fuse to form the knightly cadre of the twelfth century and later. If knighthood was one of the most distinctive aspects of the high medieval nobility, then its roots lay in the functions, fluidities, and subjective perceptions of the early Middle Ages.

Thus, although the existence of elites of some sort was a social fact at all times, membership rested on no firmly defined criteria. Nor could it, for rulers did not distribute patronage and favour according to objective test, but rather followed the pressures of the moment—political need, loyalty, ability, and friendship. The most general statement that can be made is that nobility was relational, with respect to those both higher and lower in the social hierarchy. Those who claimed to be noble, and who were recognized by their peers as noble, ranged from individuals of comfortable but not extravagant means to those of vast landed fortunes. They comprised families whose nobility extended back for many generations, alongside those of a more recent vintage, for whom royal service provided the most common ladder of social mobility. Carefully chosen marriage partners and shrewd disposition of the family patrimony made women vital links in the transmission of ancestry, land, and claims to nobility from one generation to the next, within and between amorphous kinship networks. For many, though, the relationship that mattered most was with their ruler. Those not in a position to catch the king's eye directly might at least hope to find an opening in the retinue of one of his courtiers for themselves or their sons. And, as patronage and service pulled people towards the royal court, so fashions and tastes for luxurious living diffused outwards and downwards from it.

The search for status, then, required energy and effort as well as expenditure. It drew on inherited resources but also on the strengths of friendships, and it called for adroit political manœuvring, to protect reputation, enhance honour, win high office and landed reward. When Rather of Verona conjured up a rich man for his pastoral dialogue, he was not interested in his creation's political ambitions or successes, only in the fate that awaited the soul of one so greedy as he. Nothing, from Rather's point of view, was more precious. The search for earthly status, he implied, was fraught with spiritual risk.

Around the year 890, Alfred, king of Wessex, received a visitor, who brought him some fine walrus ivory. Ohthere lived in Norway, at the northernmost limit of settled agricultural activity. One summer, he extended his hunting expedition further even than the whale-hunters went, sailing right the way round the arctic coast of Scandinavia, as far as the White Sea, to find out whether anyone lived there. His gift of the very finest ivory came from those parts, uninhabited apart from the occasional camp of the *Finnas*, the Sami hunters and fishers of arctic Scandinavia.

Ohthere's detailed description of northern geography fascinated the West Saxons. They also questioned him about himself, and discovered that 'he was among the chief men of that country, but he had not more than twenty cattle, twenty sheep and twenty pigs, and the little that he ploughed he ploughed with horses'. Their surprise that such an important man had so little arable land and very modest flocks of domestic animals was tempered by the realization that Ohthere 'was a very rich man in those possessions which their riches consist of, that is in wild deer. . . . [which] they call reindeer'. The main source of the wealth of the men of that region, Ohthere reported, was the tribute of marten fur, reindeer hide, bearskin coats, sacks of feathers, whalebone, and rawhide ropes received from the Sami, each of whom paid 'according to his rank'.[40]

Neither herds of reindeer nor the personal dependencies of tribute-givers acknowledge precise territorial boundaries. That the wealth of reindeer barons such as Ohthere came more from herding and tribute taking than from agriculture reflected the scarcity of arable land, its poor quality, and the lack of tightly organized lordships so far north. Here was an economy that did not turn on the control of land, where the labour of the hunter rather than the ploughman upheld those of higher rank. There could not be a greater contrast to the agricultural economy of northern Flanders, with its highly regulated farming, demarcated plots of land, firm subordination to royal, comital, and ecclesiastical lordship, and its rapidly commercializing exchange. They form the extreme modes of labour and lordship in the early Middle Ages, but nevertheless share important features. Both were carefully organized to exploit the natural resources of the region, whether walrus tusk and bearskin or linen, oats, and wool. Both reveal local gradations of wealth and rank, which, although very different in absolute terms, manifested themselves in social and political inequalities on a regionally significant scale. Both contributed resources that kings and their retinues valued: rare furs; ivory for jewellery, delicate caskets, and precious book covers; oats for horses; timber for warships and castles. Both are suggestive of the varied ways in which powerful men and rulers obtained the resources that sustained their lordship, and what they did with those different resources once they had acquired them. The next chapter takes up these issues in more detail.

# 6

# Getting and Giving

There is a fine fortress on the promontory,
Graciously each one there receives his share.
. . . . . .

There is a fine fortress on a height,
Lavish its feasting, loud its revelry
Beautiful all round it, that fort of champions,
Is the flying spray: its wings are long![1]

Charlemagne liked foreigners, and took great care in welcoming
them, to the extent that their great number seemed, not unjustly, to
be burdensome not only to the palace but even to the kingdom.
But because of his magnanimous nature, Charlemagne was un-
troubled by burdens of this kind, since he was compensated for the
great inconvenience by praise for his generosity and the reward of a
good reputation.[2]

CHARLEMAGNE knew that a ruler needed a reputation for generosity.
His court, like that of Bleiddudd, lord of the Welsh 'fine fortress' of Tenby,
resounded with the sounds of feasting and revelry, part of the lavish
display and conspicuous consumption that successful rulership required.
According to one contemporary estimate, the daily consumption of Otto
I's court in 968 amounted to 'one thousand pigs and sheep, ten cartloads
of wine, another ten of beer, one thousand measures of grain, eight oxen,
in addition to vast quantities of chickens, piglets, fish, eggs, vegetables and
other foodstuffs'.[3] Even if an exaggerated report, it is suggestive of the
scale on which rulership needed to be resourced. Charlemagne's generosity (although not Bleiddudd's) must have been on a similar scale: that it
generated criticism is little surprise. The truly generous ruler could afford
to ignore complaints in the expectation of reaping political rewards from
his extravagant expenditure.

Displays of generous grandeur and maintenance of an elite lifestyle were but two of the uses to which lords and rulers might put their material resources. Endowing churches; rewarding followers; supporting the administration of a kingdom; conducting warfare; building residences, palaces, or castles; engaging in diplomacy; providing for relatives: all drained them. This chapter, then, explores ways of accumulating and distributing a wide range of forms of material assets. Taking its cue from Charlemagne's feasting of so many foreigners in order to enhance his reputation, its focus is the conversion of economic capital to symbolic capital—that is, of treasure, money, cattle, and agricultural produce into honour, political success, and divine approval.

The translation of the one into the other was fraught with difficulties. Land and its produce remained the predominant source of support for all early medieval elites, yet even kings remained constrained by the vagaries of bad weather and outbreaks of disease, for food shortages might make campaigning impossible or an outbreak of disease decimate an army. Income in the form of perishable foodstuffs could not be stored in treasure chests and required conversion into something more enduring. There were, of course, other sources of wealth, but they too were often unstable. Plunder could be won in battle, or lost. Indiscriminate generosity might exhaust both resources and reputation. Inheritance and marriage might bring enhanced wealth; providing for sons and daughters might drain it. Rulers might amass great treasure in the form of diplomatic gifts—but, by the same token, had to reciprocate generously in some way. Thus, although the attributes of a successful king included a well-filled treasure chest, and although his legitimacy rested, in part, on stewardship of precious ancestral heirlooms, we should not work with static images of gold hoards in mind. Rather, the translation of wealth into political power was a dynamic process of circulation and redistribution, of constant inflow and outflow. Kings hoarded in order to be able to disburse; they gave in order to get.

The conversion of material assets into social and political advantage tended to be concentrated at particular nodes. The first part of this chapter identifies the places where wealth and power tended to cluster, situates them within geographical networks, and comments on their relationship to the polities in which they lay. This section, then, explores ways of accumulating and distributing wealth within early medieval economies, and notes ways in which kings and others took advantage of them. It notes shifting patterns of commerce, and their relationship to other forms of exchange. The second part of the chapter shifts focus from places to people, from topographical to social networks. It addresses gift giving and

6.1. Principal places mentioned in Chapter 6.

patronage as strategies central to the ways in which early medieval lords and rulers used their resources to build and maintain their power. Finally, it argues that material wealth helped organize relationships between the human and the supernatural, and that its use offers insights into early medieval cosmologies.

## Landscapes of Power, Landscapes of Wealth

In hierarchically organized agricultural societies, material resources, political leadership, and supernatural power are as liable to be unequally distributed in geographical terms as they are in social terms. Mapping textual and archaeological evidence would reveal a complex landscape, in which economic, religious, and political functions clustered in some places, but other locations had fewer roles. Making several such mental sketch maps for the early Middle Ages is the task of this section. It reveals great changes: charting these landscapes is an effective way to explore the dynamic human geography of the early Middle Ages.

We must start in the ancient Mediterranean, where the Roman Empire knitted together a mosaic of cities and their dependent territories into a vast and remarkably enduring political and economic system. Any map of this would emphasize the dominance of urban communities as political, religious, and economic focal points. Closer inspection would reveal their importance as places where local and imperial interests intersected, overlapped, or competed. Agriculture, wars, tribute, and state-organized production and supply had generated the vast resources needed to sustain this empire. Indeed, so great were the demands of the Roman state that it had sucked in resources from far beyond its political frontiers, seeking minerals such as gold and iron, prestige goods such as spices or furs and human resources, whether slaves or soldiers, wherever available. Its internal economy was a command economy, activated by imperial requisitioning, with transport systems directed to provisioning the army's many units and feeding the teeming cities of Rome and Constantinople. The massive fourth- to fifth-century bureaucracy and army had strained resources to the limit, yet lavish imperial and aristocratic spending on refined civic architecture and ceremonials continued to enhance the urban environment and project the ideology of empire against this backdrop. In late Antiquity, cities remained the central points for the consumption and display of wealth and for political activity, most visibly in the Mediterranean. Above all, Rome itself concentrated material wealth and political influence in one place, a supremacy it maintained long after the foundation of a second imperial capital on the Bosphorus at Constantinople in 324. Even the removal of the fourth-century western court first to Trier, then Milan, and finally Ravenna in 408 did little to dent Rome's predominance as the outstanding theatre of power. Nor, immediately, did the lapse of the western imperial title after 476. Although in many cases their population and inhabited areas were diminishing, the cities rimming the Mediterranean nevertheless still formed by far the wealthiest zone in Europe in *c*.500. State-driven exchange still regularly shipped large quantities of grain, wine, and oil as well as luxury items from one end of the Mediterranean to the other, replenishing imperial granaries and sustaining urban magnificence.

Crumbling imperial control in the West changed all this. The ending of imperial rule entailed the gradual unravelling—and sometimes deliberate dismembering—of its huge military and bureaucratic regime, and of the system of exactions, taxes, and coinage that had sustained it. It also left the tradition of civic munificence and imperial monument building to decay, quickly in some places, more gradually in others. In this changed climate, cities in peripheral provinces struggled to survive at all; nearer to the Mediterranean, most persisted, albeit on a reduced scale. As warrior elites carved new polities out of Roman territory, they established themselves as rural landowners, but maintained a generally respectful attitude towards cities as theatres of power, even if those urban centres were now dilapidated, partially abandoned, and economically impoverished.

The overall consequences for the fifth, sixth, and seventh centuries can be sketched. Secular elites became ever more rural and more militarized; everywhere civic display, urban lifestyle, and civilian ideologies were at best severely compromised, and in much of the West (unlike the East) collapsed altogether. Only bishops and clerics continues to build in cities; under their aegis, the multiplication of churches changed the appearance and character of the urban environment. Meanwhile, systems of exchange that had formerly moved goods over long distances disintegrated. By the mid-seventh century even the Mediterranean economy had dissolved into local zones of more-or-less autonomous activity within which a reduced volume of goods circulated, connected only by erratic sailings from one port to the next. The separate Mediterranean micro-regions did not continue to function at the same level, and in the western Mediterranean basin, in particular, economic activity slumped to far lower levels than at the eastern end. This affected Rome too: by the eighth century, the shrunken city was fed from its immediate hinterland only, and civic display had given way to ecclesiastical munificence.

The end of the Roman state-driven economy was a gradual, erratic process, which cannot be precisely dated, but whose results are clear. Although political imperatives and the need for resources had led the empire to seek raw materials and rare items far beyond its borders, the military frontier had nevertheless been the clear limit of the Roman fiscal system and its monetized economy. The end of the tax state and the cessation of regular minting of coinage effectively blurred the distinction between economic systems within and beyond the border. Furthermore, there emerged not a new, unified economy but a series of overlapping local and regional economies. Except in Italy, their characteristics and nodes were more rural than urban and their coinages switched from gold to silver.

Although these changes took place over approximately the same period as the formation of post-imperial kingdoms, the new political and economic topographies by no means coincided. This was particularly evident in Gaul, where the kings of the Franks looked south to exploit the trade in the Mediterranean and where eastern items continued to flow northwards through the trading city of Marseilles until the seventh century, but they also turned their attention north, to the mouth of the Rhine and beyond. Here, the rapidly expanding Frisian population enjoyed a gold-rich society by the late sixth century and shared in the culture common to all the North Sea littorals: by the early seventh century, Frisia was the magnet that pulled the Franks ever more into the northern European arena. The Frankish kingdom thus straddled both the Mediterranean and the North Sea economic zones.

Around the North Sea, new patterns of communication and exchange integrated regions formerly transected by the Roman political frontier. Their outlines are clear by the early seventh century. From the mouth of the Seine to the base of the Jutland peninsula on the Continent and from the Solent to the Humber Basin in England, new coastal or estuarine centres of production and exchange developed, known as emporia or *wics*. Only flourishing in the seventh, eighth, and ninth centuries, these were waterfront centres of artisanal production and trade that funnelled goods from regional hinterlands overseas to other territories and kingdoms. In this way, basalt quern stones quarried in the Eifel hills north of Trier reached the Rhine delta, travelled northwards through the Danish peninsula into the western Baltic, and crossed the Channel to the south coast of England in a traffic unbounded by political frontiers.

By *c.*800, emporia were also to be found throughout southern Scandinavia and the Baltic, whose exports of amber, furs, and ivory were exchanged for shipments of woollen cloth, wine, pottery, ceramics, and arms. Even where they did lie within the territory of the former Roman Empire, their sites were not old Roman cities but rather a new type of focal point for the distribution of goods. They were undefended, and often only seasonally occupied, mostly by men unaccompanied by women or children. Characteristically, emporia were not in themselves centres of royal or aristocratic lordship, but usually were located in close and probably direct relationship with them, as on the Solent, where *Hamwih* lay just south of the West Saxon royal centre of Winchester (itself an old Roman city), or in Frisia, where *Dorestad* was located near to the late Merovingian ecclesiastical centre in the Roman fort at Utrecht.

And, as small silver coins began to be minted in some North Sea emporia from the 670s, kings took an interest, finding ways to tap into their wealth by taxing transactions, exploiting the possibilities of acquiring prestige items for themselves and of generating income by selling the surplus produce of their own estates. Royal interest and encouragement were matched by ecclesiastical pursuit of wealth and luxury, and the emergence everywhere of cathedrals and monasteries as centres of wealth as well as of political influence is a characteristic feature of the seventh and eighth centuries. Thus, for example, the late-eighth-century rulers of the land-locked Anglo-Saxon kingdom of Mercia imposed tolls on ships trading at *Lundenwic*, 'an emporium for many nations who come to it by land and sea' on the open riverside beach to the west of the old Roman city of London.[4] (London's *wic* is probably commemorated in the street name Aldwych.) Specifically exempted from these tolls were ships belonging to certain Kentish churches and to the bishops of London and Worcester. Although details of their trading activities are unknown, these churches, like the kings who privileged them with documents of exemption, found emporia central to the development of their own wealth and power. In this way, the interests of several different groups overlapped.

The intensification of long-distance exchange at points along the eastern coast of Britain coincided with its decline around the western coast. In late Antiquity, trade had linked the Mediterranean, via the Atlantic coast of Gaul, to Brittany and then to south-western Britain and the entire Irish Sea zone. Grain, wine, and oil travelled out, and ships returned with British tin, silver, and lead plus slaves and hunting dogs from Ireland. The link into the Mediterranean persisted into the middle of the sixth century, but thereafter, until *c.*700, only the northern sector of this route remained in use, conveying salt, wine, spices, and dyestuffs from Bordeaux and Nantes in south-western Gaul to the Irish Sea region in considerable quantities.

Whether merchants ever made the entire run from the Mediterranean to Ireland and even south-western Scotland, or whether goods passed through several intermediaries, remains disputed. Although this trade was of very modest proportions in Mediterranean terms, it was of significance to the kings who competed for influence and territory around the Irish Sea. These rulers based themselves in Iron Age fortifications on commanding hilltops, sites whose population must have been numbered in dozens or, at most, hundreds and whose modest economic role was far outstripped by their political and symbolic importance. These high-status sites included centres such as Cadbury, Dinas Powys, and Dunadd in Britain and the double complex at Navan Fort and Armagh in Ireland. Those who ruled from these sites—men like Bleiddudd of Tenby—commanded labour services and military obligations from their subjects. They also retained specialist craftsmen such as goldsmiths, jewellers, and enamellers, who worked within the safety of the hillfort residences to produce the luxury artefacts through which they flaunted their elite status. And, in regulating access to the goods from the Mediterranean and south-western Gaul, they enhanced their own position.

By the early eighth century, most of these fortified hilltops had been abandoned. In Ireland, artisanal production moved to monastic sites, but its distribution, such as there was, probably remained under royal control. In due course, the Irish Sea region gradually reoriented its economic and political connections away from the Gaul and the Bay of Biscay, instead turning northwards, via the Northern Isles to Scandinavia and the Baltic. Although the causes remain uncertain and the chronology approximate, they are in some way associated with an altogether larger shift that was affecting eighth-century Europe as a whole: the temporary abatement of economic activity around the western Mediterranean and its intensification in northern waters.

Access to the wealth of the North Sea and, beyond it, of the Baltic was just one of the reasons for relentless Frankish expansion northwards in the eighth century. Under the leadership of the Carolingian dynasty, the Franks succeeded by 800 in building a polity that controlled a land mass greater than any other post-Roman polity before the sixteenth century. With its political core in the regions between the Seine and the middle Rhine, their empire stretched from the Ebro to the Danube and from the Tiber to the Elbe (Figure 8.3). It embraced dozens of economically distinct regions, ranging from the relatively urbanized Po valley to the sparsely inhabited forests of northern Germany, and it certainly controlled far greater material resources than any other early medieval polity, even if nowhere near the level of those of the Roman state. Indeed, comparison ends at that point, for the Carolingians quite lacked the apparatus of a state-run command economy. Careful exploitation of the agricultural surplus of their own vast estates; adroit taxation of the growing volume of trade both in the localities and along the inter-regional routes that criss-crossed the empire and passed beyond its boundaries; and aggressive plundering of their neighbours all facilitated high levels of accumulation. Persistent efforts to co-opt the loyalty of local aristocrats and churches involved the redistribution of a proportion of that fortune, but won the kings indirect access to both secular and ecclesiastical landed wealth, as, for example, at Ghent.

Carolingian kings and emperors shunned the urban displays of power their Roman predecessors had cultivated. The Carolingians sought game in the forests of the Ardennes in the company of a select noble entourage, whereas Roman emperors had enjoyed the hunt in metropolitan amphitheatres, watched by many thousands of spectators. They preferred to endow huge rural monasteries, which functioned as additional centres of power and accumulation of treasure, rather than lavishing patronage on civic monuments in densely populated cities. Even when their palaces were located, as Aachen, Nijmegen, Frankfurt, and Regensburg all were, on Roman foundations, these were small, semi-rural establishments or old army camps on the northern Roman periphery, not cities at its heart.

Their empire was also polyfocal. Although in the second half of his reign Charlemagne developed a showpiece palace around the thermal springs at Aachen, it was never his sole abode, except in his final years. Nor was it ever the only administrative centre, for he and his successors generally set their sons to rule one or more provinces as junior or sub-kings, and provided each with his own retinue and governing centres. In the second half of the ninth century, intra-familial rivalries hardened these temporary administrative expedients into more enduring kingdoms, whose rulers were left either to found new palaces for themselves or to impose their entourage on monastic hospitality. Though Aachen remained the most prestigious, the most coveted, of ruling sites, multiple rulers meant multiple nodes in the geography of power. In the Carolingian era, as throughout the early Middle Ages, authority remained personal, not institutional, and so the king's presence, wherever he was, identified the nerve centre of political activity.

The Carolingian dynasty managed to meld many different webs of local political influence and economic resources, each of which had its own regional hub. Ghent was one of them, as we have seen, so let us visit a rather different one: Mainz. An old Roman frontier city, it lay on the middle Rhine, the great arterial waterway that led from the North Sea towards the Alpine passes to Italy and the Mediterranean. The dominant presence here was not royal, for there was no palace; instead it was ecclesiastical, for the origins of the archbishopric of Mainz lay in the late Roman era. In person or, more commonly, through their agents, rulers, magnates, and churches tapped into the lucrative trade that passed through the city. It presented a fragmented townscape, for, within its Roman walls, ecclesiastical and secular residential complexes each formed their own compound amid areas given over to agriculture or viticulture. Regional bigwigs and the abbots of major rural monasteries all had town houses here, which were used whenever they or their estate bailiffs came to town to conduct business or take agricultural produce to the market. With a royal mint to stimulate trade and also facilitate its taxation, the city also functioned as an important centre of production and exchange. Along the riverside, the 'Frisian quarter' comprised the warehouses and workshops of a sizeable colony of Frisian merchants, whose boats plied the Rhine, exporting the wine and grain of the regional hinterland, together with the fine metalwork produced in the city itself. By the early tenth century, Mainz was also a transit point for the shipment of goods brought across the Alps, including spices from the east, and was visited by Muslim and Jewish traders. But, by then, the Carolingian political experiment had foundered on the rock of regional differentiation and local interest. In the absence of means of rapid communication and reliable methods of compulsion, effective polities generally remained smaller in scale, even as local agricultural output rose and inter-regional trade intensified. In the localities of late- and post-Carolingian Europe, economic dynamism remained unaffected by political fragmentation.

The wealth and growing population of Frankish coastal emporia, rural monasteries, riverine ports, and local markets were among the best documented of the many targets to attract the attention of the Vikings. Particularly well recorded are the attacks that their highly mobile forces staged from the late eighth century onwards on the Carolingian heartlands and British Isles. Their raids became more frequent and more devastating in the course of the ninth century: by sacking church treasuries, targeting markets, and extorting tribute from rulers, they siphoned off quantities of coin and treasure, sometimes also cattle and humans. As their war bands grew larger, the Vikings also sought land to settle, whether by outright conquest or by concessions wrung from local rulers.

Confident seamen, able traders, canny raiders, the Vikings travelled far and wide from the late eighth until the early eleventh century. In the ninth and tenth centuries Scandinavian boats dominated the coasts of the British archipelago and the Northern Isles, ranging along the western seaboard of Europe, and occasionally passing through the Strait of Gibraltar into the Mediterranean. They crossed the Atlantic to settle Iceland and even sometimes sailed onward to Greenland and Newfoundland. They criss-crossed the Baltic and travelled the river routes of eastern Europe to reach the Black Sea. There the Vikings tapped into the vast wealth of the Muslim world, thereby sucking westwards massive quantities of Islamic silver coins. Stimulated by this traffic, powerful trading centres such as Kiev, on the river Dnieper, emerged by the 860s.

The finds from the Swedish settlement at Helgö are indicative of the breadth of Viking contacts, direct or indirect: they include glassware from the Rhineland; the intricately wrought head of an Irish crozier; a silver dish and a hoard of gold coins from Byzantium; a ladle made in Coptic Egypt, and a bronze statuette of the Buddha. Explanations for this dramatic (but sometimes overdramatized) phase of northern seafaring activity remain controversial. Southern Scandinavian society underwent profound transformations in the sixth to eighth centuries, developing into a more hierarchically ordered society in which resources became accumulated in centres controlled by local leaders, such as the one we have already encountered at Borre in Vestfold. The emergence of these powerful chiefdoms seems to have been closely associated with the ability to exploit and redistribute resources derived from trade as well as local agricultural and artisanal production. The wealth of the Baltic emporia—places such as Birka, which contained 'many rich merchants, and a large amount of goods and money'[5]—certainly helped fuel their growth, as the North Sea emporia did that of seventh- and eighth-century Anglo-Saxon and Frankish kings. Among these chiefdoms, the Danish one developed earliest into a dynastic kingdom and asserted a seaborne hegemony that extended beyond the Jutland peninsula to include the southern Scandinavian chiefdoms and the Slavic communities along the Baltic shore.

The growing concentration of power and resources in the hands of Denmark's kings was contested both within their kingdom and on its borders: political rivalries encouraged the formation of aggressive warrior bands and aristocratic elites. And Charlemagne's expansion into northern Saxony not only destroyed traditional alliances between the Danes and their Slavic neighbours east of the Elbe, for an imperial politics of patronizing client-kings also fostered the emergence of dominant local dynasties of new-found status and influence. Trading contacts over a wide area and a tradition of maritime travel coupled with political upheaval and the ever-pressing need to accumulate the resources that would reward a war band: these preconditions were sufficient to unleash the Viking raids on western Europe's accumulated treasure.

From a northern perspective, the 'Viking Age' was as much about the transformation of the power structures of Scandinavia as it was about exploiting the material resources of western Europe and the Muslim lands. From a British and continental perspective, it was also about the destabilization and transformation of established political landscapes. It was not merely that Viking raiders demanded tribute or presented a military challenge. In these terms, it is relatively simple to assess their impact, for their depredations demonstrated the ability of the Carolingian and Anglo-Saxon agrarian and artisanal economies to continue generating resources year after year. They also contributed to the development of efficient Frankish and English coinages run under tight control for royal profit. In this respect, although local damage was often severe and always traumatic, the overall effect of the Viking raids was transformative not destructive. Equally significantly, Franks, Bretons, Anglo-Saxons, Welsh, and Gaels had no qualms about making common cause with the Vikings when it suited their own political purposes. Roving Viking war bands were welcome participants in Carolingian familial feuding or inter-kingdom rivalries within the British Isles to an extent that contemporary chroniclers took pains to obscure. Their presence complicated or even destroyed local political conventions, in addition to subverting the regular rhythms of agricultural production, diverting tax revenues, and releasing the wealth of church treasuries into circulation.

The Viking impact was especially far-reaching in the British Isles, where a plethora of competing kings were only too ready to call on outside help to overcome a neighbouring rival. For example, the mid-ninth-century absorption of the formerly powerful Pictish kingdom into the Gaelic kingdom of Dalriada may well have been the work of tactical alliances between Gaels and Vikings. Perhaps, inadvertently, the Vikings prompted the emergence of the kingdom of Alba out of the Gaels' domination of the Picts. Certainly by the late ninth century, north-eastern Scotland and the Orkney Islands emerged as an aggressive and powerful lordship of Norse origin whose main place of power was the former Pictish settlement at Birsay. In Ireland, Norse raiders were notable for their rapid assimilation into Irish society. As keen participants in the violent rivalries between Irish kings, the founders of several coastal trading colonies, and settlers in the hinterland of these ports, they rapidly intermarried and left their mark on language, settlement, and politics.

For the Hiberno-Norse, as for other Scandinavian groups, raiding and conquest were part of a spectrum of activities that embraced colonizing as well as trading. Dense ninth- and tenth-century Hiberno-Norse settlement in the Hebrides largely obliterated all traces of earlier cultural groups and left a legacy that endures in the place names of these islands. In Iceland, Hiberno-Norse settlers joined migrants from western and northern Norway who had found an all-but-unoccupied land and settled there in some numbers between c.870 and c.930. There they replicated the political organization of their northern Scandinavian homelands—

a patchwork of small chiefdoms whose headmen presided over largely self-regulating farming communities—and remained distinctive for their lack of any kingship until Iceland passed under the control of the Norwegian crown in 1262.

From the early tenth century until the early eleventh century, Dublin, the richest and most influential of the Norse colonies in Ireland, was effectively another small kingdom, one whose political significance was enhanced by the accumulation of considerable commercial wealth. Its rulers built it up by extending their raiding, slaving, and military campaigning into northern England and south-western Scotland. Its denizens were doubtless sustained by a regionally generated agricultural surplus, but trade—especially in slaves—across the Irish Sea and beyond integrated this flourishing port into the Scandinavian web of trade routes that straddled the North Sea and Baltic and ultimately linked with Muslim traders in the Caucasus and Transoxania. Much of the trade and tribute that moved along these routes did so in the form of hacksilver (silver collars, arm rings, and the like cut into portions of roughly uniform weight) or silver coin, but, to assist their trading ventures, the Norse first imported foreign coins into Ireland, and then started to mint their own currency in Dublin. The Mediterranean and Near East had been familiar with metallic currency as a medium of exchange and assertion of a ruler's prestige and authority since the seventh century BC: that coins were not minted in Ireland until the 997 is a measure of the cultural difference between the Mediterranean and the non-Romanized parts of Europe.

Well before that date, the West Saxon kings had cleared the Viking warlords out of England, and had incorporated the heavily Scandinavianized eastern lowlands into a refashioned monarchy that aggressively asserted overlordship over the Welsh, British, Gaels, and Norse of western and northern Britain. In the south, in and beyond their West Saxon heartland, they built large defensive centres known as burhs, which not only served strategic military purposes in the fight against the Vikings but rapidly emerged as focuses for new forms of urban development. Although retaining close links to their agricultural hinterland, these late Anglo-Saxon towns were sophisticated and populous trading communities as well as centres of royal and ecclesiastical power. They provided regional markets for locally produced agricultural surpluses and artisan manufactures, and imported growing quantities of prestige goods such as silks and wine for the fashion-conscious elite. Above all, they housed royal mints and customs collectors, by means of which the late Anglo-Saxon kings sucked very large amounts of tax, in the form of silver pennies, out of the thriving English economy.

Was Anglo-Saxon England the richest kingdom in Europe by 1000? The case can be argued. Certainly by the late tenth century, when the supply of Islamic silver into Scandinavia dwindled and a resurgent Danish monarchy found expansion into the Baltic lands blocked by the Ottonian Empire, England was the most enticing source of profit, with large amounts of silver coins in circulation and flourishing local and regional urban markets. A new wave of attacks on England, organized by the Danish kings, culminated in the fall of the West Saxon ruling dynasty in 1016 and the accession of Cnut, who soon acquired the Danish throne as well. On this basis, he built a North Sea empire stretching from Dublin, via Scotland and Scandinavia, to the Baltic, but his personal hegemony did not outlast his death in 1035 (Figure 8.4).

Cnut's North Sea empire had relied upon the maritime connections and trading wealth built up by the Danes and Norwegians over the preceding 200 years. By the early eleventh century, such a territorially far-flung hegemony was characteristic of northern Europe rather than the lands south of the Loire and the Alps, where regionally intensive rather than imperially extensive polities were emerging. The fragmentation of France into regional or local lordships was a manifestation of this. The disjuncture between traditional political topographies and newer accumulations of material wealth was, however, most acute in northern Italy.

By the start of the new millennium, Italian towns were at the hub of a rapidly expanding urban and mercantile economy and were beginning to assert their own autonomy. While urban life never disappeared in Italy to anything like the extent that it did north of the Alps, the role of Italian cities as centres of production, exchange, and consumption in the period from c.600 to c.800 is hard to assess, although it seems clear that the pace of production and exchange began to intensify only rather later than in the North Sea area. As the evidence gradually becomes more plentiful, we can trace patterns unlike those of the late- and post-Roman Mediterranean, although it remains true that the changed nature of the evidence (documentary as well as archaeological) may exaggerate the impression of an economic transformation.

Northern Italy had been absorbed into the Frankish kingdom in 774. Carolingian control fell away after 888, but, in the middle of the tenth century, the Carolingians' German heirs, the Ottonians, reasserted a transalpine lordship from their main seats of power in distant, economically backward Saxony. North-east of the Rhine, the absence of long-established towns or markets and the lack of a well-developed coin-using economy left rulers reliant on other methods of resourcing their rule: itinerant kingship, vast landed estates, the tribute of dependent peoples, and the seemingly inexhaustible plunder of frontier warfare. Little wonder, then, that northern Italy attracted them, for here urban wealth was developing apace.

Of particular note is the growth during the ninth century of new Italian coastal towns well placed to develop long-distance trading contacts but in locations unfavourable to agriculture. At the head of the Adriatic, Venice exploited its location on the frontier between the Carolingian and Byzantine empires and, from at least 840, was effectively independent, with only its own interests to foster. Venetians put their energies into a trading economy that gave them a key role in the shipment of goods between western Europe, Byzantium, and the Islamic east, so much so that by the late tenth century the Adriatic Sea was, from a Muslim perspective, simply the 'gulf of Venice'.[6] The perception is important, for much of Venice's prominence probably derived from its role as an entrepôt in the slave trade. Here, slaves captured along Europe's eastern periphery were loaded for shipment to Egypt, and then transit onwards to major Islamic cities, where, unlike in the Christian world, slavery was a fundamental social and military resource. In return, Venetian merchants imported 'all the riches of the east from across the sea' and traded these prestige items on up the Po valley.[7]

On the rocky coast of the Tyrrhenian Sea in southern Italy, Amalfi too had originated as a stronghold against land-based invaders in the late sixth century. In the ninth and tenth centuries, Amalfitans used their fleet to support their Christian neighbours against Saracen pirates or to help Arabs against Christians as best suited their own ambitions, in the process establishing lucrative trading contacts with the ports of the Islamic Mediterranean. Through such political processes, shrewd merchants fostered the growth of a new, urban, and mercantile society that attracted attention for its 'richness and opulence'.[8]

What was the situation of older Italian towns at the end of the tenth century? The Roman city of Pavia had been the capital of the Lombard kingdom since the late sixth century and its palace remained the seat of royal government in Italy under the Carolingian then Ottonian rulers. Detailed regulations emanating from the royal treasury document the city's economic life at the end of the tenth century, a time when the city was frequently visited by the emperor and his retinue. Through his treasurer, the emperor collected tolls on the trade that passed through Pavia, regulating its mint and market activities both for his own financial profit and to maintain law and order. The ordinance also tells us of the urban community and its craftsmen—fishermen with their boats, tanners, shipowners, and sailors of large ships, gold-panners and soap-manufacturers—and of the traders who passed through the city. These included Anglo-Saxons and others—probably French and German—from beyond the Alps, who traded horses, slaves, wool, linen and canvas cloth, tin and swords. Italians came too: traders from Amalfi, Salerno, and Gaeta on the Calabrian coast, and especially rich Venetians trading up the Po valley, purchasing wine and grain but bringing with them goods from Byzantium and the Muslim world—spices, ivory combs, silver mirrors, and the like. So Pavia was an outlet for local agricultural produce, a place of production for artisanal products, and a marketplace for imported luxuries as well as a centre for administration and the display of imperial power. The Ottonians, as all rulers, found tolls on trade a lucrative source of income, and their treasury in Pavia was no exception.

But this was not to last. From the late tenth century, Pavia's citizens chafed against imperial control and rebelled on several occasions. When they heard the news of the death of the emperor Henry II in 1024, they destroyed the palace so completely that its location is now unknown. Their revolt signalled the end of an era. Centralized imperial administration in Italy was virtually at an end, and the pace of efforts to achieve urban autonomy throughout Italy quickened in the course of the eleventh century. The political landscapes that had emerged in the aftermath of the disintegration of the Roman Empire could no longer easily contain the new realities of Italian urban wealth.

## Treasure, Gifts, and Patronage

The author of the Pavia toll regulations also noted a series of customary payments that were not part of the burgeoning commercial economy of Italy at the end of the tenth century. The wife of the king's treasurer could expect that merchants from other Italian cities would give her gifts of eastern manufactured goods and fine patterned silks. The treasurer himself was to make regular donations of lighting oil to Pavia's cathedral church and of clothing to its custodians. We meet here other forms of exchange, ones in which women were often expert, but in which commercial profit was not the aim. The giving of prestige gifts or of charitable donations to a religious institution signals very different forms of transactions, ones whose social, political, or religious dimension is to the fore. By shifting focus to social interactions that were characterized by patronage, gift giving, or forcible expropriation, we can understand better how material resources could be converted into symbolic capital—that is, into honour, prestige, and political influence.

The scene is set not in Rome but in imperial Ravenna. A glittering mosaic panel in the sixth-century church of San Vitale depicts Justinian (527–65), the last Latin-speaking emperor to rule in Constantinople, and the man who came near to realizing a dream of ousting the warrior kings of Italy, Spain, and North Africa and restoring these provinces to direct imperial control. Dressed in purple and gold, with a huge, heavily jew- elled diadem on his head and a matching brooch on his shoulder, he is flanked by courtiers whose rank is indicated by their dress, from the lav- ish to the more modest. His consort Theodora faces towards him across the church, equally opulently adorned, her retinue also dressed to em- phasize precise hierarchy. Both carry gifts of equal splendour: he bears a massive golden salver, she a golden cup studded with glittering gems. The representation of the imperial couple draws attention to the way in which ostentatious display and the giving of gifts were the outer trappings of power in the late Roman world. Expressed in dress, precious objects, art, and architecture, the late antique rhetoric of power and prestige included an idiom of visible wealth, expertly deployed by women and men in com- plementary ways.

Sumptuously embellished churches—gifts to the Christian God—still stand as a reminder to us of the massive disposable wealth of late Roman emperors and aristocrats. They also signal their donors' hopes that gen- erosity might be rewarded by enhanced holy patronage and protection, for building and endowing churches projected into the realm of the super- natural customs and expectations that informed human relationships. Among the Romans, gift giving consolidated friendships between indi- viduals and eased the exchange of political favours. In a culture where se- curing patronage was central to political and social advancement, gifts could cement the flow of support between patron and client. Their cent- rality reflected the basic truth that personal favours and direct contact were the real lubricants of power and influence in the late Roman world, not its cumbersome bureaucratic procedures.

On their accession, late antique emperors would shower coins into the crowds and distribute splendid silver dishes and tableware as largesse to favoured supporters. They also frequently made huge payments to neigh- bouring kings and warlords to win peace or compliance with other political goals. In this way, Roman prestige goods—gold coins and medal- lions, luxury silver tableware, the jewelled brooches that designated high rank—flooded across the imperial frontiers. Archaeologists have found their remnants everywhere from Scandinavia and the eastern Baltic to the Black Sea: the influx of fourth- and fifth-century Roman wealth into the treasure chests of the warrior chieftains of northern Europe and the Danube basin enhanced these leaders' prestige and power vis-à-vis their own followers. As they flowed through the political, social, and religious veins of the late antique empire, prestige items cloaked bureaucracy in the guise of direct personal relationships, helped win the support of the saints in heaven, conferred legitimacy, and structured the empire's relationships with its enemies and neighbours.

The post-imperial kingdoms of the early medieval West remained firmly within this political order. Kings took their cue—and much of their treasure—from the empire. Two sixth-century episodes reveal both the material richness and the political symbolism involved. The first concerns the victory of Clovis in 507 over the Goths of south-western Gaul and Spain under their king Alaric II, whom he killed. The battle enabled him to seize south-western Gaul for the Franks, thus confining the Goths to the Iberian peninsula, much to the annoyance of Alaric's father-in-law Theoderic the Great, king of Italy (493–526). Clovis's troops grabbed what they could of Alaric's treasure but, crucially, not the heirlooms that were central to his dynasty's identity. These included ancient political treasures, seized when the Goths under Alaric I had sacked Rome in 410: 'Among these were the treasures of Solomon, the king of the Hebrews, a most noteworthy sight. . . . Most of them were adorned with emeralds; and they had been taken from Jerusalem by the Romans in ancient times [i.e. the Roman sack of AD 70].'[9] These venerable markers of political identity—successively Jewish, Roman, then Gothic—signalled Alaric I's successors as legitimate players in Roman imperial politics. These treasures were far too precious to let fall into Frankish hands, so Theoderic took them into his own custody, returning them to his grandson Amalaric when he became of age to succeed to the throne. Whatever their worth as gold and gems, these heirlooms symbolized prestige, legitimacy, and dynastic continuity.

In the immediate aftermath of his victory, Clovis was rewarded with traditional imperial tokens of recognition and patronage by the Byzantine emperor Anastasius (491–548), whose political strategies his victory had also served. Clovis then signalled his increased status with a dramatic display of royal generosity directed towards his new subjects: in the course of a victory parade in Roman idiom, he made a great gift of the spoils of war to the church of St Martin at Tours and, clad in Roman dress, 'he mounted a horse and, by his own hand, and with the greatest goodwill, distributed gold and silver to the crowd along the road between the gateway of the courtyard [of St Martin's church] and the cathedral church in the city'.[10] By immediately redistributing the booty, Clovis established his credentials as a generous ruler, allied himself with one of the most important saints of the region, and put his new subjects under a moral obligation to reciprocate by giving him their support and loyalty. On this, as on many other occasions, Clovis was a shrewd manipulator of the symbolism of gifts and treasure: by giving, he gained.

Our second episode comes from near the end of the sixth century, and concerns Clovis's great-grandson, Childebert II (575–96). In 584, the Byzantine emperor Maurice (582–602) had presented him with 50,000 gold coins (*solidi*) as an inducement to invade Italy. The peninsula had been reconquered by Justinian at vast cost only a generation before, but then invaded by the Lombards under Alboin in 568, who extended their control throughout its northern half in the course of the next twenty years. Maurice's strategy was the time-honoured one of paying one warrior king to attack another; he hoped the Franks would drive the Lombards out of Italy.

To be effective, diplomatic gift giving presupposed that both giver and receiver recognized the implicit moral code, and that they had equal political interests in an exchange of treasure-for-peace. But, on this particular occasion, it failed. As Childebert marched into Italy, the Lombards avoided conflict by submitting, presenting him with gifts of their own to persuade him to leave. Maurice felt that Childebert had broken the terms of the payment and demanded its return: but the Frankish king was so confident of his power that he did not even deign to reply. In this game of political poker, Childebert was twice the winner. He had gained financially on two occasions, for Maurice's payment was approximately 227.5 kilograms of gold, and the 'many gifts' of the Lombards must also have been substantial.[11] But he had also twice enhanced his political standing: by rejecting the subordination to imperial wishes implied by Maurice's gift, and by receiving the Lombards' submission that accompanied their gifts. He had thereby increased both his material and his symbolic capital.

As the events of 507 and 584 indicate, the amounts of treasure that facilitated post-imperial politics were enormous. They also show that access to and control of treasure were intimately associated with political legitimacy in the eyes of rival kings, one's own subjects, the Byzantine emperor. Yet Maurice's experience reminds us that the giving of political subsidies was unpredictable and fraught with difficulties: it might, or might not, achieve the donor's goals.

As a means for achieving political ends, gift giving did not have to be on the scale of cartloads of gold and jewels: it could involve nothing more costly than a bunch of flowers from a meadow or a thoughtfully composed letter. To observe this, let us remain in sixth-century Gaul a moment longer. In 566, an Italian poet arrived at the court of Sigibert (561–75),

father of Childebert II. Venantius Fortunatus launched his career with
great éclat by presenting the king with a skilfully composed nuptial ode
on the occasion of his marriage to Brunhild. Fortunatus's charming Latin
verses are commonly read as an indication of the continuing appreciation
for classical literary culture in post-imperial Gaul. But, in addition to
being an able poet, the Italian was also sufficiently adroit for the patronage he attracted eventually to bring him a bishopric. As we watch him
winning friends and becoming more influential, we may also glimpse the
ways in which gift giving was part of the patronage that articulated relationships between individuals.

Food was a subject often in Fortunatus's mind. He thrived—indeed survived—on invitations to banquets or gifts of food. His counter-gifts were
poetic and laudatory:

> Nectar, wine, food, clothing, learning, opportunity:
> With your generous gifts, Gogo, you content me.[12]

Senior palace official in Sigibert's court, and man of wide-ranging contacts and influence, Gogo was a useful patron for the Italian poet. Through
the relationship, Fortunatus enjoyed the 'fruits of friendship'.[13] A poem
to Conda, a man who had risen from modest origins to become a key
financial and administrative figure in Sigibert's retinue, hints at the political realities that informed the flow of benefits. Fortunatus comments that
Sigibert has given Conda lavish gifts in reward for his able services: 'The
king, more powerful than the rest, has provided rightly better rewards, and
your case demonstrates what he values more highly.' Conda's own conduct
is modelled on the king's: 'In generosity and kindness you bestow gifts in
plenty on all, and bind men to you by your gifts.'[14] The king's example
was one to be emulated throughout the social hierarchy, for at all levels
generous giving created obligations. Power brokers such as Gogo and
Conda were well placed to manipulate the flow of royal patronage if they
chose: Fortunatus's eulogies were well aimed.

In the end, Fortunatus settled down with two particular patrons. One
was Gregory, the hard-pressed bishop of Tours. The other was Radegund
(d. 587), former queen of Chlothar I (511–61) but by this time cloistered at
Poitiers. As a nun, she continued to practise her courtly skills, and, in
pursuit of her own aims, exploited the traditionally feminine associations
of fine dress and food. At Tours, Venantius commended himself to Gregory
as a special 'humble servant'. The bishop's support for his versifying protégé
ranged from presents of shoe leather to landed estates. In return, the Italian
used his literary talent to support Gregory at moments of great
political crisis. At Poitiers, Radegund and her abbess, Agnes, frequently

sent Fortunatus gifts of food from their table—a jug of milk, dark plums, delicate titbits. Whether from the hands of a wealthy queen, a lord's wife, or a woman dedicated to monastic poverty, food was a gift that nurtured more than just a man's stomach. Fortunatus reciprocated with equally modest tokens—bunches of violets, a handmade basket of sweet chestnuts—and put his rhetorical skills to good use in furthering Radegund's plans for making peace between feuding kings and collecting earthly relics of the immortals in heaven. Behind the delicate poetic images, Fortunatus knew as well as Gregory or Radegund the unspoken rules of the courtly game of gift giving. All three were well aware that gifts, obligation, reward, and influence all went together, for they knew well how to convert material resources into social power, political influence, and saintly patronage. Shortly before 600, Fortunatus got his bishopric—in Poitiers.

The use of wealth to solidify political friendships or to maintain and refresh existing bonds of loyalty, dependence, and service was not confined to the late Roman world and its immediate heirs. Indeed, one reason why fifth- and sixth-century rulers so rapidly adapted to their own purposes the politics of redistribution and reciprocity was that analogous customs were integral to the culture of the war bands that had transformed the political map of the Roman West in the fifth century. The organization of the chiefdoms north of the Rhine–Danube frontier and in the non-Roman parts of the British Isles was undoubtedly much simpler than the bureaucratic culture of the imperial state, with its array of professional specialisms and massive military machine. Lacking administrative or coercive means of ruling, the kings of these polities could fall back on little more than bonds of personal influence and obligation.

They forged them from material wealth. The most famous expression of this occurs in *Beowulf*, but has close parallels in early medieval epics in many other languages. The good epic warlord or king is generous to his followers, rewarding valour in battle with lavish gifts, but thereby investing in the expectation of future service and support. An effective war leader will attract ambitious young warriors into his retinue, entertain them in his hall, feast them, and arm them: in the competition for power, rival lords use treasure, precious weaponry, and their own reputation to swell their own army and compete for victory. In *Beowulf*, Hrothgar son of Healfdene was a ruler of this sort:

> Then to Hrothgar was granted glory in battle,
> mastery of the field; so friends and kinsmen
> gladly obeyed him, and his band increased
> to a great company.[15]

Beowulf, a princely warrior from the land of the Geats, was among those
who sought service in Hrothgar's retinue, and his exploits form an extended commentary on the social code of martial success, treasure, reward,
honour, and rulership. When Beowulf returned from slaying the monsters
who had attacked Heorot, the Danish king declared:

> You will lack nothing
> that lies in my gift of the goods of this world:
> lesser offices have elicited reward,
> we have honoured from our hoard less heroic men,
> far weaker in war. But you have well ensured
> by the deeds of your hands an undying honour
> for your name forever.

Then the hall was prepared for the banquet—'gold-embroidered tapes-
tries | glowed from the walls'—and Hrothgar arrived to take his place:

> No people has gathered in greater retinue,
> borne themselves better about their ring-giver.
> Men known for their courage came to the benches,
> rejoiced in the feast; they refreshed themselves kindly
> with many a mead-cup.
>
>            .     .     .     .     .
>
> Then as a sign of victory the son of Healfdene
> bestowed on Beowulf a standard worked in gold,
> a figured battle-banner, breast and head-armour;
> and many admired the marvellous sword
> that was borne before the hero. Beowulf drank with
> the company in the hall. He had no cause to be ashamed of
> gifts so fine before fighting-men!

Hrothgar then added eight warhorses with gold and jewelled harness to
the array of gifts, and, through the gift giving, the reputation of both men
was enhanced:

> Thus did the glorious prince, guardian of the treasure,
> reward these deeds, with both war-horses and armour;
> of such open-handedness no honest man
> could ever speak in disparagement.[16]

Both Hrothgar and Beowulf had warded off the shame that was the
dreaded undertow of a culture of honour and reward: Beowulf had fought
his way to wealth and reputation while Hrothgar had demonstrated regal
generosity. On the hero's return to the Geats, the circulation of these precious weapons continued, for he duly made his own spirit of generosity

manifest by giving them to his kinsman, King Hygelac. Beowulf had
proved that he was fit to succeed to the throne.

*Beowulf* is a great literary epic and its heroes legendary. That its social
ethos is nevertheless a realistic indicator of the rituals and values surrounding gift giving in the highly martial culture of the early Middle Ages
is amply confirmed by a wide range of historical sources from all parts of
Europe. Their matter-of-fact narratives of plundering expeditions and
lively descriptions of gifts exchanged at feasts and other ceremonial occasions give historical specificity to the values of epic poetry. Warfare, plundering, and feasting all had their place alongside other forms of exchange:
these were the military and political complement to the concentration of
agricultural, artisanal, or trading wealth on lordly or royal sites.

The treasures that figure so prominently in the pages of *Beowulf* were
not confined to well-wrought weaponry and jewelled body armour. They
included goblets and tableware, arm rings and collars, all made of gold.
The items of personal adornment were worn and given away by women
as well as by men, for women had an integral role in the interlocking
traditions of expropriation, redistribution, and reciprocity that shaped all
early medieval societies. They too were the givers of gifts, using whatever
resources they had at their own command to exercise patronage for their
chosen political and religious purposes, as we have seen Theodora and
Radegund do. To them often fell the task of ensuring that courtly gifts
and hospitality upheld the subtleties of rank and social precedence. A
ninth-century guide to the complex organization of Charlemagne's royal
household makes this explicit. 'The good management of the palace, and
especially the royal dignity, as well as the gifts given annually to the offi-
cers (excepting, however, the food and water for the horses) pertained especially to the queen, and under her to the chamberlain.'[17] In overseeing
the selection of gifts, the queen upheld the economy of honour upon
which palace ritual depended.

In addition to being the agents of generosity, women might find themselves its objects. Hrothgar had betrothed his daughter Freawaru to the
Danes' enemy Ingeld, hoping

> thus to end all the feud and their fatal wars
> by means of the lady.[18]

Although the *Beowulf* poet doubted the effectiveness of peacemaking
marriage alliances, they are frequently attested in documentary sources of
the early Middle Ages. One early example suffices: as a countermove to
Clovis's defeat of the Iberian Goths in 507, Theoderic the Great gave
his niece Amalberga in marriage to the Franks' enemy, the Thuringian

Hermanifrid. Sealing the marriage with the exchange of 'such gifts as the royal rank requires', Theoderic declared to Hermanifrid: 'May divine favour attend your marriage, that, as friendship has allied us, so may family love bind our posterity.'[19] Hrothgar would have recognized this sentiment—but would also have accepted that marriage alliances were no more predictable in their outcomes than gift giving.

Archaeological material from sites throughout Europe confirms the skill and technical abilities of early medieval goldsmiths and weapon-forgers. It also restores to us some modest fraction of the treasure that demarcated wealth, power, and prestige. But herein lies an irony, for much of the gold and jewellery recovered by archaeologists was deliberately buried, especially in the more northerly parts of Europe. Leaving aside the many caches whose owners buried them in times of insecurity with the intention of recovering them later, intentional deposits might mark sites and actions of ritual or religious significance. One of their social functions was to provide the spectacle of deposition—for whatever group of participants was privileged to watch. Another turned on the knowledge that thereafter the treasure was hidden from view, invisibly present. This is the context of the fifth-century bog sacrifices of war booty from Jutland and southern Sweden, which offer oblique comment on the way in which warring chiefdoms commemorated victory over an enemy. Cosmological significance also attaches to many of the deposits of gold at Gudme ('home of the gods'), a fifth- to sixth-century centre of political and religious power and trade on the Danish island of Fyn. Here we encounter a range of non-Roman and non-Christian associations between wealth and the supernatural, ones whose full religious or ideological implications cannot be fully recovered owing to the lack of written evidence to reveal the cosmology that informed them. Though mute, such deposits are suggestive.

Equally intentional was the funerary deposition of objects, mundane or prestigious. Archaeologists have uncovered—and continue to find—thousands of furnished inhumation burials from England and the non-Mediterranean continent in the period from c.400 to c.700, plus small numbers from Mediterranean regions. Such graves range from very modest through to immensely wealthy assemblages. Take the example of the East Saxon cemetery at Prittlewell in south-east England, where about 20 sixth- to seventh-century graves have been found. Some had no objects deposited in them at all; others no more than a knife, brooch, or a pot or two. One grave contained an exceptional chamber, whose discovery was announced in February 2004. Accompanied by his sword and shield, a warrior had been buried in the first half of the seventh century in a large, wood-lined cell. He had been laid to rest clothed in gold-braided fabric belted with a massive gold buckle, wearing gold-buckled shoes and with two small gold-foil crosses on his chest. His burial chamber was kitted out with a wide range of items that hint at far-flung contacts: a Byzantine flagon and inscribed silver spoon; a large Coptic bowl; two gold coins from Merovingian Gaul; hanging bowls from Ireland or northern England; and two pairs of Kentish glass jars. It also contained accoutrements suggestive of a ruler who liked to entertain his retinue in high style: a Roman-type folding seat perhaps from Italy; a tall stand for a torch (or perhaps a royal standard); decorated drinking horns; wooden drinking cups with gilded mounts; a lyre; gaming pieces and dice; plus hanging cauldrons, buckets, and a casket.

Like the handful of other richly furnished, probably royal, graves known from Anglo-Saxon England, the princely grave at Prittlewell undoubtedly had both a religious and a social context. On the one hand, it hints at the complexities and contradictions that often accompanied the spread of Christianity.[20] On the other, it suggests a good funeral, with a 'master of ceremonies' to orchestrate its grandeur, surviving relatives vying for the inheritance, and onlookers impressed by the spectacle. As we saw earlier, the burial rites employed as Roman rule collapsed and new kingdoms evolved were often an occasion for lavish displays of social status, not simply that of the deceased, but equally importantly of the heirs.[21] In view of the fluidity and uncertainty of early medieval inheritance practices, the death of a leading member of a kin group might well have been a moment of great crisis for his or her surviving relatives and their wider community, all the more so if the dead person were a ruler. Decisions about the weapons, jewels, and other objects to place in an early medieval grave were then deliberate choices about the uses of valuable items. The burial of these treasures was an assertion of prestige and influence at a crucial political moment, the funeral itself a suitable theatre for renegotiating power and reconfiguring social relationships.

Whether worked into items of personal adornment, elaborate tableware, or body armour and weaponry, gold, silver, and jewels were among the most durable forms of movable wealth in the early Middle Ages. Other forms perished, leaving only indirect trace. Prominent among them were the victims of plundering and warfare along the northern and eastern fringes of Europe, where slaving was habitual. Many human cargoes were shipped by Viking slavers from the British Isles to the Baltic, whence they were traded on into the Muslim east. Other convoys were marched westwards and southwards from the Slav lands of central Europe. Some were then embarked at Venice and other Mediterranean ports for transport to the Muslim east; others were taken via Verdun and then across the Pyrenees to supply the Umayyad court at Cordoba. The only material testimony to these unfortunates' existence is the neck irons, manacles, and chains with which they were bound, such as those from the stronghold of Staré Zámky, at the western end of the Carpathians. A convoy heading westwards from there would in all likelihood have made its way to the East Frankish border toll station at Raffelstetten in Bavaria. Here, Rus and Bohemian slave-dealers sold them on, quite probably to the Jews who were prominent in the early medieval European slave trade. The commercial value of these convoys must have been considerable, for the tolls taken at Raffelstetten in 906 indicate that a female slave was of equal value to a war stallion. She was an expensive item, prestigious in her own right, valuable in reproductive terms, and, in cash terms, worth four times as much as a male slave (or a mare).

The great worth of female slaves was also recognized in Ireland, where they formed a common unit of value. For example, the honour price of a provincial king was fourteen female slaves (*cumals*) in the estimation of an eighth-century treatise. By far the commonest form of currency for making payments in Ireland, however, was cattle. Central to the Irish economy, they were equally significant in political and social contexts. Irish law tracts reveal a world where lords bound clients to themselves by grants of cattle in ways that were simultaneously economic and political investments. This could happen in one of two ways, forming relationships of either 'free' or 'base' clientship. Common to both was a system that dispersed a lord's large herd widely, thus reducing the risk of malnourishment or disease, and where, over a period of years, a lord would receive back calves and heifers equal or greater in number to the size of the original grant of stock. Although cattle were only one element in a mixed arable–pastoral economy, they had a political significance and symbolic importance that other livestock lacked, as other aspects of the clientage arrangements reveal. In the case of a base tenant, his honour became subsumed within the lord's own, in a clear relationship of subjection. In addition, the base client paid annual food renders, provided manual labour on the lord's lands and fortifications, and demonstrated his subjection both by feasting the lord and his retinue for one night each winter and by fighting for him in his military retinue. A free client, on the other hand, enjoyed an honourable relationship with his lord. He might well be of noble status himself, and more than repaid the loan of stock on terms that imply that he had considerable herds of his own on which to draw should the lord's cattle fail to breed. There are other indications of his status too.

Unlike the base client, the free client suffered no loss of independence. All he had to do to mark the relationship was to rise to his feet when his lord stood up in the local political assembly, and probably provide fairly light labour services too. Through cattle clientage, a lord did not simply make arrangements for stockbreeding. He was fed and his own arable land was farmed. He acquired dependants commensurate with his wealth and rank, and a military following. With large herds of cattle he could acquire the attributes of a 'noble of the first rank' and enjoy all the prestige and power the status implied.[22]

All this makes sense for a population who used cattle as their equivalent of a unit of currency and lived in a natural environment that was particularly well suited to stock raising. But the methodical system suggested by the law codes must have been tempered by other, harsher realities: the episodes of cattle murrain that ripped through Ireland, intense competition among lords to acquire free clients, and the cattle raiding that formed the characteristic—and often deadly—form of Irish status rivalry among the numerous lords and petty kings. Paradoxically, cattle raiding was as integral to maintaining social equilibrium as it was dangerous to life and limb. But the paradox is only apparent, for, like feuding, cattle raiding had its own conventions. As with feuding too, contemporaries took its *raison d'être* for granted. A successful foray swelled a lord's stock of breeding cattle and might thus enable him to recruit more clients. It also provided an arena for displays of the masculine ethic of courage and military skill, and the likelihood that it would trigger a retaliatory raid raised the stakes. If a raid failed, a chief risked losing prestige, possibly also his life and the cohesion of his following. Cattle raids kept resources circulating and demanded frequent reassertions of military ability and solidarity. In so doing, they provided opportunities for negotiating codes of honour and binding a lord to his followers.

The surviving evidence makes it impossible to ascertain to what extent the Irish system of cattle-based patronage changed in the course of the early Middle Ages. Elsewhere, however, notable developments in the politics of generosity are more readily traceable. Above all, they concern the growing significance of landed estates as objects of patronage—and of competition. Many reasons for this have already been encountered: rising population; the precedent of inalienable ecclesiastical endowments; concern for the fate of the Christian soul after death; the gradually increasing ability to extract a significant cash profit from the land. From the seventh century on the Continent, and the eighth in England, grants of land became increasingly prominent forms of reward. While prestige items always remained the appropriate gift for another ruler, their role in relationships between a king and his entourage shifted to accommodate the pressure to acquire land.

Immovable property was the most potent, but also the most complex, form of gift or patronage. As such, it was central to the maintenance of honour, but liable to generate particular tensions. Unlike plunder or tribute, it was everywhere yet of finite quantity—unless, perhaps, there was an open frontier that invited aggression and land seizure. As a source of income, rights of lordship, and status, it had potentially enduring importance. But it usually came hedged around with qualifications, and was generally subject to multiple interests. If granted to the laity, it might be confiscated later for misbehaviour. If given to a church, it carried reciprocal obligations of prayer and military service. Then there might be the expectations of the heirs of a former owner to counter or accommodate, or sitting tenants to consider. And benefactors usually gave land to a church not in a single, limited moment of piety, but in the hope of forging enduring spiritual bonds with a religious community and its patron saint. Intertwined secular and religious favours together with ongoing commitments thus lay at the core of the politics of landed patronage.

We gain rare, vivid insights into the insecurities inherent in a land-based patronage system by once more taking Einhard as our guide. In the fifteen years after Charlemagne's death in 814, escalating tensions among the elite about inheritance, patronage, and reward exacerbated disputes about the imperial succession, and culminated in serious revolts in 830 and again in 833–4. In this atmosphere of political uncertainty, control of land became the key to political success more than ever before: competition for landed resources hereafter fuelled politics in an unprecedented way. These are the circumstances that Einhard's correspondence illustrates so effectively.

Through his letters, we see him negotiating with his own personal assistants and administrators in order to reap the financial benefits of his property. The reader is immediately struck by Einhard's attention to detail: he writes about such minutiae as arrangements for the distribution of the offal from slaughtered cattle, or the problem of securing a supply of wax after two years when the bees had failed to produce much honey. This attentiveness was in response to the sheer challenge of getting the right resources to the right place at the right time, whether food to maintain his retinue while he attended court at Aachen, or the difficulty of obtaining the building supplies he desired for the church he was constructing at Seligenstadt. Unlike the lordship of the clergy of St Peter's, Ghent, Einhard's personal lordship lacked a single administrative centre but shifted around his estates. Vigilance was also needed, for he also had to wrestle with negligent estate bailiffs and ensure that the income due to him was collected in full and in coins of good quality. Such administrative details inevitably had a political aspect. It was traditional—indeed obligatory—for Carolingian bishops, abbots, and lords to make annual 'gifts' to the ruler, and these generally took the form of prestige objects—horses, falcons and weaponry, silver, gold, and jewelled objects. This did not merely help to keep the royal treasure chests stocked: it defined the elite group who enjoyed access to the ruler. It also marked their deference to him. So Einhard duly wrote to his deputies instructing them to prepare and deliver his offerings to the palace. He can hardly have been unique in the exertions needed to make the most of landed property: his letters are simply more explicit about the difficulties than most other sources.

Einhard also hoped for something in return, usually in the form of political favours. He wrote on several occasions to Louis the Pious or members of his family to invoke their patronage and active help in building his church at Seligenstadt. He usually brought added pressure to bear by hinting at the spiritual support that Marcellinus and Peter, the Roman martyrs housed there, would bestow on those who patronized them, for Carolingian ideas of patronage embraced the saints as firmly as in late Antiquity. At other times, contacts—'friendships'—made at the earthly court could also be invoked to secure his goals, whether further resources for his building project, or favours for his political followers. Land also featured here, for, in the uncertain political climate of the 830s, Einhard's followers feared loss of their benefices—those estates to which they had only temporary rights—and, as their patron, he used his influence and the prestige of his name to do what he could for them. And, since the politics of patronage was a reciprocal process, many of his letters also reveal that he was himself importuned by others who sought to turn his influence to their own purposes. So he also wrote to palace officials, abbots, counts, and bishops to put in a good word or argue a case here and plead for an appointment there.

Against this backdrop of uncertainty and cronyism, Einhard emerges as a man whose influence was worth courting: as ever, personal contacts, patronage, and gifts together directed the flow of power and privilege and turned friendship into politics. In this respect, there is, however, a notable disparity between his great political capital and the relatively modest landed resources available to him. Perhaps, in making himself the earthly advocate of his beloved heavenly martyrs, Einhard had acquired spiritual resources to help bridge the gap. In addition, his long years at court, brilliant talents, and unfaltering loyalty first to Charlemagne and then to Louis the Pious had served him well, for they afforded him a central place in the web of social power that was spun around the imperial court. Proximity to martyred saints and emperors alike compensated for his limited material resources.

If Einhard's careful negotiation of the quicksands of court politics emphasizes the precariousness of lay careers built upon royal favour and grants of benefices, it also underscores the interconnectedness of secular and supernatural patronage. One of the main desires of kings and lesser laity alike was to win heavenly favour and intercession. Those who secured it on their behalf, put pious wishes into practice, and turned land into prayer were commonly their widows. This was why Heregyth, Abba's widow, had left land to Christ Church, Canterbury, and why Gisela devoted so much of her energies to the monastery that she and Eberhard had founded at Cysoing.[23]

Because of their potency as heavenly patrons, saints were not only the recipients of much land and treasure but could also themselves constitute the donated objects. Henry, duke of Saxony, had been chosen as king by the German nobility late in 918 and was formally installed on the throne the following spring. Lacking any ancestral claim to the throne, Henry built his rule on shrewd negotiating, military success, and the accumulation of holy relics through royal gift exchange. In 921, he reached an accord on equal terms with Charles the Simple, the last remaining Carolingian ruler, whose recognition enhanced his prestige and helped consolidate his position. In practice, though, Charles was the much weaker man, and the following year was defeated in battle and deposed by his own subjects. Desperate for support, Charles sent Henry a 'sign of faith and truth'—part of the body of the Carolingians' especial patron, the martyr Denis.[24] The gesture was one of defiance towards Charles's West Frankish opponents—but by the same token recognized Henry I as a rightful heir of the ancient Carolingian dynasty and the protector of its religious traditions. The arm of St Denis extended the aura of generations of Frankish kings to the new German ruler.

More prestigious even than remains of saints or martyrs were relics of Christ's crucifixion. In this Henry followed in Radegund's footsteps and made a notable acquisition. In 926, he ended his enmity with Rudolf II, king of Burgundy (912–37), persuaded him to recognize his overlordship, gave him rich gifts and transferred part of Swabia to him. The pact between the two kings was sealed when Rudolf gave Henry 'that thing whereby God had joined the things of earth to the things of heaven'— namely, the 'sacred spear' believed to have been used at the crucifixion and once owned by the first Christian Roman emperor, Constantine. This 'invincible weapon against all enemies, visible and invisible', had been a gift to Rudolf during his brief adventure as king of Italy (922–6).[25] Passing from him to Henry, who in turn bequeathed it to his son Otto I, the spear became an enduring symbol of legitimate rulership and German imperial authority, as the next chapter will demonstrate. Carried into battle, regarded as a holy relic and token of empire, it was kept at Aachen until the German empire ended in 1806, when, along with the rest of the imperial regalia, it was transferred to Vienna, where it remains on display.

The symbolism of ancient weapons, secular and sacred patronage all fuse in Henry I's relic collecting. Economic capital was transformed into symbolic capital; secular lordship expressed itself through spiritual patronage. The royal politics of gift giving and alliance building deployed many currencies: material wealth, sacred objects, territorial control, prestige, and legitimacy were inter-convertible. Although Otto I's empire bore minimal resemblance to that of Justinian 400 years earlier, kings and emperors continued to use similar strategies and strove for similar goals. Successful rulers adroitly manipulated all their convertible assets.

From the middle of the eleventh century, some of these attitudes began to change. First in northern Italy, where a mercantile economy was developing rapidly, and soon thereafter elsewhere, the acquisition of material resources no longer seemed such a straightforward sign of blessing. Although early medieval moralists had condemned the immoderate thirst for riches and regarded avarice as the worst of all vices, they had never called into question either the need to accumulate in a principled way or the reciprocity of giving and getting that defined and sustained political communities. But the surge in monetary transactions and commercial profit in cities such as Milan and Pavia short-circuited the ebb-and-flow of gifts and benefits. It also eroded the consensus that sustained it. Churchmen began to worry about the spiritual purity of those who accepted gifts in return for loyalty, and, especially, for ecclesiastical office and advantage. The involvement of bishops and abbots in the exchange of gifts and patronage became equated with moral corruption: the taint of heresy was detected. Then, as levels of material wealth rose still further, poverty began to seem to some the more godly option.

None of this would have made sense before the turn of the millennium. In the early Middle Ages, material wealth and political power had flowed along channels that were secular, sacred, or both simultaneously. Both were multiform, mutable, unstable, in need of constant reinforcement. In communities at risk of dearth, earthly riches betokened divine favour. Fitting offerings for the gods and the Christian saints, treasures, like land, conferred upon their owners and donors religious as well as political advantage. In this world where resources were hard-won but easily dissipated, their possession was one of the defining characteristics of the religious and lay elite. They used their wealth to display their status; uphold and reinforce their honour; establish and strengthen their ties to lords, rulers, and the saints in heaven.

Accumulating resources and distributing them generously were thus urgent imperatives. They demanded continuous attention, and no secular or ecclesiastical power broker could afford to let his or her attention slip. Full treasure chests little availed the lord who lacked the ability to manage their contents and manipulate their symbolism to political and religious advantage; a richly equipped altar did little for a church whose patron saint was a sluggish advocate of donors' interests. Yet conventions of gift giving and patronage followed no explicit rules. Their universally recognized moral and political expectations remained implicit, a consensus embedded in social practice and absorbed as part of childhood training in the courtly exercise of power. Intensely competitive, with both earthly honour and the fate of the soul at issue, the early Middle Ages remained a customary world of getting and giving. Having watched how kings turned their resources into political advantage, we must next ask how they justified that power and made it seem natural.

# IDEOLOGIES

# 7

# Kingship and Christianity

We pray that you bestow on King Louis unending prosperity.
We pray that you bestow on him life, health, and victory. Hear us!
. . .
We pray that you restrain the heathens steadfast in their savage
   religion. Hear us!
We pray that you humble the pagan heathens. Hear us![1]

First of all, my dearest son, I counsel, advise and persuade you thus:
if you desire to honour the royal crown, you should uphold the
catholic and apostolic faith with such diligence and good care that
you set an example to all the subjects committed to you by God, and
so that all sons of the church may deservedly call you a true man of
Christian profession. Know for sure that without this you will be
called neither a Christian nor a son of the church. And because faith
without works dies, those who believe falsely or who do not imple-
ment their faith in good works neither reign honorably nor share in
the eternal kingdom and its crown.[2]

WHEN the monks of the royal monastery of Lorsch prayed to the
Christian God for 'unending prosperity . . . life, health, and victory' for
their king, Louis the German (840–76), they invoked an ideology of kingship that had already been many centuries in the making. Prosperity for
ruler and subjects alike; the defence and propagation of Christianity; victory over enemies; upholding the rule of law: together, these formed the
core of early medieval thinking about the role of kings and the place of
Christianity in politics and society. By the early eleventh century, Europe
had evolved a culture distinctive for its integration of sacred and profane
power, characterized by kings who ruled in close association with the
personnel and institutions of the Christian religion, identified themselves
as 'Christ's own deputy',[3] and presided over efforts to promote their own

particular vision of a Christian society. The model of Christian kingship that had matured by the early years of the eleventh century is captured for us in the manual of advice quoted above, written by King Stephen of Hungary (997–1038) for his infant son. Stephen offered his heir a ten-point plan in which the king himself exemplified the Christain faith and its moral agenda, supported ecclesiastical institutions, and honoured its personnel. In his short, state-of-the-art treatise, royal power and Christian religion interlocked, supplying both a powerful ideology and practical code of conduct to mould the future king into the truly Christian ruler.

Such advice was timely: Pope Sylvester II had sent both his blessing and a diadem to Stephen in 1000/1, thereby making him the first crowned Christian king of the Hungarians. Otto III had given his approval, signified with a gift of a copy of the Holy Lance that his great-grandfather had received from Rudolf of Burgundy and had brandished as the insignia of Christian rulership. In that moment, Stephen took his place in an ordered hierarchy of Christian princes at whose apex Otto, as emperor, exercised pre-eminent authority.[4] Yet only a century and a half previously, the Hungarians (Magyars, in their own language) were the very 'heathens steadfast in their savage religion' whose attacks had so terrorized Louis the German and his subjects, and for whose defeat the monks of Lorsch had prayed. Their transformation from a cluster of semi-nomadic tribes in the western Asian steppe practising shamanism and spirit worship into a single people settled west of the Carpathian mountains and cohering into a Christian kingdom happened with remarkable rapidity. Notably, Stephen's coronation and anointing in 1000/1 accompanied the establishment of an archbishopric at Esztergom, and this joint institutionalization of church authority and Christian rulership is often regarded as the founding moment of the Christian kingdom of Hungary. Further, in the years immediately following, King Stephen not only wrote his manual of advice for his son; he also issued two law codes that took additional steps to strengthen royal power, establish a church hierarchy, promote Christian beliefs, and eradicate social and religious practices unacceptable to his Christian clergy. In this perspective, he was himself the model Christian ruler whom his son should aspire to emulate, a king whose vision of a truly Christian society achieved by legislation held out the possibility of realizing many a missionary bishop's dreams. When he was formally recognized as a saint by the Hungarian bishops in 1083, half a century after his death, Stephen's role as national founding father was formalized and commemorated.

In Stephen of Hungary we find a succinct illustration of the ways in

7.1. Principal places mentioned in Chapter 7.

which kings were central to the religious life of the early Middle Ages, fostering Christianity and benefiting from the ideology that this religion in turn promoted. This chapter will track three themes that associated rulers with religion: the royal role in fostering the spread of Christianity at the expense of other religious identities; the distinctions of both practice and perception between Christianity and other early medieval religiosities and rulers' contribution to ensuring 'correct' Christian observance; and the place of kings in early medieval understanding of the relationship of the human to the sacred.

## The Spread of Christianity

When Stephen of Hungary died in 1038, the Christian religion was fully a millennium old. Its dissemination during these centuries had acquired a distinctive profile. As it became the predominant religion of the Roman world during the fourth and fifth centuries, Christianity had reached an accord with the empire, its modes of governance, and its characteristic social and cultural forms. Indeed, it was so firmly established that the demise of imperial government in the West in the course of the fifth century caused Christianity to recede or disappear only in those limited areas where prolonged military insecurity and invasion unravelled the whole fabric of the Roman way of life. Elsewhere, not least in the city of Rome itself, churchmen took over many of the functions of governance formerly fulfilled by the state. And in the provinces whose social cohesion and identity had anyway come to depend less and less on central government, Christian communities and their leaders rapidly adjusted themselves to the establishment of new kingdoms, seeing in their warrior kings the same possibilities for protection and patronage that they had been accustomed to enjoy under imperial aegis. The extent of Christianity in c.500 is indicated on Figure 7.2.

By the end of the fifth century, Christian observance was so widespread throughout and even beyond the Roman world that its presence led to a narrowing of options. In place of the religious pluralism of Antiquity, there had emerged a compulsory—even coercive—Christianity, whose essence was to deny the validity of any religious alternative. In the mid-seventh century, however, the arrival of Arab conquerors bringing the new religion of Islam into the Asian and African provinces of the Byzantine Empire both helped harden the conceptual boundaries between religions and greatly altered the geographical ones. In the face of the Arab advance, the Byzantine Empire lost the majority of its non-European territories during the course of the seventh century, and the conquest of Spain in 711 left only the mountainous north of the peninsula under Christian control. To be sure, there remained thereafter extensive Christian communities under Islamic rule, and Byzantium also managed to maintain control of ancient Christian cities in Asia Minor, but, from the later seventh century, a religious frontier effectively threaded across the Mediterranean. That frontier came to be as much cultural and political as religious, and, with only

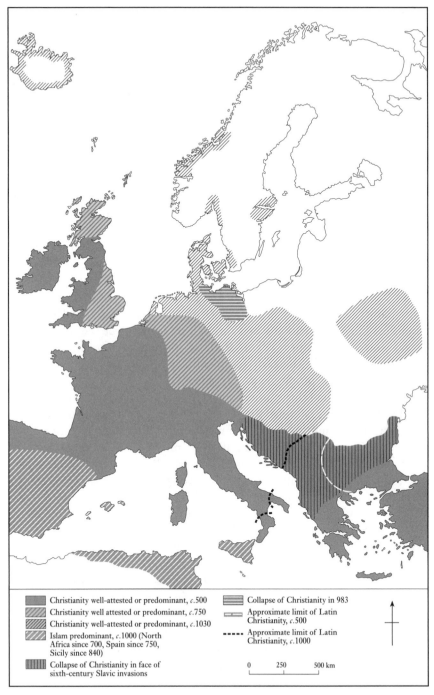

7.2. The extent of Christianity in the early Middle Ages. This map indicates the expansion of Christianity beyond its late Roman limits, as well as areas where it ceased to be a significant presence.

minor fluctuations, would remain unaltered until the eleventh century. Its presence defined identities in a new and sharper way.

North of the Mediterranean, another equally profound geographical transformation was occurring, as the old boundaries of empire along the Danube, the Rhine, and across northern Britain ceased to mark the limits of a Christian church organized to fit the Roman administrative template, with its division of the empire into dioceses and provinces. As Figure 7.2 shows, between the fourth and the seventh century, the Christian religion found its way to all corners of the British Isles; during the eighth and ninth centuries it extended from the Rhine to the Elbe, and then from the Danube to the Dnieper and the Baltic in the course of the tenth and early eleventh centuries. Indeed, Hungary was only one of several Christian kingdoms newly established around the turn of the millennium: the rulers of Poland, Bohemia, Denmark, Norway, and the Rus principality of Kiev all adopted Christianity within the decades 970–1030. Far out in the north Atlantic, even the communities of Vikings-turned-farmers who had settled on Iceland made a collective decision to adopt Christianity in 999/1000. In the course of the early Middle Ages, Christianity 'had gained many kingdoms and had triumphed over the mightiest kings and had crushed through its own power the necks of the proud and the sublime'. When Radbod, bishop of Utrecht (899–917), wrote those words in the early tenth century he cannot have known that they were as much prophetic as retrospective.[5]

How and why had this come about? Three salient characteristics of early medieval Christianity contribute to the explanation: its small-scale forms of organization, multiple social definitions, and doctrinal flexibility. As to the first, Christians had evolved a fairly standard form of organization by $c.500$, in which regional communities of worship (dioceses) were supervised by a bishop who had jurisdiction over professional ritual specialists (priests) who served local churches. The bishop of Rome—the pope—was widely acknowledged as the most senior leader of Christians in the West: if he was respected, it was out of deference, for, as the next chapter will explain, he commanded no jurisdictional obedience before $c.1050$. When groups of bishops acted in concert, they did so in a regional or sometimes a national level, but not a universal one. It became customary during the early Middle Ages for the pope to sanction the creation of new arch-bishoprics (such as Esztergom) as national or regional 'super-bishoprics', but new dioceses could be established, and new village churches built and staffed, wherever needed, without papal authorization. In addition, communities of celibate men or women living together established themselves wherever Christianity took hold. Although in the course of the early

Middle Ages these tended to become formalized to a common pattern, most monasteries nevertheless remained autonomous. In institutional terms, then, Christian modes of organization remained decentralized and could easily be replicated everywhere.

In social and doctrinal terms, early medieval Christianity evinced considerable fluidity. No consensus had emerged as to quite what being a 'Christian' meant except inasmuch as it designated a person who had made a public profession of this identity by undergoing the initiation ritual of baptism, or who had had that profession made on his or her behalf. Theologically speaking, that announcement implied that the individual was open to the possibility of eternal life after death. As Julian, bishop of Toledo (680–90), affirmed, 'everyone who is truly a Christian should in no way doubt that the flesh will be resurrected of all persons who have been born or will be born and who have died or will die'.[6] On this point, there was indeed agreement. The practical implications of the baptismal profession remained imprecise, however. More rigorous definitions of being a Christian emphasized ethical conduct, disengagement from the ties of secular society, and intellectual understanding of that belief. At its fullest, Christianity pulled all aspects of temporal, human existence into relationship with the divine in the course of a search for salvation in eternity. The precise doctrinal implications of that also remained negotiable. In the 500 years since its origins in Palestine, the religion's teachings had not been systematized into a single, coherent body of doctrine of undisputed meaning. Nor would that happen during the early Middle Ages: those who debated and wrote about its tenets had likeminded views on some but not all issues. Few indeed were equipped or inclined to participate in such learned discussions, not that these debates would have meant anything to the person baptized at birth into an isolated rural community visited occasionally by a barely literate priest. Being 'Christian' in the early Middle Ages was not susceptible to a standardized definition.

Thus, before c.1100, Christianity was organized in ways that were local but nevertheless replicable anywhere. Further, there was a spectrum of definitions of what it meant to be Christian and a range of interpretations of the core tenets of doctrine. In effect, early medieval Christianity was neither centralized nor systematized. Not a single, uniform cultural package to be adopted or rejected as an entity, it comprised a repertoire of beliefs, social practices, and organizational forms that could be adopted and adapted piecemeal. Thus Christianity jumped from one cultural and political context to another, repeatedly mutating and reconstituting itself in ways that preserved its core features. Differently put, a religion with an avowedly universal message managed to localize itself in a multitude of cultural contexts. Pluralisms and possibilities remained the hallmarks of early medieval Christianity—or, better, of early medieval Christianities— and enabled this universal religion to take endlessly varied local forms. Christianity thus reinforced the localisms so characteristic of the early Middle Ages.

Traditional narratives of the spread of Christianity do not take adequate account of these local variations. They offer a story of its diffusion from ancient Mediterranean centres of power through the work of famous men—emperors, kings, missionaries, and sometimes even popes. Inherent in this interpretation is a set of anachronistic assumptions about what constitutes normative Christianity. Those local particularities become much more evident when we start from a vantage point at the boundaries of Christendom, not at its centre. Kings and missionaries will concern us somewhat later.

As zones of cultural and economic interchange, early medieval frontiers were just as porous as Roman ones. Cross-border contacts made in the course of normal activities such as travelling and trading might be channels of encounter or dissemination through which Christianity seeped. The reception of passing merchants, missionaries, or political envoys offered moments of interaction, generating a modicum of familiarity with the Christian religion long before its adoption. Thus, when Franks and Danes met on the banks of the Eider to swear peace in 811, each group of envoys did so 'according to their own ritual and custom', the former taking an explicitly Christian oath, the latter doing something different.[7] The Magyars offer another example of a people whose contacts with Christianity preceded the arrival of Byzantine and German missionaries among them in the course of the tenth century, for in the early 880s the Greek missionary Methodius had travelled between Constantinople and the Slav lands through Hungarian territory along the Danube, where he was received with 'honor, solemnity, and joy' by their leader, who showered him with gifts.[8] Such encounters belong to the world of long-distance travel and took place at the level of elites and political leaders. But local cross-border encounters could also prompt the emergence of Christian communities in their hinterland. This is the likely explanation for the presence of organized churches in places such as Whithorn and Abercorn in the fifth and sixth centuries, north of the Roman frontier in Britain, or at Nilkheim in the early eighth century, beyond the eastern periphery of Merovingian Gaul.

Trade is a well-documented means of gaining knowledge of another religion. Doubtless the prayers and rituals of Christian merchants travelling beyond the limits of Christendom drew occasional comment. Better recorded, however, are the experiences of non-Christian merchants whose trade took them into Christian territories. Ninth-century merchants from the Scandinavian emporia encountered Christianity in the course of their travels. Some men from the Baltic emporium at Hedeby had been baptized at *Dorestad*, for example. Others recollected enough of what the Frankish missionary bishop Anskar (d. 865) had preached to suggest to the Swedes trying to sack the eastern Baltic settlement of *Apulia* that they appeal to the Christian god for help when their own deities were unwilling to assist.

Another notable form of encounter and dissemination of Christianity was cross-border raiding and slaving. Late Roman writers were well aware that Christian slaves sometimes spread Christianity to their captors: the most famous example is Patrick, the Romano-British Christian carried off into slavery by Irish raiders who escaped and later returned to Ireland to preach to his former masters at some point in the fifth century. In this respect, nothing changed with the political disintegration of the Roman Empire, for the slaving that marked the rim of all powerful polities in the early Middle Ages continued to function as a channel of religious interaction. Notably, on arrival at Birka, Anskar had found a considerable number of Christian captives. A tale from the 840s reveals how such people found themselves in transit around Europe's periphery. Fintan was a Christian, the son of a petty Irish ruler in Laigin, whose kin were busy feuding with a neighbouring warlord. To pre-empt further retaliation, his opponents resorted to guile: they invited Fintan to a feast on the beach and arranged for a group of Vikings in the neighbourhood to stage a raid and seize him. Fintan was rapidly and repeatedly sold on from one Viking to another, until he found himself the property of a man ready to return home, who shipped him off with his other captives. En route back to Scandinavia, the crew stopped overnight at an uninhabited island in the Orkneys, where Fintan managed to escape. Pledging himself never to return home, he swam to safety on a nearby island, and ended his days in 881 as a hermit in the foothills of the Alps at Rheinau.

The most notorious form of frontier violence is, of course, warfare, and this in its own way also contributed to the spread of Christianity. In the 250s, Goths living adjacent to the Roman frontier in the Crimea had frequently raided the southern, Roman shore of the Black Sea. On occasion, they returned with Christian prisoners, and from such inauspicious beginnings, the Goths acquired their first knowledge of Christianity. Some Goths converted; certainly the captive community preserved its religion for several generations until Ulfilas's imperially sponsored mission in the

340s–350s turned the Goths to the Arian interpretation of Christianity in vogue in imperial circles at that time.[9] Another perhaps more frequent scenario was the exposure to Christianity in imperial detention of prisoners and hostages taken from frontier peoples. Charlemagne's wars against the Saxons were notorious for their bloodshed and unremitting determination to crush Saxon society and religion, substituting Christianity at swordpoint.[10] A modest administrative memorandum from 805–6 records for us the names of thirty-seven Saxon hostages entrusted singly or in pairs to the safekeeping of the bishops, abbots, and counts of Alamannia. Their fates are unknown, but these were evidently men important enough to have had their lives spared—for refashioning as Christian subjects of the conquering emperor. Many other successful Carolingian and Ottonian campaigns against pagan enemies must have ended similarly.

From the late fourth century onwards, the periphery of the Christian Roman Empire was also a zone where not only individuals and small groups were in transit, but sometimes also armies and whole peoples. As warlords and their retinues crossed the frontier in search of new homes within the empire, so they found themselves settling among Christians. Some, such as the Goths and Vandals who settled within the empire in the early fifth century, were already Christians, albeit Arian Christians. For others, however, adoption of Christianity followed after migration into the empire. As the Franks expanded the area of their political control and settlement into the northern half of Gaul in the course of the fifth century, they must have had extensive contacts with the region's well-established urban Christian communities, and with such rural ones as existed. Here, religious change came not through travellers or missionaries, but through the sustained interactions of everyday life. Intermarriage was one aspect of that: whenever a Frankish warrior married a Christian woman, the household became a focus for religious change. In Gaul and elsewhere, the importance of Christian wives and mothers in spreading their religion cannot be overestimated. Only at royal level, however, does the surviving evidence enable us to track this in any detail. Clovis, the Frankish king whose acceptance of Christianity in (probably) 508 made him a trophy convert of great significance both to contemporaries and to posterity, had long been married to a Christian Burgundian princess. Chlothild's determination to have her children baptized and her personal influence over Clovis contributed to his decision to accept Christianity, earning herself a place in later legend as 'the mother of France'. From farmstead to palace, the domestic household was one of the most effective—if least well-documented—focuses for religious change and acculturation.

Except in the lower Rhineland, the gradual accommodation of the Franks to Christianity entailed no substantive disruption to Gallo-Roman Christianity. If anything, it enhanced the influence of leading churchmen. Elsewhere, however, the movement of armies and settlers often had a more deleterious effect. Christianity had spread throughout Britain by the late fourth century, but, when Anglo-Saxon settlers crossed the North Sea during the fifth and sixth centuries, its institutional organization crumbled throughout south-eastern Britain. Such Christianity as did survive here did so only as a few isolated pockets, bereft of clerical leadership. Perhaps the same happened in the Danube plain in the tenth century, for the western part of the region taken over by the Magyars included well-established Christian communities who seem to have passed their own vernacular religious terminology on to their conquerors.

In contrast to this slow, almost unchronicled cultural seepage, the political jolts that jump-started Christianity in new environments are highly visible in the sources. These form the second, quite different, means by which the religion spread: the decisive actions of powerful men and women whose impact was often rapid and wide-ranging. Whether as a narrative of rulers whose conversion harked back to that of the emperor Constantine (306–37), of queens who persuaded their consorts of a different understanding of their power, or of evangelizers obedient to Christ's injunction 'go ye and teach all nations, baptizing them in the name of the Father, the Son and the Holy Ghost' (Matt. 28: 19), the spread of Christianity is also a tale of high politics and of individuals whose fame Christian communities dutifully nurtured.

As a royal action, the acceptance—or rejection—of the new religion commonly took place against the background of a politics of hegemony. The assertion of influence by an overlord over a lesser ruler, the search by a petty king for support from a powerful neighbour, or simply the desire to emulate a proven recipe for succesful kingship all played their part. Whether on their own initiative or in response to royal instruction, preachers moved through the same channels of communication, only infrequently setting out for places unconnected even in any indirect way with their homeland. They brought with them political contacts, prestigious gifts, experience in magnificent ritual, and, not least, prior familiarity with the authoritative script for enacting successful conversion.

In these circumstances, acceptance of Christianity bore all the marks of political spectacle, carefully staged. When in 597/8 the Kentish king Æthelberht accepted Christianity from Augustine, a Roman monk working with the support of the Frankish overlords of Kent, 10,000 people, so it was claimed, were baptized as well. Demographically preposterous but rhetorically effective, the figure indicates an eye-catching occasion of immediate significance. The baptism of fourteen Bohemian princes with their retinues at the court of Louis the German at Regensburg in 845 must also have offered an impressive sight. Sometimes a superior king stood godfather to the convert ruler, sponsoring his change of identity and receiving him from the baptismal font, using baptism to assert a hierarchy of deference. Such were the circumstances in which Alfred of Wessex sponsored the baptism of his defeated enemy, the Viking leader Guthrum in 878. Royal baptism might also aim to tie future rulers into an alliance: during Otto III's visit to Gniezno in 1000, he became godfather to a newborn son of the Christian Polish prince, Boleslaw Chobry (992–1025), in a ceremony rich in symbolic importance. He also strengthened the bond by giving Boleslaw both a royal crown and another replica of the Holy Lance (still to be seen in Cracow).

To ask whether religious or political motivations underlay such baptisms is misplaced, for the distinction was meaningless in an age in which identities were as much social as personal and in which religious expression was more usually communal than individual. Petty or powerful, rulers needed to act out in visually dramatic form their political relationships with both superiors and underlings. Indeed, kings could function only with the support of their leading men. Anxieties about conversion, or conversion followed by apostasy, were thus the symptoms of conflict within a ruling group. In north-western Europe, the tensions between acceptance or rejection of the new religion could reflect choices about overlordship, perhaps also conflicts between older and younger members of a ruling elite. Æthelberht of Kent's death in 616 was followed by a reversion to pagan ways led by his son and successor, while a century later the Frisian ruler Radbod (d. 719) backed out of the baptismal font on being told that his pagan ancestors would not accompany him to the Christian heaven. Here, the issue of collective identity was expressed in terms of social cohesion between the living and the dead, but the hard reality was that Frankish aggression had fostered conflict within the Frisian elite.

Rulers in central Europe in the ninth, tenth, and eleventh centuries faced an additional dilemma in choosing between the Christianity sponsored by the Carolingian emperors and their Ottonian heirs, and that of the Byzantine emperors. As Chapter 1 emphasized, the former used Latin as its sacred language and looked to Rome for authenticity and sometimes even leadership, whereas the latter was prepared to adapt local vernacular languages for ritual use and had its jurisdictional centre at Constantinople. The choice was inevitably also one of political advantage, a dilemma particularly acute in the decades when the two empires, east and west, were actively competing for allies and influence. In the lower Danube basin, Khan Boris of the Bulgars (852–89) was a military threat and potential ally for Franks and Byzantines alike: both cultivated him and sought influence over him. This was the context of Boris's decision to adopt Christianity and of his baptism in 864/5. But political and cultural orientation remained an issue, and Boris negotiated at length with both Rome and Constantinople before opting for Greek Christianity in 870. A century or so later, the emerging Hungarian kingdom faced similar pressures. In the late tenth century, German and Byzantine missionaries worked simultaneously among the Magyars: the Greek clergy remained active long after King Stephen's coronation under papal and Ottonian auspices.

We should return briefly to Stephen's reign. He was a Christian king ruling subjects among whom local, unremarked, and unremarkable missionary work in spreading Christianity was gradually proceeding, and would long continue, interrupted by pagan revolts for some decades to come. Establishment of the archbishopric of Estzergom had to be followed by the gradual installation of the institutional infrastructure of a national Christianity—a network of bishops, the foundation and endowment of monasteries in which communities of men or women led a disciplined life of austerity and prayer, the training of local priests in ritual specialisms and the Latin language. Traditional procedures had to be renegotiated to meet the expectations of Christian clergy for legal protection and privileged status and for grants of land to be held in perpetuity. And the long, slow process of accommodation between traditional Magyar social conventions and the ethical demands of Christian doctrine had to be set in motion. In all this, Stephen of Hungary was exceptional only in the documentation that his zealous promotion of Christianity generated and in the alacrity with which he acted. His reign simply encapsulated a well-recorded, high-speed version of what many convert kings had faced in preceding centuries.

To achieve these goals took time and political determination. In areas where the spread of Christianity remained limited to informal contacts, institutionalization did not occur. In the absence of a priestly hierarchy or full literacy, we find improvisational forms of Christian living that flourished in ways that made sense to their practitioners but often met with suspicion or outright condemnation from the missionaries who finally caught up with these people. Such a one was Frideburg, a Christian woman living among the predominantly non-Christian Swedes in the middle of the ninth century. Knowing about a ritual involving wine sipped by the dying (the *viaticum*, in which consecrated wine is administered to the dying by a priest as part of rituals to ease the passage of the Christian soul to heaven), she purchased wine and set it aside with instructions to her daughter to give it to her to drink on her deathbed. Another such was Ørlygr Hrappson, a Norwegian who had been fostered in his youth by an Irish bishop in the Hebrides. In the early tenth century he journeyed to Iceland, equipped with the timbers to build a church, a liturgical book, and 'consecrated earth' to bury under its corner pillars. This last would have horrified anyone trained in the correct procedures for consecrating a new church. Ørlygr had named his church in honour of the Gaelic saint Columba, and there, three generations later, his descendants still 'believed in Columba although they were not baptized'.[11] Such 'do-it-yourself' Christianity was the concomitant of the slow seepage of religious change through informal channels of contact in the absence of an organized priesthood: although sparsely documented, it must have flourished all around the margins of institutionalized Christendom and in remote, internal pockets.

Whether we focus attention on the spread of Christianity by informal or by formal means, we are repeatedly reminded that religious change always occurred within social contexts, contexts that were frequently also political. It affected families and households, royal courts, armies, merchant communities, each in different and distinctive ways. Two general points can nevertheless be made. First, if early medieval men and women balanced views about the 'truth' of Christian doctrine against political or pragmatic motives in their acceptance of the new religion, we do not hear about it in their own terms. To be sure, deeply Christian writers believed this was what converts should do, and sometimes represented them as doing, but the actual reasoning that underlay religious change remains hidden from us. We may be sure, however, that the need to make a decision was much sharper for some than for others, sharper for rulers—or rebels—than loyal followers, for parents than children. Secondly, neither the baptism of a ruler and his retinue nor the domestic adoption of certain Christian practices necessarily resulted in a rapid and complete spiritual, moral, and social transformation. As previous chapters have made clear, shifts in burial rituals, sexual behaviour, responses to sickness, and much else besides, did occur but were slow, erratic, and extremely difficult to enforce. In neither geographical nor chronological terms can we detect an even momentum: the spread of Christianity followed many different routes and rhythms. Highly dependent on a shifting matrix of specific circumstances of place and time, it meant different things to different people. In sum, early medieval Christianity consisted of local knowledge not universal 'truth'.

## Pagans and Christians

Despite their many local forms of organization, ritual, and social practice, the Christianities of early medieval Europe nevertheless had much in common. At the heart of the Christian world view lay the claim that this religion provided the only possible truth about the relationship of the supernatural (or divine), the natural (or earthly), and the human (or social). These universalizing notions appealed to rulers and their advisers because they reordered ideas of community, shaped new identities, identified new enemies, and supplied new justifications of royal power. As a mindset that opposed Christians and non-Christians solidified, it became the task of kings and clerics everywhere to extirpate 'error' wherever they might find it. In this way, Christianity transformed the imaginative landscapes of its adoptive societies. By providing a common stock of universal values, it offered them new ways of linking together. By promising warrior kings new ideologies and modes of communication, it encouraged them towards a shared ethic and even a common purpose.[12] Indeed, it succeeded so well in offering an overarching, umbrella identity that, by the early eleventh century, 'Christendom' and 'Europe' had become virtually synonymous. By the end of the first millennium, scattered communities of Jews formed the only significant non-Christian presence in Europe; treated with an ambivalent mix of disregard, tolerance, and hostility, they tested the limits of early medieval Europe's identity as a compulsory Christian community.

Compulsory Christianity rested on notions inherited from late Antiquity that deemed it not only a universal religion but also the only 'right' one. In this triumphalist perspective, the spread of Christianity was often represented as the eradication of 'wrong' religions. Hrabanus Maurus stated this pithily: 'Christianity destroys all errors.'[13] This rhetorical position denied any validity to other religions. Their gods were simply redefined as demons, their moral teachings and cult practices condemned as depraved.

Then the devil and his servant demons . . . began to appear to humankind in various forms and speak with them and demand of them that they offer sacrifices to them on high mountains and in leafy forests and they worship them as God. . . . One demon claimed to be Jupiter, who had been a magician and involved in so many adulteries that he had taken his own sister, Juno, as his wife and had corrupted his daughters, Minerva and Venus, and had even committed foul incest with his nieces and all his female relatives. Another demon called himself Mars, who had sown quarrels and discord. . . . Another demon imagined herself to be Venus; she had been a whore and not only participated in innumerable adulteries, but had even prostituted herself with her father, Jupiter, and her brother, Mars. . . . The demons even persuaded people to build temples to them and to place therein images or statues of wicked men and to set up altars to them, on which they should pour out for them blood both of animals and even of men.[14]

By thus inverting the religious valency of the traditional Roman deities, Martin, bishop of Braga (556–79), denatured them and ridiculed any attempt to assert their authenticity. His views circulated widely in the early Middle Ages, and were reiterated in various ways. For example, when baptism was administered in Germany in the vicinity of the missionary outpost of Fulda in the late eighth–ninth centuries, new Christians who accepted Christ promised to 'forsake all the works and words of the devils Thunor, Woden and Saxnot and all the fiends that are their companions'.[15]

Another way Christians dealt with indigenous gods was by denying their suprahuman status. By reducing gods to the status of mortals, Christians attempted to render rival deities innocuous. Daniel, bishop of Winchester (c.705–44), proffered this advice to Boniface on one of his preaching missions in Germany: 'You ought not to offer opposition to them concerning the genealogy of their gods, false though they are, but allow them to assert according to their belief that some were begotten of others through the intercourse of male and female, so that you may then at any rate show gods and goddesses born after the manner of humans to have been humans, not gods, and, since they did not exist before, to have had a beginning.'[16] Thus reduced to human status, gods might find themselves relegated to the distant past. Woden, one of the most widely venerated Germanic gods, suffered this fate, particularly among the various Anglo-Saxon peoples. Two and one half centuries after Christian missionaries had introduced their religion into southern England, Woden had been demoted from god to founding ancestor of royal dynasties, and from the primordial begetter of kings to descendant of Adam, the first human whom, according to scriptural tradition, the Judaeo-Christian God had created. Elsewhere—notably Ireland, Iceland, and Scandinavia—epics, sagas, and myths often kept these figures alive for many centuries more in a literary afterlife that filtered representations of the pagan past through long Christian experience.

From the fifth century onwards, Christian oppositional rhetoric also lumped together all non-Christians, except Jews, by dismissing them pejoratively as 'pagans'. Certainly no one would ever have used this as a term of self-identification. Its deployment hides from us the great variety of the indigenous religious traditions of early medieval Europe and deliberately obscures any understanding of their true nature. In attempting to assess this, we must proceed carefully. Whereas the thoughts and voices of upholders of the non-Christian religions of the Roman world have sometimes come down to us directly in writing, there is no comparable avenue into the religious attitudes or experiences of those men and women of the early Middle Ages who were not Christian, for, as Chapter 1 made clear, literacy in anything more than terse, incised inscriptions was a Christian introduction. We can rely only on material remains that may have had a religious significance, on linguistic traces (place names, for example), or on the accounts of non-Christian beliefs and practices offered by Christian writers.

With caution, we may nevertheless posit some broad outlines of the traditional religiosities that Christian preachers encountered as they moved outside the Roman world. Unlike Judaism, Christianity, or Islam, none of them depended upon a corpus of sacred texts, a prophetic tradition, or recognition of a single, universal deity. None had any doctrine and orthodoxy to defend, or a word expressing the complex abstraction 'religion'. They did not order the cosmos around a single, all-powerful figure, or even an opposed, dualist, pair, but found it to be inhabited by innumerable spirits who both influenced mortal affairs and were open to human manipulation. Everywhere, from the deepest earth to the most distant stars, the natural and the supernatural, the physical and the spirit, interlocked and interacted. Within this, the place of humankind was secured by means of myths, rituals, stores of sacred knowledge, or the activities of practitioners such as shamans, seers, or druids. Their rituals also offered ways of understanding and trying to control the elemental forces of life and death, fertility and sickness, war and prosperity. Propitiation of gods and spirits through sacrifice, binding, or invoking them with talismans and amulets; prediction of the future by means such as divination; and regulation of human conduct through taboos all appear to have been common. Thus sacral activities were so bound up with other aspects of human existence—familial, domestic, agricultural, political, military—as to make redundant any attempt to regard 'religion' as a discrete category of experience.

Despite these generalities, and despite apparently widespread cults of a few gods (such as the Germanic Woden), religious traditions were nevertheless very much about local identity, whether of group or of place. Many of the geographical specificities elude us, especially since we are much better informed about the religious traditions of some regions than of others. It is nevertheless clear that a god might be the primordial ancestor of a warrior elite; a natural feature such as an ancient tree might encapsulate the essence of a community; or a sacred site might be the ritual heart of a polity or a place of sacrifice. Thus, seventh-century Lombards believed they acquired their name when Woden promised the Langobards, the 'long-bearded men', victory in battle, whilst the southern tip of Ireland was ruled by the Corcu Loígde, the 'family of the Calf Goddess'. The German region of Lommatsch acquired its name from a sacred spring venerated by the local populace for its ability to predict the future by announcing peace and a good harvest with a scattering of wheat, oats, and acorns, but 'when the savage storms of war threaten, it gives a clear indication of the outcome with blood and ash'.[17] Perched upon their *terpen* above the tidal marshes along the North Sea coast, eighth-century Frisians identified in the forces of the flood tide a god to be placated by human sacrifice. By contrast, in the century following their overthrow of Ottonian rule in 983, the Liutizi Slavs organized their resistance to German rulers and their religion around their chief shrine, that of the god Swarozyc in the holy compound at *Riedegost*.

Archaeology helps elaborate this sketchy account. In Scandinavia and northern-central Europe in particular, traces of ritual sacrifices—animals, humans, weaponry—have been found, sometimes in special ritual enclosures, elsewhere as deposits in bogs, beside lakes, or around trees. Material remains and textual records alike confirm that sacred precincts could also contain pillar-shaped idols of wood or stone, but only in southern Scandinavia and the western Slav lands have statues of gods in figural form been found. Finds such as the Danish site at Nydam with its huge fourth- and fifth-century ritual deposits of weaponry and a boat; the figurines of gods and the remains of tenth-century horse sacrifices from Oldenburg, a Slavic stronghold on the Baltic coast of modern Germany; or the tenth- and eleventh-century remains of animals heaped around the trunk of a tree on Frösö, an island cult centre in northern Sweden, are all a graphic reminder of beliefs and practices that Christianity would in due course annihilate.

Inasmuch as modern scholars cannot study these indigenous religiosities through internal textual evidence, they are in a formal sense prehistoric. They should not thereby be assumed to be ahistoric. Ways in which they changed over time can indeed be detected, not least through interaction with neighbouring hegemonic cultures or with Christianity. The invention of the ogam alphabet by the pre-Christian Irish is one example already encountered. In the fifth and sixth centuries, Anglo-Saxon settlers in Britain may have begun to use special cult buildings either by taking over old Roman temples and churches or by building their own wooden shrines in deliberate imitation. In late-tenth- and early eleventh-century

Denmark, rune stones sometimes invoked the power of the god Thor in formulae whose wording betrays Christian influence. And the Liutizi, the Danes' neighbours, had not always worshipped in temples, nor had one sanctuary always taken precedence over others in their territory: as opposition to German rule hardened, so their indigenous religion acquired a structure and organization that mimicked their opponents' religion. When it came to the mutual reinforcement of political and sacral power, there was no better model than Christianity.

That indigenous religious traditions responded to the influence of a neighbouring Christianity should be no great surprise, for the porous nature of early medieval frontiers has already been stressed. In practice, religious beliefs and practices are never hermetically sealed systems, but develop through creative engagement, acculturation, or opposition with their wider social milieux. Thus, however stark the triumphalist antithesis of Christian truth and pagan error became, this conceptual dichotomy did not generally inform everyday religious experience, except for Christian armies urged into battle specifically to defeat pagans. For the most part, the reality of personal circumstance did not match up to a missionary ideology that presented conversion to Christianity as a total personal reorientation accompanied by complete rejection of the pre-Christian past.

Narratives about convert kings often make this clear: we may return to Hungary to make the point. King Stephen's father, Géza (c.970–97), had come to power at a moment when the Hungarians were poised between the two empires, Byzantine and German; under his rule, they swung their political allegiance decisively westwards. German missionaries from Bavaria supplemented the Greek ones already active amongst the Hungarians and baptized Géza himself in 972. Yet, battling other chieftains as he was to confirm his own paramount leadership over the Hungarians, he took whatever route he could to consolidate his position. A murderous man of quick temper, Géza, now Christian, 'turned his rage against his reluctant subjects, in order to strengthen this faith. Thus, glowing with zeal for God, he washed away his old crimes. He sacrificed both to the omnipotent God and to various false gods. When reproached by his priest for doing so, however, he maintained that the practice had brought him both wealth and great power.'[18] Like a considerable number of other rulers importuned by missionaries, Géza preferred religious pluralism to the rejection of old ways. Christian baptism complemented rather than replaced traditional worship. He seems to have recognized that the Hungarians' inherited religious beliefs and practices were too bound up with their identity and modes of living to be jettisoned without unravelling everything he sought to build. Géza, then, reminds us that baptism did not of itself eradicate traditional practices or rewrite the past. Conversion to Christianity should be seen as an extended encounter and interaction between different religious and cultural systems, not as the substitution of one for another that triumphalist historiography implies.

In late Antiquity, Christian leaders had come to realize that membership of the Christian community as marked by baptism was not enough to distinguish a Christian from a pagan. They began to move the goalposts, arguing that all forms of human behaviour must be distinctive. 'It is not enough for us to receive the name of Christians if we do not conduct ourselves as Christians', Caesarius of Arles warned his sixth-century audience.[19] Thus Christianity gradually became a religion of quotidian morality, which, as we have seen, concerned itself with the regular rhythms of daily life—times of work and worship, feasting and fasting, sex and abstinence—as well as with its unpredictable crises, such as fevered children, lame horses, or inclement weather. Thus Caesarius remonstrated that his Christian hearers should not respond to sickness by any means other than Christian ones. The peasant mother of Provence who drank a herbal drink to procure an abortion, who took a sick child to a diviner or a woman skilled in herbs, or who hung a written charm round the child's neck doubtless relied on practices that had been known for generations to be effective. A visit to a Christian priest or saint's shrine was only one of several therapeutic strategies available to her for coping with sickness and disaster. For Caesarius, however, these other strategies were all 'the persuasion of the devil'.[20] He demanded that his hearers abandon their traditional cosmology, in which the supernatural and the human came together and interacted in a wide range of persons and places, and instead seek out only those approved by their bishop: churches, saints, and priests. Even so, it was not enough to go to the right places, for he also told his congregation that to leap around dancing outside saints' shrines was 'to come to church Christian but leave pagan'.[21]

Caesarius threw a *cordon sanitaire* around Christianity, thereby staking out a clear distinction between 'right' Christianity and 'wrong' Christianity. In formulating the difference, he extended the condemnatory rhetoric formerly applied to non-Christian practices to cover anything his baptized congregation did that met with his disapproval. This language was the traditional polemic of 'superstition' and 'error'. 'Superstition' signalled any behaviour that the ecclesiastical elite deemed detrimental to the salvation of their Christian flock. As the persons, places, rituals, and words that mediated between humankind and the supernatural gradually all became subject to ecclesiastical claims to regulate them, 'superstition' was the term of abuse for anything that escaped that control and therefore lay on the wrong side of the conceptual boundary between right and wrong Christianity.

When Hrabanus Maurus declared that 'Christianity destroys errors', he defined these as 'idolatry, avarice and other vices', not bothering to distinguish non-Christian practices from inappropriate conduct by Christians.[22] Of wrong Christianity, Hrabanus doubtless had much direct experience. But of idolatry and other non-Christian practices he had at best a second- or third-hand knowledge, acquired from his reading or from his correspondence with missionary priests. His pagans were all in the mind, but that did not stop him pronouncing on how to deal with them. The method was clear: it was a royal one. As archbishop of Mainz, Hrabanus worked in close conjunction with his king, Louis the German. That it was a key task of kings to assist churchmen in the extirpation of error had been established by Louis's grandfather, Charlemagne. By a verbal association that the English language cannot reproduce, Isidore of Seville's popular encyclopaedic handbook, the *Etymologies*, had specified the correction of his subjects as an essential duty of a king. **Reges a regendo vocati**. . . . *Non autem* **regit** *qui non* **corrigit** ('kings take their title from the act of ruling. . . . However he who does not correct does not rule').[23] The point was more than wordplay: it sketched an entire moral agenda. Converted into a vigorous legislative programme first by the Iberian Gothic kings of Isidore's own day, adopted one and a half centuries later by Charlemagne, and subsequently disseminated wherever the ideals of his reign caught on, the royal responsibility for the correction of religious error gave a new twist to the distinction between Christian and pagan. An energetic Christian king such as Louis the German not only 'humbl[ed] the pagan heathens' on the battlefield; he worked closely with his leading bishops to inculcate correct Christianity amongst his subjects.

In such an environment, the do-it-yourself Christianity of remote areas might seem suspect, however authentic it was to its practitioners. 'Superstition' and 'error' were in the eye of the beholder not the perpetrator, for, during the early Middle Ages, the ecclesiastical elite arrogated to themselves the right to specify what constituted correct Christianity. One of Hrabanus Maurus's predecessors as archbishop of Mainz, Boniface had spent the second quarter of the eighth century travelling and preaching in the Frankish Rhineland, Thuringia, and Bavaria. Here he encountered no sharp frontier between Christianity and paganism but rather a spectrum of practices. One of its extremes was the disciplined monasticism in which he himself had been trained; its other the non-Christian practices of regions too remote to have had any previous interaction with

Christendom. Most people were somewhere in between, however—easy-going bishops whose values were more those of their aristocratic kinsfolk than of an ascetic; baptized peasants who made sacrifices to Christian saints or sought to predict the future from horse dung; do-it-yourself Christians who were unaware that their children were baptized with garbled ritual formulae. By the time Boniface died in 754, he had deployed Caesarius's notion of 'superstition' to reduce this blurred spectrum to a sharp conceptual polarity of right and wrong Christianity.

Boniface is important because of the key role he took in formulating norms of correct Christianity and in encouraging rulers to throw their weight behind them. As vast areas of Europe rapidly fell under Carolingian rule in the second half of the eighth century, so these norms were promulgated and further elaborated by bishops working in tandem with kings who had taken to heart the task of 'correction'. Charlemagne and his heirs strove hard to promote correct Christianity, and the enthusiastic reception given to this ideal in late Anglo-Saxon England and in Ottonian–Salian Germany ensured that it long remained influential. By the early eleventh century, we find the task of correction even at Europe's eastern periphery, for it informed the legislation of Stephen of Hungary. Correct Christianity—as defined from Boniface onwards—was well on its way to becoming the single permissible Christianity.

But what about Europe's western extremity? Ireland, Christianized in the fifth century, remained untouched by Carolingian or Ottonian political or cultural hegemony. Christianity in Ireland had long since accommodated its modes of organization to the small-scale kingdoms and the politics of cattle and kinship, and had adapted biblical precepts in ways that made local sense. It was simply one of the many early medieval Christianities, and it proved remarkably enduring. But, in the eyes of those for whom there was only one correct Christianity, the Irish version had come to seem distinctly odd by the later eleventh century. In 1070, William the Conqueror appointed a new archbishop to the see of Canterbury. Lanfranc had been born in Pavia, the old royal capital of Italy, in c.1010, and was familiar both with the traditional responsibility of kings for the welfare of Christianity, and with novel ideals of a centrally organized, uniform Christianity that were developing from the middle years of the eleventh century onwards. In c.1074, Lanfranc took it upon himself to point out to the high king of Ireland, Toirrdelbach ua Briain, king of Munster (1063–86), that his Christianity was the wrong sort. Baptism was not administered the way Lanfranc deemed proper, marriages did not conform to the requirements formulated by continental churchmen, bishops were not consecrated in the same way as elsewhere. Toirrdelbach must 'correct' these 'appalling . . . practices' and 'evil customs'.[24] The Irish did respond, but slowly, and certainly not fast enough to counteract the view that they persisted in error. In 1155, in the changed climate of the twelfth century—changed by the emergence of claims to universal papal monarchy and fusion of the many local Christian communities of earlier centuries into a single, much more homogeneous Christendom—Pope Adrian IV authorized the invasion of Ireland by the English king Henry II (1154–89) on the grounds that it would be to Henry's eternal credit 'to enlarge the boundaries of the church, to reveal the truth of the Christian faith to peoples still untaught and barbarous, and to root out the weeds of vice from the Lord's field'.[25] The Irish, then, were all but outright pagans, outside the church: their lack of correct Christianity justified invasion and conquest. When diverse local Christianities yielded to a single, standardized, normative Christianity at swordpoint, the early Middle Ages were truly over.

## Good Kings, Bad Kings

In the spring of 961 Otto I prepared to undertake the dangerous march from Germany across the Alps to Rome. As part of his preparations, he had his 6-year-old son made king in order to secure the succession should he not return. The ceremony took place on 26 May in the chapel of the palace that Charlemagne had built at Aachen, the same spot where Otto had himself been consecrated at the beginning of his reign twenty-five years earlier. The young child, the future Otto II, found himself smeared with holy oil; then handed a symbolic sword, sceptre, and staff; crowned; and finally enthroned in a ceremony whose words, rituals, and gestures all had a long history, and which were as redolent of tradition as the location itself. At one level, the ceremony was a family affair, for, of the three archbishops who conducted the consecration, one was the new king's uncle, another his adult half-brother, and the third another relative. At another level, it bound both the junior and the senior Otto closely to the leading men of the realm, who were formally asked whether they were willing to submit to the rule of the new king, and to obey his commands. More complex still, it associated king, kingdom, and the Christian God in an intense bond, for Otto was asked, 'Do you wish to rule and defend the kingdom granted to you by God according to the justice of your ancestors?' and he replied with a formal promise that he would do so with God's help and the support of all those faithful to him.[26] As the consecration ceremony continued, it invoked all the complex ideas and ideologies of Christian kingship that had developed by the late tenth century. The king's role was to be the most strenuous of kings, the vanquisher of enemies, the guardian and defender of churches and the clergy. God was requested to crown him with 'the crown of justice and piety', to grant him victory over his enemies visible and invisible, and to bestow on him abundant harvests, health, peace, and heirs of his body. Divine help was invoked too to keep subject peoples loyal and magnates peaceable. In the course of the ceremony, Otto heard himself likened to the rulers of the ancient Israelites, leaders whom the Judaeo-Christian scriptures presented as anointed kings fighting in the name of God and ruling with justice and wisdom as mediators between God and people.

Much was going on here. Otto I had spent years crushing serious revolts led by close members of his own family—his own brothers, son, and son-in-law—and so he sought to bind his relatives and subjects to his chosen successor. But the consecration resolved the tensions by transforming a political decision into something else: it incorporated young Otto's kingship into the God-given, and thus 'natural' order of the world. By setting the new king apart from other people as a person especially close to God, it made a human choice seem beyond challenge. In a violent world, it gave one man the legitimate right to decree violence. Overall, it made acceptable the very fact of kingship, the pre-eminent power of one man over everyone else that constituted the fundamental form of political organization throughout the early Middle Ages.

Indeed, it made kingship more than acceptable: it made it desirable. In the course of the ceremony, the new ruler was instructed in the tasks, moral responsibilities, and rewards that awaited him. Here was something for everybody. He was to be a vigorous warrior, protector of churches and churchmen, of widows and the poor, and the source of all justice in his kingdom. In this, he was to promote the Christian religion both by defeating its enemies and by instructing and guiding his subjects. The purpose of warfare was to bring peace, not merely in the sense of the absence of warfare but in its much deeper meaning of a harmonious social order grounded in Christian principle and action. Here was the muscular Christianity espoused by many generations of Frankish rulers, applauded by the monks of Lorsch in their prayers for Louis the German (see quotation at head of chapter), and supported by the *potentes*. Here too was a king pledged to 'correct' his subjects by promoting the welfare of God's churches and by extirpating 'superstition' and 'error' wherever they lurked. In all this, the keynote was 'justice', a word that extended beyond its judicial meaning of rendering judgement in lawsuits to embrace the moral equity necessary to achieving that rightful social ordering. Thus kingship should be a convergence of interests between the king and his leading subjects, clerical and lay, to the advantage of all persons in the realm, the powerful and the poor. Consecration, then, articulated that consensus in magnificent ritual splendour.

The prayers intoned over the new king also hinted that fulfilment of these responsibilities would bring the divine blessings of peace, prosperity, and progeny on ruler and realm. The king who fulfilled his responsibilities—the good king—was thus the linchpin of a world view that regarded the ordering of human society as an integral part of the wider ordering of the entire cosmos. And since, by the later tenth century, that cosmos had long since been understood within a Christian frame of reference, it also demanded that the good king function within that vision of a social order whose ultimate goal was eternal salvation for all. The ruler should act, then, in the hope of winning 'eternal joys in perpetual blessedness' for himself.[27] The king thus linked the present moment to eternity. Through the explicit biblical parallels, he also joined the Old Testament past to Ottonian present, taking his place as another in the line of monarchs protected by God and ruling in his name. So consecration enacted beliefs about the right ordering of the human and the divine, the sacred and the secular.

Supercharged with political, ritual, and cosmological significance, an early medieval royal inauguration was a highly specific event. A dramatic interlude of ritual clarity in the midst of the normal contention of court politics, it made explicit that ruling was as much an ideological as a practical undertaking. As such, it both brought into sharp perspective ideas that were often much more fluid and set a standard for measuring a king's achievements. We may remain with Otto II for a moment longer, for the verdict passed on his reign by the historian Thietmar of Merseburg demonstrates this. Thietmar had lived through Otto II's reign, and assessed it by linking military failures to Christian morality and the conduct of his subjects to the condition of their king:

> Otto, the second bearer of this name . . .
> . . . was installed on the throne of his great father
> With worthy praise, he who helped all in need.
>
> .     .     .     .     .
>
> His youth was happy and fortunate, but sorrow arrived in his latter years
> Through the heavy burden of our sins.
> Then, this evil world did penance for rejecting the truth.[28]

In Thietmar's opinion, Otto II suffered because of the sins of his subjects: the king had lost good fortune, and the right ordering of society had slipped.

The high ideals of kingship that Otto strove to maintain had reached maturity in the reigns of Charlemagne and his immediate successors out of very much older traditions of both ritual and political thinking. They had congealed precisely because the unprecedented power that the Carolingians wielded required unprecedented justification. Charlemagne's power had taken many different forms—military success, attempts at regulation of many aspects of daily life, strenuous lordship manifested in vigorous economic exploitation of his lands and in successful manipulation of webs of aristocratic kinship—all of which imposed huge demands upon his subjects. The ideology and ceremonial of Christian kingship provided validation for this, deflecting attention away from the harsh realities of power. By stressing cosmic order not human oppression, divine legitimation made submission to such a strong ruler acceptable. And it offered kings access to a form of power that no quantity of treasure or fighting men could yield, for supernatural sanction was a form of legitimacy far more potent than mere political consensus, paternal designation, or success in battle. And when, from the mid-ninth century onwards, archbishops established a role—a prerogative, as they came to see it—in conveying the divine sanction to kings in the form of an ecclesiastical anointing, the synthesis of Christianity and kingship was complete. Thanks to clerical initiative, early medieval kings were the symbolic centre of a transcendent and explicitly Christian social order.

From the middle of the ninth century onwards, that Christian order also explicitly embraced a king's wife. In an innovation that lacked biblical precedent, a new ritual for consecrating a queen gave her a formal role in its maintenance. In addition to her well-attested courtly functions—domestic administration of a palace involved not only its provisioning but also regulating the flow of guests and gifts—the queen became a living icon of fertility, prosperity, and good conduct. It is no coincidence that queenship became both official and explicitly Christian in exactly the decades when Carolingian moralists were insisting on a new, tighter definition of marriage, and demanding that kings uphold it in their own lives. Through her new role as sole lifelong consort and chosen mother of the future heir, a queen's behaviour reflected directly upon her spouse. Her sexual modesty enhanced his reputation and epitomized the right ordering of society; her decorum betokened a king's wisdom in choosing her as his bride; her good counsel persuaded him to mercy; her fertility confirmed her husband's. Conversely, her barrenness might threaten political stability and seem a sign of divine disfavour; any hint of undue influence or allegation of sexual promiscuity undermined and unmanned a king's reputation for control of self, household, and society at large. Consecration, then, bestowed upon a queen heavy responsibilities for just rule and formalized her participation in upholding the transcendent order.

Once tapped in these ways, ideological power brought additional benefits. Protecting churches also meant endowing them generously. Among the Franks, the tomb of St Martin, among the Scots, the tomb of St Columba, among the Irish, the tomb of St Patrick—these and many others enjoyed landed wealth of royal origin. In return, kings and queens acquired the powerful spiritual patronage of the saints whose shrines they housed. At the same time, churches and monasteries made their huge landed wealth available to support royal power in various ways, as the clergy at St Peter's, Ghent, did for Louis the Pious. Royal nunneries had their place in these networks, as significant landowners in their own right, as homes for kings' daughters or widows, and as sources of intercessory prayer for their patroness and her family. Furthermore, churches put their considerable legal and administrative expertise at royal disposal, thereby transmitting at least some late Roman bureaucratic skills and judicial principles to early medieval rulers. The intense symbiosis of royal and ecclesiastical affairs was the practical expression of the early medieval ideologies of Christian rulership.

One corollary was the readiness of churchmen to lecture kings about their responsibilities. Whether by royal request or on their own initiative, clergy wrote letters, treatises, and admonitions to kings, encouraging, exhorting, or chastising. And there is enough evidence to suggest that at least some kings listened, and took the advice to heart. One king who certainly did was Charles the Bald, grandson of Charlemagne and ruler of the western third of his empire. And he needed to: his reign was a long struggle to deal with repeated conflicts with his brothers, nephews, and sons, worsening external threats posed by Viking raids, and diminishing internal resources. In addition, he faced assertive aristocrats and self-confident bishops. The most forceful and articulate of these was Hincmar of Reims, who had as clear views on the obligations of kings as he did on those of marriage.[29] Charles had read an earlier set of comments on kingship and questioned Hincmar about it, probably in 873. The archbishop replied with a treatise *On the Person of a King and the Royal Ministry*, whose words, he suspected, might leave the king feeling rather nettled. Its contents can be summarized thus: the Christian God appoints kings, permitting evil ones as well as enabling good ones. A good king rules in justice, punishing criminals, defending the church, and being equitable in judgement, and is thus a blessing to his subjects, bringing them peace, fruitful soil, and fertility. By contrast, a bad king brings only suffering, oppression, invasion, and famine. In another treatise, Hincmar labelled such a king as tyrannical: nevertheless, he retains a place within the cosmological whole, for God permits him to rule as a punishment for the sins of his people. Hincmar's good king is powerful and vigorous, in battle as in law. He exercises moral self-restraint, refusing to give in to flattery, partisanship, or pride. Humility is an essential precondition of good kingship, justice its daily manifestation. The king thus becomes an exemplar of good conduct to his subjects. This can be quite compatible with shedding blood, if warfare will defend Christianity or if his subjects' terrible crimes justify the death penalty. In Hincmar's opinion, then, good kingship was vigorous morality in action for the sake of the welfare of the entire Christian social order. It was a *ministerium*, a ministry: a duty of responsible service to others. By means of the rule of good kings, human society embraced divinely inspired harmony, and the king ruled as Christ's deputy on earth.

*On the Person of a King and the Royal Ministry* marks a late and sophisticated stage in the development of early medieval thinking about royal power. Within that tradition, ideas of diverse origin had gradually fused, but this tract nevertheless allows us to identify exactly what the constituent elements were, for Hincmar worked by naming his sources and quoting from them extensively. In so doing he laid bare the intellectual antecedents of his—and much other early medieval—thinking about the nature and disposition of power. In the first place was the Bible, both the Old Testament books, which expounded the relations between God, kings, and people in ancient Israel, and the New Testament exposition of the teachings of Christ and his followers on social and political obligation within the Roman Empire. In the second place were the great theologians and moralists of late Antiquity and the very early Middle Ages. Ambrose and Augustine had been writing when the Roman Empire was still a powerful political reality; Gregory the Great experienced both the enduring vigour of the eastern, Byzantine Empire and the dissolution of stability in Italy. Each in his own distinctive way, these writers combined scriptural ideas with strong Roman views on the ethics of power and the nature of law. The fourth writer from whom Hincmar drew heavily he believed, erroneously, to be Cyprian of Carthage (d. 258). He was, in fact, an anonymous seventh-century Irishman whose ideas were a fascinating *mélange* of biblical, patristic, and indigenous Irish wisdom literature.

At risk of oversimplifying, we may, therefore, locate the origins of early medieval ideas about good and bad kings in three different cultural traditions: Roman, biblical, and Irish. Three admonitions to kings, all dating from the late sixth to seventh centuries, help us to disentangle their respective contributions. The author of the first was Martin of Braga; its recipient Miro, king of the Suevi (570–83), a people who had settled in north-western Iberia in 409 and maintained an independent kingdom there until absorbed by their powerful Gothic neighbours in 585 (see Figures 0.2 and 8.2). Martin's *Formula for an Honest Life* was intended as simple advice for the king and 'those who assisted in his royal ministry', and was explicitly independent of Christian teaching. He outlined the four cardinal virtues that should inform all the king's actions: prudence, magnanimity of spirit, self-restraint, and justice. In so doing, Martin stressed the need for self-discipline, ethical conduct, service to others, and equitable behaviour in all things. Avoiding vice, the king should be the 'corrector without reproach' of others and an exemplar of good conduct. All these ideas derived directly from the writings of the Roman philosopher Seneca (*c.*4 BC–AD 65); in one way or another, all resurface in Hincmar's advice to Charles the Bald. Martin's straightforward treatise was hugely popular throughout the entire Middle Ages, a reminder of the enduring legacy of the Roman belief that self-restrained moral conduct was the necessary precondition for the exercise of authority over others.[30]

The second strand, the scriptural, was rich, complex, and subject to endless reinterpretation. Nevertheless, the letter that Gregory the Great wrote to Æthelberht of Kent in 601 shows one way in which it could be presented in straightforward terms appropriate, as here, for a warleader who had just accepted Christianity. Gregory's succinct premiss condenses the whole tenor of biblical history into a single truism: 'Almighty God raises up certain good men to be rulers over nations in order that he may by their means bestow the gifts of his righteousness upon all those over whom they are set.' Behind this sentence lies awareness of ancient Israelite cosmology, which identified the king as a sacred person, protected by God and consecrated by being anointed with oil by the priests. As Gregory implied, he was the conduit between the divine and the human; his good governance brought God's gifts of fertility, prosperity, and peace. In Gregory's thinking, certain consequences followed from this ancient premiss. First, Æthelberht has responsibilities towards God—to further the spread of Christianity, to set an example of Christian conduct, and to change his people's conduct by 'exhorting, terrifying, enticing and correcting' them.[31] Secondly, if he does this, God will reward him with honour, a glorious reputation, and eternal life promised to Christians. Here, the king is the fulcum of the Christian polity with simultaneous obligations towards both the Christian God and his own subjects. This was central to much of Gregory's thought, and he expressed his views on the responsibilities of

rulers in many other works besides this one letter. Their wide dissemination ensured that his ideas too became part of the common currency
of early medieval political thinking; Hincmar was only one of many to
acknowledge indebtedness to Gregory's contribution.

The third strand is perhaps the most unexpected. We encounter it in a
seventh-century treatise, *The Testament of Morann*, a work of instruction
from an Irish sage, the *fili* Morann, to King Feradach Find Fechtnach.
Both are legendary characters, but this is one sample of an Old Irish
wisdom literature addressed to kings. Morann's purpose is to bring to the
king 'the virtue of rectitude, | which each ruler must have'.[32] Through his
messenger, he tells Fechtnach about the *fír flathemon*, the 'king's justice',
a rich term meaning equity combined with truth and integrity.

> Tell him, it is through the justice of the ruler that plagues and great
>    lightnings are kept from the people.
> It is through the justice of the ruler that he judges great tribes and
>    great riches.
> It is through the justice of the ruler that he secures peace,
>    tranquillity, joy, ease, and comfort.
> It is through the justice of the ruler that he dispatches great
>    battalions to the borders of hostile neighbours.
> It is through the justice of the ruler that every heir plants his
>    house-post in his fair inheritance.
> It is through the justice of the ruler that abundances of great tree-
>    fruit of the great wood are tasted.
> It is through the justice of the ruler that milk-yields of great cattle
>    are maintained.
> It is through the justice of the ruler there is an abundance of every
>    high, tall corn.[33]

Morann goes on to spell out in detail how the true ruler must behave to
uphold the rightful order of society and win these abundances for his
people. He also refers to the antithesis, the 'un-ruler' or usurper whose
reign is spent in violence and warfare, against whom 'there is always
bellowing with horns'.[34]

Once again, we find that royal conduct is integrally associated with the
welfare of the people, the fecundity of the soil, and the maintenance of
peace through external warfare and internal good governance. Good rulership presupposed that the king's 'justice' would regulate social relations
effectively and fairly. These were part of a wider complex of traditions current in Ireland before the introduction of Christianity, traditions
that placed a high symbolic value on the king as the embodiment of both
social and supernatural order. As in ancient Israel, kings were perceived

to be central to a way of thinking that regarded social well-being as but one aspect of the well-being of the wider world—its soil, its weather, and its rulers—and that drew a tight analogy between political malaise and a discordant cosmos.

Not surprisingly, *The Testament of Morann* remained unknown beyond Ireland, for it was written in Old Irish. But its ideas about the true ruler as opposed to the un-ruler and about the importance of the king's 'justice' informed a Latin tract also written in seventh-century Ireland and widely read in England and on the Continent from the eighth through the twelfth century, commonly entitled *On the Twelve Abuses of the World*. This was the work that Hincmar thought had been written by Cyprian, and whose definitions of good and evil kings he quoted in full.

Now ancient Israel, pre-Christian Ireland, and the ninth-century Carolingian Empire were all very different societies. They all had kings in abundance, however, and accepted kingship as the only possible political order. All assumed the interpenetration of the supernatural, the earthly, and the social in various ways, an assumption that manifested itself differently in each culture. But they shared the presupposition that the king was one of the key nodes of this interaction and that his conduct was a conduit through which the divine, the natural, and the human affected each other. For this reason, beliefs about the nature of kingship derived both from the Old Testament and from Irish learning were readily appropriated in the warrior kingdoms that emerged out of the Roman Empire. If early Germanic-speaking peoples had ever regarded their kings within a cosmological context, the huge upheavals and transformations of the fourth and fifth centuries had been far too disruptive to sustain such beliefs. Instead, the inheritance of Roman Christianity and classical standards of ethical conduct for the exercise of power provided a cultural context receptive to the assimilation of other texts and ideas about good kings and bad kings.

That melding had commenced in the immediate aftermath of the adoption of Christianity by the Roman emperor Constantine, and the patristic theologians on whom Hincmar drew had played no small part in it. But thinking about the tasks of kingship never remained static, and the political transformation of the western Roman Empire in the fifth century provided another impetus. As empire yielded to kingdoms and as Christianity spread among them, the urge to formulate norms of Christian kingship became irresistible. Hincmar's several treatises on kingship represent the culmination of that long, slow process.

Not only his sophisticated political thought and his copious writings make Hincmar important. He also specialized in inventing royal rituals to enact in dramatic form the political theology he espoused. It was his shrewd political judgement that had introduced the king's formal promise to his people into the consecration ceremony, and, more than any single other person, he regularized the tradition of anointing kings and queens. Otto II, and the many subsequent generations of medieval rulers whose reigns were inaugurated with the same words and religious rituals, participated in a sacred drama that was in large part the product of Hincmar's fertile mind. While consecration at the hands of archbishops could not of itself make a good king, it did make a king and it did instruct him how to be a good one. And, for the ruler who was already married, unlike the young Otto II, the consecration of his queen implicated her in the maintenance of good rule.

What difference did these ideals make to the practice of rulership? They were no substitute for hard-won experience, let alone a remedy against defeat in battle. Rather, their importance lay in establishing an agreed yardstick by which to measure a king's performance, and in providing the criteria for criticism, whether by disaffected lay subjects, clerical critics, or those anxious to oust a rival. Early medieval kings were not bad simply for being sly, promiscuous, incompetent, or unsuccessful in war: they were bad when they lost the respect and cooperation of their leading subjects, lay and ecclesiastical. In short, bad kingship was the wilful destruction of the consensual partnership that made governance work. In a cosmological perspective, it was the perversion of divine order.

It could take several forms. One was sexual and gendered. A ruler's self-restraint had to start with the control of his own body lest, 'governed by lust, [he stain] the fame of [his] glory before God and men by the sin of lasciviousness and adultery'. Such conduct, Boniface warned King Æthelbald of Mercia (716–57) in 746–7, was both 'a disgrace in the sight of God and the ruin of your reputation among men'. Far more serious, though, was the accusation that Æthelbald had vented his lust on those whom he ought to protect, nuns dedicated to God in the convents of his kingdom: this conduct was 'the snare of death and the pit of hell and the whirlpool of perdition'.[35] Whereas a good ruler 'should first rule himself with reasonable and meritorious discipline; second his wife, his children, and his household; and third, the people entrusted to him', the bad king combined lack of self-control with a wanton wife. 'A foolish wife is the ruin of a household, the exhaustion of wealth, the fullness of crimes, and the abode of all evils and vices.'[36] Accusations of queenly adultery became a weapon for attacking kings, as Louis the Pious and his empress, the beautiful Judith, discovered to their joint cost in the 830s. The truth of the matter was irrelevant, for queenly modesty had become so integral to good king-ship that insinuation and allegation against the queen sufficed to identify the bad king.

Another form of bad kingship was taking bad counsel, or no counsel at all. The best advice came from God, as set out in the Bible. Two further precepts followed: 'a prudent man summons other prudent men into counsel and does nothing without their advice; but a foolish man deliberates by himself and does whatever he hastily desires without the counsel of others. . . . The third rule in counsels to be observed is that a just ruler should not have deceitful and pernicious counselors. Who, indeed, should trust the counsels of the wicked? . . . As good counselors raise the state upwards, so evil ones press it downwards in ruinous calamity.'[37] Counsellors might be condemned as evil if they blocked others' access to the king, as Hagano did in the reign of Charles the Simple, or came, as Charles the Fat's adviser Liutward of Vercelli did, from the wrong social background. The political consequences could be serious: Zwentibold of Lotharingia (895–900) was deposed not only because he plundered church property but because, 'settling the affairs of the kingdom with women and men of lower rank, he disparaged his more honourable and noble followers and stripped them of their offices and dignities'.[38]

Most dangerous of all, however, was the form of bad kingship identi-fied as early as the seventh century by pseudo-Cyprian: disregard for justice. One of the 'twelve abuses', the 'unjust king' dishonoured his subjects, disregarding their rights and interests. This was the tyranny of oppression about which Hincmar would in due course warn Charles the Bald. But Charles learned this lesson the hard way, for in his early years he had ruled so vigorously that in 858 his subjects rebelled, amid com-plaints that his rule had become 'tyranny' when, they alleged, he destroyed their property with 'evil savagery' and broke the oaths and pledges he had made to his people. In short, 'all despaired of his good faith'.[39] Charles, his opponents asserted, ruled without regard for the common welfare and ignored the even-handed identity of interests and purpose between ruler and ruled that lay at the heart of good kingship and successful governance alike.

Accusations of bad kingship made for vigorous political opposition; from the pen of a historian, they damned in posterity. Thietmar of Merse-burg—or his informant—had no time at all for the Danish king Swein Forkbeard (c.987–1014), a Christian. He condemned the Dane not only for his attacks on England, but for wasting his own kingdom: he was 'not a ruler but a destroyer. . . . he traded security for constant wandering, peace for war, a kingdom for exile, the God of heaven and earth for the Devil.'[40] In effect, Thietmar turned Swein into an icon of bad kingship, who displayed the opposite of the good ruler's qualities in a perversion of the Christian cosmological scheme.

Bad kingship reminds us that good kingship was a highly sophisticated political and ideological construct. As a moral undertaking, based upon obligation, justice, and self-restraint, it was greatly indebted to ecclesiastical visions of the right ordering of the social world, but it was not confected out of purely clerical ingredients, for kingship was far too fundamental to be left entirely to churchmen to define. It remained grounded in the harsh practicalities of leadership in war, and presupposed the consent and cooperation of the secular elite. Without that, a king could not function: he would be reduced to uselessness, an un-ruler. So we should be careful not to think in dualistic terms, of one prescription of kingship for clergy, and another for laity. Churches relied on strong warrior kings to defend their lands as well as to spread Christianity, nobles were happy to let some of the sacred aura of kingship brush off onto themselves. Principles of justice and self-restraint were as much a shrewd political strategy for aristocrats keen to enhance their own position as they were a code of conduct for kings.

After all, as Jonas of Orleans, Adalbero of Laon, and others emphasized, Christian ethics of the responsibilities of power had come to apply not only to kings but also to the *potentes* who constituted the ruling elite.[41] At its most ideologically effective, royal authority presumed a complementary balance between the just exercise of power by kings and their leading subjects: good kingship was the ideological and cosmological abstraction of a social order grounded in good lordship more generally. No one knew that better than Adalbero's contemporary, Wulfstan of York, whose association between the collapse of civil society and the moral transgressions of the Anglo-Saxons has already been quoted.[42] At about the same time as his castigation of the Anglo-Saxon elite spelled out the connection between natural disaster and social disarray, he articulated trenchantly the king's side of this same relationship:

> For the Christian king
> it is very fitting
> that he be in the position of a father
> to the Christian people.
> And in watching and warding over them
> be Christ's deputy,
> as he is called.[43]

These lines, written in about 1010, summed up centuries of reflection on the task and nature of kingship in a Christian society. A few years later, Wulfstan elaborated the underlying logic:

> Through the unwise king
> the people will be made wretched
> not once, but very often
> because of his misrule.
> Through the king's wisdom
> the people will be blessed
> and prosperous and victorious.
> And therefore the wise king
> must expand and exalt
> christendom and kingdom,
> and heathendom shall he always
> hinder and abhor.[44]

The early medieval convergence of interests that represented the king as 'Christ's deputy' reached its high point in the 1020s in England and in Germany, but was not to remain uncontested much longer. In the 1070s, fierce ideological warfare broke out, first in the German empire, then elsewhere, about the appropriate relationship of king to God and clergy. Institutional changes followed, transforming the exercise of priestly authority and the means of implementing royal justice by the end of the twelfth century. Wulfstan of York would have found it strange indeed that the role of 'Christ's deputy' had been claimed exclusively for the pope, yet the exercise of justice remained the cornerstone of Christian kingship. Hincmar of Reims, on the other hand, would have felt quite at home at the inauguration of any new ruler, for the consecration formula used for Otto II looked directly back to his inspiration but remained a living tradition for many centuries to come.

During Antiquity, 'Europe' signalled one of the three continents of the known world. But in the centuries from c.500 to c.1000, much of the continent came to adopt a new identity, as Christendom, the community of all baptized believers in Christ and the Christian God. Men and women from the Mediterranean to the Arctic Circle now had something in common. And, as is the nature of any group identity, Christendom defined itself as much vis-à-vis those outside as those within. Propagated by powerful words and sharp swords alike, Christendom did its best to silence alternative visions of the world. As a dominant core of beliefs and values, it influenced the history of Europe and the wider world for centuries to come.

This much is self-evident. But the significance of the alliance between kings and the Christian religion that emerged in the early Middle Ages is deeper than this. Early medieval Christianity was even more a religion of the powerful, the *potentes*, than of the poor, the *pauperes*. In Antiquity, Europe beyond the Roman imperial frontier had been occupied by numerous petty peoples and their fragile, shifting confederations. By the end of the millennium, however, powerful and enduring kingdoms had emerged there. Previous chapters have sketched some of the reasons for this: the impact of Christianity supplements them, for it offered resources, infrastructures, ideology, and, importantly, identity. Differently put, Christianity brought with it the late Roman legacy of institutionalized power, well resourced, ideologically justified, and of cosmological significance.

In those Mediterranean parts of Europe that had passed from imperial officials to warrior kings in the fifth century with little structural disruption, the association of Christianity and rulership was already firmly entrenched. Continuity of administration and bureaucracy in both secular and ecclesiastical life assisted this. But, even here, Christianity brought kings new justifications for ruling, new tasks and obligations, new powers to exercise. And, when effective royal government broke down in southern France and Italy in the later tenth and early eleventh centuries, the ideals and obligations of ethical power were maintained and asserted by churches. At the same time, muscular Christianity offered the small kingdoms of northern Spain a ready-made justification for beginning steady aggression against the Muslim warlords of the central and southern parts of the Iberian peninsula. However dislocating the ideological disputes and juridical reorganization of Christendom in the late eleventh and twelfth centuries were, the early medieval alliance of warrior kings and Christianity remained unassailed.

# 8

# Rome and the Peoples of Europe

The . . . mighty sea has also in its arctic region . . . a great island named Scandza, from which my tale (by God's grace) shall take its beginning. . . . Now from this island of Scandza, as from a factory of peoples or a womb of nations, the Goths are said to have come forth long ago under their king.[1]

To the king who had been intent on war came a longing for travel, bearing a pilgrim's staff. The lord, dear to the emperor, friend of Peter, reaped a portion of Rome's glory.
    Few generous princes will thus have measured the southward path with their feet.[2]

AT the centre of the Roman Empire lay the Great Sea around whose sun-drenched shores the imperial provinces sprawled. Roman geographers organized their knowledge of the world from this Mediterranean vantage point: *mare nostrum*, our sea, divided the land mass into three continents, Europe, Asia, and Africa. Around the whole of the world flowed Ocean, the tidal girdle that 'surrounds its coasts like a wreath'.[3] At the furthest edge of Europe, Ocean contained islands, with only some of which the Romans were familiar: Britain they ruled, Ireland they visited occasionally, the Orkneys they acknowledged by repute. Beyond these and 'separated from the others by an indefinite space and . . . known to barely a few' lay Thule, the island of summer midnight sun and the winter night that lasted for a full six months, where the sea was dark and frozen.[4] Also in its arctic region Ocean was believed to contain the 'great island named Scandza', also called 'Scadinavia'. Here was the outermost edge of the world.

From Rome to Scandinavia was a long stretch of the imagination. In Antiquity, Roman ethnographers filled the space beyond the imperial frontiers with 'imagined communities', whose names, numbers, physical and moral characteristics they described in detail on the basis of limited knowledge and much stereotyping. Those who lived beyond the frontiers have left ample archaeological evidence of their existence, including their characteristic forms of settlement, furnished burials, and deposits of elite riches and weapons, yet we cannot use material remains such as these to deduce with any confidence what their political organization, far less their self-perceptions, may have been.[5] In the absence of any documentary records from these communities, who employed only occasional runic or ogam literacy, the historian thus encounters them through the interpretations of Roman commentators: the mentalities and social identities that informed life beyond the frontier remain effectively unknown.

These were the peoples whom, whatever their irrecoverable individualities, Romans categorized as 'barbarians', distinguishing only the sedentary and uncultured from the nomadic and utterly alien. As has been emphasized, 'barbarians' fulfilled an important cultural role by epitomizing the absence of the beneficial effects of the Roman way of life and its more 'civilized' values.[6] Yet these groups were far more than the essential 'other' of ingrained prejudices, for they also held a crucial, if ambivalent, place in imperial politics. While their restiveness provided the ongoing *raison d'être* for the military machine of the western provinces, their manpower was nevertheless crucial to the replenishment of Roman armies. And when, in the fifth century, some of these troops crossed the frontier and eventually founded new kingdoms, the infinitely distant Scandza, where—according to Mediterranean imagination—people had nothing to do except procreate during the long winter months, took on the aspect of the 'womb of nations'. Here, then, sixth-century writers located the first cause of the movements of peoples, battles, and political upheavals that in the course of the fifth century had turned the western Roman imperial provinces into separate kingdoms under their own rulers.

Rome and Scandinavia form the geographical frame of reference of this final chapter. Its conceptual dimension is indicated by two transformations. The first concerns Scandinavia, the 'womb of nations' of late Roman ethnographical imagination, where Christian kingdoms were rapidly developing from the late tenth century. It is emblematic of the early eleventh-century state of affairs that the road from Scandinavia to Rome was a real journey for King Cnut, grandson of the first Christian king of the Danes, for it was he whom the poet Sighvatr described as the prince who 'measured the southward path with [his] feet' in 1027. By the time of his pilgrimage, the geopolitical map of Europe's cultures and polities had achieved a form that would not fundamentally alter for some centuries to come. Together with the spread of Latin Christianity, the development of kingdoms based on ethnic groupings and of new imperial hegemonies had so reorganized the political topography of Europe that the old imaginative framework was quite redundant. Once the unknown periphery, Scandinavia was now incorporated within the political community of Latin Christendom on much the same terms as other regions.

Rome had been transformed too. Although vastly diminished since its imperial maximum of approximately 0.5 million inhabitants, the population of the city that Cnut visited was nevertheless far larger than that of any other in Latin Christendom. Cnut, as so many other visitors and pilgrims, would have encountered pockets of dense settlement among gardens and vineyards on the sites of the tenements that in antiquity had housed the city's teeming population. On his way to the shrines and churches, many already venerable with age, he would also have passed the crumbling, debris-filled monuments of the city's imperial past. For Rome had undergone profound changes in the early Middle Ages. In c.500, although no longer the administrative capital of the empire, it retained its ancient prestige and remained the seat of the senate, the body that had participated in governing Rome as city, kingdom, republic, and empire since the earliest times. The city remained a forum of political life for aristocrats of ancient families, who hailed it as 'that fertile mother of eloquence, that vast temple of every virtue, that city which cannot be called an alien place',[7] and at the same time was home to the pope and Latin Christendom's holiest shrines. Ecclesiastical presence asserted steadily growing influence on the politics and material fabric of fifth- and sixth-century Rome, so that, by the later eighth century, it had become a city of the papal church. By the time of Cnut's visit, however, it was in political terms a peripheral city, a southern outpost of northern polities wedged on the volatile frontier with the Byzantines of southern Italy, and only occasionally visited by emperors whose power base lay far north of the Alps. Splendid traditions of senatorial governance had long since given way to a ruling elite who exercised control through the papal bureaucracy. In the late tenth and early eleventh centuries, interest groups that fused ecclesiastical and secular interests played for high stakes in an urban politics characterized by aristocratic factionalism, popular unrest, and occasional imperial intervention.

Even so, Rome's hold over the imagination of all the inhabitants of Christian Europe was long since assured. Northern writers dreamed on, without mundane reality interrupting their idealized visions of the 'queen of cities'.[8] 'Famed throughout the triple world by Franks, | faithful

Christians and emperors', it was secure in its reputation as 'mother of kings and glory of Italians',[9] 'the mother of martyrs, the domicile of the apostles',[10] 'the capital of the world . . . mother of all churches'.[11] By the early years of the second Christian millennium, Rome was Europe's 'imagined community' par excellence, geographically marginal but symbolically central, a powerful idea but a shabby urban experience. Rome's twin roles as historic seat of political power and contemporary Christian holy place expressed different aspects of the same past.

Between these two poles—Scandinavia and Rome—this chapter establishes how political, religious, and cultural identities were formed and re-formed throughout the early Middle Ages. Rejecting any view of the period from c.500 to c.1000 as significant primarily for the foundations of the events of later epochs, it dismisses narratives of 'the origin of nations' and 'the rise of the papacy'. It also refuses to cast the history of the early Middle Ages in terms of such Rome-centred normative evaluations as 'barbarian invasion' or 'ideals of empire'. Instead, the heart of this chapter is an exploration of Rome's role as an urban reality with such a rich political, cultural, and religious past that it exerted a powerful grip on the imagination of all who encountered it directly or indirectly. Each section presents a different aspect of this central theme; each is introduced by a journey to or from Rome. The first argues that there is nothing primordial about the ethnically based kingdoms that developed in the course of the early Middle Ages, but rather that these political identities were as much the product of specific cultural configurations and historical moments as kin-based, gendered, or religious ones. It pays particular attention to the contribution of Roman and Christian literature to the origin myths that explained and propagated early medieval ethnic identities. The second section turns from kingdoms to empires, as both concepts and polities. By asking how empires were established and legitimated, it assesses the extent to which Romanness was a political ideology that informed the early medieval political order. In this context, it also considers the transformation in Rome's role as the capital of empire. Visitors to the city form the thread through the final section. Their experience puts imperial ceremonial in context and also brings Christian Rome into focus. The chapter ends by juxtaposing the Rome experienced by the city's visitors with the evocations of Rome recreated in many parts of Christian Europe, arguing that the city's Christian identity formed a recurrent leitmotiv of early medieval cultural expression. It emerges that, in multiple ways, the political and cultural legacy of the Roman Empire formed a counterpoise to the particularisms and local identities so characteristic of Europe after Rome.

**8.1.** Principal places mentioned in Chapter 8.

# Rome, AD 500

In AD 500, a Gothic warrior king visited Rome. The unchallenged ruler of Italy since 493, Theoderic the Great had established his military court at Ravenna, headquarters of the former imperial army and, since 408, a supplemental capital to Rome. Fifth-century Rome had remained a civilian city and its guardians were still members of the senatorial aristocracy.

By the end of the fifth century, however, their traditional domination of the city's politics and patronage faced increasing challenge from papal officials and the growing wealth of the city's many Christian churches, the foremost among which housed the tomb of St Peter, leader of the apostles. So in 500 Theoderic expressed his deference by going first to St Peter's, on the opposite bank of the Tiber from the ancient city: there 'Pope Symmachus and all the senate and people of Rome came joyfully to meet him outside the city'. Only then did he enter the city itself, where he addressed the senate and 'promised that, with God's help, he would uphold inviolably everything that previous Roman emperors had decreed'. Next, in traditional imperial fashion, he paraded in triumph through the city to the palace, staged circus games for the populace, distributed food, and allocated expenses for repairing the city walls.[12]

Adept at manipulating Roman conventions of rulership, Theoderic was in origin a frontier warlord who had spent his formative adolescent years as a hostage in the imperial court at Constantinople. Probably born in 451, the son of a mother who may conceivably have been Roman and a Gothic father who at that date led part of a Gothic army settled on imperial soil in Pannonia, Theoderic died in 526, western emperor in all but name (see Figure 8.2). In 489, he had led from the Balkans into Italy his following, a heterogeneous group drawn from various ethnic war bands but which, under his strong leadership, was rapidly acquiring a coherent group identity as 'Goths'. At the request of the Byzantine emperor Zeno (474–91), he seized control of Italy from Odoacer, the warlord who had dominated the peninsula since the deposition of the western child-emperor Romulus Augustulus in 476. In due course Zeno's successor Anastasius acknowledged Theoderic as the legitimate ruler of Italy; the Goth always took care to defer to Anastasius as emperor. Governing the mixed population of Romans and 'Goths'—indigenous inhabitants and in-comers of various origins—Theoderic won a reputation as a vigorous ruler, managing for most of his reign to maintain a careful balance between the touchy pride of the old senatorial elite and his own retinue of military par-venus. During his reign, Ravenna hosted a far more stable, magnificent, and respected court than under the last emperors, while in Rome the sen-ate enjoyed an Indian summer of influence and erudition. The pope also benefited from the rapport between Goths and senators, notwithstanding Theoderic's allegiance to Arian Christianity. The contemporary verdict was firm:

A most warlike and strong man . . . outstanding and of good will in all things, he reigned thirty-three years. During his time, Italy enjoyed thirty years of good

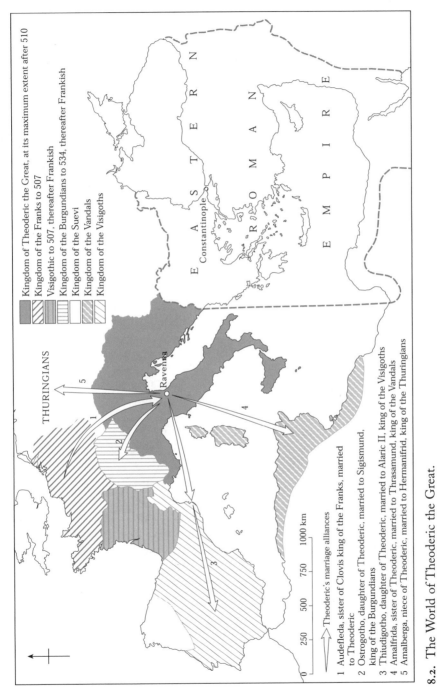

Kingdom of Theoderic the Great, at its maximum extent after 510
Kingdom of the Franks to 507
Visigothic to 507, thereafter Frankish
Kingdom of the Burgundians to 534, thereafter Frankish
Kingdom of the Suevi
Kingdom of the Vandals
Kingdom of the Visigoths

THURINGIANS

Ravenna

Constantinople

E A S T E R N   R O M A N   E M P I R E

0   250   500   750   1000 km

→ Theoderic's marriage alliances

1 Audefleda, sister of Clovis king of the Franks, married to Theoderic
2 Ostrogotho, daughter of Theoderic, married to Sigismund, king of the Burgundians
3 Thiudigotho, daughter of Theoderic, married to Alaric II, king of the Visigoths
4 Amalfrida, sister of Theoderic, married to Thrasamund, king of the Vandals
5 Amalberga, niece of Theoderic, married to Hermanifrid, king of the Thuringians

8.2. The World of Theoderic the Great.

fortune and prosperity, so that there was peace to those who were going about their business, and he did nothing improperly. Thus he ruled two peoples in one, the Romans and the Goths, and although he himself was of the Arian sect, he nevertheless attempted nothing against the Catholics, so that by the Romans he was hailed as another Trajan or Valentinian and by the Goths . . . was adjudged their most powerful king in all things.[13]

All around the western Mediterranean, other warlords had also lever-aged their military ability for institutional authority as kings in the middle and later decades of the fifth century, profiting as much from the enduring vitality of Roman administrative and legal traditions as from the effectiveness of their armed followings. In such circumstances, the distinction between Roman and non-Roman inevitably blurred in practice, if not always in ideology or rhetoric. Although arguably not the most successful from a longer perspective, Theoderic's reign is certainly the best documented of these sixth-century kingdoms. In the unremitting competition for land, influence, and reputation among their rulers, he affirmed his pre-eminence through a canny combination of military skill, ruthless politics, and dynastic marriage alliances, including those with Hermanifrid and Alaric II.

In both domestic and external affairs, therefore, Theoderic replicated traditional discourses of power and successfully inserted himself into imperial networks of influence. But from the perspective of the eastern empire's court in mid-sixth-century Constantinople, the rapidly shifting western politics half a century or so earlier came to be seen as something very different: the demise of the old order. With the benefit of hindsight, the coup against Romulus Augustulus became a turning point, as a Constantinopolitan court official emphasized towards the end of Theoderic's reign. 'With this Augustulus perished the western empire of the Roman people, which the first Augustus, Octavian, began to rule in the seven hundred and ninth year from the foundation of the city. This occurred in the five hundred and twenty-second year of the kingdom of the departed emperors, with Gothic kings thereafter holding Rome.'[14] In sum, Theoderic's life spanned three-quarters of a century of immense and irreversible political change: his visit to the city in 500 is a convenient vantage point from which to take stock of the changing interactions between Rome and the peoples of Europe.

To do this is to investigate both the relationship of political formations to collective ethnic identities and, equally importantly, early medieval perceptions of it. Viewed from the perspective of the politics and passions of nineteenth- and twentieth-century Europe, this relationship became a highly charged issue, but it is important to be clear that the conceptual distinction between polity and ethnicity had no place in early medieval thinking. Nor did the modern dichotomy between culturally constructed ethnicity and biologically determined race. Instead, it is best to begin with political vocabulary. In the first place, both Roman and Judaeo-Christian conceptions of political organization viewed the entire world as divided into many peoples. From a Roman perspective, some of these had been subsumed into their empire with its pretensions to world rule; in biblical tradition all of them shared a common descent from the sons of the mythical founding ancestor, Noah—although only those acknowledging the Judaeo-Christian God could claim to be the 'people of God'. Secondly, central to Latin and the various local languages of the early Middle Ages were words that denoted in undifferentiated fashion a group whose members shared one or more of the following: putative descent from a common ancestor; common cultural attributes; organization into a single polity. Capable of being translated as 'people', these include the Latin terms *gens, genus, natio, plebs*; in the Germanic languages *folk* (Old High German), *þiuda* (Gothic), *þeod* (Old English); in the Celtic languages *tuath, cenél* (Old Irish), *tud* (Old Welsh). Writing between 906 and 913, Regino of Prüm echoed a millennium-long tradition and encapsulated the assumptions inherent in this vocabulary when he declared: 'the various nations of peoples are distinguished from each other by descent, customs, language and laws.'[15] This conventional reformulation of a commonplace notion underlines the absence of any distinction in ancient and early medieval thinking between groups whose membership was determined by biological descent (real or fictive) and groups defined by such socially constituted features as shared behavioural traits, names, political identity, or beliefs. Nor did any of these words specify the size, internal organization, or cultural characteristics of the peoples of early medieval Europe. It must be emphatically stated that the nuances of modern political and cultural terminology would have been meaningless in early medieval perspective.

That said, earlier chapters have already hinted at some of the issues involved in assessing what constituted a people in the early Middle Ages. Of Regino's diagnostics of ethnic identity, Chapter 1 examined language and Chapters 3 and 4 dealt with law and 'customs': although sometimes linguistic and/or legal communities approximately correlated with ethnic groups, for the most part they did not. Also important is the demonstration in Chapter 3 that genealogies organized gendered claims to power, above all for kings, claims that, as Chapter 7 indicated, often had cosmological overtones. However fictional, descent thus functioned as a persuasive metaphor for the legitimate transmission of power and status among a male ruling elite; by the same token, it provided mythical cogency in explaining the identity of an entire people. As for women, their role as agents of familial and cultural reproduction usually remained implicit, but, as we shall see, myths of descent did occasionally make this explicit.

Early medieval sources recount origin myths for many—indeed most— of the peoples of Europe. Such tales link an aboriginal homeland, final place of settlement, and genealogy of the ruling dynasty of a people; they may also explain key social and moral attributes, such as hairstyle, weaponry, nobility, or bravery. Some reach us via the pens of members of the ethnic group whose history they purport to narrate: in answering the question 'who are we?' they offer a vehicle for acknowledging collective identity and legitimating leadership. Others offer the perspective of outsiders and either emphasize separateness or seek schematic explanations of the multi-ethnic reality of the early Middle Ages. Whether their perspective is internal or external, these myths assert identity through difference and manipulate the past in service of the present. By explaining the present with reference to a past generally more imagined than real, they justify the restriction of authority to certain families and conceal the flux of political life in a cloak of natural, primordial metaphor.

Inevitably, we know of these myths only when they took written form. Although they may contain elements of preliterate tradition, whether the stories were told by warriors around the camp fire, by mothers to their children, or by court poets as lordly entertainment, the genre as it has come down to us is a product of the extended encounter between Christianity and the peoples of Europe outlined in the previous chapter. Because Christianity was the main vector for the transmission of the literary culture of the Roman world and churches the main agents of its preservation, the form and content of these myths were liable to be influenced by both biblical and classical origin tales.[16] Thus, for example, writers of the seventh, eighth, and ninth centuries commonly presented the Franks as descended from the Trojans. According to Rome's own myth of origins, as retold in the first century BC by the epic poet Virgil, the Trojan hero Aeneas had come to the land of the Latins, where his heirs founded Rome. By subsuming Roman history into that of ancient Troy, Virgil's ever popular myth invited his Frankish readers to claim parity with the Romans through shared Trojan origins. By contrast, Irish mythographers emphasized that Fénius Farsaid, inventor of the Gaelic language and eponymous ancestor of the *Féni*, the Irish, enjoyed a biblical descent from Magog, son of Japhet, son of Noah.[17]

This broad cultural template—of familiar biblical and classical paradigms, sometimes with an unquantifiable admixture of oral tradition—applied in a wide range of settings. We can best survey the origin legends of the peoples of Europe by starting far beyond the former imperial boundaries, and gradually moving ever nearer to Rome itself. In the world of Gaelic language along north-western Europe's Atlantic edge, the Irish were well aware that their linguistic, legal, and cultural uniformity complemented their division into competing kingdoms, of which there were probably over 100 in the fifth and sixth centuries, although no more than a dozen of any political consequence by the tenth. They saw no tension between identifying each kingdom in genealogical terms as a descent-based group, such as the Corcu Loígde, and simultaneously expressing the common characteristics of the Irish as an ethnic group. Irish scholars achieved this by accumulating an impressive body of myth that slotted the many hundreds of Irish ruling dynasties, real and legendary, into a historical framework derived from the Bible. In the process they provided the Irish with a secure place in universal history and a known origin comparable with that of all other peoples of the world.

What began in the seventh century as scholarly manipulation of Latin texts imported into Ireland's ecclesiastical libraries culminated in a widespread origin myth by the eleventh century. This was a story of the successive migrations of heroic ancestors and their wanderings through Africa, Asia, and Europe, culminating in the settlement of the originally uninhabited island of Ireland. The method employed was threefold: narrative, chronology, and genealogical etymology. Narrative archetypes taken from the Old Testament provided the literary scaffolding; computational facility adjusted this to chime with the outlines of world history as constructed by fourth-century Christian chroniclers; plausible etymologies provided the names for founding ancestors, of whom Fénius Farsaid is one example.

By the early ninth century, all the main elements of the Irish origin myth had been formulated, and were circulating widely in various genres and with varying details, in Ireland and elsewhere. Here is the form in which part of it reached a British audience:

When the children of Israel crossed through the Red Sea, the Egyptians came and pursued them and were drowned, as may be read in the Law [i.e. the Old Testament: see Exod. 14: 21–31]. Among the Egyptians was a nobleman of Scythia, with a great following, who had been expelled from his kingdom, and was there when the Egyptians were drowned, but did not join in the pursuit of the children of God. The survivors took counsel to expel him, lest he should attack their kingdom and occupy it, for their strength had been drowned in the Red Sea. He was expelled and he wandered for 42 years through Africa, and they came to the Altars of the Philistines . . . [and many other named places] and their people multiplied exceedingly. After they had come to Spain, and 1002 years after the Egyptians had been drowned in the Red Sea, they came to the country of Dal Riada, at the time when Brutus was ruling among the Romans.[18]

Inasmuch as the Scythians of the Eurasian steppe were the archetypal noble savages (real and imagined) of Graeco-Roman ethnography and Brutus was the legendary first consul and founder of the Roman Republic, this tale deftly inserted the Irish into Roman and biblical history simultaneously. The linkage was strengthened, when ingenious etymologizing provided the anonymous Scythian nobleman with a wife: 'Scota, the daughter of Pharoah king of Egypt', herself explicitly the eponym of the *Scotti* and thus primordial mother of all the Irish.[19] Elaborated to include Scota's marriage to the Scythian, the origin myth achieved its definitive form throughout the Gaelic culture province common to Ireland and northern Britain. And in northern Britain, as the Gaelic kingdom of Alba evolved into the high medieval kingdom of the Scots, old myths served the rulers of this multi-ethnic, multilingual kingdom well, providing impeccable genealogical legitimation. Indeed, when the child-king Alexander III was consecrated king of Scots at Scone in 1249, his ancestry was proclaimed in full—all the way back to Scota, daughter of Pharoah.

Like the Irish, the British combined a strong sense of their own historical and ethnic identity with the reality of fragmentation into discrete, often competing, kingdoms. Unlike the Irish, however, they had no need to invent an attachment to the Roman past. In the legendary Brutus they identified an obvious eponym; via Brutus (or Britto, as he was sometimes called) their descent from the Trojans was easily asserted. Additionally, historical figures from Britain's era of Roman rule morphed into legendary ancestors of early Welsh dynasties, most prominently the late-fourth-century general and aspirant ursurper Magnus Maximus (d. 388). Migration, invasion, and settlement provided the political context for the development of British myths of ethnic origin, but a context in which the British were victims not victors. Faced with loss of hegemony over southern and eastern Britain to the sixth-century kingdoms coalescing around Germanic-speaking elites, the Britons' claim to be the aboriginal, rightful inhabitants of the island provided them with both an ethnic origin and the basis on which to prophesy the eventual expulsion of the hated invaders.

A remarkable Welsh monument at Llantysilio-y-Ial indicates the inseparability of British origin myth, descent-based kingship, and legitimation of territorial claims. Cyngen, king of Powys (d. 854), erected an inscribed column 2.4 metres high to the memory of his great-grandfather Eliseg, who had reconquered the inheritance of the kings of Powys from the English. Commencing by naming four generations of his own genealogy, Cyngen lauded Eliseg's achievements and spelled out his distinguished, if legendary, pedigree. This transforms the names of historical persons into ruling ancestors, legitimating Eliseg's position (and, by implication, Cyngen's) by descent not only from Britu but also from 'Maximus the king who slew the king of the Romans'.[20] Here we see clearly the appropriation of a common British legend for specific dynastic purposes in Powys, in much the same way as individual Irish kingdoms associated themselves with a common ethnic origin story.

This discussion of the Irish and British origin legends that emerged in the early Middle Ages has emphasized the significance of Roman history and Christian Latin texts as the cultural rubble out of which fundamentally different edifices could be built, even in places at or beyond the outermost margins of former imperial rule. It has also drawn attention to the theme of migration and settlement as context or content—or both—of origin myths. We find variants on both these points when we turn from the Celtic-language areas of Atlantic Europe to the Germanic-speaking peoples who had emerged amid the military imperatives and cultural porousness of the fourth- and fifth-century Rhine–Danube frontier.

This was an environment where prolonged encounter with the armies and institutions of the Roman Empire promoted the formulation of such stories—and not least because the need to assert a collective identity was enhanced by the destabilizing effect of the constant formation and reformation of ethnic groups in the course of warfare, migration, settlement, and intermarriage. Such instability characterized the fifth and early sixth centuries in particular. Thereafter—from the seventh century—origin myths developed in altered circumstances. In some instances, they provided ideological glue for successful kingdoms whose populations were in practice always a mixture of Roman and heterogeneous non-Roman elements, but that gradually came to take their political identities from the ethnic self-perception of their ruling dynasty. Notable instances of this include not only the Frankish kingdom; the kingdoms of Angles, Saxons, and Jutes in south-eastern Britain; the kingdom of the Lombards, who had established dominance over the central and northern Italian peninsula in 568; and the Iberian kingdom that emerged in the fifth and sixth centuries under the leadership of Alaric's dynasty and subsequently

acquired the designation 'Visigothic' to distinguish it from the Goths
under Theoderic's rule in Italy. In other instances, the formulation or
elaboration of persuasive Germanic origin legends was the product of
political defeat not of success, and offered a retrospective on peoples whose
cultural identity had outlasted their existence as a separate polity: this was
notably the case for the Burgundians, whose Rhone valley kingdom was
conquered by the Franks in 534. In similar fashion, the Lombard origin
myth found its literary apogee shortly after the Franks had eliminated the
Lombard kingdom in 774. Both these instances also indicate that, directly
or indirectly, the Franks' political hegemony involved manipulating the
ethnic identities of peoples absorbed into their aggressively successful
polity.

The single kingdom that fits neither model was Theoderic's. Alone of
fifth-, sixth-, and seventh-century kings, he actively encouraged the
formation of ethnic mythology that asserted his right to the Gothic
kingship by descent from founding ancestors of the Goths. Genealogy
as ideology found expression in the names he gave his offspring, which
were those of putative ancestral heroes. From Cassiodorus, the learned
Roman senator who held the senior court offices of Quaestor and
Praetorian Prefect, he even commissioned a twelve-volume history of
the Gothic people, now unfortunately lost, but which is known to have
given this new people an old history and to have flaunted Theoderic's
supposedly ancient pedigree. We can only speculate about why the king
was so determined to articulate a flawless Gothic identity for himself and
his dynasty: perhaps the insecurity of a parvenu; perhaps the political
priority of melding his fissiparous war band of disparate followers into a
more ordered whole; perhaps the challenge to a newcomer of ruling the
Roman imperial heartland, where 'Romanness' must have seemed a far
more self-evident and monolithic identity than it actually was in practice.

It remains impossible to assess how much acceptance this Gothic identity commanded beyond its proponents within Theoderic's court circle.
But it is certain that its mythological development did not cease when his
dynasty failed in 536 and sixteen years later his kingdom collapsed, fatally
undermined by a lengthy and destructive Byzantine campaign to recon-
quer the Italian peninsula. Having read Cassiodorus's Gothic History, a
bureaucrat in Constantinople, himself of Gothic extraction, marked the
resumption of Byzantine rule in Italy by writing his own account of the
'origin and deeds of the Goths'. Jordanes opened his work with Ocean's
girdle around the three known continents, for 'the same mighty sea
has also in its arctic region, that is, in the north, a great island named

Scandza, from which,' he declared, 'by God's grace my tale shall take its beginning'. From Scandza, 'as from a factory of peoples or a womb of nations, the Goths are said to have come forth long ago under their king, Berig by name. . . . And even to this day it is said to be called Gothiscandza.'[21] Claiming to prefer the rich, though inconsistent, traditions of ancient ethnography and the history of Rome that commenced with the city's mythic Trojan origins to the Goths' 'old wives' tales' that he had heard,[22] Jordanes equated the Goths with the Scythians and mentioned theories of their descent from Magog, thus fitting them into the geography and chronology of both Roman and biblical history. He endowed them with a magnificent past, one that commenced with migration from primeval beginnings in Scandza, and led, through wanderings and sufferings in the vast space between the mouth of the Danube and the boundaries of Asia, to encounter and conflict with Huns and Romans and then eventuated in Theoderic's triumphal march from the Balkans to conquer Italy. It was a past replete with the names of legendary kings— names that Theoderic's own children bore—and ancestors—'such heroes as admiring antiquity scarce proclaims its own to be'—of whose deeds 'in earliest times they [the Goths] sang . . . in strains of song'.[23]

Like Theoderic's kingdom, Jordanes's account was a product of its own time and place. Inasmuch as Theoderic and his immediate heirs were all dead and his kingdom restored to direct imperial rule, it was a product of the failure to establish a viable Gothic kingdom in Italy. For all its relentless narrative and anecdotal detail, Jordanes's vision of the past functioned as all origin tales do, by projecting the present political order into the distant past, and it achieved this so effectively that many generations of readers have been seduced by its attractive explanation of Gothic origins. Moreover, it rapidly gained such popularity that it acted as the template for subsequent origin tales for several other peoples such as the Lombards, who also came to acquire a mythic homeland in Scandza. Despite the dissimilar political context of composition, Jordanes had much in common with the anonymous Irish mythographers in purpose, narrative emplotment, balancing of oral tradition with literary sources, even some of the names out of which he spun his story. Like theirs, his work was exploited for quite different purposes in later centuries. Nevertheless, his—and their—great achievement was to show that ethnic and Roman histories cannot be disentangled and that the one presumes the other. Without Rome, its literature, legends, and Christian religion, the peoples of sixth-century Europe had no past, no present—and no future.

## Paderborn, AD 799

In the summer of 799, Pope Leo III (795–816) journeyed north, to visit
Charlemagne in Saxony at Paderborn. Not long thereafter, a skilled poet
envisioned their meeting. Writing in Latin, he began by introducing
Charlemagne, 'the beacon of Europe':

> Charles, powerful warrior, merciful victor and triumphant king,
> surpasses in goodness all the kings in the world,
> stands out as more just and more powerful than them all.
>
> .      .      .      .      .
>
> King Charles, head of the world, love and adornment of his people,
> venerable summit of Europe, very best father, hero,
> august lord in a city where a second Rome newly flowers,
> rising to great heights with its massive walls,
> touching the stars with its high domes.[24]

Then, after a vivid narration of the circumstances of Leo's journey, the
poet returned his audience's attention to Charlemagne as he awaited the
travel-weary Leo. Clad in a golden helmet, the Frankish king towered
above everyone else as he sat astride his warhorse, surrounded by the units
of his army drawn up in a circle for a full dress parade. Adjacent choirs
of priests in their long vestments held aloft banners with that most
Christian of symbols, the cross. As Leo approached, 'he is astounded how
varied in their customs, languages, clothing, and armour are the various
peoples from different parts of the world'. The ruler, now dismounted, and
the pope met: 'the king, the father of Europe, and Leo, the chief pastor
of the world' embraced.[25]

The so-called Paderborn epic used deliberately classicizing expressions
and a rich vocabulary of ancient imperial imagery in order to present
Charlemagne as the Christian world ruler, king over so many peoples
that his rule was tantamount to rule over Europe. So powerful was this
monarch that Aachen, Charlemagne's newly built prestige palace complex,
has become 'a second Rome'. Only by such imperial analogies could his
position be accurately represented. The poetic evocation of the Paderborn
'summit meeting' between Frankish king and Roman pope thus alerts us
to the appropriation of Rome's imperial past as an element of early medieval political ideas and attitudes. It opens up for inspection two themes:
the early medieval language of 'empire' in the representation of power, and
the city of Rome as the capital of empire.

To put these broad themes in context, we should take time to explore
the situations in which king and pope found themselves in 799, in order

to establish why Leo's visit to Paderborn constitutes such a useful avenue of approach. We start with the city of Rome at the close of the eighth century and the circumstances of the pope's long journey. Leo left behind him a city whose population had shrunk far below the levels of Theoderic's day, perhaps as low as 25,000, but which was nevertheless notably cosmopolitian. Its permanent population comprised families of Greek, Syrian, and Sicilian origin in addition to those of local, Roman descent. Numbers were swelled by a transient population of pilgrims—Anglo-Saxons, Irish, Frisians, Franks, Greeks—and of merchants, including Arabs, Venetians, and southern Italians.

By this time, Rome was developing into a substantial artisanal and mercantile centre, where pottery and metalwork were produced in some quantity and where eastern goods—textiles, spices, precious metals—seem to have been exchanged for slaves. Certainly, by the late eighth century there were adequate funds available for extensive renovation of the crumbling urban fabric. Following the example set by his predecessor Hadrian I, Leo III was energetically restoring the city's monuments, repairing its ancient churches and overseeing the construction of new ones. His lavish endowment of churches, old and new, marks him out as one of Rome's great builders, as does his commissioning of palatial papal accommodation on a scale of unprecedented grandeur. But Leo had nevertheless fled a city in turmoil, for earlier that year he had been physically attacked in the course of a major religious procession through the city streets. The attack, which seems to have been accompanied by a move formally to depose him and by allegations of severe misconduct, nevertheless failed to inflict the horrific and irreversible mutilation that would have disqualified him from office. The position of pope was fast becoming the target of aristocratic factional ambition in a characteristically Roman form of politics. For Leo to leave the city for the four- to five-month round trip to Paderborn was to risk his position still further.

Paderborn was also a building site, albeit of a very different nature. Since 772 Charlemagne had been conducting frequent military campaigns against the Franks' northern neighbours, the Saxons; the forced conversion to Christianity that accompanied their ruthless subjugation has already been mentioned.[26] Founded in 776 at a strategically convenient location as a base for military and missionary endeavours in Saxony, this new *urbs Karoli*, 'Charles's city', had already been twice burned by the Saxons: in 799 a new church 'of amazing size' was erected and the royal palace rebuilt, larger than before.[27] With its sturdy fortifications, stone buildings, stained glass, frescoed walls, elevated balconies, and luxury imported tableware, the church and palace complex made an

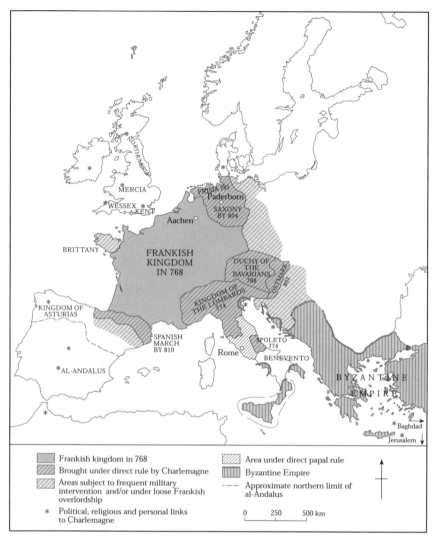

8.3. The World of Charlemagne.

unequivocal statement about the power of the Saxons' new ruler and new religion.

And powerful indeed he was (see Figure 8.3). By 799, Charlemagne had surmounted all internal Frankish opposition to his rule, successfully co-opting the loyalty and resources of secular and ecclesiastical elites. He had appropriated the rapidly crystallizing ideals of Christian kingship as his own and, as Chapter 7 noted, fashioned from them a manifesto for 'correct Christianity' that he urged on all his subjects. He patronized scholars such as the Anglo-Saxon Alcuin, the Visigoth Theodulf, the Lombard Paul the Deacon, and the anonymous author of the 'Paderborn epic' as much for his own greater renown as for their contribution towards building a Christian kingdom. Envoys and exiles from far and wide sought him out, extending yet further the range of his influence and reputation. His vast project of military and cultural imperialism is notable for its geographical scope, economic investment, and human cost—and for the prestige he thereby accrued. But at the time of Leo's visit, protracted Saxon resistance was still posing a formidable challenge to Charlemagne's ambitions, and, as Charlemagne's biographer Einhard later said, 'No war taken up by the Frankish people was ever longer, harder, or more dreadful'.[28] The reconstruction of Paderborn in 799 symbolized the king's 'greatness of spirit and steadfast determination' in the face of the 'faithlessness of the Saxons'.[29]

The conquest of Saxony was not completed until 804, and was exceptional only for its bitterness and duration. The enforcement of Frankish rule marked a new phase in the development of the political organization and ethnic identity of the Saxons, making the situation in Saxony comparable to that elsewhere in Charlemagne's vast realm. Everywhere that Charlemagne and his aristocracy extended their rule, either older ethnic identities were reformulated or new ones emerged. Frankish domination certainly did not eradicate other ethnic groupings—far from it. If anything, it strengthened them, albeit in ways that increasingly associated a particular people with a specific region and a specific legal tradition. Carolingian rule thus fostered the creation of territorially bounded ethnic groups each with their own conventions encoded in law. As for the Franks themselves, their own ethnic identity was so fluid in its expression but so politically compelling that it functioned as a 'super-ethnicity', complementary not antagonistic to the peoples pulled into its orbit. When the poet of the 'Paderborn epic' put words (lifted from Virgil) into Leo's mouth expressing amazement at the many different peoples constituting Charlemagne's army, he was merely articulating the multi-ethnic quality that made the Frankish polity so distinctive.

Leo's visit was not Charlemagne's first encounter with a pope—that had taken place in 754 when Charlemagne was only 5 years old. In that year, Stephen II (752–7) had crossed the Alps both to confer legitimacy on the coup that had brought Charlemagne's father Pippin III to the Frankish throne in 751 and to enlist Frankish political and military help for himself. In 754, the papal predicament derived from the very real threat of Lombard aggression, exacerbated by the recent collapse of the Byzantine administration of central Italy, an administration that had endured here since Justinian's reconquest of the peninsula. In seeking out the assistance of the upstart Carolingian dynasty, Stephen acknowledged that Rome's ecclesiastical bureaucrats were in no position to take adequate military measures to protect their city. In 799, however, Charlemagne was himself the king of the Lombards and in 781 and 787 had confirmed that an extensive territory in Rome's hinterland was to be under direct papal rule. Leo III was thus left to continue Hadrian I's work of puzzling out how the popes, who until around 750 had been subjects of Byzantine imperial administration, could turn themselves into autonomous territorial rulers. That the rapidly shifting and poorly defined position of the pope had led to factionalism and street fighting within Rome hints at how high the political stakes must have been.

The meeting at Paderborn brought together a hugely powerful king, well disposed by family tradition to be respectful towards the bishop of Rome, and a weakened, supplicant pope. In no sense can it have been a meeting of equals. How to characterize it more precisely is impossible, however. That we do not know what was discussed has not prevented historians' attempts at guessing. Nor do we know what relationship, if any, there was between this meeting and Charlemagne's coronation as emperor in Rome during a papal Mass on 25 December 800, when the Frankish king had travelled south to take definitive action to restore Leo's position. If the Paderborn meeting raises more questions than answers, even more so does Charlemagne's imperial coronation. The conflicting viewpoints and aspirations of the two key players themselves were promptly obfuscated by factitious and partisan reportage put around by papal and Frankish spin doctors alike. The politics of contested interpretation inherent in the very events of 799–800 was thus coupled with a calculus of retrospective significance that began immediately afterwards.

In acquiring the title of emperor, Charlemagne set a precedent that future generations were keen to emulate. It took until 850 to establish the convention that the only route to the imperial title was papal coronation in Rome, a tradition that endured, off and on, until 1452; detached from any Roman association thereafter, the imperial title persisted north of the Alps until the Napoleonic era.

Inasmuch as popes, emperors, and historians of later ages repeatedly turned to Leo's impasse and Charlemagne's coronation to justify actions or legitimate claims in quite different circumstances, the events at Paderborn in 799 and at Rome the following year have suffered from extreme teleological over-interpretation. We can avoid that, however, by maintaining the figurative perspective with which this section began, and focusing on the use of 'Rome' and 'empire' as powerful imaginative devices that shaped the cultural parameters of early medieval thinking. Another poem (quite possibly by the same poet) underscores the point that both were transferable notions, equally potent as metaphors as they were as institutions:

My Palaemon [Charlemagne] looks out from the lofty citadel of the new Rome and sees all the kingdoms forged into an empire through his victories.
Our times are transformed into the civilisation of Antiquity.
Golden Rome is reborn and restored anew to the world![30]

The transformation at work here was not, of course a transformation of the world of *c*.800 'into the civilisation of Antiquity' but rather the transformation of phrases, ideas, and values drawn from the ancient world into the grandiose rhetoric of the powerful Frankish hegemonic kingship. That Constantinople had been officially designated 'new Rome' since 381 in no way detracted from the suitability of the epithet for Aachen: 'Rome' was a cipher that stood for the capital of empire in all its architectural grandeur and political importance.

In using an imperial, Roman *mise-en-scène* to add glamour and legitimacy to the political realities of their own day, Carolingian writers tapped into long-standing habits of thought, for empire (*imperium*) was a term central to the Latin political vocabulary of Antiquity. Since early medieval authors frequently relied on Isidore of Seville's *Etymologies* as a concise guide to classical culture, we should do the same. It included a synopsis of world history that drew readers' attention to two points. In the course of identifying two polities that were 'more glorious' than all others, the Assyrian and the Roman, Isidore explained that 'other kingdoms and other kings' were held in a relationship to them 'like appendices'.[31] Overlordship or other forms of hegemony over dependent kingdoms was thus one key descriptor. The other was more specific to the history of Rome itself, the title of 'emperor'. Isidore noted, correctly, that the word *imperator* had originally referred to a general in command of an army, but that the senate had bestowed it as a title on Augustus (d. AD 14) 'in order that he would be distinguished from the kings of other peoples', and that his successors had retained the title.[32]

If 'emperor' became a distinctively Roman title for a ruler whose position was based on military conquest and rule over dependent kingdoms, then an empire was, more generally, any such polity. A reader of the Latin Bible encountered references to many ancient empires, of which the Roman was simply the most recent. Together, the Latin Bible and Isidore ensured that the idea of 'empire' was integral to Christian Latin learning.

The Old Testament, in particular, demonstrated its value as a term for any militarily powerful, multi-ethnic kingdom, especially one that had managed to subordinate other kings to its own ruler. The New Testament provided the basis on which fourth- and fifth-century thinkers had developed theological justifications for the existence of empires as integral to the Christian scheme of divinely ordained redemption of humankind.

'Empire', *imperium*, was thus a useful word for a wide range of early medieval political situations, Christian and non-Christian. It could function neutrally, to describe an exceptionally powerful ruler, as, for example, in Bede's ascription of *imperium* to a sequence of sixth- and seventh-century Anglo-Saxon kings who managed to 'rule over all the southern kingdoms [of Britain], which are divided from the north by the river Humber and the surrounding territory'.[33] Similarly, writing of events much nearer his own day but on the Continent, Bede described Pippin of Herstal, 'duke of the Franks', as exercising 'imperial authority' in southern Frisia after having expelled its ruler and annexed his territory in 690.[34] Alternatively, a king's admirers and propagandists could use the word as a 'puff', to talk up the influence and prestige of kings such as Theoderic the Great.

The word *imperator*, 'emperor', could also be used for laudatory purposes, especially in military situations. The Northumbrian king Oswald (634–42) certainly exercised hegemony over much of the northern half of Britain, and his reign had commenced with a great victory over 'the most powerful king of the Britons', Cadwallon of Gwynedd, in 634. After Oswald's death, emphatic significance was placed on his success: 'Oswald returned as victor after battle and was afterwards ordained by God as emperor of all Britain.'[35] In tenth-century Germany, Otto I's defeat of the Magyars at the river Lech in 955 was afterwards deemed to have been similarly decisive: 'Seizing his shield and the Holy Lance, he turned his horse to face the enemy fulfilling the role of the strongest soldier and the best commander (*imperator*).'[36]

The benefit of hindsight was not an essential prerequisite for such flattery, however. Brian Boru, king of the Dál Cais in Munster (976–1014), broke the traditional mould of Irish politics by defeating not only the minor kings of southern parts of the island and the Hiberno-Norse colony of Dublin but also the traditional overkings of the northern half Ireland, the Uí Néill. Taking tribute, hostages, and plunder wherever he went, Brian asserted a vigorous overlordship throughout Ireland. In 1005, he put a generous gift of gold on the altar of St Patrick at Armagh, a shrine normally under the patronage of the Uí Néill. A priest recorded the donation in the church's ancient gospel book 'in the sight of Brian, emperor of the

Irish'.[37] Brian certainly did not hold any formally bestowed office or title of emperor, but clerical bombast accurately captured the essence of his position as the king who dominated all other Irish kings of his day.

In sum, empire and emperors were often in the eye of the beholder. Oswald, Otto I as he rode into battle against the Magyars, and Brian Boru were emperors in the opinion of the learned men of their times, in much the same way as Theoderic, Pippin of Herstal, and others enjoyed *imperium*. Those who knew their Bible and their Isidore had at their disposal a vocabulary well suited to describe a characteristic early medieval political formation, one built upon dependent peoples. Their subordination might be established through battle, maintained by taking tribute, hostages, and troops from sub-kings, or consolidated by direct annexation and the removal of local kings: all were normal early medieval forms of *imperium*. When Charlemagne dismounted to meet Leo III at Paderborn, his kingship was exactly analogous. Only Charlemagne's ceremonial installation as emperor in Rome the next year was novel. It supplemented the traditional, descriptive vocabulary of empire and emperorship with an appointed office that was redolent of Roman Antiquity, and it gave the pope a vital role in bestowing that title.

Centuries earlier, the warlords who established kingdoms within the provinces of the crumbling western Roman Empire had legitimized their position by eagerly appropriating symbols of Roman rule—portraits on coins, seals, dress, insignia of office, flattering epithets. As Theoderic had said to Anastasius: 'Our kingship is an imitation of yours, modelled on your good design, a copy of the only Empire. By as much as we follow you, so much we precede all other peoples.'[38] If direct imperial imitation was the sincerest form of flattery in Italy in *c*.500, the aggressively competitive kings of later generations and more distant places also did their best to cash in on the act. Wrenched from its original context, imperial symbolism was thus transmitted across the centuries as a repertoire of royal procedures and attributes.

Charlemagne's installation as emperor in 800 gave renewed impetus to this much older practice, for papal officials were experts in Byzantine imperial ceremonial. Increasing diplomatic contact between the Frankish and Byzantine courts also enabled direct observation and emulation, for the prestige of the *Romaioi*, the Romans, as the Byzantines understood themselves to be, elicited a mixture of grudging admiration and keen imitation throughout the early Middle Ages—and for long thereafter. Whether at the Carolingian or, later, the Ottonian imperial court, appropriation of aspects of Byzantine court culture and ceremonial took place in an atmosphere of mutual edginess, a rivalry sharpened by the competition for political and religious influence all the way from the Balkans to the Baltic.

Just as the cultural prestige of the Byzantine court was a reflex of its political influence, so we find the same at the courts of the western—Carolingian and Ottonian—emperors. Alongside Charlemagne's lavish entertainment of visitors at Aachen, Paderborn, and elsewhere can be placed the appropriation of Carolingian styles of government in other kingdoms. In the ninth century, Alfonso II of Asturias (791–842) and Alfred of Wessex both found useful precedent in Carolingian ideologies of royal authority; at the end of the tenth century, the influence of Ottonian hegemony on the newly Christian kingdoms of central Europe—Poland, Hungary, and Bohemia—was also marked.

Thus we should not think of 'empire' only with reference to the two specific early medieval polities, Byzantine and (after 800) western, whose rulers were formally vested with the title of emperor. Far more than that, 'empire' was a widely used term for a particular kind of successful kingdom. It implied domination and hegemony—military, political, cultural. Furthermore, imperial practices provided a repertoire of inherited ways of presenting and enacting royal power for showy display and enhanced legitimacy: almost everywhere, kings avidly drew upon this stock of motifs, adding an imperial lustre to less grandiose realities.

Although rulers commonly took contemporary empires as their point of reference, on occasion they turned to the past, above all to the Roman Empire. When Charlemagne placed the motto 'the renewal of the Roman Empire' on his seal in the spring of 801, he had already left Rome, never to return—and was certainly not outlining a practical political programme. Rather, he was investing his new-found title with the rhetorical mantle of historical authentication. Subsequent emperors generally followed his example and spent minimal time in Rome itself, except for Otto III. Having revived Charlemagne's slogan, in the slightly but significantly altered form of 'the renewal of the empire of the Romans', Otto attempted to take it literally rather than metaphorically. In 998, he rebuilt the old imperial palace in Rome and set about governing from there, the first emperor to do so since the early fourth century. But no amount of 'renewal' could save him from the rough-and-tumble of Rome's urban politics, and the city's traditional rulers soon put paid to his ambition, expelling him early in 1001.

Otto died before he could learn the lesson that, for a transalpine emperor, Rome was more useful as an idea than as a centre of government. As an idea, it drew on the antique past to confer a potent form of legitimacy; as a place of power, it was best left well alone, distant but powerfully evocative. Though the rhetoric of Romanness added a patina of ancient respectability to the new forms of hegemonic kingship that emerged in northern Europe from the end of the eighth century onwards, most early medieval ideologues knew very well how to distinguish 'Rome' from 'empire'. In their separate ways, both were powerful master ideas: but we can never know precisely what part Leo III's visit to Paderborn may have played in the decision to conflate them into a novel institutional form.

## Rome, AD 1027

We come, finally, to Cnut's journey from Scandinavia to Rome. King of Denmark by inheritance, of England by conquest, and aspirant ruler of Norway, he strove to protect and extend his North Sea empire. This gave him occasion to assert overlordship or take military action everywhere from the Irish Sea to the southern eastern Baltic (Figure 8.4). In 1025, he had come to an agreement with the newly elected German king Conrad II about their joint strategic interests in Poland and the Baltic Slav peoples; Cnut then spent the summer of 1026 in southern Sweden confronting a joint Norwegian and Swedish attack. Thereafter, he 'measured the southward path with [his] feet',[39] all the way to Rome. 'Generous prince' that he certainly was, Cnut showered gifts on the churches he visited en route, and arrived in Rome in time for the celebration of Easter in 1027. Together with King Rudolf III of Burgundy (993–1032), the German and Italian nobility and around seventy archbishops, bishops, and abbots, Cnut was in the audience in St Peter's on Easter Sunday when Pope John XIX (1024–33) crowned Conrad and his wife Gisela. The festivities were more magnificent than any previous early medieval imperial coronation, perhaps because of the persistent challenges to Conrad's rule. To impress the rebellious German and Italian aristocracy, he needed all the external political support he could muster: in an imposing display of imperial dignity, his two royal neighbours Cnut and Rudolf escorted the new emperor as he processed out of the basilica to his lodgings and the banquet that doubtless awaited them there.

If Conrad was an emperor who needed to be seen with a retinue of kings, Cnut too had much to gain from his place of honour at Conrad's side. Heading back to Denmark, he wrote to his English subjects, announcing that he had just been to Rome.

I would have you know that there was a great gathering of nobles there at the Easter solemnity with our lord Pope John and the Emperor Conrad, to wit, all the princes of the peoples from Monte Gargano [southern Italy] to this nearest sea [the North Sea], who all gave me a respectful welcome and honoured me with

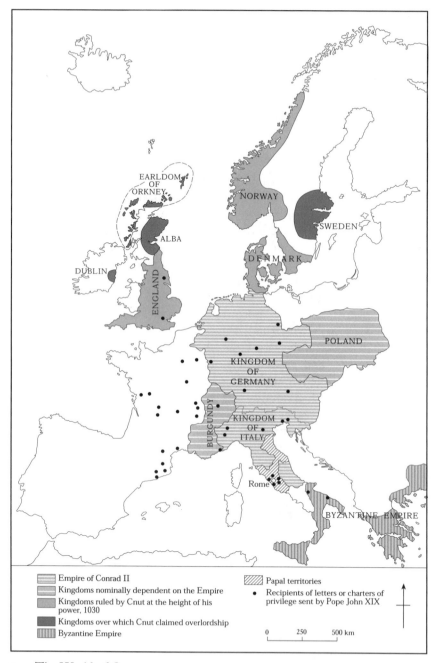

8.4. The World of Cnut.

magnificent gifts. In particular I was honoured by the emperor with sundry gifts and precious presents: vessels of gold and silver and very precious fabrics and robes.[40]

Imperial gifts and papal honour enhanced the regality of a king whose rule over the English was based on conquest: those who were not in Cnut's retinue in Rome should nevertheless be aware of the prestige that accrued to their king. 'Dear to the emperor', Cnut had indeed 'reaped a portion of Rome's glory'.

For many of those in Rome that Easter, Conrad's coronation was an opportunity to conduct business. Whether at local, national, or imperial level, early medieval governance was not a constant process but rather the subject of intense bursts of activity on specific occasions of limited duration: the Easter gathering of 1027 was one such. For the three weeks of Conrad's visit, Rome functioned as Europe's political centre. Indeed, the flurry of activity on this occasion was all the greater because of the exceptionally large number of secular and ecclesiastical notables in attendance. When tenth- and early eleventh-century rulers summoned their subjects to debate major decisions or issued formal written documents, it was most usually done in the context of important religious festivities, and Conrad's coronation gathering was no exception. In the first place, pope and emperor presided together in a large ecclesiastical assembly in the Lateran basilica in an attempt to resolve two disputes about status and precedence between proud Italian prelates. The archbishops of Milan and Ravenna had suddenly erupted into unseemly rows as to which of them should lead Conrad into St Peter's, while the acrimony between the archbishops of Aquileia and Grado had been rumbling on for centuries already. A formal record detailed the names of the council's many participants, their deliberations and decisions. Such procedural and documentary grandeur was itself a form of political action, an expression of consensus far more important than the subsequent—contested—outcome.

In addition, bishops and abbots from far and wide petitioned the pope and the emperor on behalf of their own churches, requesting confirmation of their landholdings, the renewal or extension of their legal rights and privileges. In the course of Conrad's stay in Rome, both he and John XIX issued many such charters. Large in format, florid in the conventions of their bureaucratic prose, and formal in appearance, both the imperial and papal documents ultimately derived from standard late Roman bureaucratic procedures, as has been indicated.[41] For pope and emperor alike, the act of issuing such a charter was a mark of political goodwill and a means of ordering networks of alliance; for the recipients, the value of these documents as trophies of momentary closeness to the centres of power usually outstripped their ability to turn papal or imperial graciousness into any meaningful political advantage. Very often, it took the proximity of pope or emperor to enforce the contents of such privileges. Such opportunities were rare: while Conrad II's court was ceaselessly peripatetic, John XIX's entourage restricted its movements to Rome and its immediate hinterland, and few of those who left Rome clutching grants and confirmations can have had any idea whether they would ever see the issuer again.

Cnut was amongst those who pursued political ends amidst the festivities—and the street brawling—that accompanied the imperial coronation. He negotiated with both Conrad and Rudolf to secure a reduction in the tolls paid by Anglo-Saxon and Danish merchants and pilgrims travelling across the Alps to Italy, and with John XIX about the huge sums extorted from Anglo-Saxon archbishops whenever one of them collected his *pallium* (the item of dress bestowed by the pope on each incoming archbishop as a symbol of office). 'All the requests which I made of my lord the pope and of the emperor and of King Rudolf and the other princes through whose territory we have to pass on the way to Rome, for the benefit of my own people, were readily granted, and the concessions confirmed on oath, on the testimony of four archbishops and twenty bishops and an immense multitude of dukes and nobles who were present', he proudly reported to the English.[42] Public formalities and many witnesses offered the only real hope that the deals that Cnut had struck would be honoured in the future.

As well as alerting us to the integration into Europe's politics of emerging Scandinavian and Slav polities, Cnut's visit to Rome reminds us of the centrality of honour and gift giving to early medieval politics. It also offers an excellent example of dramatically staged Christian rulership in action. It concerns us here for an additional reason, however—its religious dimension. In writing to his English subjects, Cnut opened by announcing his spiritual concerns: 'I give you notice that I have lately gone to Rome to pray for the redemption of my sins and the salvation of my kingdoms and of the peoples who are subject to my rule.' Made in fulfilment of a long-standing vow, his journey was a pilgrimage that took him not only to the churches of Rome's two apostolic patrons, Peter and Paul, but also to 'every sanctuary that I could learn of within the city of Rome or outside it'.[43] For Cnut, as for many others in the early Middle Ages, Rome's importance was above all religious.

The Christian city had two contrasting dimensions, that of popes and that of pilgrims, which we will consider in this order. Whatever the broader political context, each pope was, first and foremost, Rome's bishop, whose time and energies were split between two main challenges. One task was to direct the elaborate ceremonies of worship around which the city's ritual life turned and to oversee its many churches, numbering approximately 200. The other was to administer the bishopric's extensive lands, direct their revenues to the upkeep of the urban fabric and the sustenance of the inhabitants and, in so doing, cope with the tendency of ecclesiastical lands to fall under the control of local bigwigs. Additional responsibilities accumulated when direct rule of the region around Rome passed to the pope in the 780s. Not only were there the intricacies of aristocratic politics to negotiate, as Leo III had found to his cost, but since, from the late eighth century, popes anyway came from local aristocratic families, there were also their relatives' affairs to foster. Defence of the papal lands formed another priority. From the early ninth until the early eleventh centuries, the main threat came in the form of Saracen plundering and slaving raids launched from Muslim north Africa and Sicily: the sack of St Peter's basilica in 846 jolted popes into action up and down the Italian coast. From the late tenth century onwards, resurgent Byzantine rule in southern Italy posed somewhat different problems. In this context, building urban defences, mustering troops, equipping ships, and negotiating military alliances all became urgent papal activities.

Faced with these local and regional priorities, it was of no direct relevance to tenth- and early eleventh-century popes that in the distant past, between c.400 and c.700, their predecessors had also been preoccupied with claiming pre-eminent status within an empire no longer directly governed from Rome, or that they had taken a leading part in the heated late antique debates about the correct definition of Christian doctrine. Certainly, no one doubted that the pope ranked first among the clergy, but in the early Middle Ages this high dignity neither conferred general authority nor commanded obedience. If early medieval bishops, abbots, lay persons, and kings chose to seek papal advice or support on specific matters, popes responded. But it was not their role to intervene in the wider world unless asked, far less to initiate. Nor, indeed, had they any means of enforcing their decisions, except perhaps in the vicinity of Rome: when a papal privilege for one church upset another's interests, or advice on a point of Christian conduct conflicted with established local norms, papal pronouncements frequently remained a dead letter.

In all this, John XIX was entirely typical. Son of the count of Tusculum near Rome, he abandoned a secular career as senator to succeed his brother as pope in 1024, and turned his considerable political skills to papal ends. Like other early medieval popes, he had no contact with large parts of western Christendom, for it was only in Anglo-Saxon England, the lands that had once comprised the Carolingian Empire, and those now ruled by the German emperor where there was any tradition of even occasional liaison with Rome. Most of the churchmen who obtained an audience with him simply sought confirmation of existing ecclesiastical lands and privileges; the most favoured returned home with their rights forcefully restated and their ceremonial splendour enhanced. A few others brought with them charters issued locally, in the hope that a papal countersignature would strengthen their legitimacy. Figure 8.4 indicates the extent of these contacts. Only in and around the city of Rome did the pope have anything more than fine words to give, when the senior clergy of his own entourage were the beneficiaries. Conrad II's coronation was the only occasion known to have brought any of Europe's rulers into direct personal contact with John XIX; the remainder of the time his channels of contact beyond the duchy of Rome were much the same as those of his predecessors. In addition to ecclesiastical delegations, his visitors from north of the Alps included a few powerful laymen who had broken ecclesiastical norms of conduct regarding marriage or the use of violence. Some had been excommunicated by their local bishop but came to Rome in search of papal absolution; others sought a penitential sentence directly from the pope rather than risking justice at the hands of local courts and clergy. But, for the most part, John XIX conducted the church services required of him, reorganized the bureaucratic hierarchy of the churches around Rome, and, in conjunction with his family, administered the papal lands to his and their mutual benefit.

Of the early medieval visitors to Rome, only a proportion sought out the pope. Most came not as petitioners to the pontiff but as pilgrims, to pray in its many shrines. We have met a few of them in other contexts, including Gerald of Aurillac, Fintan of Rheinau, and Cyngen, king of Powys. One of many centres of pilgrimage in the early Middle Ages, the city was sometimes in active competition with other shrines, such as St Martin's at Tours, but the great number of martyr saints venerated in churches in and around Rome exerted a cumulative attraction greater than anywhere else. From the time of Damasus I (366–84) onwards, popes had encouraged worship at the scores of early Christian graves in the extramural cemeteries and associated churches. Its martyrs were the city's spiritual adornment, its link with the early Christian era and an earthly anticipation of a heaven populated with saints. At their head were the apostles Peter and Paul: 'O lucky Rome, stained purple with the precious blood of such great princes, you excel all the beauty of the world, not in your praise but in the merits of your saints, whom you slew with bloody swords.'[44]

By the sixth century, Rome was no longer just the centre of local or regional pilgrimage (Figure 8.5). Worshippers were travelling increasing distances, and, by the first half of the seventh century, the Roman clergy were organized for their reception, providing accommodation and guidebooks. Arriving in Rome in 631, Irish monks found themselves 'in one lodging in the church of St Peter with a Greek, a Hebrew, a Scythian and an Egyptian';[45] by the end of the eighth century, Anglo-Saxons, Franks, Frisians, Greeks, and Lombards each had their own permanent establishment catering to their needs. From their hostels, pilgrims set out to tour the holy sites, equipped with precise itineraries. 'You go east until you reach the holy martyr Emerentiana, who is buried in the upper church, with two martyrs in the catacomb below, Victor and Alexander. Then follow the street *via Numentana* to the church of St Agnes, which is beautiful, in which she rests alone. Pope Honorius restored this with wonderful craftsmanship.'[46] This is typical of the careful detail with which a guidebook from the pontificate of Honorius I (625–38) steered pilgrims round the city. To visit all the catacombs and churches would have required a protracted stay, which not all chose to make, and concentrations of pilgrim graffiti suggest that some sites were indeed more popular than others. In the seventh and eighth centuries, women such as the Anglo-Saxon Fagihild and the Greek Anastasia joined men such as the Lombard Anwald, the Frank Lotharius, and many others in scratching their names onto the walls of the catacomb of Marcellinus and Peter on the *via Labicana*, an enduring testimony to the popularity of this particular site.

'. . . and thus you enter the street *via Vaticana* until you come to the basilica of St Peter, which Constantine, emperor of the whole world, built and which stands out above all other churches. At the western end of this beautiful church his holy body lies.' Any visit to Rome culminated at the tomb of St Peter, where the visitor would 'pour our tears of penitence'.[47] 'Friend of Peter', as Sighvatr described him, Cnut was blunt about the advantages of praying here: 'I have learnt from wise men of the great power which the holy Apostle Peter had received from our Lord of binding and loosing, and that it is he who bears the keys of the kingdom of Heaven; and for this I thought it very profitable to seek his advocacy in particular with God.'[48] Cnut's words echo those of Christian scripture, which claimed that Christ had said to his follower Peter: 'I will give to thee the keys of the kingdom of heaven. And whatsoever thou shalt bind upon earth, it shall be bound also in heaven: and whatsoever thou shalt loose on earth, it shall be loosed also in heaven' (Matt. 16: 19). A Bavarian song of *c*.900 expressed in simple but strong terms the underlying beliefs that made St Peter's 'advocacy' so desirable:

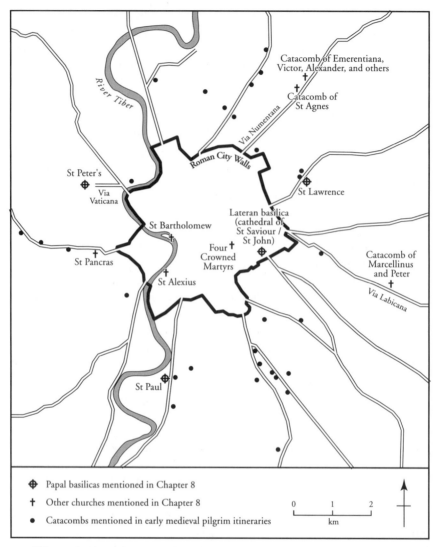

8.5. The ecclesiastical topography of early medieval Rome. Of the approximately 200 churches in early medieval Rome, this map shows four of the five papal basilicas and those churches and shrines mentioned in Chapter 8. Based on R. Valentini and G. Zucchetti, *Codice topografico della città di Roma*, 2, Fonti per la Storia d'Italia, 88 (Rome, 1942).

Our Lord has transmitted authority to St Peter,
that he may save the man who places hope in him.
Lord have mercy, Christ have mercy.

He keeps guard by his words over the gates of heaven
and can place therein him whom he would save.
Lord have mercy, Christ have mercy.

Let us beseech God's beloved, all together, in full voice,
that he may deign to have mercy on us sinners.
Lord have mercy, Christ have mercy.[49]

In short, within the Christian cosmology of a world permeated by sin, St Peter's was the help most likely to aid the sinner achieve salvation. For this reason more than any other, men and women made the arduous journey to Rome, risking Alpine brigands; Saracen pirates; profiteers and prostitutes out to turn a quick penny from gullible foreigners.

City of St Peter, Rome was intensely familiar even to those who never visited it. To worship 'in the Roman manner' was to adopt the most authentic possible form of liturgy.[50] Narratives of the sufferings of Rome's martyrs and of the lives of the early popes circulated widely in the early Middle Ages: to read them was to enter the city in the mind's eye. One monk whose experience was entirely in the mind was an unnamed Irishman in the monastery of Kilbarry. He had vowed to go on pilgrimage to Rome, but had failed to obtain his superior's permission. The concerned abbot called the monk into his cell, so that they could pray and fast together for three days and nights. But, while his master prayed, the disciple fell asleep. When he awoke, he recounted what he had seen as he slept:

'I saw myself undertaking the pilgrim's journey, on which a very beautiful young man accompanied me. Having crossed the ocean, I reached Rome, with the same companion leading me along the right way. With the young man, I completed in due order the pilgrimage that I had vowed to undertake, in accordance with my intention. The same young man led me back here by the same road. Departing from me with great cheerfulness, he declared that he was the angel of God and he also stated that I had completely fulfilled the pilgrimage that I had vowed to undertake.'[51]

At Europe's outer margins, Rome was impossibly distant for all save the wealthiest few. But, as a place of holiness where the pious Christian dead lay buried in their multitudes, it could nevertheless be replicated and rendered accessible. The Irish did this by using the word 'Rome' to refer to a monastic cemetery. On Devenish island on Loch Erne, Molaisse (d. 564/71) had established 'a common cemetery [*ruaim*] for the Gaels':

here was 'God the Father's own domain'.[52] The same was done in west-ernmost Britain. Bardsey Island lies off the north-west coast of Wales, and is difficult of access. A twelfth-century Welsh writer explained why this was 'the Rome of Britain':

In ancient British custom, it is proverbially called 'the Rome of Britain' on ac-count of the length and difficulty of the sea crossing, for it is situated on the very edge of the country, and also on account of the holiness and attractiveness of the place; holiness because the bodies of twenty thousand saints—confessors and martyrs—lie buried there; attractiveness because it is surrounded on all sides by the sea, with a high cliff on the eastern side and flat, fertile land with a spring of sweetly flowing water on the western side. The coast abounds with dolphins and the island is completely lacking in snakes and frogs.[53]

This Rome was paradise on an Atlantic island. Other recreations em-phasized different aspects of the earthly city, most notably its buildings, church dedications, or topography. Remaining in the British Isles for a little longer, we shall switch attention to the Anglo-Saxon communities along the eastern seaboard, where papal missionaries were active for most of the seventh century. Canterbury, itself a former Roman city of regional importance, was the centre from which the earliest missionaries worked. Here, Augustine and his fellow Roman monks made for themselves a home from home. As Figure 8.6 indicates, they did so by dedicating the churches they founded to the principal patrons of Rome's own churches, old and new, and by copying their topographical relationship to the walled urban area. Rome's cathedral, the Lateran, lay within the city walls and was dedicated to Christ the Saviour, and its adjacent baptistery church was dedicated to St John: thus Augustine built his cathedral, Christ Church, within Canterbury's Roman defences, next to which his succes-sor Cuthbert (740–60) added the church of St John the Baptist. At Rome, the papal basilicas of St Peter and St Paul both lay outside the city walls: at Canterbury, Augustine founded an extramural burial church, dedicated to Sts Peter and Paul together. And, since the popes who sent the mis-sions to Canterbury, Gregory I and Honorius I, were especial patrons of Rome's extramural church of St Pancras and the city-centre church of the Four Crowned Martyrs, so too seventh-century Canterbury soon acquired an external church to St Pancras and an intramural one honouring the Four Crowned Martyrs. In all these churches, Augustine and his immediate successors placed relics of Rome's martyrs and followed the distinctively Roman way of singing the liturgy: the ruins of Roman-era Canterbury had been transformed into a replica of Christian Rome.

    The presence of a ruined Roman city was nevertheless not essential for

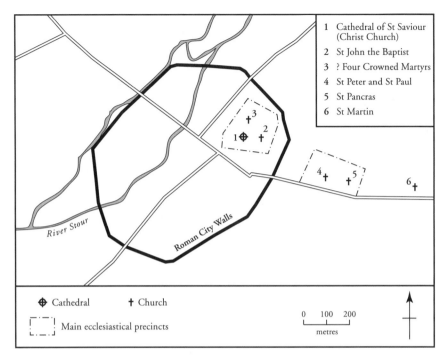

1 Cathedral of St Saviour (Christ Church)
2 St John the Baptist
3 ? Four Crowned Martyrs
4 St Peter and St Paul
5 St Pancras
6 St Martin

⊕ Cathedral      † Church

⌐ ‾ ¬
¦ _ ¦ Main ecclesiastical precincts
⌐ . ¬

0   100   200
metres

8.6. The ecclesiastical topography of seventh-century Canterbury. Based on N. P. Brooks, 'Canterbury, Rome and the Construction of English Identity', in Julia M. H. Smith (ed.), *Early Medieval Rome and the Christian West: Essays in Honour of Donald Bullough* (Leiden, 2000), with permission of Brill Academic Publishers and the author.

this sort of imitation of Rome. Much further north, where in former times the Roman Empire had shaded off into a militarized frontier zone, a Northumbrian monk founded twin monasteries near the mouth of the river Tyne, at Wearmouth in 674 and Jarrow in 681. Benedict Biscop had already travelled repeatedly to Rome and was determined to replicate the visual splendour and modes of worship he had observed there. To achieve this, he imported stonemasons and glaziers to build his churches 'in the Roman style he had always loved so much' and stocked them with the books, liturgical vestments, and pictures he had brought back with him.[54] He fetched a Roman singing master to teach his Northumbrian novices to sing Roman chant and dedicated his churches to Rome's two most important patrons, Wearmouth to St Peter and Jarrow to St Paul.

From this Northumbrian Rome, another followed. In *c.*713/14 Nechtan, king of the Picts, wrote to the abbot of Wearmouth–Jarrow requesting details of Roman liturgical procedure and builders 'to build a church of stone for his people after the Roman fashion, promising that it should be dedicated in honour of the blessed chief of the apostles'. A passing twelfth-century reference to a place called *Egglespethir* (Peter's church) near Restenneth is all that remains of this Scottish Rome. 'Remote though they were from the Roman people and their language', Nechtan promised that the Picts would replicate the practices of the Roman church. [55] In the far north, where no Roman missionary ever ventured and where local building techniques relied on wattle and timber, a stone church dedicated to St Peter in which Roman ecclesiastical customs prevailed would indeed have been a powerful evocation of Rome itself.

Such local renditions of Rome were not confined to the British archipelago. But they were characteristic of regions where Christian communities lacked their own direct link to the Roman era, whether that association was expressed through the veneration of their own local martyrs in ancient churches or an unbroken sequence of bishops stretching back to the third or fourth century. The replication of Rome through name transference, building forms, liturgy, dedications, and imported martyrial relics signalled a strong desire for attachment to authoritative narratives of Christian origins and apostolic authenticity in the absence of locally available proofs.

The main other region where Christian communities found imaginative ways to import Rome to their own locality was Germany. In the ninth century, abbots and bishops sometimes went to great lengths to acquire corporeal relics of Roman martyrs as one expression of this. Some also directly copied the most distinctive feature of Rome's ecclesiastical architecture: the ground plan of St Peter's, with its unusual western orientation and circular crypt around the apostle's tomb. To build such a crypt was to build in a deliberately Roman style. By the tenth century, German bishops were finding even more elaborate ways of transporting Rome to their own locality. A good example of this is Konstanz, a city on the banks of the upper Rhine, illustrated in Figure 8.7. Here, Bishop Conrad (934–75) rebuilt his see, in much the same way as Augustine had established Canterbury, reflecting the spiritual topography of Rome but also revealing his close links with Otto I. Next to the cathedral of St Mary a new church in honour of St John the Evangelist and St John the Baptist evoked the Lateran, whose dedication to Christ the Saviour had been superseded by the cult of both Johns by the late eighth century. Beyond the built-up area, foundations to St Lawrence and St Paul recalled Rome's extramural papal basilicas dedicated to these saints. Together with St Maurice, St

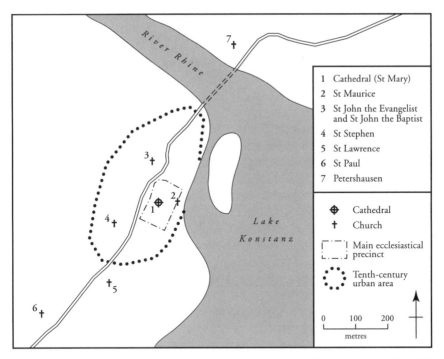

8.7. The ecclesiastical topography of late-tenth-century Konstanz. Based on H. Maurer, *Konstanz als ottonischer Bischofssitz*, Veröffentlichungen des Max-Planck-Instituts für Geschichte, 39 (Göttingen, 1973), with permission of the Max-Planck-Institut für Geschichte.

Lawrence had brought victory over the Magyars to Otto I in 955, so a rotunda in honour of Otto's especial patron, St Maurice, completed Conrad's building activities. His successor but one, Gebhard (979–95), went even further. Since St Peter's lay on the opposite bank of the Tiber from the city of Rome, Gebhard went to great effort to acquire a site on the opposite bank of the Rhine from his cathedral city. Here he founded a monastery 'constructed in accordance with the layout of the church of the prince of the apostles at Rome'—with a western orientation and a relic crypt—'and for this reason he called the place Petershausen [Peterhouse]'. Gebhard affirmed the Roman connection by enshrining part of the head of Pope Gregory I in it.[56]

We end back in Paderborn, where a fire had razed the town in 1000. Bishop Meinwerk (1009–36) set about rebuilding it on a far grander scale then ever before and in a way that reflected his own earlier career as one

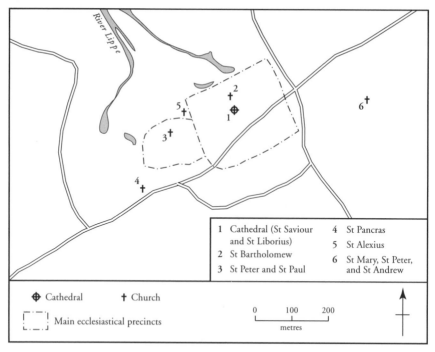

**8.8.** The ecclesiastical topography of early eleventh-century Paderborn. This map shows the city as Meinwerk left it on his death in 1036; he did not live to complete his plan for two further churches, one to the north and one to the south of the town. Based on E. Herzog, *Die ottonische Stadt: Die Anfänge der mittelalterlichen Stadtbaukunst in Deutschland* (Berlin, 1964).

of Otto III's most trusted clerical courtiers. Figure 8.8 shows the town as he left it on his death. He planned to build five churches 'in the manner of a cross', with the rebuilt cathedral at its centre and four religious communities to mark the arms: thus through prayer 'the city might be marked by the crucifix and defended against all the darts of the Enemy'.[57] Of the new churches, the eastern one was a replica of the Church of the Holy Sepulchre in Jerusalem: dedicated to the Virgin Mary and Sts Peter and Andrew and housing relics fetched back from the Holy Land, it encapsulated Christ's life story and offered an earthly reflection of the heavenly Jerusalem. Opposite it, to the west, was a miniature of early Christian Rome, a Benedictine monastery dedicated to Sts Peter and Paul, with a western apse and a circular relic crypt. In it, Meinwerk placed an altar that

Leo III had dedicated on his visit in 799. With its strong papal associations, he used this as the espicopal funerary church where he reinterred
his predecessors' remains, and where in due course he was himself buried.
To the north and south of Paderborn were to be a further two churches.
In laying out his cathedral city, Meinwerk also made precise reference to
contemporary Rome, that of Otto III, by dedicating two other new
chapels to saints whose cults Otto had himself launched in Rome, St
Alexius and St Bartholomew. Meinwerk's death before he could complete
his ambitious Christian theme park in no way detracts from the point that
Rome, and indeed Jerusalem, could be relocated at will. Through architectural analogy, saints' relics, and episcopal liturgy, the holiest places in
Christendom could be rebuilt and the events associated with them re-
enacted elsewhere. In the early Middle Ages, Rome was the ideal type of
a Christian holy place.

Rome was the city that, so legend held, the heirs of the Trojan hero
Aeneas had founded and that had gone on to conquer an empire span-
ning most of the known world. It was the city that had made martyrs of
its earliest Christian inhabitants and then become the capital of a Christian empire. The history, myth, and legend of its long past, bloody and
glorious, weighed heavily on the men and women of the early Middle
Ages. First the foundation of a new imperial capital at Constantinople,
then the formation of new kingdoms and ethnic identities in and around
the western provinces, had rendered obsolete Rome's role as the capital of
that ancient empire—but yet its central significance lived on.

From his Scandinavian perspective, Sighvatr unerringly identified the
'glory' that Cnut reaped in Rome. It came from being 'dear to the emperor, friend of Peter'. However much the political map of Europe had
been transformed between c.500 and c.1000, Rome could not shake off its
association with empire. Rather, its imperial dimension was reconfigured,
formed anew to suit the needs of the powerful warrior kings of early
medieval northern Europe. Glory, legitimacy, a secure past, and a cultural
heritage—Rome provided aspiring emperors and their subjects with all
these and more in abundance. Above all, the very notion of empire offered a way of organizing political life that might stand some chance of
overcoming the local roots of all early medieval political power.

And, if empire was the city's enduring political attribute, Peter remained
at the heart of its religious identity. From his tomb on the Vatican hill on
the opposite bank of the Tiber, the prince of the apostles influenced the
beliefs and devotions of early medieval Christians in their local churches
and in their long journeys in search of Christian salvation. Manifested in

liturgy and ritual, place names and architecture, affection for St Peter
transcended the localisms and particularities that so characterized early
medieval society.

Those identities and attachments found resonances far and wide. Not
only in their travels but also in their stories and libraries, buildings and
ceremonies, early medieval men and women transposed Rome, gave its
history new meanings, imagined it in new ways, constructed it afresh.
Whether encountered in books and documents or in bricks and mortar,
it formed a storehouse of every conceivable kind of cultural resource, a
repository of ideas and artefacts to be transvalued and transported wherever and however people wished. By stocking the imagination, the city—
unique and particular as it was—was suggestive of a shared culture. In
Rome, the peoples of Europe found a common fascination.

# Epilogue

IN 1049 another pope named Leo crossed the Alps. With Leo IX's journey to Reims, a different story begins. It tells of the formation of a papal monarchy, exercising authority throughout Latin Christendom by means of a centralized judicial and administrative machinery of government. This story reaches its apogee in the thirteenth century, when the city of Rome functioned as the jurisdictional headquarters of an international ecclesiastical institution, regulating theological doctrines, social norms, political procedures, and rituals of worship throughout the Latin west. It interprets conflict between popes and rulers as the opportunity to shed supposedly archaic notions of monarchy, as the first step towards specifically western—and thus more modern—modes of power. Additional strands in the narrative emphasize a striving towards a particular vision of conformity—expansion at the expense of Islam and Byzantium, elimination of Europe's last pagans, intolerance of internal dissent, and persecution of Jews. Its traditional corollaries are the celebration of cosmopolitan high culture and professional national governments, developments made possible by rapid urbanization and the formation of a self-sustaining, international mandarin class. In an echo of the vigorous rhetoric of novelty and new beginnings employed by eleventh- and twelfth-century writers, this version of the history of Europe is often presented in triumphalist terms, as a phase of enduring significance whose religious, institutional, and cultural parameters long outlived the Middle Ages. It identifies the period from approximately the turn of the first millennium as the decisive era of fresh starts in virtually every field of human endeavour—agricultural, economic, religious, institutional, military, literary, artistic. In this paradigm, the location of power shifted, forever, in the course of the long twelfth century.

Change the perspective, however, and this becomes a story of loss—of diversity, local identities, customary habits, plural solutions to common problems. Turned around, the traditional narrative recounts the erosion of the varied complexities of early medieval Europe's cultures. Its inversion tracks the ways in which presumptions of local knowledge faded as aspirations towards uniformity grew. It suggests that local values and regional issues lost out to lay and ecclesiastical hierarchs whose centralizing

ambitions became the main agents of change. It marks the waning of
diversity and the waxing of deviance.

This reorientation is not simply an intellectual exercise. The thematic
tension in European historiography between diversity and uniformity derives its creative vigour from the strong, if oblique, relationship that has
always existed between the content of historical writing and its immediate political context. Certainly, the familiar story of the high Middle Ages
served the nation states of nineteenth- and twentieth-century Europe
well, for they found in the medieval past resonances of more modern preoccupations. But, at the start of the third millennium, when the very notion of the nation state is being eroded from all directions, that well-worn
narrative can no longer be sustained. A Europe in which regional identities of early medieval origin are being rediscovered—Mercia, Burgundy,
Fife, Lombardy, Carinthia, and many others—needs a different story.
So too does a Europe urgently striving for new forms of pluralism and
coexistence in cultural, religious, social, and economic affairs.

This book has sought to offer that with respect to the centuries from
500 to 1000. It has balanced exploration of the ways in which common
themes were manifested in diversity of experience with arguments for the
cultural dynamism of these centuries. In 500, the many differences that
distinguished one region of Europe from another all mapped onto a
single spectrum. At one end, around the western Mediterranean, lay
profoundly Roman but nevertheless post-imperial polities—Christian,
relatively urbanized and populous, wealthy, literate, internally divided by
steep gradients of status, wealth, and gender. Beyond them, around
or straddling the former frontiers, new polities of rather weaker Roman
character, which marched with those beyond the border, where Roman
influence was always indirect. At its furthest reach, far away from the
Mediterranean in an arc from the northern Atlantic to the Baltic and on
to the Black Sea, were thinly populated polities characterized by shallow
social hierarchies, some of whom made occasional use of inscriptional
literacy (in runic or ogam) but which otherwise exercised power in
non-literate, non-bureaucratic, non-urban modes. Their contacts with the
Roman world were spasmodic, but so prestigious that power congealed
around those very few with access to Roman contacts, Roman goods,
Roman religion.

By 1000, that simple spectrum had dissolved. While varying population densities doubtless still existed, plague and de-urbanization around
the Mediterranean had reduced the differential with more northern areas;
in any case, the population was rising rapidly everywhere long before the
millennium. Across the western Mediterranean there had come to be a

shifting zone where Christianity shaded off into the dominance of Islam. To its north, the cultural hegemony of the Roman way of life had yielded to a matrix shaped by Christianity, a religion into which many separate Roman cultural elements had been gradually subsumed. Its dominance demanded vast landed resources, treasures, ideological reinforcements. It called for a reordering of daily life, sexual relationships, and family bonds. Its language, technologies of power, cosmology, and far-flung web of contacts together sharpened distinctions of status and gender and fostered new, steeply graduated, hierarchies of power, at whose apex were rulers whose wealth, power, and prestige lacked precedent in those localities. It prompted the emergence of new imperial polities whose centres lay in that northern arc; while to its south, around the western Mediterranean, the large kingdoms of post-imperial times had mostly disintegrated into numerous tiny polities. Lacking any injection of new ideologies or techniques of ruling, the latter competed bitterly among themselves for access to limited resources and prestige, for only some of them were in a position to profit from trading with Byzantium and the Islamic world, and even fewer had any scope for territorial aggrandizement at the expense of a non-Christian neighbour.

In short, from a world of Roman culture within which Christianity was one element in 500, by 1000 Europe had become a Christian world of which Roman cultural attributes formed one aspect. From a world of large polities in the south and small, simpler ones to the north and west, Europe had turned into a world of territorially extensive northern but modest southern ones.

In arguing this, I have adopted a perspective that has neither the city of Rome as its focal point nor the imperial frontiers as its frame. To do that would have simply reinstated the greatest Roman conceit of all, that of the dissemination from Rome of the benefits of a 'superior' civilization. In chronological terms, my emphasis on Europe after the collapse of imperial rule in the West has also been a concentration on Europe before the emergence of Rome as the seat of a European papal monarchy. Nor—except in my title—have I allowed the word 'Rome' to stand for anything other than the city of that name, in contrast to its frequent shorthand usage to designate the Roman Empire, bundled with its cultural attributes. This mode of presentation makes visible many different reinterpretations and imaginative appropriations of the Roman legacy—multiple strands and shifting patterns of coloured threads interwoven through a rich tapestry of cultural diversity.

This tapestry does not have neatly hemmed edges: in both geographical and chronological terms they are ragged, and deliberately so. I have defined the early Middle Ages by a cluster of phenomena whose common characteristics are, on the one hand, regional diversity and localism and, on the other, the omnipresence of aspects of the Roman cultural, religious, and political inheritance. In so doing, I have also demonstrated that, in the dynamic cultures of early medieval Europe, the location, pace, and direction of flux were far from uniform. And I have emphasized not generalized change, but multiple changes—abrupt or gradual, deliberate or contingent—in order to bring into focus both the social constraints that framed men's and women's lives and the many active choices each person made about his or her own affairs.

Viewed in this way, the early Middle Ages cannot be said to have begun, or ended, at particular dates on a time line, or to have been confined to this or that place or region. This approach avoids any necessity to privilege political, or economic, or religious, or any other theme as the determinant of periodization. By the same token, it blurs any attempt sharply to differentiate one historical period from another. Arguments that suggest that the eleventh century was the decisive period that ushered in a 'take-off' or 'first European revolution' in many—or all—aspects of European life misrepresent the dynamism of preceding centuries and cannot be allowed to stand. As I have presented them here, the early Middle Ages can in no way be seen as static, primitive, or underdeveloped, as simply the launch pad for take-off. Of the various novelties claimed for the eleventh and twelfth centuries, only a shift in the modalities of change remains, a shift in which centralizing institutions, lay and ecclesiastical, emerged as new, vigorous agents of change.

Instead, I have posited an early medieval 'syndrome' whose symptoms appeared early in some places, acquired a particular intensity in others, lingered longer elsewhere. The list is long, and could easily be lengthened: generally low population levels despite spasmodic growth; distinct but overlapping local economies combining low-output peasant agriculture and variable levels of urban activity with lavish conspicuous consumption by the elite; strongly gendered hierarchies of domination that commonly conflated the familial and official; the heavy presence of the past as a source of authenticity, legitimization, and meaning; polities incapable of harnessing sufficient economic, political, and cultural resources to overcome their innate tendency to collapse under the weight of their own success; the role of Christianity as a transmitter of many other aspects of Roman culture besides its normative creed. All of these are subsidiary, however, to its critical diagnostic: a cluster of dominant ideologies in which Rome held a central, inspirational place but no ascendant political role as it once had in Antiquity and would again, differently conceived, under papal guidance. To that extent, Europe *after* Rome is also Europe *before* Rome—after the crumbling of the political hegemony of the western Roman Empire but before the ecclesiastical hegemony of the international Roman Church. As I have presented the half millennium from 500 to 1000, we are freed from the historiographical tyranny of institutional frameworks and their teleologies, freed to focus on the ways in which men and women, peasants and lords, rulers and clergy experienced their world, endowed it with meaning and shaped it by their actions—freed to fashion a new cultural history for a new Europe.

# Notes

## CHAPTER I. SPEAKING AND WRITING

1. Gregory the Great, *Moralia in Iob*, XI.xlv.61 and XXXIII.iii.7, ed. M. Adriaen, 3 vols. with continuous pagination, CCSL 143, 143A, 143B (Turnhout, 1979–85), 620; also at 1675.
2. *The Blickling Homilies*, 10 (Rogation Wednesday), ed. and trans. Richard J. Kelly (London, 2003), 78–9.
3. Above, n. 1.
4. M. Coens, 'Un miracle posthume de S. Martin', *Analecta Bollandiana*, 50 (1932), 284–94, quotations at 291, 293, 294. For the religious context, see p. 73.
5. 'Genesis A', lines 1684–90, ed. A. N. Doane, *Genesis A: A New Edition* (Madison, WI, 1978), 161; cf. Gen. 11: 7.
6. Isidore, *Etymologiae*, IX.i.1, cf. IX.i.14, ed. W. M. Lindsay, 2 vols. (Oxford, 1911), i. 343, 345.
7. *Armes Prydein*, lines 172–4, ed. Ifor Williams and trans. Rachel Bromwich (Dublin, 1982), 12–13.
8. *The Text of the Book of Llan Dâv*, ed. J. G. Evans and J. Rhys (Oxford, 1893), 181.
9. Adomnan of Iona, *Life of St Columba*, II.32, trans. Richard Sharpe (Harmondsworth, 1995), 179 (*Adomnan's Life of Columba*, ed. A. O. Anderson and M. O. Anderson (Edinburgh, 1961), 396).
10. Paul the Deacon, *History of the Lombards*, I.27, trans. William Dudley Foulke (Philadelphia, 1974), 52 (*Historia Langobardorum*, ed. G. Waitz, MGH SRL (Hanover, 1878), 70).
11. *The First Grammatical Treatise*, ed. and trans. Hreinn Benediktsson (Reykjavik, 1972), 208–9.
12. *La Vie de Jean, abbé de Gorze*, 119, ed. Michel Parisse (Paris, 1999), 146.
13. Claudius of Turin, *Chronicle*, cited by Michael Idomir Allen, 'The Chronicle of Claudius of Turin', in Alexander Callander Murray (ed.), *After Rome's Fall: Narrators and Sources of Early Medieval History* (Toronto, 1998), 288–319 at 305. I have slightly adapted Allen's translation.
14. MGH Poetae V, pt. 2, p. 337, lines 11–12.
15. Bruno of Querfurt, *Vita quinque fratrum*, 9, 10, 13, MGH SS XV, pt. 2, pp. 725, 727, 729.
16. Ratramnus of Corbie, Letter to Rimbert, MGH Epp. VI, pp. 155–7.
17. Prudentius, *Contra Symmachum*, II.816–17, ed. Maurice P. Cunningham, *Aurelii Prudentii Carmina*, CCSL 126 (Turnhout, 1966), 239.

18. Salvian, *De gubernatione Dei*, V.ii.8, ed. G. Larrigue, *Salvien de Marseille: Œuvres*, 2 vols., SC 176, 220 (Paris, 1971–5), ii. 316. Cf. the English translation by Eva M. Sanford, *On the Government of God* (New York, 1930).

19. Priscus of Panium, fragment 11, ed. R. C. Blockley, *The Fragmentary Classicising Historians of the Later Roman Empire*, ii (Liverpool, 1983), 266, slightly adapted from translation in Alexander Callander Murray, *From Roman to Merovingian Gaul: A Reader* (Peterborough, ONT, 2000), 145.

20. See pp. 95, 127–30.

21. See pp. 225–6.

22. *Etymologiae*, IX.i.3, ed. Lindsay, i. 343.

23. Council of Clovesho of 747, clause 10. *Councils and Ecclesiastical Documents Relating to Great Britain and Ireland*, ed. A. W. Haddan and W. Stubbs, 3 vols. (Oxford, 1869–71), iii. 366.

24. Bede, Letter to Egbert, *EHD*, 799–810, at 801 (*Councils and Ecclesiastical Documents*, ed. Haddan and Stubbs, iii. 314–25).

25. Ælfric, *Praefatio Genesis anglice*, ed. Jonathan Wilcox, *Ælfric's Prefaces* (Durham, 1994), 116.

26. On Fénius Farsaid see also p. 262.

27. *Life of Constantine*, 16, trans. Marvin Kantor, *Medieval Slavic Lives of Saints and Princes* (Ann Arbor, 1983), 71.

28. *Conversio Bagoariorum et Carantanorum*, 12, ed. Fritz Lošek, *Die Conversio Bagoariorum et Carantanorum und der Brief des Erzbischofs Theotmar von Salzburg*, MGH Studien und Texte, 15 (Hanover, 1997), 130.

29. Liudger, *Vita Gregorii abbatis Traiacensis*, 2, ed. O. Holder-Egger, MGH SS XV, pt. 1, pp. 67–8.

30. Caesarius of Arles, *Sermones*, 6, ed. G. Morin, 2 vols., CCSL 103–4 (Turnhout, 1953), i. 31. Cf. the translation by Mary Madeleine Mueller, *Saint Caesarius of Arles: Sermons*, 3 vols. Fathers of the Church, 31, 47, 66 (Washington, 1956–73).

31. *Vita Fructuosi*, 2, *AASS Apr.* II, col. 431. Cf. the translation by A. T. Fear, *Lives of the Visigothic Fathers* (Liverpool, 1997).

32. See pp. 135–46.

33. 'Berrad Airechta: An Old Irish Tract on Suretyship', trans. Robin Stacey, in T. M. Charles-Edwards, M. E. Owen, and D. Walters (eds.), *Lawyers and Laymen: Studies in the History of Law Presented to Professor Dafydd Jenkins* (Cardiff, 1986), 210–33, at 221.

34. Narbonne judgement of 955, cited by Patrick Geary, 'Oblivion between Orality and Textuality in the Tenth Century', in Gerd Althoff, Johannes Fried, and Patrick J. Geary (eds.), *Medieval Concepts of the Past: Ritual, Memory, Historiography* (Cambridge, 2002), 111–22, at 120.

35. The point is developed on pp. 239–47.

36. See p. 13.

37. *La Règle de S. Benoît*, ed. Jean Neufville and trans. Adalbert de Vogüé, SC 181–186a (Paris, 1971–7), i. 412. Many English translations are available.

38. Hrabanus Maurus, *De institutione clericorum*, III.2, ed. Detlev Zimpel (Frank-furt am Main, 1996), 438.
39. Hrabanus Maurus, 'To Eigilus on the book he had written', in Helen Waddell (ed. and trans.), *Medieval Latin Lyrics* (Harmondsworth, 1952), 119 (*Carmina* 21, MGH Poetae II, p. 186).

## CHAPTER 2. LIVING AND DYING

1. Lament attributed to Egil Skalla-Grimsson (d. *c*.990), from *Egil's Saga*, trans. Hermann Pálsson and Paul Edwards (Harmondsworth, 1976), 205 (*Egils Saga Skalla-Grímssonar*, ed. S. Nordal, Íslenzk Fornrit, 2 (Reykjavik, 1933), 247).
2. *The Annals of Fulda*, trans. Timothy Reuter (Manchester, 1992), 31 (*Annales Fuldenses*, a. 850, ed. F. Kurze, MGH SRG (Hanover, 1891), 40).
3. *Vita altera Bonifatii*, 9, ed. W. Levison, *Vitae Sancti Bonifatii archiepiscopi Moguntini*, MGH SRG (Hanover, 1905), 68.
4. *Annals of Ulster (to AD 1131)*, ed. S. Mac Airt and G. Mac Niocaill (Dublin, 1983), 203; *The Annals of Saint-Bertin*, trans. Janet L. Nelson (Manchester, 1991), 185 (*Annales de Saint-Bertin*, ed. F. Grat, J. Vielliard, and S. Clémencet (Paris, 1964), 195).
5. *Annals of Saint-Bertin*, trans. Nelson, 42 (*Annales de Saint-Bertin*, ed. Grat, Vielliard, and Clémencet, 28).
6. Widukind, *Res gestae Saxonicae*, I.20, ed. P. Hirsch and H.-E. Lohmann, MGH SRG 60 (Hanover, 1935), 29–30.
7. Cf. pp. 22, 31–2 on alternative explanations, and pp. 262–7 on origin myths.
8. *Venantius Fortunatus: Personal and Political Poems*, trans. Judith George (Liverpool, 1995), 9–15 (*Carmina*, IV. 26 in *Opera poetica*, ed. F. Leo, MGH AA IV, pt. 1, pp. 95–9), quotation from lines 46, 56, and 64.
9. Sixth-century inscription from Narbonne, cited by Mark A. Handley, *Death, Society and Culture: Inscriptions and Epitaphs in Gaul and Spain, AD 300–750* (Oxford, 2003), 92.
10. See further pp. 186–8.
11. Gregory of Tours, *Libri historiarum decem*, IV.31, ed. B. Krusch and W. Levison, MGH SRM I, pt. 1 (Hanover, 1937–51), 165–6. Cf. the inaccurate translation by L. Thorpe as *The History of the Franks* (Harmondsworth, 1974).
12. Paul the Deacon, *History of the Lombards*, VI.5, trans. William Dudley Foulke (Philadelphia, 1974), 255 (*Historia Langobardorum*, ed. G. Waitz, MGH SRL (Hanover, 1878), 166).
13. Bede, *Life of St Cuthbert*, 33, in *Two Lives of Saint Cuthbert*, ed. and trans. Bertram Colgrave (Cambridge, 1940), 258–61.
14. *Annals of Fulda*, trans. Reuter, 118 (*Annales Fuldenses*, a. 889, ed. Kurze, 117).
15. *Annals of Ulster*, ed. Mac Airt and Mac Niocaill, 159.

16. *Anglo-Saxon Chronicle* for 1005, *EHD*, 240 (*Two of the Saxon Chronicles Parallel*, ed. C. Plummer, 2 vols. (Oxford, 1892–9), i. 136).

17. *Poenitentiale Baedae*, IV.12, ed. A. W. Haddan and W. Stubbs, *Councils and Ecclesiastical Documents Relating to Great Britain and Ireland*, 3 vols. (Oxford, 1869–71), iii. 330 (cf. the translation of another version of this same text under the less misleading title of 'Penitential of Ps-Bede', II.11, in *Medieval Handbooks of Penance*, trans. John T. McNeill and Helena M. Gamer (New York, 1938, repr. 1990), 225).

18. For a specific example see p. 172.

19. See pp. 192–4 on the Vikings.

20. See pp. 16–17.

21. *Annales Xantenses*, a. 873, ed. B. von Simson, MGH SRG (Hanover, 1909), 33. The 'ancient plague of the Egyptians' refers to the plague of locusts in Exod. 10: 14–15.

22. As quoted by Gregory of Tours, *Libri historiarum decem*, X.1, ed. Krusch and Levison, 479. The biblical citations are Ps. 95: 2 and Lam. 3: 41.

23. 'Edict when the "Great Army" came to England', *EHD*, 447–8 (F. Liebermann, (ed.), *Die Gesetze der Angelsachsen*, 3 vols. (Halle, 1898–1916), i. 262).

24. *Annales Xantenses*, a. 869, ed. von Simson, 26.

25. Gregory of Tours, *Libri historiarum decem*, VII.45, ed. Krusch and Levison, 365.

26. Bede, *Ecclesiastical History of the English People*, III.30, ed. and trans. Bertram Colgrave and R. A. B. Mynors (Oxford, 1969), 322–3.

27. Bruno of Querfurt, *Vita Adalberti*, 25, ed. G. H. Pertz, MGH SS IV, p. 608.

28. *Documentos de época visigoda escritos en pizarra (siglos VI–VIII)*, ed. Isabel Velázquez Soriano, Monumenta Palaeographica Medii Aevi, series hispanica, 2 vols. (Turnhout, 2000), no. 104, i. 113–15, ii. 124–6.

29. See pp. 42–3.

30. *Byrhtferth's Manual*, ed. and trans. S. J. Crawford, Early English Text Society, 177 (London, 1929), 132–3.

31. Wulfstan of York, *Sermo Lupi ad Anglos*, in *EHD*, 929–34, quotations from pp. 929–30 and 934 (*The Homilies of Wulfstan*, ed. Dorothy Bethurum (Oxford, 1957), no. xx (version in mss E, I), 266–75).

32. *Annales Hildesheimenses*, ed. G. Waitz, MGH SRG (Hanover, 1878), 28.

33. For the political significance of this see p. 276.

34. *Miracula Alexii*, 9, *AASS Jul.* IV, col. 259.


## CHAPTER 3. FRIENDS AND RELATIONS

1. 'The Rune Poem', lines 59–63, ed. and trans. T. A. Shippey, *Poems of Wisdom and Learning in Old English* (Cambridge, 1976), 82–3.

2. Wipo, *The Deeds of Conrad II*, trans. Theodor E. Mommsen and Karl F. Morrison, *Imperial Lives and Letters of the Eleventh Century*, 2nd edn. (New

York, 2000), 63 (*Wiponis opera*, ed. H. Bresslau, MGH SRG (Hanover, 1915), 17).

3. 'Hildebrandlied', trans. Patrick J. Geary, *Readings in Medieval History*, 3rd edn. (Peterborough, ONT, 2003), 118 (ed. Wilhelm Braune, *Althochdeutsches Lesebuch*, 16th edn. (Tübingen, 1979), 84–5).

4. William of Malmesbury, *Vita Wulfstani*, I.1, ed. and trans. M. Winterbottom and R. M. Thomson, *William of Malmesbury: Saints' Lives. Lives of SS. Wulfstan, Dunstan, Patrick, Benignus and Indract* (Oxford, 2002), 14–15.

5. Quoted by John V. Kelleher, 'The Pre-Norman Irish Genealogies', *Irish Historical Studies*, 16 (1968–9), 138–53 at 145.

6. See p. 34 on the nature of Irish legal treatises.

7. *Beowulf: A Verse Translation*, trans. Michael Alexander, 2nd edn. (Harmondsworth, 2001), lines 2597–8 and 83–4, pp. 93 and 6, with line numbering specific to this edition (*Beowulf: A Student Edition*, ed. George Jack (Oxford, 1994, rev. 1997), lines 2600–1 and 84–5, pp. 178 and 33, with line numbering following the manuscript).

8. *The Laws of the Salian Franks*, trans. Katherine Fischer Drew (Philadelphia, 1991), 123, slightly adapted (*Pactus Legis Salicae*, title LX.1, ed. K. A. Eckhardt, MGH Leges Nationum Germanicarum IV, pt. 1, p. 225).

9. Sigebert of Gembloux, *Vita Deodorici episcopi Mettensis*, MGH SS IV, p. 465, quoted by Régine Le Jan, *Famille et pouvoir dans le monde franc (VIIe–Xe siècle): Essai d'anthropologie sociale* (Paris, 1995), 84 n. 184.

10. Marc Bloch, *Feudal Society*, trans. L. A. Manyon, 2nd edn., 2 vols. (London, 1965), i. 123–4.

11. *Beowulf*, lines 1324–8, trans. Alexander, p. 49 (ed. Jack, lines 1325–29, p. 107).

12. *Beowulf*, lines 1016–18, trans. Alexander, p. 38 (ed. Jack, lines 1017–19, p. 86).

13. VI Æthelstan 8.2–3, *EHD*, 425 (F. Liebermann (ed.), *Die Gesetze der Angelsachsen*, 3 vols. (Halle, 1898–1916), i. 178–9).

14. Above, n. 1.

15. Paulinus of Aquileia, *Liber exhortationis*, 49, *PL* 99, col. 253.

16. *Pactus Legis Salicae*, title XXX.1–5, ed. Eckhardt, 118–19, following translation suggested by Guy Halsall, *Warfare and Society in the Barbarian West, 450–900* (London, 2003), 11.

17. *Laws of the Alamans and Bavarians*, trans. Theodore John Rivers (Philadelphia, 1977), 129 (*Lex Baiwariorum* III.1, ed. E. von Schwind, MGH Leges Nationum Germanicarum V, pt. 2, p. 313).

18. Drew, *Laws of the Salian Franks*, 78 (*Pactus Legis Salicae*, title XIII.11, ed. Eckhardt, 62–3).

19. *EHD*, 819 (ed. M. Tangl, *Die Briefen des hl. Bonifatius und Lullus*, no. 73, MGH Epp. Sel. I (Berlin, 1916), 146–55).

20. Gregory of Tours, *Libri historiarum decem*, VI.36, ed. B. Krusch and W. Levison, MGH SRM I, pt. 1 (Hanover, 1937–51), 307.

21. II Cnut 53, *EHD*, 463 (Liebermann (ed.), *Gesetze*, i. 348).

22. *Sedulius Scottus: On Christian Rulers and the Poems*, trans. Edward Gerard Doyle (Binghamton, 1983), 60 (*De rectoribus christianis*, 5, ed. S. Hellmann,

*Sedulius Scottus*, Quellen und Untersuchungen zur lateinischen Philologie 1, pt. 1 (Munich, 1906), 35).

23. Laws of Liutprand, clause 135, trans. Katherine Fischer Drew, *The Lombard Laws* (Philadelphia, 1973), 204–5 (*Leges Langobardorum*, ed. F. Bluhme and A. Boretius, MGH Legum IV, p. 466).

24. *Handbook for William: A Carolingian Woman's Counsel for her Son*, trans. Carol Neel (Lincoln, NE, 1991), 21, 33 (Dhuoda, *Manuel pour mon fils* III.1, 9, ed. Pierre Riché, SC 225 bis, 2nd edn. (Paris, 1997), 134, 170–2).

25. *Handbook for William*, 35–6, slightly adapted (*Manuel pour mon fils*, III.10, ed. Riché, 178).

26. *Waltharius*, lines 177, 696–7, ed. and trans. Dennis M. Kratz, in Waltharius *and* Ruodlieb (New York, 1984), 11, 35.

27. Ibid., lines 629–31, trans. Kratz, 33.

28. Ibid., lines 1079–80, trans. Kratz, 53.

29. Ibid., lines 1089–96, trans. Kratz, 53–5.

30. *The Battle of Maldon*, lines 205–8, trans. Michael Alexander, *The Earliest English Poems*, 3rd edn. (Harmondsworth, 1991), 107–8 (*The Battle of Maldon*, ed. D. G. Scragg (Manchester, 1981), 63).

31. *EHD*, 863–4 (Alcuin, *Epistolae* 231, 232, ed. E. Dümmler, MGH Epp. IV, pp. 376–7).

32. *Cath Maige Tuired*, quoted by Philip O'Leary, 'The Honour of Women in Early Irish Literature', *Ériu*, 38 (1987), 24–44 at 37.

33. Asser, *Life of Alfred*, trans. Simon Keynes and Michael Lapidge, *Alfred the Great: Asser's* Life of Alfred *and other Contemporary Sources* (Harmondsworth, 1983), 74 (*Asser's Life of King Alfred, Together with the Annals of St Neots Erroneously Ascribed to Asser*, ch. 18, ed. William Henry Stephenson with introduction by Dorothy Whitelock (Oxford, 1959), 17–18).

34. Adomnan, *Life of St Columba*, II. 39, trans. Richard Sharpe (Harmondsworth, 1995), 189 (*Adomnan's Life of Columba*, ed. A. O. Anderson and M. O. Anderson (Edinburgh, 1961), 422).

35. Gregory of Tours, *Libri historiarum decem*, X.27, ed. Krusch and Levison, 519–20.

36. Edict of Rothari, clause 74, trans. Drew, *Lombard Laws*, 65 (*Leges Langobardorum*, ed. Bluhme and Boretius, 23–4).

37. Gregory of Tours, *Libri historiarum decem*, VIII.5, ed. Krusch and Levison, 374.

## CHAPTER 4. MEN AND WOMEN

1. Gregory the Great, *Moralia in Job*, XI.xlix.65, ed. M. Adriaen, 3 vols. with continuous pagination, CCSL 143, 143A, 143B (Turnhout, 1979–85), 623.

2. 'Maxims I', lines 24–6, ed. and trans. T. Shippey, *Poems of Wisdom and Learning in Old English* (Cambridge, 1976), 64–5.

3. See Ch. 1.

4. See pp. 89–92, 105.

5. See Chs. 5, 7, and 8.

6. See p. 40.

7. 'Maxims II', lines 11–12, ed. and trans. Shippey, *Poems of Widsom and Learning*, 76–7.

8. For wergeld as an expression of rank see pp. 100–1.

9. Edict of Rothari, clause 204, trans. Katherine Fischer Drew, *The Lombard Laws* (Philadelphia, 1973), 92 (*Leges Langobardorum*, ed. F. Bluhme and A. Boretius, MGH Legum IV, p. 466).

10. P. D. King, *Charlemagne: Translated Sources* (Kendal, 1987), 218–19 (*Admonitio generalis*, clause 81, MGH Capitularia I, ed. A. Boretius (Hanover, 1883), 61).

11. Above, n. 1.

12. Isidore, *Etymologiae*, XI.ii.17–19, ed. W. M. Lindsay (Oxford, 1911), ii. 23.

13. Ambrose of Milan, Letter IV.15. *Sancti Ambrosii opera*, x: *Epistularum libri I–VI*, ed. Otto Faller, CSEL 82 (Vienna, 1968), 112–13. The biblical quotations are Deut. 22: 5, 1 Cor. 14: 34–5, and 1 Tim. 2: 11–12.

14. Odo of Cluny, *The Life of St Gerald of Aurillac*, trans. Thomas F. X. Noble and Thomas Head, *Soldiers of Christ: Saints and Saints' Lives from Late Antiquity and the Early Middle Ages* (University Park, PA, 1995), 313 (*Vita Geraldi*, I.21, *PL* 133, col. 656).

15. *Capitula* of Arichis of Benevento, 12 (*Leges Langobardorum*, ed. Bluhme and Boretius, 209).

16. Adam of Bremen, *History of the Archbishops of Hamburg-Bremen*, trans. Francis J. Tschan (New York, 1959), 203 (*Gesta Hammaburgensis ecclesiae pontificum*, IV.21, ed. B. Schmeidler, MGH SRG (Hanover, 1917), 251).

17. Quoted by T. M. Charles-Edwards, *Early Irish and Welsh Kinship* (Oxford, 1993), 462.

18. Quoted by Fergus Kelly, *A Guide to Early Irish Law* (Dublin, 1988), 70.

19. Ibid. 70–1.

20. Ibid. 71.

21. Letter 167 to Rusticus, bishop of Narbonne, in 459, *PL* 54, col. 1204.

22. 1 Cor. 7: 2 and 6: 9–10.

23. Quoted from a law tract on privileged ranks by Donnchadh Ó Corráin, 'Marriage in Early Ireland', in Art Cosgrove (ed.), *Marriage in Ireland* (Dublin, 1985), 5–24 at 19.

24. See pp. 238–9.

25. 'Visio Baronti', 12, trans. J. N. Hillgarth, *Christianity and Paganism, 350–750: The Conversion of Western Europe* (Philadelphia, 1969), 199 (ed. W. Levison, MGH SRM V, p. 386).

26. Jonas, *Life of St Columbanus*, 32, trans. Edward Peters, *Monks, Bishops and Pagans: Christian Culture in Gaul and Italy, 500–700* (Philadelphia, 1975), 94 (*Vita Columbani*, I.19, ed. B. Krusch, MGH SRM IV, p. 87).

27. For a full discussion see Ch. 7.
28. All quotations from Hincmar, *Epistolae*, 136, ed. E. Perels, MGH Epp. VIII, pt. 1, pp. 87–107 at 88–9.
29. See p. 127.
30. *Annales Quedlinburgenses*, a. 1020, MGH SS III, p. 85.
31. See pp. 29–30, 41–2, 85–6.
32. See p. 134.
33. F. E. Harmer (ed.), *Select English Historical Documents of the Ninth and Tenth Centuries* (Cambridge, 1914), no. 2, pp. 3–5 with translation pp. 40–2.
34. See pp. 65–8.
35. Quoted in translation by Birgit Sawyer, *Property and Inheritance in Viking Scandinavia: The Runic Evidence* (Alingsås, 1988), 17.
36. *EHD*, 602–3 (ed. A. J. Robertson, *Anglo-Saxon Charters*, 2nd edn. (Cambridge, 1956), 150–3).
37. *Codice Diplomatico Longobardo*, v, ed. H. Zielinski, Fonti per la Storia d'Italia, 66 (Rome, 1986), no. 50, pp. 177–80.
38. See also p. 44.

## CHAPTER 5. LABOUR AND LORDSHIP

1. *Aelfric's Colloquy*, ed. G. N. Garmonsway, 2nd edn. (Exeter, 1978), 20–1. Cf. the translation by Michael Swanton, *Anglo-Saxon Prose* (London, 1975), 108–9.
2. Old Irish verse, cited by Jane Stevenson, 'The Beginnings of Literacy in Ireland', *Proceedings of the Royal Irish Academy of Ireland*, 89C (1989), 127–65 at 159.
3. *Responsa misso cuidam data*, clause 1, MGH Capitularia I, no. 158, ed. A. Boretius (Hanover, 1883), 145.
4. See p. 169.
5. Survey of the manor of Tidenham (between 956 and 1061), *Anglo-Saxon Charters*, 109, ed. and trans. A. J. Robertson, 2nd edn. (Cambridge, 1956), 204–7.
6. See p. 76.
7. *Laws of the Alamans and Bavarians*, trans. Theodore John Rivers (Philadelphia, 1977), 162, slighted adapted (*Lex Baiwariorum*, XVI.11, ed. E. von Schwind, MGH Leges Nationum Germanicarum V, pt. 2, p. 439).
8. W. de Gray Birch, *Cartularium Saxonicum*, 3 vols. (London, 1885–93), iii. 358–9.
9. Lichfield memoranda, no. 5, in *The Text of the Book of Llan Dâv*, ed. J. G. Evans and J. Rhys (Oxford, 1893), p. xlvi.
10. *Lex Baiwariorum*, VIII.22–3, ed. von Schwind, 365. Cf. the translation by Rivers, *Laws of the Alamans and Bavarians*, 142.

11. Jonas of Orleans, *De institutione laicali*, II.xxii, *PL* 106, col. 215.

12. Walburg Boppert, *Die frühchristlichen Inschriften des Mittelrheingebietes* (Mainz, 1971), 108–18, at 109.

13. Adalbero of Laon, *Poème au Roi Robert*, ed. C. Carozzi (Paris, 1979), lines 290–4, p. 22.

14. Palladius, *Opus agriculturae*, I.6.3, quoted by C. R. Whittaker and P. Garnsey, 'Rural Life in the Later Roman Empire', *The Cambridge Ancient History*, xiii, ed. Averil Cameron and Peter Garnsey (Cambridge, 1998), 296.

15. Caesarius of Arles, Sermon 154, quoted with minor adaptations from William E. Klingshirn, *Caesarius of Arles: The Making of a Christian Community in Late Antique Gaul* (Cambridge, 1994), 205–6 (*Sermones*, ed. G. Morin, 2 vols., CCSL 103–4 (Turnhout, 1953), ii. 629).

16. See pp. 143–5.

17. From the so-called *Rectitudines Singularum Personarum*, trans. Swanton, *Anglo-Saxon Prose*, 22–3, under the title 'Duties and Perquisites' (F. Liebermann (ed.), *Die Gesetze der Angelsachsen*, 3 vols. (Halle, 1898–1916), i. 447–8).

18. *The Complete Works of Rather of Verona*, trans. Peter L. D. Reid (Binghamton, NY, 1991), 52, with adaptations (*Praeloquia*, I.33, *Ratherii Veronensis opera*, ed. Peter L. D. Reid, 2 vols., CCCM 46 (Turnhout, 1976–84), ii. 34).

19. See pp. 44, 139–40, 143–5 and 169.

20. Lives of the Fathers of Merida, 3: Nanctus, trans. A. T. Fear, *Lives of the Visigothic Fathers* (Liverpool, 1997), 57 (*Vitas sanctorum patrum Emeretensium*, ed. A. Maya Sánchez, CCSL 116 (Turnhout, 1992), 23).

21. Bede, *Ecclesiastical History of the English People*, IV.22, ed. and trans. Bertram Colgrave and R. A. B. Mynors (Oxford, 1969), 402–3.

22. 'Astronomer', *Vita Hludowici*, 28, ed. E. Tremp, *Thegan, Die Taten Ludwigs des Frommen (Gesta Hludowici imperatoris). Astronomus, Das Leben Kaiser Ludwigs (Vita Hludowici imperatoris)*, MGH SRG 64 (Hanover, 1995), 378.

23. Odo of Cluny, *The Life of St Gerald of Aurillac*, trans. Thomas F. X. Noble and Thomas Head, *Soldiers of Christ: Saints and Saints' Lives from Late Antiquity and the Early Middle Ages* (University Park, PA, 1995), 310 (*Vita Geraldi*, I.16, *PL* 133, col. 653).

24. *Codex Carolinus*, 81, MGH Epp. III, ed. W. Gundlach, 614.

25. Donizo of Canossa, *Vita Mathildis*, I.10, line 806, MGH SS XII, p. 368.

26. See pp. 70–1.

27. *Capitulare missorum* of 819, clause 29, MGH Capitularia I, p. 291.

28. Notker, *Gesta Karoli*, II.18, ed. H. F. Haefele, MGH SRG, NS 12 (Berlin, 1959), 88.

29. *Ottonian Germany: The Chronicle of Thietmar of Merseburg*, trans. David A. Warner (Manchester, 2001), 282 (*Thietmari Merseburgensis episcopi chronicon* VI.65, ed. R. Holtzmann, MGH SRG, NS 9 (Berlin, 1935), 354).

30. Ekkehard of St Gall, *Casus Sancti Galli*, 48, ed. H. F. Haefele (Darmstadt, 1980), 108–10.

31. *Crith Gablach*, clause 112, trans. Eoin MacNeill, 'Ancient Irish Law: Law of Status or Franchise', *Proceedings of the Royal Irish Academy*, 36C (1923), 281–311.
32. *Geþyncðo*, *EHD*, 469 (ed. Liebermann, *Gesetze*, i. 456).
33. Odo of Cluny, *The Life of St Gerald of Aurillac*, trans. Noble and Head, *Soldiers of Christ*, 298 (*Vita Geraldi*, I.1, PL 133, cols. 642–3).
34. See pp. 100–8.
35. *The Annals of Fulda*, trans. Timothy Reuter (Manchester, 1992), 101 (*Annales Fuldenses*, a. 887, ed. F. Kurze, MGH SRG (Hanover, 1891), 105).
36. Gregory of Tours, *Libri historiarum decem*, V.48, ed. B. Krusch and W. Levison, MGH SRM I, pt. 1 (Hanover, 1937–51), 258.
37. See pp. 88–9 on Gregory's ancestry.
38. Thegan, *Die Taten Ludwigs des Frommen*, 44, ed. Tremp, 23. Cf. the translation by Paul Edward Dutton, *Carolingian Civilization: A Reader* (Peterborough, ONT, 1993), 151.
39. Richer, *Histoire de France*, I.15, ed. Robert Latouche, 2nd edn., 2 vols. (Paris, 1964–7), i. 38.
40. *Two Voyagers at the Court of King Alfred: The Ventures of Ohthere and Wulfstan together with the Description of Northern Europe from the Old English Orosius*, ed. Niels Lund and trans. Christine E. Fell (York, 1984), 20.

## CHAPTER 6. GETTING AND GIVING

1. 'Etmic Dinbych', lines 33–4, 84–51, trans. Ifor Williams, in *The Beginnings of Welsh Poetry: Studies by Sir Ifor Williams*, ed. Rachel Bromwich, 2nd edn. (Cardiff, 1972), 163–6.
2. Einhard, *Vita Karoli*, 21, ed. O. Holder-Egger, MGH SRG (Hanover, 1911), 26. Many English translations are available.
3. Annalista Saxo, a. 968, MGH SS VI, p. 622.
4. Bede, *Ecclesiastical History of the English People*, II.3, ed. and trans. Bertram Colgrave and R. A. B. Mynors (Oxford, 1969), 142–3.
5. C. H. Robinson, *Anskar, Apostle of the North, 801–865: Translated from the Vita Anskarii by Bishop Rimbert his Fellow Missionary and Successor* (London, 1921), 65 (*Vita Anskarii auctore Rimberto*, 19, ed. G. Waitz, MGH SRG (Hanover, 1884), 41).
6. Ibn Hauqal, *Configuration de la terre (Kitab surat al-Ard)*, ed. and trans J. H. Kramers and G. Wiet, 2 vols. (Beirut, 1946), i. 196.
7. Notker, *Gesta Karoli*, II.17, ed. H. F. Haefele, MGH SRG, NS 12 (Berlin, 1959), 86.
8. Ibn Hauqal, *Configuration de la terre*, 197.
9. Procopius, *History of the Wars*, V.xii.42, ed. and trans. H. B. Dewing, *Procopius*, 7 vols. (Cambridge, MA, 1914–40), iii. 128–9.
10. Gregory of Tours, *Libri historiarum decem*, II.38, ed. B. Krusch and W. Levison, MGH SRM I, pt. 1 (Hanover, 1937–51), 88–9.

11. Gregory of Tours, *Libri historiarum decem*, VI.42, ed. Krusch and Levison, 314.

12. Venantius Fortunatus, *Carmina*, VII.2, lines 1–2, ed. F. Leo, MGH AA IV, pt. 1, p. 154.

13. Ibid., VII.3, line 6, ed. Leo, 155.

14. *Venantius Fortunatus: Personal and Political Poems*, trans. Judith George (Liverpool, 1995), 66–7 (Venantius Fortunatus, *Carmina*, VII.16, lines 43–4, 55–7, ed. Leo, 170–2).

15. *Beowulf: A Verse Translation*, trans. Michael Alexander, 2nd edn. (Harmondsworth, 2001), lines 63–6, p. 5 (*Beowulf: A Student Edition*, ed. George Jack (Oxford, 1994, rev. 1997), lines 64–7, p. 32).

16. *Beowulf*, trans. Alexander, lines 948–54, 993–4, 1010–14, 1019–25, 1045–8, pp. 35–6, 37, 37–8, 38, 39 (ed. Jack, lines 949–55, 994–5, 1011–15, 1020–6, 1046–9, pp. 83, 85, 86, 86–7, 88–9).

17. Hincmar of Reims, *On the Governance of the Palace*, trans. Paul Edward Dutton, *Carolingian Civilization: A Reader* (Peterborough, ONT, 1993), 493 (*De ordine palatii*, 22, ed. R. Schieffer, MGH Fontes iuris Germanici antiqui in usum scholarum separatim editi (Hanover, 1980), 72).

18. *Beowulf*, trans. Alexander, lines 1027–8, p. 73 (ed. Jack, lines 2028–9, p. 146).

19. *The Variae of Magnus Aurelius Cassiodorus Senator*, IV.1, trans. S. J. B. Barnish (Liverpool, 1992), 74 (*Variae*, ed. T. Mommsen, MGH AA XII, p. 114).

20. See pp. 235–6.

21. See pp. 119–20.

22. See p. 176.

23. See pp. 140 and 145.

24. Widukind, *Res gestae Saxonicae*, I.33, eds. P. Hirsch and H.-E. Lohmann, MGH SRG (Hanover, 1935), 45–6.

25. *Liudprand of Cremona: The Embassy to Constantinople and Other Writings*, trans. F. A. Wright, ed. John Julius Norwich (London, 1993), 114–15 (*Antapodosis*, IV.25, in *Liudprandi opera*, ed. J. Becker, MGH SRG (Hanover, 1915), 119).

## CHAPTER 7. KINGSHIP AND CHRISTIANITY

1. Prayer to be said over Louis the German, quoted from the MS by Eric J. Goldberg, '"More devoted to the equipment of battle than the splendor of banquets": Frontier Kingship, Martial Ritual and Early Knighthood at the Court of Louis the German', *Viator*, 30 (1999), 41–78 at 71.

2. Stephen of Hungary, *Libellus de institutione morum*, 1, ed. J. Balogh, in *Scriptores rerum Hungaricarum tempore ducum regumque stirpis Arpadianae gestarum*, gen. ed. E. Szentpétery, 2 vols. (Budapest, 1937–8), ii. 621.

3. Ælfric of Eynsham, Homily IX, line 48, ed. J. C. Pope, *Homilies of Ælfric: A Supplementary Collection*, 2 vols., Early English Text Society, 259–60 (Oxford, 1967–8), i. 380.

4. For the notion of emperor, see pp. 274–5.

5. Radbod of Utrecht, *Libellus de miraculo sancti Martini*, MGH SS XV, pt. 2, p. 1240, trans. Wolfert van Egmond, 'Converting Monks: Missionary Activity in Early Medieval Frisia and Saxony', in Guyda Armstrong and Ian Wood (eds.), *Christianizing Peoples and Converting Individuals* (Turnhout, 2000), 40.

6. Julian of Toledo, *Prognosticon futuri saeculi*, III.14 (quoting Augustine of Hippo, *Enchiridion*, 84). *Sancti Iuliani Toletanae sedis episcopi opera, pars I*, ed. J. N. Hillgarth, CCSL 115 (Turnhout, 1976), 90–1.

7. *Annales regni Francorum*, ed. F. Kurze, MGH SRG (Hanover, 1895), 134. Cf. English translation by Bernhard Scholz, *Carolingian Chronicles* (Ann Arbor, 1972).

8. *Life of Methodius*, 16, trans. Marvin Kantor, *Medieval Slavic Lives of Saints and Princes* (Ann Arbor, 1983), 125. (Kantor's identification of the 'king' in this passage with the Frankish Charles the Fat is erroneous.)

9. See p. 34.

10. See pp. 57–8, 269–71.

11. *Landnámabók*, 15, ed. Jakob Benediktsson, 2 vols. (Reykjavik, 1968), i. 52–5. Cf. English translation by Hermann Pálsson and Paul Edwards, *The Book of Settlements: Landnámabók* (Manitoba, 1972), 23–4.

12. See Ch. 1 on new, literate modes of communication, and pp. 239–51 on ideologies.

13. Hrabanus Maurus, *Expositio in Epistolam I ad Corinthios*, 2, PL 112, col. 23.

14. Martin of Braga, *Reforming the Rustics*, trans. Claude W. Barlow, *Iberian Fathers*, i: *Martin of Braga, Paschasius of Dumium, Leander of Seville* (Washington, 1969), 74–5, slightly adapted (*De correctione rusticorum*, 7–8, ed. Claude W. Barlow, *Martini episcopi Bracarensis opera omnia* (New Haven, 1950), 186–8).

15. *Niederdeutsche Taufgelöbnis*, ii, in *Althochdeutsches Lesebuch*, ed. Wilhem Braune, 16th edn. (Tübingen, 1979), 39.

16. *EHD*, 795, translation slightly altered (ed. M. Tangl, *Die Briefen des hl. Bonifatius und Lullus* 23, MGH Epp. Sel. I (Berlin, 1916), 38–41).

17. *Ottonian Germany: The Chronicle of Thietmar of Merseburg*, trans. David A. Warner (Manchester, 2001), 69 (*Thietmari Merseburgensis episcopi chronicon*, I.3, ed. R. Holtzmann, MGH SRG, ns 9 (Berlin, 1935), 7).

18. *Chronicle of Thietmar of Merseburg*, trans. Warner, 364 (*Chronicon*, VIII.4, ed. Holtzmann, 496).

19. Caesarius of Arles, *Sermones*, 16, ed. G. Morin, 2 vols., CCSL 103–4 (Turnhout, 1953), i. 77.

20. Ibid. 52, ed. Morin, i. 230–3, quotation at p. 232.

21. Ibid. 13, ed. Morin, i. 67.

22. Above, n. 13.

23. *Etymologiae*, IX.iii.4, ed. W. M. Lindsay, 2 vols. (Oxford, 1911), i. 362.

24. Lanfranc, letter 10, *The Letters of Lanfranc, Archbishop of Canterbury*, ed. and trans. Helen Clover and Margaret Gibson (Oxford, 1979), 70–3.

25. Privilege of Adrian IV, preserved in Gerald of Wales, *Expugnatio Hibernica*, ed. and trans. A. B. Scott and F. X. Martin (Dublin, 1978), 144–5.

26. *Ordo ad regem benedicendum* (= Ordo LXXII), *Le Pontifical romano-germanique du dixième siècle*, ed. Cyrille Vogel and Reinhard Elze, 3 vols., Studi e Testi 226, 227, 269 (Rome, 1963–72), i. 246–61, quotation at p. 249.

27. Ibid. 253.

28. *Chronicle of Thietmar of Merseburg*, trans. Warner, 126 (*Chronicon*, III, prol., ed. Holtzmann, 94).

29. See p. 132.

30. *Formula honestae vitae*, in *Martini episcopi Braracensis opera omnia*, ed. Barlow, 236–50; quotations from pp. 237, 244. Cf. translation by Barlow, *Iberian Fathers*, i. 87–97.

31. Bede, *Ecclesiastical History of the English People*, I.32, ed. and trans. Bertram Colgrave and R. A. B. Mynors (Oxford, 1969), 111–13.

32. *Audacht Morainn*, ed. and trans. Fergus Kelly (Dublin, 1976), 2–3.

33. Ibid. 6–7.

34. Ibid. 18–19.

35. *EHD*, 817–18 (ed. Tangl, *Die Briefen des hl. Bonifatius* 73, pp. 146–55).

36. *Sedulius Scottus: On Christian Rulers and the Poems*, trans. Edward Gerard Doyle (Binghamton, NY, 1983), 59–60 (*De rectoribus christianis*, 5, ed. S. Hellmann, *Sedulius Scottus*, Quellen und Untersuchungen zur lateinischen Philologie 1, pt. 1 (Munich, 1906), 35).

37. *Sedulius Scottus: On Christian Rulers*, trans. Doyle, 61–2 (*De rectoribus christianis*, 6, ed. Hellmann, 38).

38. *Reginonis abbatis Prumiensis chronicon*, a. 900, ed. F. Kurze, MGH SRG (Hanover, 1890), 148.

39. *The Annals of Fulda*, trans. Timothy Reuter (Manchester, 1992), 42 (*Annales Fuldenses*, ed. F. Kurze, MGH SRG (Hanover, 1891), 49–50).

40. *Chronicle of Thietmar of Merseburg*, trans. Warner, 333 (*Chronicon*, VII.36, ed. Holtzmann, p. 442).

41. See pp. 159–60.

42. See p. 78.

43. Wulfstan of York, *Institutes of Polity*, version I, §1–2, ed. Karl Jost, *Die 'Institutes of Polity Civil and Ecclesiastical'*, Schweizer anglistische Arbeiten, 47 (Bern, 1959), 40, quoting MS D.

44. Ibid., version II, §§13–15, p. 47, quoting MS X.

## CHAPTER 8. ROME AND THE PEOPLES OF EUROPE

1. *The Gothic History of Jordanes*, trans. C. C. Mierow (Princeton, 1915), 53, 57, with minor adaptation (*Getica*, I.9, IV.25, ed. T. Mommsen, MGH AA V, pp. 55–6, 60).

2. Sighvatr, 'Knútsdrápa (Tøgdrápa)', verses 10–11, *EHD*, 338 (ed. Finnur Jónsson, *Den Norsk-Islandske Skjaldedigtning*, 4 vols. (Copenhagen, 1912–15), vol. B–1, p. 234.

3. *Gothic History of Jordanes*, trans. Mierow, 52 (*Getica*, I.6, ed. Mommsen, 55).

4. Orosius, *Seven Books of History against the Pagans*, trans. Roy J. Deferrari (Washington, 1964), 16 (*Histoire (contre les païens)*, I.2.79, ed. Marie-Pierre Arnaud-Lindet, 3 vols. (Paris, 1990–1), i. 32).

5. See pp. 56–7, 119–20, 206–7 for the material evidence.

6. See p. 31.

7. *The Variae of Magnus Aurelius Cassiodorus Senator*, trans. S. J. B. Barnish (Liverpool, 1992), 76 (Cassiodorus, *Variae*, IV.6, ed. T. Mommsen, MGH AA XII, p. 117).

8. *Liudprand of Cremona: The Embassy to Constantinople and Other Writings*, trans. F. A. Wright, with introduction by J. J. Norwich (London, 1993), 22 (*Antapodosis*, I.25, in *Liudprandi opera*, ed. J. Becker, MGH SRG (Hanover, 1915), 21).

9. *Sedulius Scottus: On Christian Rulers and the Poems*, trans. Edward Gerard Doyle (Binghamton, NY, 1983), 107 (*Carmina*, II.7, lines 62–4, ed. L. Traube, MGH Poetae III, p. 174).

10. Bruno of Querfurt, *Vita Adalberti*, 12, MGH SS IV, p. 600.

11. *Ottonis III. Diplomata* no. 389, ed. T. Sickel, MGH Diplomata regum et imperatorum Germaniae II, pt. 2, pp. 819–20.

12. 'Anonymus Valesianus', 65–7, ed. Ingemar König, *Aus der Zeit Theoderichs des Grossen: Einleitung, Text, Übersetzung und Kommentar einer anonymen Quelle* (Darmstadt, 1997), 82–4.

13. 'Anonymus Valesianus', 58–60, ed. König, 78–80.

14. *The Chronicle of Marcellinus*, ed. and trans. Brian Croke (Sydney, 1995), 27.

15. *Epistola ad Hathonem archiepiscopum missa*, in *Reginonis abbatis Prumiensis chronicon*, ed. F. Kurze, MGH SRG (Hanover, 1890), p. xx.

16. See pp. 30, 47–9.

17. See p. 36 and cf. Gen. 10: 1–2.

18. *Historia Brittonum*, 15, ed. and trans. John Morris, *Nennius: British History and the Welsh Annals* (London, 1980), 21, with Latin p. 62.

19. *Sanas Cormaic (Cormac's Glossary)*, line 1162, ed. Kuno Meyer, Anecdota from Irish Manuscripts, 4 (Halle 1912), 102.

20. http://www.ucl.ac.uk/archaeology/cisp/database/site/ltysl.html. See also 'The Pillar of Eliseg', *Early Welsh Genealogical Tracts*, ed. and trans. P. C. Bartrum (Cardiff, 1966), 1–3.

21. Above, n. 1.

22. *Gothic History of Jordanes*, trans. Mierow, 60 (*Getica*, V.38, ed. Mommsen, 64).

23. *Gothic History of Jordanes*, trans. Mierow, 62 (*Getica*, V.43, ed. Mommsen, 65).

24. *De Karolo rege et Leone papa*, lines 12, 27–9, 92–6, ed. Franz Brunhölzl, Studien und Quellen zur westfälischen Geschichte, 36, Beiheft (Paderborn, 1999), 10, 16. Cf. the translation of the first third of this poem in Peter

Godman, *Poetry of the Carolingian Renaissance* (London, 1985), no. 25, pp. 196–207.

25. *De Karolo rege et Leone papa*, lines 495–6, 504, p. 44.
26. See p. 226.
27. *Annales Petaviani*, a. 776, *Annales Laureshamenses*, a. 799, ed. G. H. Pertz, MGH SS I, pp. 16, 38.
28. *Vita Karoli*, 7, ed. O. Holder-Egger, MGH SRG (Hanover, 1911), 9.
29. Ibid. 9–10.
30. Modoin, *Ecloga*, lines 24–7, ed. and trans. Godman, *Poetry of the Carolingian Renaissance*, 192–3.
31. *Etymologiae*, IX.iii.2–3, ed. W. M. Lindsay, 2 vols. (Oxford, 1911), i. 362.
32. Ibid., IX.iii.14, ed. Lindsay, i. 364.
33. Bede, *Ecclesiastical History of the English People*, II.5, ed. and trans. Bertram Colgrave and R. A. B. Mynors (Oxford, 1969), 148–9.
34. Ibid., V.10, ed. and trans. Colgrave and Mynors, 480–1. Translation adapted.
35. Adomnan of Iona, *Life of St Columba*, I.1, trans. Richard Sharpe (Harmondsworth, 1995), 110–11 (*Adomnan's Life of Columba*, ed. A. O. Anderson and M. O. Anderson (Edinburgh, 1961), 198–200).
36. Widukind, *Res gestae Saxonicae* III.46, ed. P. Hirsch and H.-E. Lohmann, MGH SRG (Hanover, 1935), 127–8.
37. *Liber Ardmachanus: The Book of Armagh edited with Introduction and Appendices* by John Gwynn (Dublin 1913), 32.
38. Cassiodorus, *Variae* I.1, ed. Mommsen, 10.
39. Above, n. 2.
40. Letter of Cnut to the English, as quoted by William of Malmesbury, *Gesta regum Anglorum*, II.183, ed. and trans. R. A. B. Mynors, R. M. Thomson, and M. Winterbottom, 2 vols. (Oxford, 1998–9), ii. 326–7.
41. See pp. 29–30.
42. Letter of Cnut to the English, ed. and trans. Mynors, Thomson, and Winterbottom, 326–7.
43. Ibid. 324–5.
44. Paulinus of Aquileia, *Carmina*, V.7, ed. E. Dümmler, MGH Poetae I, p. 137.
45. *Cummian's Letter 'De controversia paschali' together with a Related Irish Computistical Tract*, ed. Maura Walsh and Dáibhí Ó Cróinín (Toronto, 1988), 93–5.
46. *Notitia ecclesiarum urbis Romae*, ed. Roberto Valentini and Giuseppe Zucchetti, *Codice topografico della città di Roma*, 4 vols., Fonti per la Storia d'Italia, 80, 88, 90, 91 (Rome, 1940–53), ii. 78–9.
47. Ibid. ii. 94, 97.
48. Letter of Cnut to the English, ed. and trans. Mynors, Thomson, and Winterbottom, 324–7.
49. 'Petruslied', trans. Cyril Edwards, in 'German Vernacular Literature', in Rosamond McKitterick (ed.), *Carolingian Culture: Emulation and Innovation*

(Cambridge, 1994), 162 (ed. Wilhelm Braune, *Althochdeutsches Lesebuch*, 16th edn. (Tübingen, 1979), 131).

50. Ps-Alcuin, *De divinis officiis*, 17, *PL* 101, col. 1209.
51. 'Vita Berachi', 25, ed. C. Plummer, *Vitae Sanctorum Hiberniae*, 2 vols. (Oxford, 1910; repr. Dublin, 1997), i. 85–6.
52. *Félire Óengusso Céli Dé: The Martyrology of Oengus the Culdee*, ed. Whitley Stokes (London, 1905), 206–7.
53. *The Text of the Book of Llan Dâv*, ed. J. G. Evans and J. Rhys (Oxford, 1893), 83–4.
54. Bede, *Lives of the Abbots of Wearmouth and Jarrow*, trans. J. F. Webb, *The Age of Bede* (rev. edn., Harmondsworth, 1988), 191 (*Historia abbatum*, 5, ed. C. Plummer, *Venerabilis Bedae opera historica*, 2 vols. (Oxford, 1896), i. 368).
55. Bede, *Ecclesiastical History*, V.21, ed. and trans. Colgrave and Mynors, 532–3, slightly adapted.
56. *Vita Gebhardi*, 13, ed. W. Wattenbach, MGH SS X, p. 587.
57. *Vita Meinwerci episcopi Patherbrunensis*, 218, ed. F. Tenckhoff, MGH SRG (Hanover, 1921), 131.

# Further Reading

## ORIENTATION FOR ENGLISH-LANGUAGE READERS

### General

Anglophone readers are now well served by volumes addressing part or all of the period covered in this book. Overviews include Peter Garnsey and Caroline Humfress, *The Evolution of the Late Antique World* (Cambridge, 2001); Rosamond McKitterick (ed.), *The Early Middle Ages: Europe 400–1000* (Oxford, 2001), and Heinrich Fichtenau, *Living in the Tenth Century: Mentalities and Social Orders*, trans. Patrick J. Geary (Chicago, 1991). *The Cambridge Ancient History* and *The New Cambridge Medieval History* are authoritative and large-scale statements by leading experts, containing both political narrative and detailed analytical approaches to a comprehensive range of subjects plus detailed bibliographical guidance. The period *c.*500–1000 is covered by the following: *The Cambridge Ancient History*, xiv: *Late Antiquity. Empire and Successors, AD 425–600*, ed. Averil Cameron, Bryan Ward-Perkins, and Michael Whitby (Cambridge, 2000); *The New Cambridge Medieval History*, i: *c.500–c.700*, ed. Paul Fouracre (forthcoming); ii: *c.700–c.900*, ed. Rosamond McKitterick (Cambridge, 1995); iii: *c.900–1024*, ed. Timothy Reuter (Cambridge, 1999).

In the absence of any firm chronological distinction between 'late Antiquity' and the 'early Middle Ages' there is considerable debate about the place of the early Middle Ages in wider conceptions of pre-modern European history. See Peter Heather, 'Late Antiquity and the Early Medieval West', in Michael Bentley (ed.), *Companion to Historiography* (London, 1997), 69–87; Lester K. Little and Barbara H. Rosenwein (eds.), *Debating the Middle Ages: Issues and Readings* (Maldon, MA, 1998); R. I. Moore, *The First European Revolution, c.970–1215* (Oxford, 2000).

### Sources

Editions of sources are listed in the above-mentioned volumes of *The Cambridge Ancient History* and *The New Cambridge Medieval History*. A convenient listing of available English-language translations can be found in McKitterick (ed.), *The Early Middle Ages*.

### Electronic Resources

Much useful material is now available on the Internet. Images of early medieval objects in museums and libraries can be found on the websites of several major institutions including The British Library, The British Museum, The Dumbarton Oaks Museum, and The Cloisters branch of the Metropolitan Museum of Art.

There are also many university-based websites dedicated to medieval resources, especially translations of texts, subject-specific bibliographies, and some maps. The following websites are well maintained and reliable access points:

http://www.fordham.edu/halsall/sbook.html
A public-access website based at Fordham University, the Internet Medieval Sourcebook has a large number of online English translations of late antique and early medieval texts. It also provides links to many other useful sites.

http://labyrinth.georgetown.edu
Based at Georgetown University, this is the oldest, and most sophisticated, portal for accessing online medieval resources.

http://www.netserf.org
An index of links to thousands of other sites with medieval resources.

http://www.wmich.edu/medieval/research/rawl/index.html
The Rawlinson Center of Western Michigan University hosts a wide range of useful research tools (bibliographies, texts, etc.) for Anglo-Saxon England and Old English studies.

http://www.medievalsources.co.uk
Subscriber-only access to electronic versions of translations published by Manchester University Press, plus public-access portal with links to a range of other medieval sites.

http://www.itergateway.org
A University of Toronto-based bibliographical database for the Middle Ages and Renaissance, part of which is public access.


## Regional Approaches

Regional and national historiographies have a strong presence in writing on the early Middle Ages, with many books being devoted to the medieval antecedents of modern polities. The following is a short English-language selection. Where relevant, they all provide bibliographic guidance to foreign-language titles.

British Isles, including Ireland
*After Rome*, ed. Thomas Charles-Edwards (Oxford, 2003) and *From the Vikings to the Normans*, ed. Wendy Davies (Oxford, 2003), both volumes of 'The Short Oxford History of the British Isles'; *The Oxford Companion to Scottish History*,

ed. Michael Lynch (Oxford, 2001); *The Oxford Companion to Irish History*, ed. S. J. Connelly, 2nd edn. (Oxford, 2002); *The Blackwell Encyclopaedia of Anglo-Saxon England*, ed. Michael Lapidge, John Blair, Simon Keynes, and Donald Scragg (Oxford, 1999); David Hill, *An Atlas of Anglo-Saxon England* (Oxford, 1981).

France

Edward James, *The Origins of France: From Clovis to the Capetians, 500–1000* (London, 1982); Ian Wood, *The Merovingian Kingdoms 450–751* (Harlow, 1994); Pierre Riché, *The Carolingians: A Family who Forged Europe*, trans. M. I. Allen (Philadelphia, 1993); Jean Dunbabin, *France in the Making, 843–1180*, 2nd edn. (Oxford, 2000).

Spain

Roger Collins, *Early Medieval Spain: Unity in Diversity, 400–1000*, 2nd edn. (Basingstoke, 1995); Thomas F. Glick, *Islamic and Christian Spain in the Early Middle Ages* (Princeton, 1979).

Italy

Chris Wickham, *Early Medieval Italy: Central Power and Local Society, 400–1000* (London, 1981); Cristina La Rocca (ed.), *Italy in the Early Middle Ages, 476–1000* (Oxford, 2002); *Medieval Italy: An Encyclopedia*, ed. Christopher Kleinhenz, 2 vols. (New York, 2004).

Germany

Timothy Reuter, *Germany in the Early Middle Ages, 800–1056* (London, 1991); Benjamin Arnold, *Medieval Germany 500–1300: A Political Interpretation* (Basingstoke, 1997); *Medieval Germany: An Encyclopedia*, ed. John M. Jeep (New York, 2001).

Scandinavia

Birgit Sawyer and Peter Sawyer, *Medieval Scandinavia: From Conversion to Reformation, circa 800–1500* (Minneapolis, 1993); *The Cambridge History of Scandinavia*, i: *Prehistory to 1520*, ed. Knut Helle (Cambridge, 2003); *Cultural Atlas of the Viking World*, ed. James Graham-Campbell (New York, 1994); *Vikings: The North Atlantic Saga*, ed. William Fitzhugh and Elisabeth Ward (Washington, 2000).

Central Europe

John V. A. Fine, Jr., *The Early Medieval Balkans: A Critical Survey from the Sixth to the Late Twelfth Century* (Ann Arbor, 1983); P. M. Barford, *The Early Slavs* (London, 2001); Pál Engel, *The Realm of St Stephen: A History of Medieval Hungary, 895–1526*, trans. Tamás Pálosfalvi (London, 2001); Paul R. Magosci,

*Historical Atlas of East Central Europe from the Early Fifth Century to the Present*, 2nd edn. (Seattle, 2002).

## CHAPTER I. SPEAKING AND WRITING

Marco Mostert (ed.), *New Approaches to Medieval Communication* (Turnhout, 1999), offers useful methodological reflections and an extremely full bibliography of themes covered in this chapter.

The history of the languages and non-Latin literatures of the early Middle Ages have naturally attracted much attention; an accessible overview is Philippe Wolff, *Western Languages, AD 100–1500*, trans. Frances Partridge (London, 1971). Vivien Law, *The History of Linguistics in Europe from Plato to 1600* (Cambridge, 2003), takes an accessible and stimulating look at how language was conceptualized and studied.

Recommended introductions to Old English are Albert C. Baugh and Thomas Cable, *A History of the English Language*, 4th edn. (London, 1993), and *The Cambridge Companion to Old English Literature*, ed. Malcolm Godden and Michael Lapidge (Cambridge, 1991). Catherine Hills, *Origins of the English* (London, 2003), outlines the controversies surrounding the historical circumstances in which Latin and British gave way to Old English.

J. Knight Bostock, *A Handbook of Old High German Literature*, 2nd edn. (Oxford, 1976), remains the only English-language discussion of this corpus and is usefully supplemented by Wolfgang Haubrichs, *Geschichte der deutschen Literatur*, vol. 1 pt. 1, *Die Anfänge: Versuche volkssprachiger Schriftlichkeit im frühen Mittelalter (ca. 700–1050/60)* (Frankfurt, 1988). D. H. Green, *Language and History in the Early Germanic World* (Cambridge, 1998), offers a comparative approach. For Slavonic, see Alexander M. Schenker, *The Dawn of Slavic* (New Haven, 1995).

The Celtic regions are surveyed by Thomas Charles-Edwards, 'Language and Society among the Insular Celts, 400–1000', in Miranda J. Green (ed.), *The Celtic World* (London, 1995), 703–36. For ogam, see Damian McManus, *A Guide to Ogam* (Maynooth, 1991); for runes, Ralph W. V. Elliott, *Runes: An Introduction*, 2nd edn. (Manchester, 1989), and David N. Parsons, *Recasting the Runes: The Reform of the Anglo-Saxon futhorc* (Uppsala, 1999).

On Latin, two historically sensitive interpretations are Michel Banniard, *Viva voce: Communication écrite et communication orale du IVe au IXe siècle en Occident latin* (Paris, 1992), and Roger Wright, *A Sociophilological Study of Late Latin* (Turnhout, 2002), both of which offer technical guidance on the philological issues underlying the transition from Latin to Romance.

Much scholarly attention has recently focused on a range of issues clustered around the 'orality'—'literacy' antithesis, with 'memory' bridging them. The poles of the debate are marked by Michael Richter, *The Formation of the Medieval West: Studies in the Oral Culture of the Barbarians* (Dublin, 1994), Rosamond

McKitterick, *The Carolingians and the Written Word* (Cambridge, 1989), and Patrick J. Geary, *Phantoms of Remembrance: Memory and Oblivion at the End of the First Millennium* (Princeton, 1994). Several volumes of essays from the 1990s are of central methodological importance, commencing with Rosamond McKitterick (ed.), *The Uses of Literacy in Early Medieval Europe* (Cambridge, 1990). Alan K. Bowman and Greg Woolf (eds.), *Literacy and Power in the Ancient World* (Cambridge, 1994), includes late Antiquity and the successor kingdoms, while Huw Pryce (ed.), *Literacy in Medieval Celtic Societies* (Cambridge, 1998), has much to say on regions too readily ignored in the debates.

Other useful collections of essays are A. N. Doane and Carol Braun Pasternak (eds.), *Vox Intertexta: Orality and Textuality in the Middle Ages* (Madison, 1992), Ursula Schaefer (ed.), *Schriftlichkeit im frühen Mittelalter* (Tübingen, 1993), Rudolf Schieffer (ed.), *Schriftkultur und Reichsverwaltung unter den Karolingern* (Opladen, 1996), and Walter Pohl and Paul Herold (eds.), *Vom Nutzen des Schreibens: Soziales Gedächtnis, Herrschaft und Besitz im Mittelalter* (Vienna, 2002). Monographic approaches include Seth Lerer, *Literacy and Power in Anglo-Saxon Literature* (Lincoln, NE, 1991); Nicholas Everett, *Literacy in Lombard Italy, c.568–774* (Cambridge, 2003); Michel Zimmermann, *Écrire et lire en Catalogne du IXe au XIIe siècle* (Madrid, 2003). For women's literacy, see Rosamond McKitterick, 'Women and literacy in the early Middle Ages' in ead., *Books, Scribes and Learning in the Frankish Kingdoms, 6th–9th Centuries* (Aldershot, 1994), ch. XIII.

The challenge of Christian, Latin literacy in the insular world was put on a new footing by Bernhard Bischoff, 'Wendepunkte in der Geschichte der lateinischen Exegese im Frühmittelalter', in id., *Mittelalterliche Studien: Ausgewählte Aufsätze zur Schriftkunde und Literaturgeschichte*, i (Stuttgart, 1966), 205–73, and has been approached rather differently by G. Hardin Brown, 'The Dynamics of Literacy in Anglo-Saxon England', *Bulletin of the John Rylands Library*, 77 (1995), 109–42, and Roy Liuzza, 'Who Read the Gospels in Old English?', in Peter S. Baker and Nicholas Howe (eds.), *Words and Works: Studies in Medieval English Language and Literature in Honour of Fred C. Robinson* (Toronto, 1998), 3–24.

On reading, there are insightful contributions in Jonathan Boyarin (ed.), *The Ethnography of Reading* (Berkeley, 1993), and Guglielmo Cavallo and Roger Chartier (eds.), *A History of Reading in the West*, trans. Lydia Cochrane (Cambridge, 1999). D. H. Green, *Listening and Reading: The Primary Reception of German Literature, 800–1300* (Cambridge, 1994), Armando Petrucci, *Writers and Readers in Medieval Italy: Studies in the History of Written Culture*, trans. Charles Radding (New Haven, 1995), and Simon Franklin, *Writing, Society and Culture in Early Rus, c.950–1300* (Cambridge, 2002), are all of wider significance than their titles suggest.

On monastic reading, Jean Leclercq, *The Love of Learning and the Desire for God*, trans. Catherine Misrahi (New York, 1961), retains its classic status. Pierre Riché, *Education and Culture in the Barbarian West, 6th–8th Centuries*, trans. John J. Contreni (Columbia, SC, 1975), and *Écoles et enseignement dans le haut moyen âge, fin du Ve siècle–milieu du XIe siècle*, 3rd edn. (Paris 1999), survey schools and curricula. Bernhard Bischoff, *Manuscripts and Libraries in the Age of Charlemagne*, trans. Michael Gorman (Cambridge, 1994), is important on the transmission of classical texts and much else.

While law and administration have traditionally been seen as aspects of constitutional and institutional history, newer approaches place them at the centre of subjects addressed in this chapter. In particular, see Patrick Wormald, '*Lex scriptum* and *verbum regis*: Legislation and Germanic Kingship from Euric to Cnut', in P. H. Sawyer and Ian N. Wood (eds.), *Early Medieval Kingship* (Leeds, 1977), 105–38; Robin Chapman Stacey, 'Law and Order in the Very Old West: England and Ireland in the Early Middle Ages', in B. T. Hudson and V. Ziegler (eds.), *Crossed Paths: Methodological Approaches to the Celtic Aspect of the European Middle Ages* (Lanham, MD, 1991), 39–60, and T. M. Charles-Edwards, 'Law in the Western Kingdoms between the Fifth and the Seventh Century', in *The Cambridge Ancient History*, xiv. 260–87. The accommodation of Roman law and associated documentary forms to the social practices of the successor kingdoms is a complex subject, but two accessible articles, both germane to the subject matter of Chapters 3 and 4, are: Patrick Wormald, 'The *Leges barbarorum*: Law and Ethnicity in the Post-Roman West', in H.-W. Goetz, J. Jarnut, and W. Pohl (eds.), *Regna and Gentes: The Relationship between Late Antique and Early Medieval Peoples and Kingdoms in the Transformation of the Roman World* (Leiden, 2003), 21–53, and Antti Arjava, 'The Survival of Roman Family Law after the Barbarian Settlements', in Ralph W. Mathisen (ed.), *Law, Society, and Authority in Late Antiquity* (Oxford, 2001), 33–51. Patrick Wormald, *The Making of English Law: King Alfred to the Twelfth Century* (Oxford, 1999), has much to say on continental as well as Anglo-Saxon law.

The study of charters in their socio-political context was opened up by the ground-breaking essays edited by Wendy Davies and Paul Fouracre, *The Settlement of Disputes in Early Medieval Europe* (Cambridge, 1986); Karl Heidecker (ed.), *Charters and the Use of the Written Word in Medieval Society* (Turnhout, 2000), contains several valuable contributions on the earlier Middle Ages. Useful studies of document-mindedness are Kathryn A. Lowe, 'Lay Literacy in Anglo-Saxon England and the Development of the Chirograph', in Phillip Pulsiano and Elaine M. Treharne (eds.), *Anglo-Saxon Manuscripts and their Heritage* (Aldershot, 1998), 161–204; and Cristina La Rocca, 'La legge e la pratica: Potere e rapporti sociali nell'Italia dell' VIII secolo', in Carlo Bertelli and Gian Pietro Brogiolo (eds.), *Il futuro dei Longobardi: L'Italia e la costruzione dell'Europa di Carlo Magno: Saggi* (Milan, 2000), 45–69. See also Warren Brown, 'When Documents are Destroyed or Lost: Lay People and Archives in the Early Middle Ages', *EME* 11 (2002), 337–66. Patrick J. Geary, 'Land, Language and Memory in Europe, 700–1100', *Transactions of the Royal Historical Society*, 6th ser., 9 (1999), 168–84, and Robin Chapman Stacey, 'Texts and Society', in *After Rome*, ed. Charles-Edwards, 221–57 (p. 315 above), put due emphasis on the oral, performative nature of texts.

The slate documents discussed on pp. 42–3 are published by Isabel Velázquez

Soriano, *Documentos de época visigoda escritos en pizarra (siglos VI–VIII)*, Monumenta Palaeographica Medii Aevi, series hispanica, 2 vols. (Turnhout, 2000). The Redon charters discussed on pp. 43–4 were edited by Aurélien de Courson, *Cartulaire de l'Abbaye de Redon en Bretagne* (Paris, 1863). For Hrabanus and Fulda, see Raymund Kottje and Harald Zimmermann (eds.), *Hrabanus Maurus: Lehrer, Abt und Bischof* (Mainz, 1982), and Gangolf Schrimpf (ed.), *Kloster Fulda in der Welt der Karolinger und Ottonen* (Frankfurt, 1996).

## CHAPTER 2. LIVING AND DYING

A judicious introduction that puts many of the issues discussed here into a broad perspective is E. L. Jones, *The European Economic Miracle: Environments, Economies and Geopolitics in the History of Europe and Asia* (Cambridge, 1981). Packed with graphs, maps, and plans, and provocative but not always accurate, is Klaus Randsborg, *The First Millennium AD in Europe and the Mediterranean: An Archaeological Essay* (Cambridge, 1991). For an emphatic word-sketch of the human dimension, see Karl Leyser, 'The Tenth-Century Condition', in his *Medieval Germany and its Neighbours, 900–1250* (London, 1982), 1–9. A wide-ranging survey incorporating the fruits of recent scholarship on themes covered in Chapters 2–6 is Philippe Depreux, *Les Sociétés occidentales du milieu du VIe à la fin du IXe siècle* (Rennes, 2002).

The environmental history of the early Middle Ages is in its infancy, although settlement studies and landscape history often address many of the same issues. For an accessible introduction to scientific approaches, see Petra Dark, *The Environment of Britain in the First Millennium AD* (London, 2000). Matthew Stout, 'Early Christian Ireland: Settlement and Environment', in Terry Barry (ed.), *A History of Settlement in Ireland* (London, 2000), 80–109, reviews issues and evidence for Ireland. A contrasting approach is Paolo Squatriti, *Water and Society in Early Medieval Italy, AD 400–1000* (Cambridge, 1998). See also Squatriti (ed.), *Working with Water in Medieval Europe: Technology and Resource-Use* (Leiden, 2000). On Europe's climate, consult Hubert H. Lamb, *Climate, History and the Modern World* (London, 1982), esp. ch. 9, and also 'Climate from 1000 BC to 1000 AD', in Martin Jones and Geoffrey Dimbleby (eds.), *The Environment of Man: The Iron Age to the Anglo-Saxon Period*, British Archaeological Reports British Series, 87 (Oxford, 1981), 53–65.

There are various approaches to settlement history. Helena Hamerow, *Early Medieval Settlements: The Archaeology of Rural Communities in North-West Europe, 400–900* (Oxford, 2002), surveys continental and Anglo-Saxon settlement sites. For a well-illustrated study of a single site, see *Un Village au temps de Charlemagne: Moines et paysans de l'abbaye de Saint-Denis du VIIe siècle à l'an Mil* (Paris, 1988). Chris Wickham, 'European Forests in the Early Middle Ages: Landscape and Land Clearance', *L'ambiente vegetale nell' alto medioevo*, 2 vols. Settimane, 37 (1990), ii. 479–545, is important (repr. in id., *Land and Power: Studies in Italian and European Social History, 400–1200* (London, 1994), 155–200); for al-Andalus, see Thomas F. Glick, *Islamic and Christian Spain in the Early Middle Ages* (Princeton, 1979), esp. ch. 2, and Andrew M. Watson, *Agricultural Innovation in the Early Islamic World: The Diffusion of Crops and Farming Techniques, 700–1100* (Cambridge, 1983). Though dated, Jean Chapelot and Robert Fossier, *The Village and House in the Middle Ages*, trans. H. Cleere (London, 1985), remains useful.

There is no satisfactory overview of early medieval demographic issues. Instead, readers should consult a range of key articles. On the plague, J.-N. Biraben and J. Le Goff, 'The Plague in the Early Middle Ages', in Robert Forster and Orest Ranum (eds.), *The Biology of Man in History: Selections from Annales* (Baltimore, 1975), 48–80, is of central importance. Controversy surrounding the geographical range and demographic significance of the plague is clear from Dick Harrison, 'Plague, Settlement and Structural Change at the Dawn of the Middle Ages', *Scandia*, 59 (1993), 15–48, and J. R. Maddicott, 'Plague in Seventh-Century England', *Past and Present*, 156 (1997), 7–54. Peter Sarris, 'The Justinianic Plague: Origins and Effects', *Continuity and Change*, 17 (2002), 169–82, argues for its catastrophic impact.

Epigraphical evidence from the post-Roman West is presented by Mark A. Handley, *Death, Society and Culture: Inscriptions and Epitaphs in Gaul and Spain, AD 300–750*, British Archaeological Reports International Series, 1135 (Oxford, 2003), with comments on its demographic implications; post-750 demography is best approached through the incisive survey of Pierre Toubert, 'The Carolingian Moment', in André Burguière, Christiane Klapisch-Zuber, Martine Segalen, and Françoise Zonabend (eds.), *A History of the Family*, i: *Distant Worlds, Ancient Worlds*, trans. Sarah Hanbury Tenison, Rosemary Morris, and Andrew Wilson (Cambridge, 1996), 379–406, and Jean-Pierre Devroey, *Économie rurale et société dans l'Europe franque (VI–IXe siècles)* (Paris, 2003), both with further bibliographic guidance. G. M. Schwartz, 'Village Populations According to the Polyptyque of the Abbey of St Bertin', *Journal of Medieval History*, 11 (1985), 31–41, is one of the few English-language contributions to debates about how to handle the ninth-century estate survey evidence. In the absence of any documentary base from which to proceed prior to the Domesday Book of 1086, there has been no demographic study of any part of the British Isles in the early Middle Ages.

The debate over female infanticide was sparked by Emily Coleman, 'Infanticide in the Early Middle Ages', in Susan Mosher Stuard (ed.), *Women in Medieval Society* (Philadelphia, 1976), 47–70, and supported by Carol Clover, 'The Politics of Scarcity: Notes on the Sex Ratio in Early Scandinavia', *Scandinavian Studies*, 60 (1988), 147–88. The detailed counter-arguments have mostly been in French: Monique Zerner, 'La Population de Villeneuve-Saint-Georges et de Nogent-sur-Marne au IXe siècle d'après le polyptyque de Saint-Germain-des-Prés', *Annales de la Faculté des Lettres et Sciences Humaines de Nice*, 37 (1979), 17–24, and Jean-Pierre Devroey, 'Les Méthodes d'analyse des polyptyques du haut moyen âge', *Acta Historica Bruxellensia*, 4 (1981), 71–88. There are sane comments on infanticide together with a fundamentally important discussion of the practice of contraception and abortion in John M. Riddle, *Contraception and Abortion from the Ancient World to the Renaissance* (Cambridge, MA, 1992). Ecclesiastical teaching is set out by J. T. Noonan, *Contraception: A History of its Treatment by the Catholic Theologians and Canonists* (Cambridge, MA, 1986). Intentional or accidental infanticide in the ninth century is the subject of Gerhard Schmitz, 'Schuld und Strafe: Eine unbekannte Stellungnahme des Rathramnus von Corbie zur Kindestötung', *Deutsches Archiv für die Erforschung des Mittelalters*, 38 (1982), 363–87.

Discussions of early medieval agriculture and productivity have often been too preoccupied with controversies about the dating of technological change; for a clear and concise appraisal, see Adriaan Verhulst, 'The "Agricultural Revolution" of the Middle Ages reconsidered', in B. S. Bachrach and D. Nicholas (eds.), *Law, Custom and the Social Fabric in the Middle Ages: Essays in Honour of Bryce Lyon* (Kalamazoo, 1990), 17–28. This can usefully be supplemented by *La Croissance agricole du haut moyen âge: Chronologie, modalités, géographie*, published by the Centre culturel de l'abbaye de Flaran (Auch, 1990). The implications of early medieval agriculture for nutrition and health are explored by M. Montanari, *L'alimentazione contadina nell'alto medioevo* (Naples, 1979), for Italy, and Kathy L. Pearson, 'Nutrition and the Early Medieval Diet', *Speculum*, 72 (1997), 1–32, for north-western Europe.

The essential work on famine remains F. Curschmann, *Hungersnöte im Mittelalter: Ein Beitrag zur deutschen Wirtschaftsgeschichte des 8. bis 13. Jahrhunderts* (Leipzig, 1900), though there is a detailed discussion of Charlemagne's response to the famines of his reign by Adriaan Verhulst, 'Karolingische Agrarpolitik: Das Capitulare de Villis und die Hungersnöte von 792/3 und 805/6', *Zeitschrift für Agrargeschichte und Agrarsoziologie*, 13 (1965), 175–89. Food taboos are examined by Pierre Bonnassie, 'Consommation d'aliments immondes et cannibalisme de survie dans l'occident du haut moyen âge', *Annales: Economies, Sociétés, Civilisations*, 44 (1989), 1035–56.

For archaeological evidence of sickness and disease, see K. Manchester, 'Resurrecting the Dead: The Potential of Palaeopathology', in E. Southworth (ed.), *Anglo-Saxon Cemeteries: A Reappraisal* (Stroud, 1990), 87–96, and, for more detail, A. Czarnetzki, C. Uhlig, and R. Wolf, *Menschen des frühen Mittelalters im Spiegel der Anthropologie und Medizin*, 2nd edn. (Stuttgart, 1983). On the social and cultural history of disease, Peregrine Horden, 'Disease, Dragons and Saints: The Management of Epidemics in the Dark Ages', in Terence Ranger and Paul Slack (eds.), *Epidemics and Ideas: Essays on the Historical Perception of Pestilence* (Cambridge, 1992), 45–76, is stimulating. See also the papers on a wide range of aspects of early medieval medical history in 'The Year 1000' issue of *Social History of Medicine*, 13/2 (2000), 197–321, ed. Peregrine Horden and Emilie Savage-Smith. M. L. Cameron, *Anglo-Saxon Medicine* (Cambridge, 1993), is also valuable.

Of the huge literature on early medieval saints' cults, Peter Brown, *The Cult of the Saints: Its Rise and Function in Latin Christianity* (Chicago, 1981), has become a classic; two collections of studies indicate more recent approaches: James

Howard-Johnston and Paul Anthony Hayward (eds.), *The Cult of Saints in Late Antiquity and the Early Middle Ages* (Oxford, 1999), and Alan Thacker and Richard Sharpe (eds.), *Local Saints and Local Churches in the Early Medieval West* (Oxford, 2002).

Early medieval cosmologies have also attracted attention. Monica Blöcker, 'Wetterzauber: Zu einem Glaubenskomplex des frühen Mittelalters', *Francia*, 9 (1981), 117–31, is essential. Valerie Flint, *The Rise of Magic in Early Medieval Europe* (Princeton, 1991), is a vigorous and controversial attempt to explore a wide range of strategies for handling illness, bad weather, and much else. On apocalyptic thinking, see the essays edited by Richard Landes, Andrew Gow, and David C. Van Meter, *The Apocalyptic Year 1000: Religious Expectation and Social Change, 950–1050* (New York, 2003).

The demographic details on pp. 66–8 are derived from Don Brothwell, 'Palaeodemography and Earlier British Populations', *World Archaeology*, 4 (1972), 75–87; Vera I. Evison, *Dover: The Buckland Anglo-Saxon Cemetery* (London, 1987), and Jürg Schneider, Daniel Gutscher, Hansueli Etter, and Jürg Hanser, *Der Münsterhof in Zürich*, 2 vols. (Olten, 1982).

## CHAPTER 3. FRIENDS AND RELATIONS

The best introduction to the subjects of Chapters 3 and 4 is Burguière et al. (eds.), *A History of the Family*, (p. 321 above), esp. chs. 8–9, 'Barbarian Europe' and 'The Carolingian Moment'. Geoffrey S. Nathan, *The Family in Late Antiquity: The Rise of Christianity and the Endurance of Tradition* (London, 2000), guides the reader through the late Roman heritage. David Herlihy, *Medieval Households* (Cambridge, MA, 1985), and Jack Goody, *The Development of the Family and Marriage in Europe* (Cambridge, 1983), are both important and contentious. Newer approaches, more alert to intra-familial interactions, are Katrien Heene, *The Legacy of Paradise: Marriage, Motherhood and Women in Carolingian Edifying Literature* (Frankfurt, 1997), Sally Crawford, *Childhood in Anglo-Saxon England* (Stroud, 1999), and Pauline Stafford, 'Parents and Children in the Early Middle Ages', *EME* 10 (2001), 257–71.

Naming practices in the ancient world are outlined by B. Salway, 'What's in a Name? A Survey of Roman Onomastic Practices from c.700 BC to AD 700', *Journal of Roman Studies*, 84 (1994), 124–45; late Roman conventions are explored in detail by Martin Heinzelmann, 'Les Changements de la dénomination latine à la fin de l'antiquité', in G. Duby and J. Le Goff (eds.), *Famille et parenté dans l'occident médiéval*, Collection de l'École Française de Rome, 30 (Rome, 1977), 19–24.

The most accessible introduction to Germanic names remains H. B. Woolf, *The Old Germanic Principles of Name-Giving* (Baltimore, 1939), now supplemented by Régine Le Jan, 'Personal Names and the Transformation of Kinship in Early Medieval Society (6th–10th centuries)', in G. T. Beech, M. Bourin, and P. Chareille (eds.), *Personal Names Studies of Medieval Europe: Social Identity and*

*Familial Structures* (Kalamazoo, MI, 2002), 31–50. Dieter Geuenich, Wofgang Haubrichs, and Jörg Jarnut (eds.), *Nomen et gens: Zur historischen Aussagekraft frühmittelalterlicher Personennamen* (Berlin, 1997), presents a range of new approaches to personal onomastics. Women's names are exhaustively analysed by Hans-Werner Goetz, 'Nomen Feminile: Namen und Namengebung der Frauen im frühen Mittelalter', *Francia*, 23/1 (1966), 99–134; peasants' names by Carl I. Hammer, 'Servile Names and Seigneurial Organisation in Early Medieval Bavaria', *Studi Medievali*, 3rd ser., 36 (1995), 917–28, and J. Bessmerny, 'Les Structures de la famille paysanne dans les villages de la Francia au IXe siècle', *Le Moyen Âge*, 90 (1984), 165–93.

For Irish names (which lack any clear connection with patterns of kinship), see Brian Ó. Cuív, *Aspects of Irish Personal Names* (Dublin, 1986).

Introductions to burial archaeology are Guy Halsall, *Early Medieval Cemeteries: An Introduction to Burial Archaeology in the Post-Roman World* (Glasgow, 1995), and Edward James, 'Burials and Status in the Early Medieval West', *Transactions of the Royal Historical Society*, 5th ser., 39 (1989), 23–40. Megan McLaughlin, *Consorting with Saints: Prayer for the Dead in the Early Middle Ages* (Ithaca, NY, 1994), ch. 2, outlines Christian rituals for commemorating the dead. For kinship in this context, see C. Bouchard, 'Family Structure and Family Consciousness among the Aristocracy in the Ninth to Eleventh Centuries', *Francia*, 14 (1986), 639–58.

L. Génicot, *Les Généalogies*, Typologie des sources du moyen âge occidental, 15 (Turnhout, 1975), offers a general introduction to genealogies; for more detailed discussion, see Kenneth Sisam, 'Anglo-Saxon Royal Genealogies', *Proceedings of the British Academy*, 39 (1953), 287–348; D. N. Dumville, 'Kingship, Genealogies and Regnal Lists', in P. H. Sawyer and I. N. Wood (eds.), *Early Medieval Kingship* (Leeds, 1977), 72–104, and David Thornton, 'Orality, Literacy and Genealogy in Early Medieval Wales and Ireland', in Pryce (ed.), *Literacy in Medieval Celtic Societies*, 83–98 (p. 318 above). Gender issues of commemoration, memory, and identity are discussed by Matthew Innes, 'Keeping it in the Family: Women and Aristocratic Memory, 700–1200', in Elisabeth van Houts (ed.), *Medieval Memories: Men, Women and the Past, 700–1300* (Harlow, 2001), 17–35, and Ian Wood, 'Genealogy Defined by Women: The Case of the Pippinids', in Leslie Brubaker and Julia M. H. Smith (eds.), *Gender in the Early Medieval World: East and West, 300–900* (Cambridge, 2004), 234–56.

Much has been written on early medieval kinship, often informed by outdated or inappropriate legal and anthropological models: the sane comments on method and conceptualization of Anita Guerreau-Jalabert should be heeded in 'Sur les structures de parenté dans l'Europe médiévale', *Annales: Economies, Sociétés, Civilisations*, 36 (1981), 1028–49, and 'La Désignation des relations et des groupes de parenté en latin médiéval', *Archivum Latinitatis Medii Aevi*, 66–7 (1988), 65–108. Outdated notions of early medieval 'clans' are attacked by Pierre Guichard, 'De l'antiquité au moyen âge: Famille large et famille étroite', *Cahiers d'Histoire*, 24 (1979), 45–60, and definitively demolished by Alexander C. Murray, *Germanic*

*Kinship Structure: Studies in Law and Society in Antiquity and the Early Middle Ages* (Toronto, 1983).

Fundamental to the approaches and issues of this book are Isabelle Réal, *Vies de saints, vie de famille: Représentation et système de la parenté dans le royaume mérovingien (481–751) d'après les sources hagiographiques* (Turnout, 2001), Régine Le Jan, *Famille et pouvoir dans le monde franc (VIIe–Xe siècle): Essai d'anthropologie sociale* (Paris, 1995), and Karl Leyser, 'The German Aristocracy from the Ninth to the Early Twelfth Century: A Historical and Cultural Sketch', *Past and Present*, 41 (1968), 25–53. For a good example of a heavily Romanized culture, see P. D. King, *Law and Society in the Visigothic Kingdom* (Cambridge, 1972), ch. 8, 'The Family'.

On Anglo-Saxon England, Lorraine Lancaster, 'Kinship in Anglo-Saxon Society', *British Journal of Sociology*, 9 (1958), 230–50, 359–77, is central; H. R. Loyn, 'Kinship in Anglo-Saxon England', *Anglo-Saxon England*, 3 (1974), 197–209, remains useful. T. M. Charles-Edwards, *Early Irish and Welsh Kinship* (Oxford, 1993), repays careful attention.

On peasant households and kinship, see T. M. Charles-Edwards, 'Kinship, Status and the Origins of the Hide', *Past and Present*, 56 (1972), 3–33, supplemented by Carl I. Hammer, 'Family and *familia* in Early Medieval Bavaria', in R. Wall, J. Robin, and P. Laslett (eds.), *Family Forms in Historic Europe* (Cambridge, 1983), 217–48.

Important studies of the forms of artificial kinship promoted by Christianization are Joseph H. Lynch, *Godparents and Kinship in Early Medieval Europe* (Princeton, 1986), and id., *Christianizing Kinship: Ritual Sponsorship in Anglo-Saxon England* (Ithaca, NY, 1998). On kinlessness, T. M. Charles-Edwards, 'The Social Background to Irish *peregrinatio*', *Celtica*, 11 (1976), 43–59, is important.

For friendship, Verena Epp, *Amicitia: Zur Geschichte personaler, sozialer, politischer und geistlicher Beziehungen im frühen Mittelalter* (Stuttgart, 1999). Gerd Althoff, *Family, Friends and Followers: Political and Social Bonds in Early Medieval Europe*, trans. Christopher Carroll (Cambridge, 2004), and id., *Amicitiae und Pacta: Bündnis, Einung, Politik und Gebetsdenken im beginnenden 10. Jahrhundert*, MGH Schriften, 37 (Hanover, 1992), are valuable.

Except for Celticists, early medieval historians have been reluctant to tackle issues of honour and shame, which otherwise generally remain the preserve of literary analysis; see T. M. Charles-Edwards, 'Honour and Status in Some Irish and Welsh Prose Tales', *Eriu*, 29 (1978), 123–41, and M. E. Owen, 'Shame and Reparation: Women's Place in the Kin', in D. Jenkins and M. E. Owen (eds.), *The Welsh Law of Women* (Cardiff, 1980), 40–68. Judicious cautions against oversimplistic use of poetic sources are to be found in Katherine O'Brien O'Keeffe, 'Heroic Values and Christian Ethics', in *Cambridge Companion to Old English Literature*, ed. Godden and Lapidge, 107–125 (p. 317 above). Nira Pancer, *Sans peur et sans vergogne: De l'honneur et des femmes aux premiers temps mérovingiens* (Paris, 2001), provides the only detailed attempt to extend the analysis to the Continent and is restricted to the sixth century.

The seminal work that first addressed early medieval feuding remains essential: J. M. Wallace-Hadrill, 'The Blood-Feud of the Franks', in his *The Long-Haired Kings* (London, 1962), 121–47. To this should now be added W. I. Miller, 'Choosing the Avenger: Some Aspects of the Bloodfeud in Medieval Iceland and England', *Law and History Review*, 1 (1983), 159–204, and *Bloodtaking and Peacemaking: Feud, Law and Society in Saga Iceland* (Chicago, 1990), which, although primarily concerned with 12th–13th-century Iceland, nevertheless has much of general value to the early medievalist. Guy Halsall, 'Violence and Society in the Early Medieval West: An Introductory Survey', in Halsall (ed.), *Violence and Society in the Early Medieval West* (Woodbridge, 1998), 1–45, offers an unduly restricted understanding of 'feud'. Richard Fletcher, *Bloodfeud: Murder and Revenge in Anglo-Saxon England* (London, 2002), is an accessible, colourful piece of eleventh-century micro-history.

## CHAPTER 4. MEN AND WOMEN

Gendered analysis of early medieval society is largely the work of anglophone scholars. For the issues involved, see Janet L. Nelson, 'Family, Gender and Sexuality in the Middle Ages', in Bentley (ed.), *Companion to Historiography*, 153–76 (p. 314 above); Pauline Stafford and Anneke Mulder-Bakker (eds.), *Gendering the Middle Ages* (Oxford, 2001), and Brubaker and Smith (eds.), *Gender in the Early Medieval World: East and West, 300–900* (p. 324 above), all with full references to additional bibliography. Contrasting approaches are sketched by Julia M. H. Smith, 'Did Women have a Transformation of the Roman World?', in Stafford and Mulder-Bakker (eds.), *Gendering the Middle Ages*, 22–41, and Guy Halsall, 'Gender and the End of Empire', *Journal of Medieval and Early Modern Studies*, 34 (2004), 17–39.

There are several books specifically on early medieval women, none of which is entirely reliable; these include Suzanne F. Wemple, *Women in Frankish Society: Marriage and the Cloister 500–900* (Philadelphia, 1981); Christine Fell, *Women in Anglo-Saxon England* (London, 1984); Lisa M. Bitel, *Land of Women: Tales of Sex and Gender from Early Ireland* (Ithaca, NY, 1996); ead., *Women in Early Medieval Europe, 400–1100* (Cambridge, 2002), and Patricia Skinner, *Women in Medieval Italian Society, 500–1200* (Harlow, 2001). There is much of value in Hans-Werner Goetz, *Frauen im frühen Mittelalter* (Cologne, 1995).

For men, see J. J. Cohen and B. Wheeler (eds.), *Becoming Male in the Middle Ages* (New York, 1997), D. M. Hadley (ed.), *Masculinity in Medieval Europe* (London, 1999), and Mathew Kuefler, *The Manly Eunuch: Masculinity, Gender Ambiguity and Christian Ideology in Late Antiquity* (Chicago, 2001). Carol Clover, 'Regardless of Sex: Men, Women and Power in Early Northern Europe', *Speculum*, 68 (1993), 363–87 (repr. in Nancy Partner (ed.), *Studying Medieval Women: Sex, Gender, Feminism* (Cambridge, MA, 1993)), offers a thoughtful comparative perspective based on early Icelandic evidence.

The key studies of burial, gender, and life cycle are Guy Halsall, 'Female Status and Power in Early Merovingian Austrasia: The Burial Evidence', *EME* 5 (1996), 1–24; id., *Settlement and Social Organization: The Merovingian Region of Metz* (Cambridge, 1995), and N. Stoodley, *The Spindle and the Spear: A Critical Enquiry into the Construction and Meaning of Gender in the Early Anglo-Saxon Burial Rite*, British Archaeological Reports British Series, 288 (Oxford, 1999).

The gendered aspects of domestic and agricultural work are analysed by Ludolf Kuchenbuch, '*Opus feminile*: Das Geschlechtsverhältnis im Spiegel von Frauenarbeit im früheren Mittelalter', in H.-W. Goetz (ed.), *Weibliche Lebensgestaltung im frühen Mittelalter* (Cologne, 1991), 139–75, and Jean-Pierre Devroey, 'Femmes au miroir des polyptyques: Une approche des rapports du couple dans l'exploitation rurale dépandante entre Seine et Rhin au IXe siècle', in Stéphane Lebecq, Alain Dierkens, Régine Le Jan, and Jean-Marie Sansterre (eds.), *Femmes et pouvoirs des femmes à Byzance et en Occident (VIe–XIe siècles)* (Villeneuve-d'Ascq, 1999), 227–49.

Marriage and sexual relationships are surveyed from the perspective of legal sources in James A. Brundage, *Law, Sex and Society in Medieval Europe* (Chicago, 1987). Key discussions of forms of marriage are Raymund Kottje, 'Eherechtliche Bestimmungen der germanischen Volksrechte (5.-8. Jh.)', in Werner Affeldt (ed.), *Frauen in Spätantike und Frühmittelalter: Lebensbedingungen, Lebensnormen, Lebensformen* (Sigmaringen, 1990), 211–20, and the papers in *Il Matrimonio nella società altomedioevale*, Settimane, 24, 2 vols. (1977). The late Roman background is evaluated by Judith Evans Grubb, *Law and Family in Late Antiquity: The Emperor Constantine's Marriage Legislation* (Oxford, 1995). For Anglo-Saxon England, Margaret Clunies Ross, 'Concubinage in Anglo-Saxon England', *Past and Present*, 108 (1985), 1–34, is crucial, while, for Ireland, Donnchadh Ó Corráin's articles, 'Marriage in Early Ireland', in Art Cosgrove (ed.), *Marriage in Ireland* (Dublin, 1985), 5–24, and 'Women and the Law in Early Ireland', in Mary O'Dowd and Sabine Wichert (eds.), *Chattel, Servant or Citizen: Women's Status in Church, State and Society* (Belfast, 1995), 45–57, are accessible complements to Charles-Edwards, *Early Irish and Welsh Kinship* (p. 325 above). See also Ruth Mazo Karras, 'Concubinage and Slavery in the Viking Age', *Scandinavian Studies*, 62 (1990), 141–62.

Mayke de Jong, 'To the Limits of Kinship: Anti-Incest Legislation in the Early Medieval West', in Jan Bremmer (ed.), *From Sappho to de Sade: Moments in the History of Sexuality* (London, 1989), 36–59, introduces the attempts to restrict choice of marriage partner, a subject surveyed in more detail by Patrick Corbet, *Autour de Burchard de Worms: L'Église allemande et les interdits de parenté (IXe–XIIe siècle)* (Frankfurt, 2001). Comparative analyses include: Bart Jaski, 'Marriage Laws in Ireland and on the Continent in the Early Middle Ages', in Christine Meek and Katharine Simms (eds.), *'The Fragility of her Sex'? Medieval Irishwomen in their European Context* (Dublin, 1996), 16–42, and Daffyd Walters, *The Comparative Legal Method: Marriage and Divorce and the Spouses' Property Rights in Early Medieval European Law and in Cyfraith Howel* (Aberystwyth, 1982).

Two studies by Carl I. Hammer address the issue of sexual relationships and marriage involving slaves, and of marriages among slaves: 'The Handmaid's Tale: Morganatic Relationships in Early-Mediaeval Bavaria', *Continuity and Change*, 19 (1995), 345–68, and 'A Slave Marriage Ceremony from Early Medieval Germany: A Note and a Document in Translation', *Slavery and Abolition*, 16 (1995), 243–9. Catalan comital marriage practices are surveyed in Martin Aurell, *Les Noces du comte: Mariage et pouvoir en Catalogne (785–1213)* (Paris, 1995).

Women, property, and inheritance are no longer the preserve of legal historians. For the late Roman background and the legislation of the successor kingdoms through to the seventh century, Antti Arjava, *Women and Law in Late Antiquity* (Oxford, 1996), is thorough, and can be supplemented by Karl Kroeschell, 'Söhne und Töchter im germanischen Erbrecht', in Götz Landwehr (ed.), *Studien zu den germanischen Volksrechte: Gedächtnisschrift für W. Ebel* (Frankfurt, 1982), 87–116.

There is now important work available on marital property transfers, women's access to property, and their role in familial inheritance strategies. Two recent conference volumes take thematic approaches to many different regions: 'Les Transferts patrimoniaux en Europe occidentale, VIIIe–Xe siècle: Actes de la table ronde de Rome, Mai 1999', published as *Mélanges de l'École Française de Rome— Moyen Age*, 111 (1999), pt. 2, and François Bougard, Laurent Feller, and Régine Le Jan (eds.), *Dots et douaires dans le haut moyen âge*, Collection de l'École Française de Rome, 295 (Rome, 2002).

Additional studies include Cristina La Rocca, 'Pouvoirs des femmes, pouvoirs de la loi dans l'Italie lombarde', in Lebecq et al. (eds.), *Femmes et pouvoirs des femmes*, 37–50 (p. 327 above); Brigitte Pohl-Resl, '"Quod me legibus contanget auere": Rechtsfähigkeit und Landbesitz langobardischer Frauen', *Mitteilungen des Instituts für Österreichische Geschichtsforschung*, 101 (1993), 201–27; Ingrid Heidrich, 'Besitz und Besitzverfügung verheirateter und verwitweter freier Frauen im Merowingischen Frankenreich', in Goetz (ed.), *Weibliche Lebensgestaltung*, 119–38 (p. 327 above). Inscriptional evidence from tenth- to eleventh-century Scandinavia is analysed by Birgit Sawyer, *Property and Inheritance in Viking Scandinavia: The Runic Evidence* (Alingsås, 1988). For late Anglo-Saxon England, the work of Pauline Stafford is crucial: see *Queen Emma and Queen Edith: Queenship and Women's Power in Eleventh-Century England* (Oxford, 1997), and references there to her earlier work on a wide range of issues.

The key study of the connections between family, commemoration, and inheritance strategy is Barbara Rosenwein, *To be the Neighbor of Saint Peter: The Social Meaning of Cluny's Property, 909–1049* (Ithaca, NY, 1989). The central role of women in commemoration and inheritance in Anglo-Saxon England is emphasized in two papers by Julia Crick: 'Women, Posthumous Benefaction, and Family Strategy in Pre-Conquest England', *Journal of British Studies*, 38 (1999), 399–422, and 'Posthumous Obligation and Family Identity', in William O. Frazer and Andrew Tyrrell (eds.), *Social Identity in Early Medieval Britain* (Leicester, 2000), 194–208. Brigitte Pohl-Resl, 'Vorsorge, Memoria und soziales Ereignis:

Frauen als Schenkerinnen in den bayerischen und alemannischen Urkunden des 8. und 9. Jahrhunderts', *Mitteilungen des Instituts für Österreichische Geschichtsforschung*, 103 (1995), 265–87, argues along similar lines.

Recent work suggests that widows hold the key to understanding many of these issues: see Janet L. Nelson, 'The Wary Widow', in Wendy Davies and Paul Fouracre (eds.), *Property and Power in the Early Middle Ages* (Cambridge, 1995), 82–113; Rolf H. Bremmer, 'Widows in Anglo-Saxon England', in Jan Bremmer and Lourens van den Bosch (eds.), *Between Poverty and the Pyre: Moments in the History of Widowhood* (London, 1995), 58–88, and Emmanuelle Santinelli, *Des Femmes éplorées? Les Veuves dans la société aristocratique du haut moyen âge* (Villeneuve-d'Ascq, 2003).

The argument that strategies of heirship changed in the eleventh century to permit the transfer of a family's entire inheritance from eldest son to eldest son was propounded by Georges Duby in a famous series of articles during the 1960s and 1970s; see chs. 3 and 6 of his *The Chivalrous Society*, trans. Cynthia Postan (London, 1977) for English versions. Criticisms of this outdated orthodoxy are Theodore Evergates, 'Nobles and Knights in Twelfth-Century France', in T. N. Bisson (ed.), *Cultures of Power: Lordship, Status and Process in Twelfth-Century Europe* (Philadelphia, 1995), 11–35, and Pauline Stafford, 'La Mutation familiale: A Suitable Case for Caution', in Joyce Hill and Mary Swan (eds.), *The Community, the Family and the Saint: Patterns of Power in Early Medieval Europe* (Turnhout, 1998), 103–25.

The figures on pp. 138–9 for the percentage of property owned by women are derived from the following studies: Arjava, *Women and Law in Late Antiquity* (p. 328 above); David Herlihy, 'Land, Family and Women in Continental Europe, 701–1200', *Traditio*, 18 (1962), 89–120, and Marc A. Meyer, 'Women's Estates in Later Anglo-Saxon England: The Politics of Possession', *Haskins Society Journal*, 3 (1991), 111–29.

The will of Eberhard and Gisela and associated charters used on pp. 143–5 are edited by Ignace de Coussemaker, *Cartulaire de l'abbaye de Cysoing et ses dependences*, 2 vols. (Lille, 1880), i. 1–11; see also the detailed analysis of Cristina La Rocca and Luigi Provero, 'The Dead and their Gifts: The Will of Eberhard, Count of Friuli and his Wife Gisela, Daughter of Louis the Pious (863–864)', in Frans Theuws and Janet L. Nelson (eds.), *Rituals of Power from Late Antiquity to the Early Middle Ages* (Leiden, 2000), 225–80.

## CHAPTER 5. LABOUR AND LORDSHIP

The literature on early medieval social hierarchies is piecemeal and remains constrained by national historiographies. Almost the sole exception is Werner Rösener, *The Peasantry of Europe* (Oxford, 1994). For Anglo-Saxon England, see Pauline Stafford, *Unification and Conquest: A Political and Social History of England in the Tenth and Eleventh Centuries* (London, 1989); W. G. Runciman,

'Accelerating Social Mobility: The Case for Anglo-Saxon England', *Past and Present*, 104 (1984), 3–30; and Rosamond Faith, *The English Peasantry and the Growth of Lordship* (Leicester, 1997). David Pelteret, *Slavery in Early Medieval England from the Reign of Alfred to the Twelfth Century* (Woodbridge, 1995), is important. On Ireland, N. B. Aitchison, 'Kingship, Society and Sacralisation: Rank, Power and Ideology in Early Medieval Ireland', *Traditio*, 49 (1994), 45–75, and Paul Holm, 'The Slave Trade of Dublin, 9th–12th Centuries', *Peritia*, 5 (1986), 317–45, are both fresh and stimulating.

For the Continent, the standard but now outdated work on slavery is Charles Verlinden, *L'Esclavage dans l'Europe médiévale*, 2 vols. (Bruges, 1955; Ghent, 1977). The debate about the transition from slavery to serfdom has at times been intense, but still generally takes its cue from Marc Bloch, 'How and Why Ancient Slavery Came to an End', in *Slavery and Serfdom in the Middle Ages: Selected Essays by Marc Bloch*, trans. William R. Beer (Berkeley, 1975), 1–31. An important polemical contribution originally published in French in 1985 is Pierre Bonnassie, 'The Survivival and Extinction of the Slave System in the Early Medieval West (Fourth to Eleventh Centuries)', in id., *From Slavery to Serfdom in South-Western Europe*, trans. Jean Birrell (Cambridge, 1991), 1–59. Carl I. Hammer, *A Large-Scale Slave Society of the Early Middle Ages: Slaves and their Families in Early Medieval Bavaria* (Woodbridge, 2002), continues the debate. Wendy Davies, 'On Servile Status in the Early Middle Ages', in M. L. Bush (ed.), *Serfdom and Slavery: Studies in Legal Bondage* (London, 1996), 225–46, is both a sane analysis and a unique attempt to discuss continental and insular societies in tandem.

Nobility has inspired no such comparative treatment. Continental issues are well served by wide-ranging survey discussions in English that will guide the reader to all the relevant foreign-language literature. See Timothy Reuter, 'The Medieval Nobility in Twentieth-Century Historiography', in Bentley (ed.), *Companion to Historiography*, 177–202 (p. 314 above), J. B. Freed, 'Reflections on the Medieval German Nobility', *American Historical Review*, 91 (1986), 553–75, and Jane Martindale, 'The French Aristocracy in the Early Middle Ages: A Reappraisal', *Past and Present*, 75 (1977), 5–45 (repr. in ead., *Status, Authority and Regional Power: Aquitaine and France, 9th to 12th Centuries* (Aldershot, 1997), ch. IV). Paul Fouracre, 'The Origins of the Nobility in Francia', in Anne J. Duggan (ed.), *Nobles and Nobility in Medieval Europe: Concepts, Origins, Transformations* (Woodbridge, 2000), 17–24, is a concise update.

Le Jan, *Famille et pouvoir dans le monde franc* (p. 325 above), is important for all aspects of the continental nobility. Karl Ferdinand Werner, *Naissance de la noblesse* (Paris, 1998), is stimulating on cultural aspects and controversial on institutional ones. See also Hans-Werner Goetz, '"Nobilis": Der Adel im Selbstverständnis der Karolingerzeit', *Vierteljahrschrift für Sozial- und Wirtschaftsgeschichte*, 70 (1983), 153–91; Karl Bosl, '*Potens* und *pauper*: Begriffsgeschichtliche Studien zur gesellschaftlichen Differenzierung im frühen Mittelalter und zum "Pauperismus" des Hochmittelalters', in id., *Frühformen der Gesellschaft im mittelalterlichen Europa* (Munich, 1964), 106–34; Karl Leyser, 'Early Medieval Canon Law and the Beginnings of Knighthood', in Lutz Fenske, Werner Rösener, and Thomas Zotz (eds.), *Institutionen, Kultur und Gesellschaft im Mittelalter: Festschrift für Josef Fleckenstein zu seinem 65. Geburtstag* (Sigmaringen, 1984), 549–66 (repr. in id., *Communications and Power in Medieval Europe*, i: *The Carolingian and Ottonian Centuries*, ed. Timothy Reuter (London, 1994), 189–213).

Important essays on elite lifestyle are Timothy Reuter, 'Nobles and Others: The Social and Cultural Expression of Power Relations in the Middle Ages', in Duggan (ed.), *Nobles and Nobility*, 85–98 (p. 330 above), and Robin Fleming, 'The New Wealth, the New Rich and the New Political Style in Late Anglo-Saxon England', *Anglo-Norman Studies*, 23 (2000), 1–22.

Landlordship has generated a vast literature for the early medieval continent. See, in general, the sensitive if now somewhat old analysis of Georges Duby, *Rural Economy and Country Life in the Medieval West* (London, 1968). It is updated well by Philippe Contamine, Marc Bompaire, Stéphane Lebecq, and Jean-Luc Sarrazin, *L'Économie médiévale* (Paris, 1993), and Devroey, *Économie rurale et société* (p. 321 above). David Herlihy, 'Church Property on the European Continent, 701–1200', *Speculum*, 36 (1961), 81–105, attempts to assess how much land was in ecclesiastical hands, region by region, while Davies and Fouracre (eds.), *Property and Power in the Early Middle Ages* (p. 329 above), explores how land sustained political authority.

Most of the literature on estate organization deals only with the Frankish empire; an excellent introduction is Jean-Pierre Devroey, 'The Large Estate in the Frankish Kingdoms: A Tentative Dynamic Definition', in id., *Études sur le grand domaine carolingien* (Aldershot, 1993), ch. I. Adriaan Verhulst, *The Carolingian Economy* (Cambridge, 2002), is a useful overview, with detailed bibliography of the extensive technical literature. The following are particularly stimulating discussions: Ludolf Kuchenbuch, 'Die Klostergrundherrschaft im Frühmittelalter: Eine Zwischenbilanz', in Friedrich Prinz (ed.), *Herrschaft und Kirche: Beiträge zur Entstehung und Wirkungsweise episkopaler und monastischer Organisationsformen* (Stuttgart, 1988), 297–343; Fred Schwind, 'Zu karolingerzeitlichen Klöstern als Wirtschaftsorganismen und Stätten handwerklicher Tätigkeit', in Fenske et al. (eds.), *Institutionen, Kultur und Gesellschaft im Mittelalter*, 101–23 (above); Pierre Toubert, 'Il sistema curtense: La produzione e lo scambio interno in Italia nel secoli VIII, IX e X', in *Storia d'Italia: Annali, 6: Economia naturale, economia monetaria* (Turin, 1983), 5–63 (and reprinted in id., *Histoire du haut moyen âge et de l'Italie médiévale* (London, 1987), ch. VIII); Wickham, 'European Forests in the Early Middle Ages' (p. 320 above).

For the military aspects of lordship, Dick Whittaker, 'Landlords and Warlords', in John Rich and Graham Shipley (eds.), *Warfare and Society in the Roman World* (London, 1993), 277–302, is useful on the militarization of late Roman society throughout the empire. For a succint summary of debates about early medieval military recruitment, see Timothy Reuter, 'The Recruitment of Armies in the Early Middle Ages: What Can We Know?', in Anne Nørgård Jørgensen and Birthe L. Clausen (eds.), *Military Aspects of Scandinavian Society in a European*

*Perspective, AD 1–1300* (Copenhagen, 1997), 32–7. See also Edward James, 'The Militarisation of Roman Society, 400–700', in ibid. 19–24; Bernard S. Bachrach, *Merovingian Military Organisation, 481–751* (Minneapolis, 1972); id., *Early Carolingian Warfare: Prelude to Empire* (Philadelphia, 2000); Richard Abels, *Lordship and Military Obligation in Anglo-Saxon England* (Berkeley, 1988); F. Prinz, *Klerus und Krieg im früheren Mittelalter: Untersuchungen zur Rolle der Kirche beim Aufbau der Königsherrschaft* (Stuttgart, 1971); Guy Halsall, *Warfare and Society in the Barbarian West, 450–900* (London, 2003).

The various networks of lordship that linked localities and regions, and then came together in the Carolingian polity, have received much attention recently in anglophone scholarship. Contrasting configurations, all with ample reference to foreign-language bibliography, are presented by Wendy Davies, *Small Worlds: The Village Community in Early Medieval Brittany* (London, 1988), Paul Fouracre, *The Age of Charles Martel* (Harlow, 2000), Matthew Innes, *State and Society in the Early Middle Ages: The Middle Rhine Valley, 400–1000* (Cambridge, 2000), and Simon MacLean, *Kingship and Politics in the Late Ninth Century: Charles the Fat and the End of the Carolingian Empire* (Cambridge, 2003). Susan Reynolds, *Fiefs and Vassals: The Medieval Evidence Reinterpreted* (Oxford, 1994), is refreshingly controversial on early medieval benefices.

Intense controversy currently swirls around the late tenth and early eleventh centuries. The emergence of knighthood, castles, and local lordships are specific themes within much larger debates about the relationship of social and political order, above all in France. Their flavour can be gauged from *Debating the Middle Ages*, eds. Little and Rosenwein, 105–210 (p. 314 above). The essays in Pierre Bonnassie and Pierre Toubert (eds.), *Hommes et sociétés dans l'Europe de l'an mil* (Toulouse, 2004), are thoughtful evaluations.

Details of the lands of St Peter's, Ghent, at the time of Einhard and Arnulf I, discussed on pp. 164–72, are derived from *Diplomata belgica ante annum millesimum centesimum scripta*, ed. M. Gysseling and A. C. F. Koch, i (Brussels, 1950), documents 49–56, pp. 123–49. See also Adriaan Verhulst, 'Over de stichting en vroegste geschiedenis van de Sint-Pieters en de Sint-Baafsabdijen te Gent', *Maatschappij voor Geschiedenis en Oudheidkunde te Gent*, niewe reeks, 7 (1953), 3–53, and Georges Declercq, 'Einhard und das karolingische Gent', in Hermann Schefers (ed.), *Einhard: Studien zum Leben und Werk* (Darmstadt, 1997), 223–46. For the town of Ghent, see Adriaan Verhulst and Georges Declercq, 'Early Medieval Ghent between Two Abbeys and the Count's Castle', in G. Decavele (ed.), *Ghent: In Defence of a Rebellious City* (Antwerp, 1989), 1–52 (repr. in Verhulst, *Rural and Urban Aspects of Early Medieval Northwest Europe* (Aldershot, 1992), ch. XII), and, for the broader context, David Nicholas, *Medieval Flanders* (London, 1992).

All this is but the tip of a bibliographical iceberg with vast dimensions and a deeply embedded historiographical problematic. Those interested in the latter can get a flavour of the issues from Otto Brunner, 'Feudalism: The History of a

Concept', in Frederic L. Cheyette (ed.), *Lordship and Community in Medieval Europe: Selected Readings* (New York, 1968), 32–61; J. W. Burrow, '"The Village Community" and the Uses of History in Nineteenth-Century England', in Neil McKendrick (ed.), *Historical Perspectives: Studies in English Thought and Society in Honour of J. H. Plumb* (London, 1974), 255–84, and Walter Pohl, 'Herrschaft', *Reallexikon der germanischen Altertumskunde*, 14 (1999), 445–57.

## CHAPTER 6. GETTING AND GIVING

The literature on early medieval trade and exchange remains divided into many subspecialities, archaeological or historical, urban or rural, late antique or medieval. As an exercise in formulating an overview, Richard Hodges and David Whitehouse, *Mohammed, Charlemagne and the Origins of Europe: Archaeology and the Pirenne Thesis* (London, 1983), is stimulating and always controversial. For important new approaches, see Richard Hodges and William Bowden (eds.), *The Sixth Century: Production, Distribution and Demand* (Leiden, 1998), in conjunction with Inge Lyse Hansen and Chris Wickham (eds.), *The Long Eighth Century: Production, Distribution and Demand* (Leiden, 2000).

On the socio-economic aspects of the end of the western Roman Empire, I have taken my cue from Chris Wickham, 'The Other Transition: From the Ancient World to Feudalism', *Past and Present*, 113 (1984), 3–36, and 'Italy and the Early Middle Ages', in Klaus Randsborg (ed.), *The Birth of Europe: Archaeology and Social Development in the First Millennium AD* (Rome, 1989), 140–51 (both repr. in Wickham, *Land and Power* (p. 320 above). See also Michael Hendy, 'From Public to Private: The Western Barbarian Coinages as a Mirror of the Disintegration of Late Roman State Structures', *Viator*, 19 (1988), 29–78. For the contrary position, see Jean Durliat, *Les Finances publiques de Dioclétien aux carolingiens (284–889)* (Sigmaringen, 1990).

Michael McCormick, *The Origins of the European Economy: Communications and Commerce, AD 300–900* (Cambridge, 2001), combines important work on the Mediterranean region with a controversial argument about the centrality of the slave trade to economic change. For some of the issues it raises, see Edward James et al., '"Origins of the European Ecomony": A Debate with Michael McCormick', *EME* 12 (2003), 259–323. Peregrine Horden and Nicholas Purcell, *The Corrupting Sea: A Study of Mediterranean History* (Oxford, 2000), emphasizes Mediterranean micro-economies and webs of local 'connectivities'. The older study of Dietrich Claude remains crucial: *Untersuchungen zu Handel und Verkehr der vor- und frühgeschichtlichen Zeit in Mittel- und Nordeuropa, ii: Der Handel im westlichen Mittelmeer während des Frühmittelalters* (Göttingen, 1985).

Northern trading networks are the focus of *Untersuchungen zu Handel und Verkehr der vor- und frühgeschichtlichen Zeit in Mittel- und Nordeuropa, iii: Der Handel des frühen Mittelalters*, and iv: *Der Handel der Karolinger- und*

*Wikingerzeit*, both edited by Klaus Düwel, Herbert Jankuhn, Harald Siems, and Dieter Timpe (Göttingen, 1985 and 1987). The important contribution of Frisian traders is documented by Stéphane Lebecq, *Marchands et navigateurs frisons du haut moyen âge*, 2 vols. (Lille, 1983). Olivier Bruand, *Voyageurs et marchands aux temps carolingiens: Les Réseaux de communication entre Loire et Meuse aux VIIIe et IXe siècles* (Brussels, 2002), emphasizes the interplay of local, regional, and long-distance trade.

For the Irish Sea zone, see the contrasting interpretations of Jonathan M. Wooding, *Communication and Commerce along the Western Sea Lanes, AD 400–800*, British Archaeological Reports International Series, 654 (Oxford, 1996), and Ewan Campbell, 'The Archaeological Evidence for External Contacts: Imports, Trade and Economy in Celtic Britain, AD 400–800', in Kenneth R. Dark (ed.), *External Contacts and the Economy of Late Roman and Post-Roman Britain* (Woodbridge, 1996), 83–96. Mary A. Valante, 'Reassessing the Irish "Monastic Town"', *Irish Historical Studies*, 31 (1998), 1–18, offers a cautious assessment of exchange in pre-Viking Ireland. Sally Foster, Allan Macinnes, and Ranald MacInnes (eds.), *Scottish Power Centres from the Early Middle Ages to the Twentieth Century* (Glasgow, 1998), and Stephen T. Driscoll and Margaret R. Nieke (eds.), *Power and Politics in Early Medieval Britain and Ireland* (Edinburgh, 1988), pay proper attention to hillforts and other high-status sites.

Towns—attempts to define them, the fate of Roman cities, urban origins in non-Roman Europe—are the subject of intense debate. J. H. W. G. Liebeschuetz, *The Decline and Fall of the Roman City* (Oxford, 2001), draws a huge specialist literature together; a contrasting, succinct overview is S. J. B. Barnish, 'The Transformation of Classical Cities and the Pirenne Debate', *Journal of Roman Archaeology*, 2 (1989), 385–400. Richard Hodges, *Towns and Trade in the Age of Charlemagne* (London, 2000), argues enthusiastically for a new Carolingian economic order. Italian cities have their own special debates: Bryan Ward-Perkins, 'Continuists, Catastrophists and the Towns of Post-Roman Northern Italy', *Papers of the British School at Rome*, 65 (1997), 157–76, and Ross Balzaretti, 'Cities and Markets in the Early Middle Ages', in G. Ausenda (ed.), *After Empire: Towards an Ethnology of Europe's Barbarians* (Woodbridge, 1995), 113–42.

*The Cambridge Urban History of Britain*, i: *600–1540* (Cambridge, 2000), ed. David Palliser, includes judicious overviews of the large literature on Anglo-Saxon towns; on relationships between towns and regional economies, see Christopher Scull, 'Urban Centres in pre-Viking England?', in John Hines (ed.), *The Anglo-Saxons from the Migration Period to the Eighth Century: An Ethnographic Perspective* (Woodbridge, 1998), 269–310, and Robin Fleming, 'Rural Elites and Urban Communities in Late Saxon England', *Past and Present*, 141 (1993), 3–37. Trading privileges in London are discussed by Susan Kelly, 'Trading Privileges from Eighth-Century England', *EME* 1 (1992), 3–28.

Adriaan Verhulst, *The Rise of Cities in North-West Europe* (Cambridge, 1999), reviews recent work on towns and emporia throughout the Low Countries. Details of Scandinavian emporia are accessible in either Helen Clarke and Björn

Ambrosiani, *Towns in the Viking Age* (Leicester, 1991), or Johan Callmer, 'Urbanization in Scandinavia and the Baltic Region, 700–1100: Trading Places, Centres and Early Urban Sites', in Helen Clarke and Björn Ambrosiani (eds.), *The Twelfth Viking Congress: Developments around the Baltic and the North Sea in the Viking Age*, Birka Studies, 3 (Stockholm, 1994), 50–90. On non-Roman Europe, see H. B. Clarke and Anngret Simms (eds.), *The Comparative History of Urban Origins in Non-Roman Europe: Ireland, Wales, Denmark, Germany, Poland and Russia from the Ninth to the Thirteenth Century*, British Archaeological Reports International Series, 255, 2 vols. (Oxford, 1985).

The extensive, specialized literature on coinage is best approached through Peter Spufford, *Money and its Uses in Medieval Europe* (Cambridge, 1988), and Philip Grierson and Mark Blackburn, *Medieval European Coinage with a Catalogue of the Coins of the Fitzwilliam Museum, Cambridge*, i: *the Early Middle Ages (5th–10th centuries)* (Cambridge, 1986).

All discussions of giving and getting go back, in various ways, to Philip Grierson, 'Commerce in the Dark Ages: A Critique of the Evidence', *Transactions of the Royal Historical Society*, 5th ser., 9 (1959), 123–40 (repr. in Grierson, *Dark Age Numismatics* (London, 1979)). On gift exchange, see also Jürgen Hannig, '*Ars donandi*: Zur Ökonomie des Schenkens im früheren Mittelalter', in Richard van Dülmen (ed.), *Armut, Liebe, Ehre* (Frankfurt, 1988), 11–37, and Arnoud-Jan Bijsterveld, 'The Medieval Gift as Agent of Social Bonding and Political Power: A Comparative Approach', in Esther Cohen and Mayke de Jong (eds.), *Medieval Transformations: Texts, Power and Gifts in Context* (Leiden, 2001), 123–56.

Critical approaches to treasure are set out in Sauro Gelichi and Cristina La Rocca (eds.), *Tesori: Forme di accumulazione della ricchezza nell'alto medioevo (secoli V–XI)* (Rome, 2004). Some of the papers in E. M. Tyler (ed.), *Treasure in the Medieval West* (York, 2000), are also relevant. A wide range of textual and material evidence is assessed by Matthias Hardt, 'Royal Treasures and Representation in the Early Middle Ages', in Walter Pohl and Helmut Reimitz (eds.), *Strategies of Distinction: The Construction of Ethnic Communities, 300–800* (Leiden, 1998), 255–80. On changing forms and uses of material wealth, see Cristina La Rocca, 'Segni di distinzione: Dai corredi funerari alle donazioni "post obitum" nel regno longobardo', in L. Paroli (ed.), *L'Italia centro-settentrionale in età longobarda* (Florence, 1997), 31–54. Timothy Reuter, 'Plunder and Tribute in the Carolingian Empire', *Transactions of the Royal Historical Society*, 5th ser., 35 (1985), 75–94, is now classic.

For women's participation in gift giving, see Michael J. Enright, 'Lady with a Mead Cup', *Frühmittelalterliche Studien*, 22 (1988), 170–203; also Bonnie Effros, *Creating Community with Food and Drink in Merovingian Gaul* (New York, 2002), and the Further Reading for Chapter 7 on queens. Additional aspects of the social context are suggested by Donald A. Bullough, *Friends, Neighbours and Fellow-Drinkers: Aspects of Community and Conflict in the Early Medieval West*, H. M. Chadwick Memorial Lecture (Cambridge, 1990).

The social and symbolic values of weapons are discussed by Régine Le Jan,

'Frankish Giving of Arms and Rituals of Power: Continuity and Change in the Carolingian Period', and Heinrich Härke, 'The Circulation of Weapons in Anglo-Saxon Society', both in Theuws and Nelson (eds.), *Rituals of Power*, 281–309, 377–99 (p. 329 above). See also Charlotte Fabech, 'Booty Sacrifices in Southern Scandinavia: A Reassessment', in P. Garwood, D. Jennings, R. Skenates and J. Toms (eds.), *Sacred and Profane: Proceedings of a Conference on Archaeology, Ritual and Religion, Oxford 1989* (Oxford, 1991), 88–99.

Irish cattle-clientage is analysed in Nerys Patterson's stimulating and controversial *Cattle Lords and Clansmen: The Social Structure of Early Ireland*, 2nd edn. (Notre Dame, IN, 1994). A. T. Lucas, *Cattle in Ancient Ireland* (Kilkenny, 1989), and Fergus Kelly, *Early Irish Farming* (Dublin, 1998), are both thorough, technical assessments.

Details on pp. 197–8 of the royal treasury in late-tenth-century Pavia are recorded in the *Instituta Regalia*, incorporated into the *Honorantiae Civitatis Papiae*, ed. Carlrichard Brühl and Cinzio Violante, *Die 'Honorantie Civitatis Papie'* (Cologne, 1983).

For the 'Prince of Prittlewell' described on pp. 206–7, see the feature on 'Prittlewell: Treasures of a King of Essex', *Current Archaeology*, 16/10 (February 2004), 430–6, and, for updates as post-excavation work continues, the regularly maintained website of the Museum of London Archaeology Service, http://www.molas.org.uk .

The sketch of Einhard on pp. 210–12 is derived from his letters, trans. in Paul Edward Dutton, *Charlemagne's Courtier: The Complete Einhard* (Peterborough, ONT, 1998), 131–64, and ed. K. Hampe, MGH Epp. V, pp. 105–42; see also Julia M. H. Smith, 'Einhard: The Sinner and the Saints', *Transactions of the Royal Historical Society*, 6th ser., 13 (2003), 55–77.

The Holy Lance discussed on pp. 212–13 is studied by Percy Ernst Schramm, 'Die "Heilige Lanze", Reliquie und Herrschaftszeichen und ihre Replik in Krakau', in his *Herrschaftszeichen und Staatssymbolik*, MGH Schriften 13, 3 vols. (Stuttgart, 1954–6), ii. 492–537.


## CHAPTER 7. KINGSHIP AND CHRISTIANITY

In view of the fact that Christianity and Christian monarchy were hugely influential in shaping medieval and modern national identities, the bibliography on this subject is vast. Valuable surveys are Richard Fletcher, *The Conversion of Europe: From Paganism to Christianity, 371–1386 AD* (London, 1997), and Arnold Angenendt, *Das Frühmittelalter: Die abendländische Christenheit vom 400 bis 900* (Stuttgart, 1990). Peter Brown, *The Rise of Western Christendom: Triumph and Diversity, AD 200–1000*, 2nd edn. (Oxford, 2003), is a magisterial summation from a cultural history perspective.

Pre-Christian religious traditions are hard to grasp, and should not be confused with the retrospective mythologies presented by literary sources of the twelfth century and later. Beliefs and practices in Ireland and other Celtic-speaking regions are especially elusive, owing to a lack of archaeological evidence for cult practices from the immediately pre-Christian period. For Slavic regions of central-northern Europe, see Lleszek Paweł Słupecki, 'Au déclin des dieux slaves', in Michel Rouche (ed.), *Clovis: histoire et mémoire. Le Baptême de Clovis, son écho à travers l'histoire*, Actes du colloque internationale d'histoire de Reims, 2 vols. (Paris, 1997), ii. 289–314, and id., *Slavonic Pagan Sanctuaries* (Warsaw, 1994). Michael Müller-Willer, *Opferkulte der Germanen und Slawen* (Stuttgart, 1999), is an excellent photographic record and brief discussion of cult places and sacrifices.

Germanic religious traditions have been intensively studied since the early nineteenth century. Among recent work, see Green, *Language and History*, chs. 1, 15 (p. 317 above), Ian Wood, 'Pagan Religions and Superstitions East of the Rhine from the Fifth to the Ninth Century', in Ausenda (ed.), *After Empire*, 253–79 (p. 334 above), and Heinrich Beck, Detlev Elmers, and Kurt Schier (eds.), *Germanische Religionsgeschichte: Quellen und Quellenprobleme* (Berlin, 1992). A judicious survey of the Anglo-Saxon textual material is J. D. Niles, 'Pagan Survival and Popular Belief', in Godden and Lapidge (eds.), *Cambridge Companion to Old English Literature*, 124–41 (p. 317 above).

Ian Wood, *The Missionary Life: Saints and the Evangelisation of Europe, 400–1050* (Harlow, 2001), explores early medieval literary representations of missionary achievements. See also Richard E. Sullivan, *Christian Missionary Activity in the Early Middle Ages* (Aldershot, 1994), and Knut Schäferdiek (ed.), *Kirchengeschichte als Missionsgeschichte*, ii: *Die Kirche des früheren Mittelalters* (Munich, 1978). Conversion within the household and women's contribution more generally is the subject of Cordula Nolte, *Conversio und Christianitas: Frauen in der Christianisierung von 5. bis 8. Jahrhundert* (Stuttgart, 1995). Parts of this book's arguments can be sampled in ead., 'Gender and Conversion in the Merovingian Era', in James Muldoon (ed.), *Varieties of Religious Conversion in the Middle Ages* (Gainesville, FL, 1997), 81–99.

Regional and national approaches to the spread of Christianity are as follows: *British Isles*: Charles Thomas, *Christianity in Roman Britain to AD 500* (London, 1981); T. M. Charles-Edwards, *Early Christian Ireland* (Cambridge, 2000); Richard Gameson (ed.), *St Augustine and the Conversion of England* (Stroud, 1999); John Blair, *The Church in Anglo-Saxon Society* (Oxford, 2005); Barbara E. Crawford (ed.), *Conversion and Christianity in the North Sea World* (St Andrews, 1998).

*Frankish lands*: of the vast literature on the baptism of Clovis, Danuta Shanzer, 'Dating the Baptism of Clovis: The Bishop of Vienne vs the Bishop of Tours', *EME*, 7 (1998), 29–57, is crucial and has extensive references to earlier bibliography. J. M. Wallace-Hadrill, *The Frankish Church* (Oxford, 1983), surveys

Merovingian and Carolingian Christianity. An alternative approach is Lutz E. von Padberg, *Mission und Christianisierung: Formen und Folgen bei Angelsachsen und Franken im 7. und 8. Jahrhundert* (Stuttgart, 1995). On Frisia and Saxony, see, respectively, Stéphane Lebecq, 'Les Frisons entre paganisme et Christianisme', in *Christianisation et déchristianisation*, Publication du Centre de Recherches d'Histoire Religieuse et d'Histoire d'Idées, 9 (Angers, 1986), 19–45, and Ruth Mazo Karras, 'Pagan Survivals and Syncretism in the Conversion of Saxony', *Catholic Historical Review*, 72 (1986), 553–72.

*Norse world*: Birgit Sawyer, Peter Sawyer, and Ian Wood (eds.), *The Christianisation of Scandinavia* (Alingsås, 1987), can now be accompanied by Birgit Sawyer, *The Viking-Age Rune Stones: Custom and Commemoration in Early Medieval Scandinavia* (Oxford, 2000), ch. 6 ('Conversion'). For Iceland, Jenny Jochens, 'Late and Peaceful: Iceland's Conversion through Arbitration in 1000', *Speculum*, 74 (1999), 621–55, is illuminating.

*Central Europe*: the best survey is in J.-M. Mayeur, C. Pietri, L. Pietri, A. Vauchez, and M. Venard (eds.), *Histoire du Christianisme*, iv: *Évêques, moines et empereurs, 610–1054* (Paris, 1993), pt. IV, chs. 1–2. See also Premysław Urbańczyk, *Early Christianity in Central and East Europe* (Warsaw, 1997), and Michael Müller-Wille (ed.), *Rom und Byzanz im Norden: Mission und Glaubenswechsel im Ostseeraum während des 8.–14. Jahrhunderts*, 2 vols. (Mainz, 1997–8).

The evolution of norms of correct Christianity from their late antique origins can be tracked through William Klingshirn, *Caesarius of Arles: The Making of a Christian Community in Late Antique Gaul* (Cambridge, 1994), and Robert Markus, 'From Caesarius to Boniface: Christianity and Paganism in Gaul', in Jacques Fontaine and J. N. Hillgarth (eds.), *Le Septième Siècle: Changements et continuités* (London, 1992), 154–72. On their Carolingian implementation from Boniface onwards, see Rosamond McKitterick, *The Frankish Church and the Carolingian Reforms, 789–895* (London, 1977). Dieter Harmening, *Superstitio: Überlieferungs- und theoriegeschichtliche Untersuchungen zur kirchlich-theologischen Aberglaubensliteratur des Mittelalters* (Berlin, 1979), is crucial on the concept of 'superstition'.

The best introduction to early medieval political thinking is *The Cambridge History of Medieval Political Thought c.350–c.1450*, ed. J. H. Burns (Cambridge, 1988). For an emphasis on kingship, see J. M. Wallace-Hadrill, *Early Germanic Kingship in England and on the Continent* (Oxford, 1971), Marc Reydellet, *La Royauté dans la littérature latine de Sidoine Apollinaire à Isidore de Séville* (Rome, 1981), and Hans Hubert Anton, *Fürstenspiegel und Herrscherethos in der Karolingerzeit* (Bonn, 1986). There has been much discussion of whether early medieval kingship was in some sense 'sacral'. Wallace-Hadrill, *Early Germanic Kingship*, ch. 1, cautiously restates the traditional view, but see now Green, *Language and History*, ch. 7 (p. 317 above), and Eve Picard, *Germanisches Sakralkönigtum? Quellenkritisches Studien zur Germania des Tacitus und zur altnordischen Überlieferung* (Heidelberg, 1991). The highly technical literature on royal consecration rituals is best approached through the articles of Janet L. Nelson, assembled in her *Politics and Ritual in Early Medieval Europe* (London, 1996), esp. ch. 12, 'Inauguration Rituals'.

On queens and queenship, see Pauline Stafford, 'The King's Wife in Wessex, 800–1066', *Past and Present*, 91 (1981), 3–27; ead., 'Queens, Nunneries and Reforming Churchmen: Gender, Religious Status and Reform in Tenth- and Eleventh-Century England', ibid. 163 (1999), 3–35; Janet L. Nelson, 'Early Medieval Rites of Queen-Making and the Shaping of Medieval Queenship', in Anne Duggan (ed.), *Queens and Queenship in Medieval Europe* (Woodbridge, 1997), 301–15; Geneviève Bührer-Thierry, 'Les Reines adultères', *Cahiers de Civilisation Médiévale*, 35 (1992), 299–312.

The connections between ideology and politics are underlined by Pauline Stafford, 'The Laws of Cnut and the History of Anglo-Saxon Royal Promises', *Anglo-Saxon England*, 10 (1981), 173–90, and Janet L. Nelson, 'Bad Kingship in the Earlier Middle Ages', *Haskins Society Journal*, 8 (1996), 1–26. On Hincmar of Reims, see Nelson, *Politics and Ritual*, ch. 7, 'Kingship, Law and Liturgy in the Political Thought of Hincmar of Rheims', and Jean Devisse, *Hincmar, archevêque de Reims, 845–882*, 3 vols. (Geneva, 1975–6). For the influence of the Bible on political ideas, see Raymund Kottje, *Studien zum Einfluss des Alten Testamentes auf Recht und Liturgie des frühen Mittelalters* (Bonn, 1970), and, more recently, 'The Power of the Word: The Influence of the Bible on Early Medieval Politics', a collection of articles in *EME* 7 (1998).

An overview of kingship in the Celtic-language zone is Wendy Davies, 'Celtic Kingships in the Early Middle Ages', in Anne Duggan (ed.), *Kings and Kingship in Medieval Europe* (London, 1993), 101–24. A succinct assessment of Irish conceptions is Philip O'Leary, 'A Foreseeing Driver of an Old Chariot: Regal Moderation in Early Irish Literature', *Cambridge Medieval Celtic Studies*, 11 (1986), 1–16; for a fuller discussion, see Bart Jaksi, *Early Irish Kingship and Succession* (Dublin, 2000). On similarities and differences between Irish and Germanic kings, Patrick Wormald, 'Celtic and Anglo-Saxon Kingship: Some Further Thoughts', in Paul E. Szarmach (ed.), *Sources of Anglo-Saxon Culture* (Kalamazoo, MI, 1986), 151–83, is fundamental.

Hincmar's treatise *De regis persona et regio ministerio* discussed on pp. 243–4 is edited in *PL* 125, cols. 833–56. One of Hincmar's other treatises on kingship is available in English translation: 'On the Governance of the Palace', in either David Herlihy, *A History of Feudalism* (New York, 1970), 209–27, or Paul Edward Dutton, *Carolingian Civilization: A Reader* (Peterborough, ONT, 1993), 485–99.

Pseudo-Cyprian, mentioned on pp. 247 and 249, is edited by Sigmund Hellmann, *De duodecim abusivis saeculi*, Texte und Untersuchungen zur altchristlichen Literatur, 3rd ser, 4 (Leipzig, 1909), and is ably assessed by Rob Meens, 'Politics, Mirrors of Princes and the Bible: Kings and the Well-Being of the Realm', *EME* 7 (1998), 345–57.

The law codes of Stephen of Hungary referred to on p. 218 are translated in *The Laws of the Medieval Kingdom of Hungary*, ed. and trans. G. Bónis, J. M. Bak, and J. R. Sweeney, 2 vols. (Bakersfield, CA, 1985–90); Hartvic's *Life of St Stephen* is available in *Medieval Hagiography: An Anthology*, ed. Thomas Head (New York, 2000).

## CHAPTER 8. ROME AND THE PEOPLES OF EUROPE

The study of the formation of early medieval kingdoms has been transformed in recent years by attention to ethnicity as a complex, shifting, social phenomenon involving the cultural and political projections of notions of self and others. In the absence of any full new synthesis, the best introduction in English is the short, suggestive essay of Walter Pohl, 'The Barbarian Successor States', in Leslie Webster and Michelle Brown (eds.), *The Transformation of the Roman World, AD 400–900* (London, 1997), 33–47. On images of 'barbarians', see Peter Heather, 'The Barbarian in Late Antiquity: Image, Reality and Transformation', in Richard Miles (ed.), *Constructing Identities in Late Antiquity* (London, 1999), 234–58, and Yves-Albert Dauge, *Le Barbare: Recherches sur la conception romaine de la barbarie et de la civilisation* (Brussels, 1981).

On the emergence of early medieval ethnicities, recent debates owe much to the stimulus of German and Austrian conceptualizations, and generally take the continental 'Germanic' peoples as their frame of reference. The starting point for all recent work is Reinhard Wenskus, *Stammesbildung und Verfassung: Das Werden der frühmittelalterlichen Gentes* (Cologne, 1961). Wenskus's approach has now been developed into a theory of ethnogenesis; see Patrick Geary, 'Ethnic Identity as Situational Construct in the Early Middle Ages', *Mitteilungen der anthropologischen Gesellschaft in Wien*, 113 (1983), 15–26, and, with more sophistication, Walter Pohl, 'Tradition, Ethnogenese und literarische Gestaltung: Eine Zwischenbilanz', in Karl Brunner and Brigitte Merta (eds.), *Ethnogenese und Überlieferung: Angewandte Methoden der Frühmittelalterforschung*, Veröffentlichungen des Institut für Österreichische Geschichtsforschung, 31 (Vienna, 1994), 9–26. Herwig Wolfram, '*Origo et religio*: Ethnic Traditions and Literature in Early Medieval Texts', *EME* 3 (1994), 19–38, is a succinct English-language expression of the views of one of the leading exponents of ethnogenesis theory. Wolfram's approach also informs the recent general, though controversial, overview of Patrick Geary, *The Myth of Nations: The Medieval Origins of Europe* (Princeton, 2001). For ethnicity in the Carolingian period, see Walter Pohl, 'Zur Bedeutung ethnischer Unterscheidungen in der frühen Karolingerzeit', *Studien zur Sachsenforschung*, 12 (1999), 193–208.

To sample the debates and criticisms surrounding the 'ethnogenesis' approach, the following volumes of essays are useful: Pohl and Reimitz (eds.), *Strategies of Distinction* (p. 335 above); Andrew Gillett (ed.), *On Barbarian Identity: Critical Approaches to Ethnicity in the Early Middle Ages* (Turnhout, 2002), and Hans-Werner Goetz, Jörg Jarnut, and Walter Pohl (eds.), *Regna and Gentes: The*

*Relationship between Late Antique and Early Medieval Peoples and Kingdoms in the Transformation of the Roman World* (Leiden, 2003).

A traditionally important line of approach is philological—and it is only modern linguistic classification that imposes a unified view on Europe's invaders as 'Germanic': see Green, *Language and History* (p. 317 above), and Walter Pohl, *Die Germanen* (Munich, 2000). On literary representations of identity and origin legends, see Walter Goffart, *The Narrators of Barbarian History (AD 550–800)* (Princeton, 1988); specifically on Jordanes, see Peter Heather, *Goths and Romans, 332–489* (Oxford, 1991), 3–67, which supersedes previous discussions.

Archaeologists contribute complementary approaches, which are crucial for northern Europe. Lotte Hedeager, *Iron Age Societies: From Tribe to State in Northern Europe, 500 BC to AD 700* (Oxford, 1992), led the way; in addition see Howard B. Clarke, Máire Ní Mhaonaigh, and Ragnall Ó Floinn (eds.), *Ireland and Scandinavia in the Early Viking Age* (Dublin, 1998), and Tania Dickinson and David Griffiths (eds.), *The Making of Kingdoms* (Oxford, 1999).

The insular world is well represented in the archaeological literature but largely absent from the 'ethnogenesis' debates. Exceptions from an Anglo-Saxon perspective are John Moreland, 'Ethnicity, Power and the English', in William O. Frazer and Andrew Tyrrell (eds.), *Social Identity in Early Medieval Britain* (London, 2000), 23–51, Nicholas Brooks, 'The English Origin Myth', in his *Anglo-Saxon Myths: State and Church, 400–1066* (London, 2000), 79–89, and Patrick Wormald, '*Engla Lond*: The Making of an Allegiance', *Journal of Historical Sociology*, 7 (1994), 1–24. Approaches to Scottish, Welsh, and Irish material remain predominantly text-historical, conceptualized with reference to shifting historiographies of the British Isles and the heavy weight of English hegemony within them. On Ireland, see Donnchadh Ó Corráin, 'Nationality and Kingship in Pre-Norman Ireland', in T. W. Moody (ed.), *Nationality and the Pursuit of Independence* (Belfast, 1978), 1–35, and John Carey, *The Irish National Origin-Legend: Synthetic Pseudohistory*, Quiggin Pamphlets on the Sources of Medieval Gaelic History, 1 (Cambridge, 1994). On Wales, there are valuable comments in P. P. Sims-Williams, 'Some Functions of Origin Stories in Early Medieval Wales', in Tore Nyberg, Iørn Piø, Preben Meulengracht Sørensen, and Aage Trommer (eds.), *History and Heroic Tale: A Symposium* (Odense, 1985), 97–131; and for Scotland, a recent important contribution is Dauvit Broun, 'The Origin of Scottish Identity', in Claus Bjørn, Alexander Grant, and Keith Stringer (eds.), *Nations, Nationalism and Patriotism in the European Past* (Copenhagen, 1994), 34–55.

In addition to the Further Reading on political ideas cited for Chapter 7, for the concept of 'empire', see Karl Ferdinand Werner, 'L'Empire carolingien et le Saint Empire', in Maurice Duverger (ed.), *Le Concept d'empire* (Paris, 1980), 151–202. Three articles by Steven Fanning take a helpful look at the use of the word *imperium*: 'Jerome's Concept of Empire', in Loveday Alexander (ed.), *Images of Empire* (Sheffield, 1991), 239–50, 'Bede, *imperium* and the Bretwaldas', *Speculum*, 66 (1991), 1–26, and 'Clovis Augustus and Merovingian *imitatio imperii*', in Kathleen Mitchell and Ian Wood (eds.), *The World of Gregory of Tours*

(Leiden, 2002), 321–35. For the appropriation of imperial vocabulary and rituals of rulership in the successor kingdoms, see Michael McCormick, *Eternal Victory: Triumphal Rulership in Late Antiquity, Byzantium and the Early Medieval West* (Cambridge, 1986).

Of the vast literature on Charlemagne and his imperial coronation, the best overview remains Donald Bullough, *The Age of Charlemagne* (London, 1965). The sumptuous catalogue from the 1999 exhibition at Paderborn is accompanied by many valuable essays on a wide range of subjects: Christoph Stiegemann and Matthias Wemhoff (eds.), *799: Kunst und Kultur der Karolingerzeit. Karl der Grosse und Papst Leo III. in Paderborn*, 3 vols. (Mainz, 1999). For the empire and cultural world of Otto I, see the equally lavish catalogue and essay volume from the 2001 exhibition at Magdeburg: Matthias Puhle (ed.), *Otto der Grosse: Magdeburg und Europa*, 2 vols. (Mainz, 2001). On Otto III, Gerd Althoff, *Otto III.* (Darmstadt, 1996), is now available in English translation (University Park, PA, 2003). Otto III's empire building in central Europe is put into broad cultural context by the third major international exhibition catalogue of recent years, Alfried Wieczorek and Hans-Martin Hinz (eds.), *Europas Mitte um 1000*, 3 vols. (Darmstadt, 2000); *Europe's Centre around 1000*, 2 vols. (Stuttgart, 2000), is an English translation of the essays but lacks the illustrations. Stefan Weinfurter, *The Salian Century: Main Currents in an Age of Transition*, trans. Barbara M. Bowlus (Philadelphia, 1999), takes Germany into the eleventh century. Detailed accounts are available of both Cnut and Conrad II: M. K. Lawson, *Cnut: the Danes in England in the Early Eleventh Century* (Harlow, 1993), and Herwig Wolfram, *Konrad II. 990–1039: Kaiser dreier Reiche* (Munich, 2000).

The place of Rome in medieval imagination is the subject of Andrea Giardina and André Vauchez, *Rome: L'Idée et le mythe du moyen âge à nos jours* (Paris, 2000), and, for the insular world, should be supplemented by Éamon Ó Carragáin's important essay, *The City of Rome and the World of Bede* (Jarrow, 1994). Richard Krautheimer's classic presentation of the city itself, *Rome: Portrait of a City, 312–1308* (Princeton, 1980), is now significantly modified by recent archaeological and architectural work. Several volumes of essays make this, and much more, accessible: Julia M. H. Smith (ed.), *Early Medieval Rome and the Christian West* (Leiden, 2000); *Roma nell'alto medioevo*, Settimane, 48, 2 vols. (Spoleto, 2001), and *Roma fra oriente e occidente*, Settimane, 49, 2 vols. (Spoleto, 2002). All these have useful material on pilgrimage to Rome; see also Clare Stancliffe, 'Kings who Opted out', in Patrick Wormald, Donald Bullough, and Roger Collins (eds.), *Ideal and Reality in Frankish and Anglo-Saxon Society: Studies Presented to J. M. Wallace-Hadrill* (Oxford, 1983), 154–76, and Kathleen Hughes, 'The Celtic Church and the Papacy', in C. H. Lawrence (ed.), *The English Church and the Papacy in the Middle Ages* (London, 1965), 3–28 (repr. in Hughes, *Church and Society in Ireland, AD 400–1200*, ed. David Dumville (London, 1987), ch. XV).

No subject has suffered from the search for the linear antecedents of later developments more than the papacy, a problem that not even the best recent survey, Bernhard Schimmelpfennig, *The Papacy*, trans. James Sievert (New York,

1992), has avoided. An alternative approach is sketched by Thomas F. X. Noble, 'Morbidity and Vitality in the History of the Early Medieval Papacy', *Catholic Historical Review*, 81 (1995), 505–40, while the papers in Michele Maccarrone (ed.), *Il primato del vescovo di Roma nel primo millennio: Ricerche e testimonianze* (Vatican City, 1991), offer context-sensitive evaluations of papal ideology and practice. Peter Llewellyn, *Rome in the Dark Ages* (London, 1971), remains useful. Important recent studies of specific issues include: Federico Marazzi, *I 'Patrimonia sanctae Romanae ecclesiae' nel Lazio (secoli IV–X): Stuttura amministrativa e prassi gestionali* (Rome, 1998); Thomas F. X. Noble, *The Republic of St Peter: The Birth of the Papal State, 680–825* (Philadelphia, 1984); Arnold Angenendt and Rudolf Schieffer, *Roma—caput et fons: Zwei Vorträge über das päpstliche Rom zwischen Altertum und Mittelalter* (Opladen, 1989); Gerd Tellenbach, 'Zur Geschichte der Päpste im 10. und früheren 11. Jahrhundert', in Fenske et al. (eds.), *Institutionen, Kultur und Gesellschaft im Mittelalter*, 165–77 (p. 331 above).

Details of the recipients of John XIX's letters and charters as plotted on Fig. 8.4 can be found in Harald Zimmermann (ed.), *Papsturkunden 896–1046*, 2 vols., Österreichische Akademie der Wissenschaften, philosophisch-historische Klasse, 174, 177 (Vienna, 1984–5), ii. 1043–126.

# Chronology

| | |
|---|---|
| 508 | Probable date of Clovis's acceptance of Christianity |
| 511 | Death of Clovis; division of his kingdom among his four sons |
| 526 | Death of Theoderic the Great |
| 534 | Frankish takeover of Burgundian kingdom in Rhone valley |
| 536 | Justinian, Byzantine emperor since 527, invades Italy, having re-conquered North Africa from the Vandals |
| c.540 | Benedict of Nursia (d. 560) composes his monastic *Rule*, which becomes the normative guide to monastic observance from c.800 |
| 541 | Bubonic plague erupts in Egypt |
| 542 | Death of Caesarius, bishop of Arles since 502, author of many sermons and other works |
| 542–3 | Bubonic plague reaches western Mediterranean; subsequent serious outbreaks in 570–1, 580, 590, and 654 |
| 552 | Completion of Byzantine conquest of Italy and final collapse of Ostrogothic kingdom |
| 561 | Death of Chlothar I, last remaining son of Clovis; division of the Frankish kingdom among four of his sons, Charibert, Sigibert I, Chilperic, and Guntram |
| 563 | Irish monk Columba (c.521–97) founds island monastery of Iona in Scottish Dalriada and from there preaches to Picts |
| 565 | Death of Justinian, having returned North Africa, south-eastern Spain and Italy to imperial (Byzantine) rule |
| 566 | Italian poet Venantius Fortunatus arrives at court of the Frankish king Sigibert I (561–75) in Reims |
| 568 | Lombards invade northern Italy under King Alboin (d. 572); by 574 in control of Po valley cities and by 580 of Tuscany. Spoleto and Benevento established as independent Lombard duchies |
| 584 | Maurice, Byzantine emperor (582–602), pays subsidies to Childebert II, king of the Franks (575–96), who invades Po valley at Maurice's request but promptly settles with the Lombards and retreats, to imperial annoyance |
| 585 | Leovigild, king of the Visigoths (568–86), takes over the Suevic kingdom |
| 589 | Under Reccared (586–601), Visigoths renounce Arian Christianity and accept Catholicism |
| 591–615 | Irish monk Columbanus active on the Continent, founding monasteries and warning kings |
| 594 | Death of Gregory, bishop of Tours since 573, author of *Ten Books of Histories* and many hagiographical works |

| | |
|---|---|
| 597 | Augustine arrives in Kent to preach Christianity to the Anglo-Saxons, having been sent by Pope Gregory I in 595/6; establishes his see at Canterbury |
| 597/8 | Æthelbert, king of Kent, accepts Christianity and is baptized by Augustine; subsequently issues law code in Old English |
| c.600– | Fitful spread of Christianity to other Anglo-Saxon kingdoms; conversion of last pagan region, the Isle of Wight, in 686–7 |
| 604 | Death of Gregory I (the Great), pope since 590, author of widely read pastoral and exegetical works |
| 616 | Death of Æthelbert of Kent; successor Eadbald at first rejects Christianity but then converts |
| 634 | Oswald, king of Northumbria, defeats Cadwallon, king of Gwynedd, and establishes domination over the northern half of Britain |
| 636 | Death of Isidore, bishop of Seville since 599, author of the *Etymologies* and numerous other works |
| 639 | Death of Dagobert I, king of the Franks since 623 |
| 642 | Death of Oswald, king of Northumbria |
| 643 | Rothari, king of the Lombards (636–52), issues his Edict |
| 664 | Serious epidemics in Britain and Irelandn peninsula |
| 674 | Benedict Biscop founds monastery of Wearmouth (Northumbria) |
| 678/9 | The vision of Barontus |
| 681 | Benedict Biscop founds monastery of Jarrow (Northumbria) |
| 711 | Muslim invasion of Iberian peninsula |
| 713/14 | Envoys of Nechtan, king of the Picts, come to Wearmouth–Jarrow for advice about Roman liturgical practices and building techniques |
| 716 | Boniface, Anglo-Saxon monk, begins missionary activity on the Continent, preaching to the Frisians and reforming the Christian communities in Germany |
| 721 | Ecclesiastical council in Rome begins changes to marriage legislation |
| 735 | Death of Bede, monk of Wearmouth–Jarrow, author of the *Ecclesiastical History of the English People* and biblical commentaries, translator of St John's Gospel |
| 744 | Boniface founds monastery of Fulda in central Germany |
| 744 | Death of Liutprand, king of the Lombards since 712 |
| 751 | Deposition of last Merovingian king of the Franks; accession of Pippin III marks start of Carolingian dynasty |
| 754 | Pope Stephen II (752–7) crosses the Alps to consecrate Pippin III |
| 754 | Boniface martyred by the Frisians at Dokkum |

| 756 | Establishment of Umayyad dynasty in Cordoba |
| 757 | Death of Æthelbald, king of Mercia since 716; accession later that same year of Offa (d. 796) |
| 767 | Last recorded outbreak of bubonic plague, in southern Italy |
| 768 | Death of Pippin III; division of his kingdom between his two sons Charlemagne and Carloman; on the latter's death in 771, entire Frankish kingdom passes to Charlemagne |
| 772 | Charlemagne commences campaigning against the Saxons |
| 774 | Charlemagne conquers and annexes the Lombard kingdom and duchy of Spoleto; duchy of Benevento remains independent into the eleventh century |
| 776 | Paderborn founded |
| 781, 787 | Charlemagne agrees limits of territory under direct papal rule; subsequently confirmed by Louis the Pious and Otto I |
| 786–94 | Alcuin of Northumbria (d. 804) among the scholars resident at Charlemagne's court |
| 788 | Charlemagne annexes Bavaria |
| 789 | Charlemagne begins to develop Aachen into a showpiece palace complex; from 802 in semi-permanent residence there. After Charlemagne's death, Aachen retains a highly symbolic role as the centre of legitimate kingship until 1804 |
| 789 | Charlemagne promulgates the 'General Admonition', a full statement of 'correct Christianity' |
| 792–3 | Severe famine in the Frankish kingdom; Charlemagne legislates to alleviate it |
| 793 | Vikings raid the Northumbrian island monastery of Lindisfarne, the first securely dated Viking raid on western Europe. Increasingly frequent raids on Ireland, Scotland, and the isles thereafter |
| 795 | Death of Hadrian I, pope since 772, close friend of Charlemagne and energetic rebuilder of Rome |
| 796 | Assassination of Æthelred I, king of Northumbria |
| 799 | After an attempt to depose him, Pope Leo III (795–816) visits Charlemagne at Paderborn |
| 800 | In Rome, Leo III crowns Charlemagne emperor (25 December) |
| c.800– | Vikings trade with Byzantium and Islam via the river routes between the Baltic and the Black and Caspian Seas |
| 804 | Deportation of Saxons from Elbe valley marks conclusion of Charlemagne's Saxon wars |
| 810 | Viking raids on Frisia and Flanders begin; Charlemagne orders construction of a fleet at Boulogne and Ghent |
| 811 | Franks and Danes make peace on banks of river Eider |

| 814 | Death of Charlemagne and burial at Aachen; accession of his son Louis the Pious |
| 815 | Einhard becomes abbot of St Peter's monastery, Ghent |
| 819 | Death of Louis the Pious's first wife, Irmingard, and his remarriage to Judith; birth of her son Charles the Bald in 823 threatens his adult half-brothers' succession rights and contributes to political unrest |
| 829 | Frankish monk Anskar begins missionary work in Scandinavia; becomes bishop of Hamburg in 831 |
| 830 | Revolt against Louis the Pious |
| 830s | Viking raids extend to southern England, interior of Ireland, and Atlantic coast of Gaul |
| 832 | Foundation of monastery of Redon (Brittany) |
| 833 | Revolt against Louis the Pious; deposed by his sons but restored to full power in 834 |
| 833–9 | Abba, reeve of Kent, makes his will |
| 840 | Death of Einhard, counsellor of Charlemagne and Louis the Pious, author of *Life of Charlemagne*, lay abbot of St Peter's, Ghent and founder of Seligenstadt |
| 840 | Death of Louis the Pious; contention between his sons is temporarily resolved by the partition of 843, which confirms Lothar I (840–55) as emperor and king of the middle kingdom, Louis the German (840–76) as king of the East Frankish kingdom, and Charles the Bald (840–77) as king of the West Frankish kingdom |
| 841 | Vikings establish base at Dublin; despite their temporary expulsion 902–17, Dublin develops into important urban centre and seat of a Hiberno-Norse kingdom, stretching until 954 across both sides of the Irish Sea |
| 841–3 | Dhuoda writes her *Handbook* for her son William |
| 842 | Death of Alfonso II, king of Asturias since 791, who established Asturias as a powerful Christian kingdom following Visigothic and Carolingian precedents and successfully defended it from Muslim attack |
| 843 | Kenneth mac Alpin ousts last Pictish king as Viking attacks on Scotland intensify |
| 845 | Vikings destroy Hamburg; Anskar becomes bishop of Bremen and resumes missionary work in Scandinavia |
| 846 | Saracens sack St Peter's, Rome |
| 856 | Death of Hrabanus Maurus, abbot of Fulda (822–42) and archbishop of Mainz since 847, author of numerous biblical commentaries |

| | |
|---|---|
| 860 | Frankish bishops adjudicate the marriage of Stephen, count of the Auvergne |
| 860s | Kiev emerges as major Rus settlement and from *c*.880 extends rule over east Slavic peoples |
| 862 | First recorded Magyar raid, on the East Frankish kingdom |
| 863 | Constantine and Methodius commence preaching to the Slavs; Constantine dies in 869; Methodius dies in 885 |
| 864 | Eberhard of Friuli and Gisela make their will |
| 864 | Baptism of Khan Boris of the Bulgars (852–89); turns to Pope Nicholas I for advice about Latin Christianity |
| 865 | Death of Anskar |
| 866 | Viking conquest of East Anglia soon followed by takeover of Northumbria in 876 and eastern Mercia in 877 |
| 870 | Khan Boris decides in favour of Greek Christianity |
| *c*.870–930 | Vikings settle in Iceland |
| 871 | Accession of Alfred, king of Wessex and exponent of Carolingian-style kingship |
| 873 | Plague of locusts devastates much of Europe |
| 878 | Alfred, king of Wessex, wins victory over Vikings and stems their advance; Danish leader Guthrum submits to baptism, with Alfred as his godfather |
| 881 | Death of Fintan, an Irishman captured by Vikings in the 840s, who escaped in the Orkneys and later became a monk at Rheinau |
| 882 | Death of Hincmar, archbishop of Reims since 845, counsellor of kings, liturgical impressario, and author of treatises on kingship, marriage, and much else |
| 884–7 | Carolingian Empire reunited by Emperor Charles the Fat (d. 888) |
| 888 | Carolingian dynastic crisis; election of non-Carolingian kings in Italy, Provence, and, temporarily, west Francia |
| *c*.894 | Magyars move west of the Carpathian mountains and begin to settle in the Danubian plain, taking over eastern Bavaria in 900 and Moravia in 902; Magyar raids on East Frankish kingdom become frequent |
| 899 | Death of Alfred of Wessex; accession of his son Edward the Elder, who commences conquest of East Anglia and eastern Mercia from the Vikings |
| 909 | Death of Gerald, count of Aurillac and holy man; his life and miracles subsequently described by Odo, abbot of Cluny (927–42) |
| 911 | Accession of Conrad I, first non-Carolingian king of the East Franks (Germans) |

| 911 | West Frankish king Charles the Simple (898–922) cedes Rouen and adjacent region to the Viking leader Rollo, thus establishing the duchy of Normandy |
| 918 | Death of Conrad I |
| 919 | Accession of Henry I, duke of Saxony, as king of the Germans |
| 921 | Charles the Simple sends Henry I the arm of St Denis |
| 922 | Defeat and deposition of Charles the Simple |
| 924 | Death of Edward the Elder, having extended West Saxon rule as far north as the river Humber; accession of Æthelstan |
| 926 | Henry I gives Swabia to Rudolf II, king of Burgundy (912–37), and acquires the Holy Lance in exchange |
| 927 | Æthelstan asserts his overlordship over the northern half of Britain and in 934 campaigns into Alba; hereafter West Saxon kings commonly referred to as kings of the English |
| 936 | Death of Henry I; accession of his son Otto I as king of Germany |
| 939 | Death of Æthelstan; accession of Edmund as king of England |
| 941 | Arnulf I, count of Flanders (918–65), begins reform of St Peter's, Ghent, and makes rich donations to the clergy |
| 946 | Death of Edmund; accession of Eadred as king of England |
| 951 | Otto invades Italy and is installed as king in Pavia |
| 953 | Embassy of John of Gorze to the court of Abd al-Rahman III (912–61) at Cordoba |
| 954 | King Eadred's capture of York ends Viking rule within England |
| 955 | Death of Eadred; accession of Edgar as king in Mercia and Northumbria; then, in 957, in Wessex |
| 955 | Otto I defeats Magyars at the battle of the river Lech; thereafter Magyar attacks diminish |
| 961 | Otto I has his 6-year-old son Otto II crowned king of Germany at Aachen, and then crosses Alps into Italy |
| 962 | Otto I crowned emperor in Rome |
| 967 | Gerbert of Aurillac visits Ripoll |
| 967 | Otto II crowned emperor |
| 972 | Baptism of Géza, king of Hungary (c.970–97) |
| 973 | Death of Otto I; sole rule of Otto II |
| 975 | Death of Edgar, king of England since 957, having fostered Carolingian-style 'correct Christianity' within England; accession of Edward 'the Martyr' |
| 978 | Assassination of Edward 'the Martyr'; accession of Æthelred II 'the Unready' to the English throne |
| 980 | Viking raids on England resume |

| | |
|---|---|
| 980 | Otto II meets Hugh Capet |
| 983 | Death of Otto II; accession of 3-year-old Otto III |
| 983 | Liutizi Slavs revolt against German dominance and reject Christianity |
| 985–7 | Abbo of Fleury teaches at Ramsey |
| 987 | Death of last Carolingian king of West Francia; coronation of Hugh Capet as king of the West Franks (French) |
| c.988 | Prince Vladimir of Kiev and the Rus accept Christianity |
| 991 | Anglo-Saxon defeat by the Vikings at Maldon on coast of Essex; subsequently commemorated in the epic poem *The Battle of Maldon* |
| 996 | Having come of age in 994, Otto III crowned emperor in Rome |
| 997 | Adalbert of Prague martyred by the Prussians at Gdansk |
| 997 | Accession of Stephen of Hungary |
| 997–1016 | Date of the sole manuscript of the Old English epic poem *Beowulf* |
| 998 | Otto III rebuilds former imperial palace in Rome in an attempt to make Rome his permanent capital |
| 999 | Death of Gregory V, the first German pope |
| 999/1000 | Icelanders adopt Christianity |
| 1000 | Otto III visits Gniezno to inaugurate the cult of Adalbert of Prague, bestow a crown and a replica of the Holy Lance on Boleslaw Chobry (992–1025), and stand godfather to his son; establishment of Polish archbishopric at Gniezno |
| 1000/1 | Pope Sylvester II sends a crown to Stephen of Hungary and Otto III sends a replica of the Holy Lance; establishment of Hungarian archbishopric at Esztergom |
| 1001 | Otto III expelled from Rome |
| 1002 | Death of Otto III; succession crisis ends when Henry II elected king in Germany |
| 1004 | Henry II elected king in Italy |
| 1005 | Great famine throughout Europe |
| 1005 | Brian Boru (976–1014) visits Armagh and makes gifts to shrine of St Patrick |
| 1009 | Bruno of Querfurt martyred by the Prussians |
| 1013 | Swein Forkbeard, king of Denmark, conquers all England north of the river Thames; Æthelred II exiled |
| 1014 | Death of Swein Forkbeard; Danish army in England recognizes his son Cnut as king but Anglo-Saxons recall Æthelred II from exile |

| | |
|---|---|
| 1014 | Defeat at the battle of Clontarf ends Brian Boru's dominance of Ireland |
| 1014 | Henry II crowned emperor |
| 1016 | Cnut, son of Swein Forkbeard, conquers England; death of Æthelred II |
| 1018 | Death of Thietmar, bishop of Merseburg since 1009, chronicler |
| 1018–23 | Hammerstein marriage dispute |
| 1023 | Death of Wulfstan, archbishop of York since 1002, homilist and counsellor of kings |
| 1024 | Death of Henry II without heir; election of Conrad II |
| 1024 | Death of Benedict VIII, pope since 1012; accession of his brother John XIX |
| 1026 | Cnut fights the Norwegians and Swedes at the battle of Holy River in southern Sweden |
| 1027 | Conrad II crowned emperor in Rome, with Cnut and Rudolf III of Burgundy in attendance |
| 1032 | Death of Rudolf III, king of Burgundy since 993 |
| 1033 | Death of John XIX |
| 1035 | Death of Cnut, king of England, Denmark, and Norway |
| 1036 | Death of Meinwerk, bishop of Paderborn since 1009, leaving his rebuilding of Paderborn unfinished |
| 1038 | Death of Stephen of Hungary; canonized in 1083 |
| 1039 | Death of Conrad II |

# Index

Page numbers in italic refer to maps and diagrams in the text.